MW00679812

Rural Voices

Editor: Chris Gustafson

Reviewers: John Allen, Lyn DeNaeyer, Chris Gustafson, Kara Heidemann, Fran Kaye, Jim King, Carol McDaniels, Jill Mulligan, Don Ralston, Jarrod Tremayne, Eileen Wirth

In addition, the following people/organizations deserve thanks for their help with the book: The Center for Applied Rural Innovation, the Center for Rural Affairs, Dr. Chuck Francis, Dr. Sam Cordes, Dr. Eileen Wirth, and Dr. John Allen, who devoted much time and energy helping me figure out the process of collecting, compiling, and publishing a book.

Writers retain all copyrights to their own work.

Copyright © 2002
Dirt Road Press
1020 CR Q, Mead, NE 68041

This book may not be reproduced by any means, mechanical or electronic, without written permission of the publisher, aside from quotes used in reviews.

ISBN: 0-9719030-0-X

Printed in the United States by Morris Publishing
3212 East Highway 30 • Kearney, NE 68847 • 1-800-650-7888

Introduction
The Earth

The Gift of Agriculture

Between the Lines

Introduction

It is very easy to take the beauty of the Great Plains for granted. We have no rugged mountains, no mysteriously dark, reluctant oceans, and no ancient, stately forests. Our landscape is relatively bare, simple and straightforward, and although most would not describe it as stunningly beautiful, there is a pleasing aestheticism in the simplicity of the modestly rolling hills and the verdant fields. The creator of these lands was a minimalist, but practiced this craft with great skill, and gave Nebraskans the sense to recognize the subtle strokes of beauty.

I have heard Nebraska described as a drive-through state: stick to I-80 and get to the other side as quickly as possible. It's common sense that you won't see much if your gaze is fixed straight ahead, and much of Nebraska exists in the periphery. Many people in our society have become accustomed to having anything and everything worthwhile handed to them; no searching involved.

It is advisable not to shove a wild rose or a rolling field down one's throat. None of Nebraska's features, with the possible exception of Scott's Bluff or Chimney Rock in its more formidable days, are overly impressive in size or scale, but that doesn't mean that there is no worth in it.

Those of us lucky enough to live here deal with the stigma of being Nebraskans and the condescension or pity that comes with it, but we can deal with it. Working the land isn't always easy, and we've learned not to take that personally, so disregarding those who are unobservant and misinformed is no problem.

This earth requires an intimacy with the land before it becomes an amicable colleague. Working with the land is much more satisfying than covering it with concrete and metal, avoiding it or regarding it as an adversary. Jeep's catch phrase, "Jeep: It kind of evens up that whole man versus nature thing," illustrates this sad point, if Americans actually buy into this insalubrious philosophy.

I'm from a small town, I'm from Nebraska, and I'm proud of it. I suppose that point is fairly obvious; I wouldn't be doing this if that weren't true. However, the number of young people in this state who are willing to make such a brazen claim is dwindling. Rural youth are leaving small towns for the "big-city glamour" of Omaha and Lincoln, and once they grow weary of that arena, are off to Kansas City or Denver, New York or Los Angeles.

Everyone is entitled to their own opinion, but I wonder how much our vision has been distorted by the media and the entertainment business? How many of our kids have been indoctrinated into feeling inferior about their rural background and upbringing? Life isn't always easy, especially in an agricultural land where each new spring offers the specter of crop failure or drought, the hours are long, and the motivation to work is largely internalized. It is probably easier to work 9 to 5 and be done with it until the next morning, but does the same feeling of satisfaction exist? I would suspect not. Many people take jobs based on money or opportunity of future advancements and are happy to leave a company or even a profession if it looks like it will benefit them.

The land can be gentle and caring, but it is also seductive and cruel. Nebraska was called the Great American Desert by early explorers, considered unfit for living, a belief that is still held by some. It may be that the derogation directed towards small town folks is the product of a disbelief that people moved out here and survived.

The "floodgates" to the Midwest really opened with the passage of the Homestead Act of 1862; a bill that provided 160 acres to anyone who would live on and cultivate the land for five years. It sounds like a great deal now, but the conditions were severe, and the consequences for those who failed were often dire. Many people came to the territories, leaving families, risking lives, and ignoring reports of angry savages, to settle and live out dreams of independence. Many people failed, but those that fought through the hardship developed an unequaled work ethic and communal bonds to help each other in times of sickness or failure.

After decades of family ownership, our bonds to the land strengthen with each season. We know every rise, every curve, and we eventually find every spot that tends to remain wet long after the rest of the field has dried. It's a process of learning, of innovating, of starting over every spring, whether the previous crop was good or bad, with the same expectations and enthusiasm. It's a process of love. It's a process with which I'm very familiar.

As with any process, there is a metamorphosis. My change in attitude began as an early teen, from a position of rural self-consciousness to a love for my bucolic homeland. Early on, I was convinced that I needed to be with "it." I didn't know necessarily what or where "it" was (I suspected it was in California somewhere), but I knew life in Mead didn't qualify.

Any time the opportunity arose to visit my cousins in California, I jumped at it, even if it meant leaving Dad to do the majority of the farm work by himself. I certainly didn't expect to still be in Nebraska after high school.

But around the time I turned 16, I saw Nebraska differently. Instead of looking past the plains and small towns in search of something larger and more ostentatious, I saw the richness all around me.

I involved myself in the community and the school, belonging to the FFA, working with the NCIP program, helping at the cemetery. I also developed a much better work ethic after observing how much time and effort my parents and grandparents put into their endeavors.

At first, I was a victim of the stereotype and the negative publicity of a rural life, even though I was surrounded constantly by evidence that contradicted my ideas. Most of what is reported in the newspaper or on the local news is bad. News of the farm crisis, weather disasters, the exodus of youth; what sort of image would one draw?

I am very thankful that I lost my prejudices, that I now see the beauty of rural places, and that I enjoy the tranquility of country life. I pity those people who never leave the Lincoln/Omaha area and couldn't place Pender from Palisade, those people never learn what this state has to offer, and never know what living with nature takes, never figure out the difference between a tractor and a combine.

Many people are realizing that there is something about country life, an intrinsic satisfaction that comes with working the land, breathing fresh air, and having unobstructed views of the sunsets that look like someone lit all of Wyoming afire.

I was in the doctor's office at St. Joseph hospital this morning and the nurse taking my temperature and blood pressure asked me where I lived. I told her. After confusing Mead with Murray, she said she and her husband had been looking for land in the country for years, but could never find any at a price they could afford. They had recently had a drive-by shooting in their neighborhood, she said she knew there had been some violence in rural areas recently, but...she couldn't take the city any more.

I sympathize with her, but with many others holding the same philosophy, Omaha and Lincoln have been expanding rapidly, gorging on farmland like a voracious fat man not unlike Mr. Creosote of Monty Python's Meaning of Life, a man who ate so much that he eventually exploded. With the expansion of the cities and the emigration of youth from rural communities, the countenance of rural Nebraska is changing; whether the character and flavor is polluted by this trend remains to be seen, but the possibility is there.

My own ethnocentricity along with the threat of a drastic mutation of rural life is the impetus behind this book. I wanted to capture the Nebraska I have come to love. I want future generations to be able to read about the traditions and travails of their ancestors; I want to share the values of hard work, dedication, family, and community held by rural Nebraskans with anyone unfamiliar with our lifestyle.

Most of all, I wanted to compile a record of the people of the best state in the United States. There, I said it. It's not very diplomatic, but the truth isn't always what people want to hear. The stories and poems contained within are very good, but not stuffed with the pomposity that is so commonplace in literature. And with that, I hope you enjoy this book.

The Earth

Curt Arens   Ab's Place

I was late that morning to my parents' farmstead for chores. My muscles were sore from playing basketball in town the night before. But they weren't too sore to hit the snooze button on my alarm clock several times.

I finally rolled out of bed and drove the half mile from my house to the home place where my parents lived. When I walked into the house, Dad immediately announced, "Well, we've got a job to do already this morning."

I had seen the bulldozers parked on Ab and Ceil's place across Bow Creek from my house. I had also seen graders and dozers parked near the thicket of 100-year-old cottonwood trees a few hundred yards from my driveway. Now it was time for the bulldozers to do their thing.

Dad explained that the new owner of Ab and Ceil's old farmstead planned to demolish the entire place and plant crops where the buildings once stood. "The house and barn on Ab's are going down today. He's gonna light the fire this morning," Dad proclaimed.

The new owner told Dad we could have anything of value left in the house. Dad had bought the electrical box in the house and installed it just before the land was sold four years earlier. He wanted to remove the box before they set the house afire.

Dad had farmed the 160 acres surrounding Ab and Ceil's for thirty years after Ab retired from farming. He had sublet the house to several families over the years after Ab and Ceil passed away. Then the land and farmstead were sold, and our family couldn't afford to purchase the ground. Now it had been sold again.

Cecelia Arens Reifenrath was my Dad's sister. She and her husband, Albert, or Ab as everyone knew him, had lived on the place all their married lives. The place was just a quarter mile from my parent's farmstead.

Since Ab and Ceil had passed away, many others had resided in that old yellow house. However, all the neighbors still referred to it as Ab and Ceil's or Ab's place because it had that distinction for nearly half a century. I just couldn't call the place Kleinschmidt's or Shoat's or Ibach's. It was always Ab's place.

13

I fed the sows and did a few other chores while Dad hastily gathered some tools before we took off for Ab's place.

I drove the pickup onto the place. I hadn't been on the place for about four years. I drove by it everyday but didn't pay much attention to the condition of the house or barn. It's like the changing of the seasons. You notice the air becoming cooler as summer changes to autumn. You see the geese flying south overhead. You might even see a yellow leaf or two on the cottonwood trees. But you never stop to think about the season changing. Then suddenly when the tree leaves are blazing with color, a fierce northwest wind blows through the night and when you peer outside the next morning, all the leaves are gone and you know fall is over and winter is around the corner.

It was the same with the house on Ab's place. I hadn't noticed that the windows in the bedroom were broken out. I hadn't noticed the weeds growing six feet tall around the house. I hadn't noticed how that old willow tree on the east side of the house had been reduced to a few weak branches.

Some things were the same. Ceil's tulips were still there, nearly ready to burst into spring color. The old cottonwood was standing above the place, but it wasn't the majestic, stately monument I remembered it to be. The barn was still there, but it had been altered and remodeled several times, so it didn't even resemble the building in which Ab and Ceil raised their broiler chickens each summer.

I had barely noticed the deterioration. Now the northwest wind would come along and feed the fire that would destroy the entire farmstead practically overnight.

Dad and I didn't open the door to the porch to enter the house. It had been torn off long ago. Fly strips hung from the ceiling of the kitchen. I remembered how warm that kitchen always was. Ceil would have homemade bread in the oven or cookies that were warm out of the oven. When my brother and I visited them as kids, we'd look forward to Ceil's baked goods. Sometimes the cookies she gave us were so hot they would burn our mouths. They tasted better that way. The sweet smells of that kitchen were gone. They had given way to the odors of mice, dust, and mildew.

The bulldozer operator burst into the house and said he was ready to start working on the house as soon as we were finished. He hovered over Dad and I like a vulture waiting on his prey. There wasn't much time.

I began cutting wires and unscrewing lag bolts from the electrical box we were trying to salvage. I smashed my hand against the wall and my knuckles began to bleed. I used my

14

pliers to unfasten the lags in the back of the box. I pinched my thumb between the arms of the pliers as it slipped from the head of the lag. The blood blister that resulted sent pain up my arm. I cussed at the box and the pliers and the house and the situation. I didn't like being rushed into saying "goodbye" to Ab's place.

Dad rushed to the basement to see if the hot water heater was worth salvaging. He sprung up the stairs to check on my progress. He was a flurry of activity.

I asked myself if he felt anything. I asked if he had a peculiar feeling of loss like I did. All he seemed to care about was getting that hot water heater or electrical box. Finally, the wires were all cut and the lags loosened. We pried to release the box from the wall, but it was stubborn. Dad used a pry bar to pull the wood paneling away from the wall. Large chunks of the finish flew from the walls. The demolition of the walls seemed so violent. There were faded spots on the paneling where maybe a family photo hung. Or maybe it was a painting that Ceil liked or a fishing plaque Ab picked up on one of their many trips.

We tore at that wall to release the electrical box. After freeing the box, we rushed to the basement to haul the hot water heater up the steep concrete stairway. The heater was rusted, so it was a loss. We removed two old pressure tanks and an outlet. That was it. That was all we could find to salvage. The cupboards were gone. The photos gone. The chairs, the tables, even the bathtub were all gone. A few ragged curtains remained.

Dad and I walked through the house silently. I peered into the living room. I could see the image of Ab lying in the hospital bed that sat in the living room for several months as he withered away with cancer.

I remembered visiting him almost everyday. Ceil was so strong to care for him at home all those months. I remembered when two of their grandchildren were baptized in that very living room. Ab was proud that day and his pain subsided for a little while.

I remembered sitting beside him while my parents visited about old times. Every now and then he'd wince in pain. He'd cough up some horrible yellow phlegm. I knew, even as a teenager, that he would die.

I always admired Ceil's strength throughout Ab's illness. She was determined to keep him at home as long as she could. The long nights of listening to Ab cough and trying somehow to comfort him must have been overwhelming for her. Watching them together at that dark time in their lives was a lesson in the meaning of true, unconditional love for me.

After Ab died that next spring, Ceil felt very alone. She went on with life as best she could, but she missed her lifelong partner terribly. On my Dad's birthday, the summer after Ab passed away, Ceil had a heart attack. A few days later she had joined her husband.

We walked into their bedroom. The windows were smashed out. Two beer cans lie in the middle of the floor.

Dad still said nothing.

We walked outside. The dozer man said he was ready to start and asked if we were done.

"When do ya think this old house was built?" he asked. "Probably 100 years old, don't ya think?"

"I don't know," Dad replied. "The basement is made of rock and mortar, so it's pretty old."

I looked over toward the barn. The fishtank was still there. When I was a youngster, Ab kept minnows in that tank and sold bait to passing fishermen. A pump kept fresh water flowing into the tank.

"Look at the peonies coming up," the dozer man observed. "She must've liked plants with all the different stuff growing around here."

He was right. Ceil loved moss roses and tulips and peonies. She loved flowers and trees and shrubs. Dad pointed out the location of the old well to the dozer man, who was almost jovial about the whole ordeal. His mood was a bit too sunny for me.

"A lot of these old places are gone now," the dozer man commented. "Everybody needs more acres to make a living, but there just aren't many farmers left in the country who need houses."

He was right again. There are fewer farmers and fewer homesteads. The farmsteads stand for a few years. The memories of the past fade silently during the breezy spring days. When the land changes hands, the use of the land sometimes changes too. The economy of the day dictates the use. The memories disappear.

My stomach was sick. The dozer man had already pushed many of the trees including the old willow into the side of the house.

Dad climbed into the pickup beside me. We began to drive away, but stopped at the end of the driveway. We both looked back as the dozer man started the fire. The smoke billowed up into the blue spring sky. Suddenly the flames

16

broke through the windows and the siding. The building was engulfed in the fire. Dad raised his hand and waved "goodbye" to the place.

He turned to me and moisture welled up in his eyes. This place was no longer Ab's place.

I still see shadows of Ab's place when I drive by almost daily. All that remains now are a few cedar trees along the highway. But one day two years ago, as I drove by, I noticed something peculiar growing in the midst of the soybeans planted where Ceil's garden once grew. A single peony flower Ceil had planted long ago bloomed almost defiantly among the crops.

Ceil's flower reminded me of the lessons of love and caring I had learned from Ab and Ceil. Because of those lessons, there's a place in my heart that will always belong to Ab and Ceil. The farmstead is gone, but that special place will never fade away.

Peter Beeson Fall in the Sandhills

Along drainage gullies and river bottoms
the oaks slowly give up their acorns and
the cottonwoods sparkle with bright yellow.
Silver tone clouds float in crisp blue skies;
fall is fading and winter is coming.
The river runs clear and cold,
swiftly carrying a cargo of fallen leaves
that spin and swirl as they dance in
the current that meanders side to side,
tugging at the crumbling river bank and
frolicking among the snags and sandbars.
On higher ground the lodgepole pines
stand like a hunting party on horseback;
surveying the silent, empty farmstead
where the darting barn swallows play tag
in the shadows cast by out-buildings.
Rolling away from the river bluffs,
red topped hills spread out like waves;
endless, treeless, peopleless expanses
dotted by clear blue lakes and ponds.
Above the fading green and yellow valleys
the sky is a super highway filled with
great flocks of snow geese and Canadas;
ducks of every conceivable ilk;

17

wave after wave of Sand Hill Cranes and
the stately, upright flight of pelicans.
The stillness is populated with sound;
the squawking conversation of geese,
the warbling echoes of southbound cranes,
the chirps of meadow lark and jay and
the movement of wind through the grasses.
Little school houses bustle with warmth;
ranchers linger over coffee at the cafe;
grain stands in colorful little mountains
next to overstuffed tall white elevators
and everyone complains about prices.
The new north wind carries with it
a dusting of snow and a blast of cold;
cattle and pheasants began to bunch up
and men work furiously putting up hay.
Ranch wives break out decks of cards;
invite the kin and neighbors over;
steel themselves for the long loneliness
that will last until branding time.

10-25-92

Elaine Frasier   **The Enlightenment**

She hadn't planned to attend the rural women's retreat,
but a friend had persuaded her. She was taking a break from
her suburban home and had returned to visit the farm where
she had grown up. As a young woman, she had left to attend
college and develop a career. As time passed, she married a
man from the city. When her parents died, the farm was left to
her and her sister. There were no intentions of either of them
ever returning to the area to live but they still shared the
inheritance—the land.

Her voice was low as she spoke, haltingly, as though
unsure of what thoughts and words would emerge.

In her earlier years, she had been quite cavalier about
her roots—never thinking of them as anything more than a
starting point in her life.

But, as the years progressed, she was surprised to find
herself feeling a slight nostalgia about the property. She mused
that her husband didn't understand her awakening feelings for
the land. And she was resigned to his detachment.   She would
return alone during their vacation times.

Her sister, co-owner of the property, was ready to call a

real estate agent to have it listed, but she found herself unwilling to divest her inner self of that which she belatedly called home. She had first returned as an absentee landowner, but now shared her soul with the land.

She didn't think anyone in the group would understand what she was trying to say...but I understood.

She couldn't put into words how, when she now looked at the land, she could return in an instant to her childhood...I understood.

And, she hadn't realized how unchanging, yet always in change, the land was...I understood.

That, after all these years, the land was a part of her.

I understood, very well.

Dick Schanou   Old Storms

The pear tree grew ten years.
Then three more staked after a high wind.
It fell again the first unstaked spring.

Grandfather fell, pigeon proofing the hayloft.
Hip-staked, south-bedroomed, he withered,
Screamed three years at the shaded sun.

In summer, propped in a back seat, he'd stare,
Hawk-nosed, behind flashing glass,
As his sons said, "Corn looks good, don't it?"
Meanwhile, in the silent, stifled room, his wife
Threw open the single window.

In winter, from an ancient recliner, he'd stare snow.
That forth-year Christmas, he asked about the corn,
Staring at a drawn rest-home shade.

When I put in the summer screens, my reclining
Father complains about the dust and about the
Breeze moving his wispy hair.

My new trees are well staked. Sometimes,
From my recliner, next to the drapery pull,
I watch them bend in the wind.

We are adults now, three daughters gathered around the kitchen table at the farm in central Nebraska where we grew up. Holidays occasionally call us back to the farm. For those events we're able to engineer in advance what's left of our family to meet at this place we will always refer to as "home." No matter how many different cities and states we've occupied with our own adult households since the time when we left the nest, we still call this place "home." Funerals, weddings and high school reunions beckon one or two of us home at various times, but it is a rare event when all three sisters sit across from one another at this table without the usual competition from spouses, children, or our mother. This is the kitchen table that holds a databank of memories for each of us. Some are shared memories that would be recognizable if told by each of us separately, but most are from our distinct perspectives as oldest child, middle, or youngest, so that the listener might be surprised to finally learn they had been told of the exact same event.

Take, for example, the afternoon coffee break ritual that occurred around this table every afternoon at approximately 4 o'clock for nearly forty years. This was a time established by our father when he, the hired man, and sometimes our grandfather would come in for coffee and some dessert left over from the noon meal. As he once explained to me, those breaks weren't solely to give him and the help a chance to take the load off their feet. He felt that most farm accidents occurred in the late afternoon because the mind grew weary and the body fatigued by that time in the day, unless there was some way to become refreshed. It's important to be thinking clearly when your bare hands are mere inches from grain augers, power take-off implements, and unpredictable livestock. To his credit, safety incidents on our farm were minimal. But today, the adult Cynthia would recall that the coffee breaks meant one thing and one thing only—she, as the eldest, would be burdened with the responsibility of baking something for the men to eat. She would probably tell you that baking was just one of the many chores that fell onto her slim shoulders, that setting a standard of excellence in all that she did so that her younger siblings would see a good example, was a heavy load indeed. Melanie, the middle daughter, might remember taking part in the interesting conversations that transpired during the coffee breaks. She might work a deal to get the hired man to hitch up the horse trailer for her 4-H meeting that evening; she might be alert to some political innuendo expressed around the table by her elders. But to the youngest child, there is no recollection of responsibility or burden of having to think or of needing to assert her views in an articulate manner. I simply remember it as something I anticipated with glee every afternoon when I saw the men come toward the house, swinging greasy straw hats in their hands. Despite my mother's chastisement of the possibility that caffeine would stunt a child's growth, I would be allowed to sit on my father's lap and sip my very own cup of rich coffee, overly sweetened and creamed. Modern day farmers in Custer County surely enjoy some type of a mid-afternoon respite like these coffee breaks. I'd like to think that the men and women who manage and toil over the land today might still take time to enjoy the simple pleasure of a time when they're not so preoccupied with the task of farming to appreciate their family and the rare lifestyle they've chosen.

On this quiet July afternoon, hours after our late lunch but still too early to qualify as cocktail hour, we three sisters sit at the kitchen table and talk with one another in low, confidential tones with only an occasional exaggerated drawl or burst of laughter. The conversation bounces erratically between present tense and reminisces of our growing up years. We are three middle-aged women whose lives have so little in common today except for the undeniable fact that we are bound together by the fiber of sibling relationship. We are sitting precisely on what is practically our only other literal common ground—this place where we grew up—this place our father sometimes referred to in his humble but strong voice as "just a small diversified family farm." We have to watch ourselves in this situation, as we know from experience that we too easily slip back into old patterns of the pecking order, competition for parental praise, and other behaviors that we wouldn't assert onto even bare acquaintances in our lives away from this farmstead. We are careful to talk about only the things that we're pretty sure are still "safe," things like our political views, the local gossip, and our heritage that took a turn on this farm. We each chose a different path when we left this farm—that of lawyer, teacher and mother, and corporate marketer. But the roots we have in common seem to outweigh all the variances that have transpired in our lives.

This is the place where we grew up, this farm just outside of Arnold where our parents took out first and second and third mortgages to finance their start in the livelihood of gambling against all odds, otherwise known as crop and livestock farming. It must have looked so different then, in 1959, when they moved to the farm sitting just at the edge of the Sandhills in Custer County. At the time there were no paved roads leading into the village of roughly a thousand people and anything east of Lexington might well have been called no mans land. Paved highways formed the main intersection in Arnold shortly after my parents and oldest sister moved here. The sign at the edge of town boasting the latest population count had to be replaced more and more often as rural America felt an economic blight that sent her people searching elsewhere for prosperity. By the time I left for college in 1979, the sign read 800-some people, and on this most recent return trip, I noticed that it had dipped by another hundred.

The first thing my parents did when they bought this farm was to tear down the existing decrepit farmhouse and use the old lumber to have their very first new home built. Such a bold proclamation of affluence must have struck a nerve with their new neighbors. The locals might have been irked by what they saw through their conservative lens: a young family sailing into town with an almost cosmopolitan assertiveness and apparently money enough to erect a modern, all-electric ranch style home within their first year here. Hardly enough time to have paid their proverbial dues of hard work and struggle and "making do" with whatever house came with the farm.

But what did the neighbors know? They didn't know that moving to this farm was a new beginning of hope for a young couple who were still trying to grapple with the death of their only son—a death that ended 4 ½ years of asthma and allergies so severe that hospitals had become more familiar to him than his own home. The locals couldn't have known that the move to Arnold represented a new feeling of freedom, surely to our mother but especially to our father. Our father, the World War II Navy veteran who prematurely ended his studies at the Chicago Theological Seminary when he was called back to his own father's farm in Lexington to assume the role of a dutiful son. The move from Lexington to Arnold may have been only 62 miles, but our father was leaving behind the role of hired hand and finally, at age 38, had the chance to become his own boss. He was ready to start all over again and beamed with hope when he invested in this farm near the South Loup River; rich with sandy loam soil that held the promise of bountiful crops and full feedlots of cattle. He used what was left of his savings that hadn't gone towards medical and funeral expenses and did something that established a pattern that would play for the rest of his life—that of spending beyond his means with the aim of giving comfort and luxury to his family. He must have been embarrassed at what he knew his new neighbors were saying about this new upshot who was changing the look of the old Downing place with that fancy new house with the hardwood floors and "radiant heat" panels that were built into the ceilings. But he must have gotten accustomed to the feeling of being a different breed of farmer, or perhaps he just accepted it and was sure enough in his own skin and character to not give it a second's concern.

In all of his 74 years, if our father had deep regrets, he so rarely voiced them. He made a point of telling us that he never had second thoughts about the investments he made in our comfort, in our future. He used some of the last strength remaining in his weary, cancer-ridden body to tell us how proud he was of each of us. So it was fitting that one of the last things he heard was from his daughter, Melanie, at his hospital bedside. She assured him that she and her husband would take good care of his farm, the farm he had tended with deliberate stewardship and quite a lot of anguish and sweat for forty-odd years.

Our father farmed right up to the beginning of the end, until the day came when he could no longer hoist himself up and onto the tractor seat, so instead gratefully turned to his middle daughter and son-in-law to resume the daily chores. I believe without a doubt that the people in my father's life meant more to him than a piece of land. But I also believe that my sister's final assurance gave him the solace he needed to close his eyes and turn in a focused way to the chore of dying.

It is inevitable that we three sisters, when given this rare time of being unhurried with each other, will bring up something about our father, affectionately known to all three of us as "Daddy." It is just as inevitable that we will acknowledge our mother's role as a catalyst for some of the most powerful memories we hold. She is the sole resident of the family farm now, unless you count her collection of spoiled house cats. We remark to each other that she has shown more strength in recent years than we ever imagined she could muster without our father's rock of support. Some of her friends have inquired to us as to why she elects to stay on the farm in a house much too large but so full of her possessions and memories. We suppose it's because like us, she sees this as her only home.

It is, after all, still a working farm that turns enough profit to pay her living expenses. But the scale of farming has changed so much that the possibility of it netting enough income to pay expenses *plus* finance three resource-heavy children with college expenses is not even considered. My brother-in-law, who actively plants the crops and tends the livestock, today has another, more lucrative, business on the side that banks whatever savings his children will need for their future. He and my sister move as rapidly as jackrabbits when they drive into the farmyard at dusk to do the cattle feeding and irrigating each evening. Income from her teaching job at the community college an hour away helps them to get ahead, but at the price of weary long drives, complicated child care plans, and new sets of tires every year. Yes, so much has changed since our growing up years on this productive farm.

The late afternoon light has faded from where we sit and the dimness signals us to move out to the front yard where we can get a better view of what's left of the original farmstead. We stroll out towards the old red barn, the centerpiece of the farm. Weeds surround it, but it stands erect and still sports most of the paint from 1989 when Daddy went to considerable expense to have the roof reinforced, re-shingled, and invested in paint and new boards for the siding where time had taken it's toll. This is the barn where the eldest of us, Cynthia, invented dangerous rites of initiation for her new Arnold friends by showing them how to jump from the lowest side of the roof onto the corrals below. This barn was grand central station during the years when Melanie, middle daughter, was heavily into 4-H horse competitions and rodeo queen contests. But to me, the youngest, the barn was the place where I retreated when someone yelled at me for breaking a crystal goblet or when the hands of the dining room clock neared the appointed hour of my weekly piano lesson. It was the place where they always forgot to look before giving up and calling Mrs. Quig to cancel my lesson. It was where I found comfort by sitting in a hay manger, stroking one of the many tame barn cats that my sisters and I had nurtured from kitten-hood to old age. Even today as an adult, I can recreate the sweet smell of prairie hay mingled with the dust and animal odor of that barn by just closing my eyes and thinking about it.

Our time of peacefulness together as sisters has come to an end as a car wheels into the circular drive and jabbering kids, my niece and nephew, jump from it before the engine is turned off. They run toward their mother, Melanie, with exuberance and delight, briefly acknowledging their aunts before inquiring what's for dinner and announcing the name of the video they want us to watch with them later this evening. As I make the mental transition from talking with the only two people in the world who will ever understand what this place means to me, I can't help but wonder if this next generation will come to associate something sentimental with this particular piece of real estate, this family farm I call home, this icon of not just a residence for my first 17 years but a lifestyle that molded my view of everything else on the planet.

J.V. Brummels   Bones

The backhoe man wears black. I suppose
the dirt and grease of his work don't show
that way. Today, he plays undertaker

for the first horse I ever bought.
For this man it's a pretty good fit.
He sympathizes. I wouldn't pay

for a hole for just any horse, but this mare
carried my kids when they were little,
and the cowboys I know knew her well.

They'll want to pay their respects. I just
don't want the dogs dragging her
piece by piece up to the house, I say.

What I don't tell him is she died pawing
at the ground and staring off to the south,
the distance something only she could see.

                 *   *   *

Still, by the next spring the coyotes
have made a den of the grave's soft earth,
and they've drug these few dark long bones

out to bleach in the sun. The truth is,
I don't much mind. If I know anything
it's that flesh feeds the living.

Death instructs us. These bones
are rock in their heft, a weight
far greater than cow or dog or bird,

a dense history of evolution
from some soft-soled, multi-toed swamp-dweller
to leg and hoof that hammer down distance.

I gather these, one by one into the cradle
of my arms, carry back to the hole what carried me
so many miles, lay them back away,

and stand bareheaded before this grave.
Death questions us. New grass
is the soft, shining hide draped

over the flesh of earth, and rock her bones.
Or this hole is just another hungry mouth,
and earth the final carnivore who feeds

on flesh that's only meat, gnaws bones to dust.
I stomp dirt down to keep the light at bay.
mount the impatient horse that today

carries my flesh through these hills.

—For Paul Zarzyski and for Liz Brummels

Steven P. Schneider   **Butte Country**

On a gray morning
we drive Highway 20 West
from Chadron to Crawford,
wild sunflowers growing by the roadside,
rolls of hay
stacked in fields,
pine-studded buttes
all around us.

What is a butte
but a peak,
an alpha wave on the horizon,
a survivor of wind's pull on the earth,
an escarpment,
a lookout onto the past and future?

When we arrive at Fort Robinson,
we ride out in a van to the buffalo camp,
pay homage to these monks of the Northern Plains
big bulls with shaggy beards and wooly shoulders,
tufts of fur around their legs.
They are crunching on wild prairie grass,
silent,

impenetrable
gazing at us
gazing at them.

In late afternoon
the sun breaks through cloud cover,
and we ride Smoky and Bandit
past Canadian thistle and tall grass
up a windy rock path
to the ridge atop Red Cloud Butte.
We gaze long at the pink clays
and thick layers of the bluff's flanks,
identify birds
we read about in the guide
to Pine Ridge:
red-tailed hawk, killdeer, yellow-breasted chat.

Our horses lead us
up,
then down.
We feel the wind
kick the dust and silt
that has carved
these bluffs
for thousands of years.

Elizabeth Barrett   Nebraska's Horizons

Nebraska poet Don Welch once told about a professor
from Pennsylvania who had visited the state and described it as
"dispiriting."

Welch went on to say that the professor did not have the
right eyesight and insight to appreciate the subtle beauty of this
glorious state.

Younger Nebraskans often have an inferiority complex
about where they live, especially when in the company of people
from states with magnificent mountain scenery or breathtaking
views of the ocean or who are from cities that never sleep.

I used to plan and plot when I would make my escape
from this boring state. The funny thing is that the longer I
stayed, the more Nebraska became part of my being.

Years ago an intense experience brought home this
knowledge loud and clear. On a trip to Hong Kong with a dog-
eared copy of "Southeast Asia on a Shoestring" tucked under

my arm and a worn pack strapped to my back, I hopped a bus to a section of the city known as Kowloon where accommodations where rumored to be cheap.

There I followed a New Zealand couple to a dilapidated high-rise apartment building called Chungking Gardens where we shared a room for $15 a night. Interestingly enough that was on the high end of what most of the backpacking crowd likes to pay.

After several days of sight-seeing around the city, I became restless and ill at ease and decided to take a ferry to a special place in the South China Sea called Lantau Island.

As we bobbed out of the harbor, voila, I could see the horizon. The unsettled feeling experienced in the bustling city evaporated as quickly as the splash of sea spray against the boat.

The next few days were enjoyable ones as I sat on the beach with the sea lapping at my toes.

My soul was at peace.

Years later, a student of mine from Nepal told me how he sometimes felt a need to escape from the plains of Nebraska to the Rocky Mountains of Colorado where he found his peace in surroundings similar to where his soul had taken root.

Where you grow up is always part of you.

To me, a city thronged with people and cluttered by sky-scraping superstructures becomes dispiriting after a few days.

As a woman of the prairie, being able to see those beautiful Nebraska sunsets and sunrises and all of the wide-open vistas in-between is salve for my soul.

Diana Lambson   **Friday, May 21, 1999**

Blue-green day.
Sprinkled down, pressed
by Thursday's temper
tantrum weather.

Breezes,
new as Adam's first breath,
squeak across leaves,
grass, calf faces,
strewing winsome whispers.

Only surface tension holds
water at pond's lip
where yesterday it was pulled back

28

like a prissy girl's skirts,
from mud.

Tractors wait
with bated exhaust at field gates,
tugging at steering wheels,
accelerators anxious to dance hope's ritual planting.
Certain of promise yet again.

Jack Ostergard   Feelings

I drove to the ranch today
Far from the traffic and lights,
To a place where I'd spent my life
And I drank in old sounds and old sights.

So it's me back out on the prairie
Somewhere miles from a town,
Where it's safe for old worn out cowboys
To go native and let their hair down.

And I realize how fortunate
I have been to have lived all of this,
And now that I have forsaken it
There are things that I'm going to miss.

Let me ride my horse to a windmill
And pause for a time to drink.
Let me survey God's Kingdom
And take a few moments to think.

I have stood on the crest of these hills
And watched this panorama pass,
I have seen the wildlife and fauna
And heard the wind in the grass.

I've seen cows and calves in these valleys
Standing in grass belly deep.
I've seen months go by with no rain
And cause strong men to weep.

Even the snow had its beauty
As blizzards sculpted the drifts
And changed the hills and the valleys
Into chasms, caverns, and cliffs.

It's a hard life that offers no quarter
And tests every weakness of men.
It challenges those who need people
And it's lonesome only to them.

I was never here to make money
Getting rich was never my goal.
It's the land and the feeling it gives you
That somehow fits into your soul.

I watch now as other men
Ride down trails I have ridden,
But to turn back the clock and go back
In this life time I find is forbidden.

So I will come back time and again
Because I am drawn to the Land
And for those who never have lived it,
It is something they can't understand.

You become one with all creatures
As you watch the hawk and the dove,
And you realize you are a small part
Of the Kingdom of God up above.

Jean Groth   Trout Calling

The demands of a farmer must have a place where all things
take recess.
One of those such places would be the Snake River.
When the call of the trout is heard, it is much too difficult to
ignore.

southeast corner of the porch
is the place they are stored.
carefully staged
to be snatched in a moment's time.
the fly rod and reel,
nymphs and hand tied flies for any weather,
hip waders and the lucky hat.
...the rain is falling.
...the hay is wet.
...the cultivating will wait.
the trout appear too loud this morning.
before I change my mind

I must heed their call.
swiftly load the white dodge truck
and get rolling down the road.
hoping my conscience
does not seize the victory.
the farming will be here
upon my return,
and my spirit will be rejuvenated.
my farm needs me, but it needs all of me.
trout fishing completes me.

Faye Tanner Cool   Journey Into a Quiet Land

I revel in the aloneness of Nebraska's Sandhills. Some people would call its vastness too lonely, but I call it welcome space. Space enough to really be...space enough to observe the land and the sky all at once...space enough to feel what it is like to be the "only person in the world."

I think a good example of this is a time when I drove Highway 2 from our small central Nebraska ranch to Alliance— a trip of over 170 miles....

It is 5:15 in the morning when I leave the house. The air is moist-warm in this early summer morning. A giant, orangish sun is rising over my right shoulder where I can see it in my rear view mirror. The moon, a gloriously full one, perches on the west horizon ahead of me, ready to dip into the dark on the other side of the world.

No cars ahead of me, no cars behind me. No car zipping by ten miles over the speed limit. No car jockeying for first place on this still empty highway.

Just over the next hill, I come upon the first traffic of the morning—a mother Bobwhite trailing a thread of little ones. She quickens her pace as she hears my engine, but she doesn't exceed the speed limit.

I come to the sleepy-looking town of Dunning. The highway bypasses most of it.

At Halsey, a huge mist of emerald green cedar spires poke into the deep blue morning sky. The forest is edged by the lighter green of the grassy hills. It is a manmade forest, the only one in the world. At its entrance a sign says it is a national forest. There is a tall tower in the midst of the trees, which houses a ranger who is there to report the fires, usually caused by lightning or some careless cigarette-tossing individual.

As I travel through them, these Sandhills appear to be

31

uninhabited, but there is evidence of life other than cattle and deer and game animals and fowl. At the highway's edge, where narrow graveled side roads wind off into the beyond, stand mailboxes. People live out there in these quiet hills. Not to say there are no ranches along the highway. I have passed a few spread out behind a windbreak of cedars or boxelders, or underneath a stand of great cottonwoods.

Other subtle clues that someone else travels this highway are an occasional bullet-riddled road marker, or a spray-painted "i" over an "a" on a NO PASSING sign. Typical rural graffiti.

Here and there along the way, I have been passing the small lakes this region is noted for. I think this adds to the sereneness of the Sandhills. Domed "breadloaf" stacks, huge round bales and some small square bales—some new, some from previous haying—dot the different meadows. An attention-getting windmill comes into view. Its wheel of red, white and blue fans spins lazily, pumping into a very much dented galvanized tank. No water shimmers from the depths, nor spills over the side. Instead the tank "overflows" with a stand of weeds.

Thedford's café has its lights on, but I don't stop.

Near Seneca, I cross into an earlier time zone and live again through the hour I've just left.

It isn't until I leave Mullen and approach Whitman—over 100 miles from home—that I meet a pickup. More than likely the driver is a rancher bound for a coffee shop and people contact after he's finished his morning's work.

On through the almost ghost town communities of Ashby, Bingham, Ellsworth, Lakeside and Antioch I go, knowing that Antioch was once a busy mining area for potash during World War II. Now, just an old building hugs the edge of the highway.

About ten miles out of Alliance and from here on into the city, I meet "heavy" traffic: nine vehicles in all. For all of these 170 miles, I have not encountered a single incident of road congestion, road jockeying, or road rage. It has been a restful trip.

On my way home, nearly eleven hours later, I find nothing much has changed. The same traffic, perhaps a little heavier this time, thins to nothing about five miles out of the city. At Seneca I lose my gained hours as I pass back into my own time zone. The red, white, and blue windmill wheel still pumps invisible water. At Halsey, the forest still pushes its dark greenery into a now faded denim-colored sky. This time I have met a few cars, and two pickups have swung around me and buzzed on, but mostly I've had the highway to myself. I do not meet the mother Bobwhite with her skein of little ones, but I do see the same sun/moon scene: the sun setting in my rear view mirror, blood red, and the brilliant full moon rising in the east in front of me, smack-dab in the middle of the highway. A sight forever etched on my memory.

It is this wealth of space I crave...

It is this only-person-in-the-world feeling that impresses me...

It is this wonderful aura of aloneness that inspires me...again...again...and again.

Mark Gustafson Land in the Country

Water tank ecology, the moss, the bugs and snails to see
    Under tiny waves wafted up by a southwesterly.
The scrap-wood boat sails the tank's green sea
    Made by grandpa and my son who's three.
We love living on our land in the country.

Her vegetable garden by the apricot tree
    Beside which grow the wild rose later steeped as hip tea.
Black birds fighting for a worm or seed pea
    And fresh turned earth that smells heavenly.
We love living on our land in the country.

The windmill creaks late on a moonlit night
    The pond's lovesick frogs sing with all their might.
A great horned owl hoots in a cottonwood out of sight
    And our son runs in the dark just for the fright.
It's why living on the land feels so right
    In the country.

Robert Richter Home Again

In the pre-dawn mist barn cats
Head home from the hunt, having
Prowled the golden dew, heard
The meager midnight moans of men and mice
In the dark, feeding on just enough
To survive the day's coming heat. The fields
Sing sweet birdsong and cricket cries.
The horizon lies half-hidden, distance
Deceiving like the heaving heart. Roads overland

33

Lead nowhere unless a destination
Is conceived, the spirit relieved of darkness.
The sun rises like a promise, but
Desert heat is the day's destiny. Barn cats
Seek shadows and sleep.

Mary Borm   The Nebraska Sandhills

In 1987 my son left home to attend boot camp at the
Great Lakes Naval Training Center in Illinois. The stories he
told on returning were a bit surprising. A few of the young men
he talked to had never heard of Nebraska and didn't know it
was part of the United States. Others thought we still had
uncivilized Native Americans fighting to turn back encroaching
white men. They thought we had no electricity or indoor
plumbing, no TV or telephone and certainly no improved
roadways. Although I shake my head at their innocence, in my
opinion, the less some of these innocents know about our
Nebraska, the happier I will be. My husband, Dewey Keys, and
I live on a small ranch in the Nebraska Sandhills. We're located
on the North Loup River in the southeast corner of Cherry
County. This is the largest, least populated county in the state.
Our closest 'city' of Purdum, supports a population of around
twenty-five, depending on the year, a Church, an old time
Mercantile, a bank, Post Office, and a well drilling company.
There is hardly ever a need for an unplanned run into town, but
when the necessity arises, we travel over eleven miles of some of
the most horrendous roads imaginable. In dry seasons, the
sand blows up around you restricting vision as well as
breathing. The washboard effect at the corners threatens to
dislodge everything from eyeglasses to shirt buttons and dental
work. When we have snow and mud, we find it necessary to
use the 4-wheel drive vehicles the city folk covet for
entertainment.

Any doctors, dentists, or major shopping centers are
over an hour away. We learn quickly to stock up on groceries
since most trips to the more populated areas are planned
around parts runs or the cattle auction. Our mail is delivered
only three days a week, a fact that is hotly argued by the postal
workers in Omaha. We get TV with the aid of a satellite receiver
and radio reception only when we hold our mouth right. About
the time the news and weather comes on, the signal fades and
we are again left in ignorance. If we choose to fight this
dilemma, we can turn on the television and get our news right
out of Chicago, our weather from New York! We've come to

34

believe those folks who report the changes in our climate, may be more interested in body English than meteorology. They stand directly in front of our state, and with beautiful, sweeping motions of the hands, report on the surrounding regions. Since they rarely move their feet, it's no wonder some folks don't know Nebraska exists. We can, of course, call neighbors to learn of the latest news and weather, but we'd best do it when the weather is dry. Our end of the telephone cable seems to malfunction every time it rains.

Since our closest neighbors are two miles away, we aren't bothered by loud parties or someone mowing the grass before the alarm goes off at 6:00 AM. We aren't compelled to keep our lawns perfectly groomed or leaf-free in fear of what the neighbors might think. If window peeping was a concern in our area, we'd be in big trouble since we are very sparing with curtains. We want the view of our beloved Sandhills as unrestricted as possible. We are simple people with simple needs. We can sit for hours watching the wild turkeys that claim our ranch as their home. We marvel at the ability of those heavy bodied creatures to fly from the ground to the tops of the trees. Then wonder how they can possibly stay there, especially when the wind is bending the trees near double. One time, Dew came to wake me at 2:00 AM just to watch the deer grazing on the tender grass in the house yard. The sight and sounds of pheasants and grouse feeding on corn the calves have spilled is always a pleasant sight each fall. We never tire of watching the newborn calves take their first breath, their first steps. Then roar with laughter as they learn to run and play with their peers, much as human babies do. Each spring when most of the new calves are on the ground, we travel around to neighboring ranches to help with the branding. These are the old time rope and drag brandings. The sights, the sounds, the fellowship with friends makes one's heart swell with pride.

I grew up in the Platte River Valley of central Nebraska and have lived in the Sandhills only nine years. Now, instead of seeing mile after mile of unchanging fields, I see rolling hills and green meadows. An endless, undulating sea of grass. Thousands of differing varieties of grasses and wildflowers that wave and bow as I pass. They seem to say, "Come. See, smell and feel this life that is mine. Understand that God put me here to share His beauty with you. I will fall to the earth and die, but next year, my seeds will sprout and I will return. I am part of Nature's eternal circle. I am Life."

I could go on through infinity telling of spacious blue skies, cloud formations that cause you to stop and stare, sunrises and sunsets that daily renew your faith in God. The creek of the windmill lulling one to sleep on soft summer evenings, the chevron of geese effortlessly slicing through the atmosphere. Then there is the song of the river as it frolics between its banks, the scream of the ice breaking up in the Spring. The doe cautiously, tentatively leading her fawn to the meadow, the cry of hawk and eagle as they soar high above the trees.

Ranch life is not easy. It's a continual conflict between you and the elements. Too much summer rain and you don't get enough hay for your cattle. In dry years, the grass doesn't grow, forcing us to constantly move cattle and, of course, raises the fire index to terrifying levels. An over abundance of cold weather and snow during calving season and you have a higher death loss. If the price of our neighbor's corn goes up, the price of our calves goes down. In my personal experience, the words rich and rancher do not belong in the same sentence. Our riches come from the beauty of our surroundings, the love of family and friends. The people in rural communities are friendlier, more giving. They are quick to offer a hand, a word of sympathy, a prayer. You don't have to size them up, trying to determine if they are genuine; you already know. Although we may poke fun at the condition of our roads and the fact that we are isolated, we like things just as they are. We take care of our land, it takes care of us. We don't want it opened to developers, huge hog confinements or cattle feeders destined to push out the old time rancher.

Although I can point at a map and say, "This is where I live," the Sandhills is more than a place on a geographical chart. It's a place in my heart. This is my home. These are my hills. I will never leave them. But when the time comes for me to go, I too will be planted here. I only pray that while I was here, I sewed enough seeds, enriched enough lives to make me worthy of my final resting place.

Lyn DeNaeyer   **Baby Talk**

"So there Bossy... now so!
Y' ol' hide, let the little guy suck!
'Nother fit or two like that 'un
Yer sorry carcass'll be on the truck.

*****

36

He'd soon be a goner, I reckon.
His mama run off in the storm.
Poor baby. She's a tough go in this world.
Well, rub 'im down a bit. Let's get 'im warm.

*****

Now, ain't that a sight fer sore eyes?
A filly. Got her ma's pretty head.
A star and a deep little chest.
You'll go a piece to find one better bred.

*****

Aw, Mother, she ain't gonna hurt none.
This ol' blanket'll do fer a bed.
Ain't fit fer man or beast out there.
Day old pups 'ud sure freeze in the shed.

*****

Looky there Honey... feel how soft!
Careful! Don't squeeze 'em so hard!
Their peepin's got mama hen worried.
Here she comes on the run, 'cross the yard.

*****

Sure, that's my boy over there on the bay.
Don't he put you in mind of my dad?
Seems to have a way with a colt.
Quite a hand, an' his ropin' ain't bad.

*****

Yeah, she's growed up an' ready fer leavin';
Full of dreamin', I hope so's' an' 'maybe's.
'S'cuse me, guess there's some dirt in my eye.
Aw, y' know how ol' men get 'bout their babies.

*****

Now Sister, that boy never meant no harm.
He's just a lad in need of a nap.

It's hard work helpin' Uncle Joe feed the calf.
Come here Tiger, up on Granddaddy's lap!"

"Well Mama, let's you and me go mix up the bread.
Dad gets that look; it's no more use talkin'!
And you know how he is with his babies.
They'll both nod off soon's he starts in to rockin'!"

For Tom McBeth and his "babies"

Renee Lanik   Platte River Awakening

Walking all day, we'd seen
everything from our feet,
covering the spring-engorged
woods as if we were as young as
our son leading the way. Whichever trail

we chose, the way was rich
in color. Cushions of moss encrusted
paths matted with lace-trampled
leaves pad our steps. Sunlit hills cool
into damp recession under a ceiling
of oak and ash. Water seeps,

falling, through sculpted,
limestone-paved shafts, a staircased
well-winding into perfectly still,
green water, spilling over
into infinity. The thrush

overhead affirms
both dawn and dusk as we
hop from rock to rock.

Fredrick Zydek   Building a Scarecrow for the Wind

We must trap this straw
like a thought and stuff
it up his sleeves,
fill his belly one fistful
at a time, use binder twine
to define his elbows and knees.

We must rub earwax into his
gloves and sleep three nights
without bathing
in the old clothes
with which we shall dress him
right down to his shorts.

We will prop him up somewhere
between the shedding place
of adolescence and the ornery task
of becoming a full-grown man.
We must give him a hat
and a Tom Waits smile,

a fair bulge in his crotch,
and a pair of shoes
that tells the world
this is a walking man,
a man whose ankles have grown
thick with sadness.

From that day on we must speak
in a hush when we pass him
and leave the wind
to explain what hatched
once we left him alone
in the world to fend for himself.

Marjorie Saiser   **Going to See the Homeplace**

This morning the grass is wet, and the wind
is blowing songs through the handles
of the Clorox bottles in the garden.

We climb into the pickup,
going to see the home place,
although, as my father says,
there's nothing there.

Two miles south of town
I open the gate. A calf watches,
his black and white face
new and stark,
all the edges undefiled.

39

Until things changed, my father says,
the house was there, west of the trees.
The barn, it was beautiful,
red and white stripes
on the cupola. The spring

inch and a quarter pipe,
cold water day and night
flowing into the barrel,
spilling over the top.

Almost at the gate I remember
to ask where the strawberries were.
I find the clump of trees at
the end of my father's pointing finger.
Not the first draw, but the second.
Strawberries, he says,
carried out by the dishpanful.

The old place at the far reaches of his finger
rolls down to the river
rolls high and pretty
rolls with his hand

blows with the wind:
I myself am seeing it, taking
the measure of it with my arms,

as if his grandmother, with my uncalloused hands,
unfurled a farm
like a sheet
into clean cold air.

LoRee Peery A Slice of 1950's Farm Life

One's growing up experience is a powerful, personal
enlightenment. Like most children, I was oblivious to the
unique time in which I grew up. It was a time when children
could still be innocent, as they really were straight off the farm
when they met maturity, whenever that coming of age would
strike.
I consider it a privilege to have grown up on a farm. My
parents, Merlin and LaVera Mosel, each came from a family of
seven children, and I am the oldest of seven. A lot can be said
for character traits, not to mention old-fashioned work ethics,

which ensue from that environment. There was no time for selfishness, laziness, disobedience, or complaint. We each had our place and there were expectations.

If Nebraskans and other Midwesterners listened to their elders, at some time they heard stories of the Blizzard of '49. As I was growing up Mom would tell how she and Dad only had a gallon of peaches to eat for a week. Then she would go on to tell how I came to be. She was a town girl and lonely stuck out in the country by herself all day. Dad was in the field or out doing chores from before dawn till after the cows were milked at night. Somewhere along the line, I concluded that I had been planned.

I was born between blizzards in the spring of 1949. Because Mom had toxemia she was so swollen up that even Dad's overalls wouldn't fit. She sewed her own dresses and it was a dress she was wearing when I was ready to make my entrance into the world. Mom and Dad were renting a farmhouse close to my dad's home place near Orchard, Nebraska. The driveway was a long one, about a half mile from the road, and impassable by car or truck. The only vehicle to make it, between mountains of snowdrifts, and over frozen ruts, was the old Oliver tractor. In labor, in a dress, and in the relentless north wind, Mom stood on the back of that tractor. She's gone now, so I can't ask if there was a car at the end of the lane, or if they drove the tractor to Grandpa Mosel's house, but I arrived a few hours later at the hospital in Norfolk. Mom not only got me, but she got frostbite on her legs.

I must have helped occupy Mom's time because she loved to read to me and I could read at age four. She designed and sewed my clothes until I started sewing my own.

My first real memory is of a big white farmhouse south of Brunswick that had narrow stairs. I had a room of my own at the top of those stairs where Mom had made me a dresser from orange crates and trimmed it in a skirt made of yellow calico with red flowers.

I turned five in the spring of 1954 and remember the first time I entered the tiny old farmhouse where I grew up. Of course, it didn't seem tiny to me at age five. A loosely woven wire fence determined the difference between the back and front porches, which each faced east, separated by a few feet and a window. The porches were enclosed and a concrete stoop rested outside each door. On the left an ornamental gate opened into the front yard.

We went through the back porch door, on the right side of the fence, off the farm yard. The first thing I saw on the other side of the door was the hand pump, too hard for me to use, where water flowed icy cold from the windmill out next to the corral, and pumped into a basin or tub. The next thing I remember is the etched and beveled glass picture window in the dining room.

The 160 acres I still call home is in Antelope County, five miles east and three north of Neligh, Nebraska. The land consists of highly erodable soil, from sand to clay and most anything in between but black loam. Dad planted dryland crops such as corn, alfalfa, and grains for silage to feed the cows. Digging into the silage pile during chores in the winter was an unforgettable experience. The fermentation would steam up, engulfing the digger with the potency of strong drink fumes.

Over the years, Dad concluded that those acres weren't meant for cropland. He wised up and seeded all acres that weren't already pasture. Now there are varied grasses where cattle graze from May to October. In a wet spring the brome hits me mid-thigh. During a dry August, cracks appear in the native grass pasture between tufts of yucca, sage, and tumbleweeds, and the prairie flowers are only a memory.

When the crops were nonproductive we survived because of livestock. Dad was an excellent pig farmer. Hogs in a pen eat everything in sight. What they don't eat they dig up with their snouts and wallow in. Hogs are intelligent and when they got out of the pen it would take the whole family to herd, holler, cuss, and chase them back in.

During farrowing time we kids were not allowed inside the pen that kept gigantic 500-pound Yorkshire sows who would put out litters of nine to 14 piglets. A few were vicious animals even when they didn't have piglets to feed. The pen was west of the house, behind the outhouse and beyond the fruit trees. The sows gave birth in A-framed shelters that had corrugated tin roofs and were scattered throughout the pen. Runt piggies were brought into the house and warmed in the oven or near the heating stove. Then they would be bottle fed. When things became more sophisticated Dad built a hog shed over a concrete slab east of the barn. Then the farrowing was done in pens and the piglets could scamper around in clean straw, escaping the ponderous weight of their mothers, which often killed a few. If Dad were alive today, I could see him with one of those self-contained, odorless facilities.

Dad also raised cattle. Some city people call all cattle cows. To me a cow is a Holstein (that's black and white), with a ponderous bag stretched pink with bulging veins and ready to pop its milk. The brother closest to me in age, Gaylen, can tell how many cows we milked, how we milked them, and how old he was during those times. I have a physical reminder. An old triangular milk stool from our barn leans on my kitchen floor next to a Holstein cow made of plywood.

Before we had running water in the house, we took Saturday night baths in a galvanized tin washtub. Dad was pretty innovative. One hot summer Saturday after the cows were milked and the cream separator bowl cleaned, he rigged up a shower for us. He parked the pickup next to the wellhouse and not far from the yard light. He laid support boards across the pickup rack, just behind the cab. On the boards he rested the separator bowl and filled it with water.

At the turn of the spigot we got water on our heads and a memory to last a lifetime.

We also raised stock cattle, white-faced with black or red bodies. The males (steers), are castrated and usually go to market as yearlings. Some females (heifers), were put in with the Black Angus bull for calving in the spring. The second time around heifers become cows. Calves have to be dehorned and vaccinated and are fed and sold at the discretion of the farmer. Some cows and their calves don't take to one another, or something happens to the mother, and the calf has to be nursed along. We would feed the calf by first letting it suck on a finger, then trick it into going for the calf bucket, which held milk and sported a false teat.

We ate rich because we ate off the land—beef, pork, chicken, and eggs; whole milk, butter, and cream. Mom always had a garden, with potatoes as a staple of our daily menu. I helped Mom clean, cut, and can shelves full of fruits and vegetables that were stored in Mason jars on the cave shelves. The cave was also a shelter at the times tornadoes threatened to strike.

There were lean times too. Twice in the fifties our farm was mortgaged. Dad worked out west in a faraway place called Gothenburg, where he was on a crew that paved the streets. That left Mom, Gaylen, and me to do the chores. Standard procedure in feeding the animals was hefting a filled five-gallon bucket in each hand and off we'd go to feed or water various critters. In the cold of winter we would finish long after dark and stay out too long. I can still see tears running down Mom's cheeks as she rubbed our frostbit hands till they were warm.

The chickens were my responsibility. At five, I only had to gather the eggs. When I was a little bigger I held a bucket and scattered grain. I closed them in at night when they were roosting, and when I was big enough, I even scooped out the coop.

Then there was a year that we lived in Neligh while Mom and Dad managed the Hilltop Cafe. I finished my fourth grade year and began my fifth grade year at two different schools in town. My schoolmates told me later how jealous they were because I had returned to that one-roomed country school a bit too citified.

Not many Nebraskans my age can claim the memories of kindergarten through eighth grade years in a one-room country school. Twelve pupils was average, counting the older boys who had to skip school to help in the fields during harvest.

Black Lake School, District #56, sat a little past three miles north of our corner. The school had a well pump and a flagpole out front to the south. The older students took turns, as they did raising and lowering the flag, carrying the water into the hallway in a big crockery cooler. We ladled water into our personal cups with a common dipper. I still have my little tin cup. That water was cold naturally, but in the winter it was icy.

The school was heated by a big oil stove that stood in the middle of the stage. The stage was a platform surrounded by chalkboards where we did math problems and diagramed sentences. In the spring we would stand on stage and practice for the spelling bee.

We went through school hearing about the young teacher who had lost her diamond engagement ring out in the coal shed. At least once each spring we would spend our recesses for a week trying to find the treasure.

Behind the school were two outhouses. Girls on the left, and boys on the right. If we couldn't wait until recess we would raise our hand with either one or two fingers extended. Number one would be a quick run out back. Number two meant we might be a few minutes. One recess I was locked in the outhouse from the outside. A couple of the girls were jealous of my red can-can, one of the special garments Mom made for me.

The days began with the Pledge of Allegiance and singing from our green songbook, *On Wings of Song*. When my work was caught up and I couldn't help the teacher, I would read. I went through the whole series of *Pollyanna* books. I went down the Mississippi with Tom and Huck, and escaped into every other antique novel that was standing on a shelf. There were floor to ceiling bookshelves in two corners and other shelves and bookcases that held the secrets of far away places and adventure sometimes beyond imagination.

Christmas programs were quite an event. "Curtains" were hung by stretching wool army blankets over a wire to create our stage. I sang a solo most every year, played in skits, and memorized classics like "'Twas the night before Christmas." Santa would burst through the door after we were finished frolicking, and those brown paper sacks were the best ever. Peanuts in the shell, a few other nuts, haystacks—chocolate covered mints—filled hard candy, an apple, and an orange.

At the end of the year we would have a school picnic. Tables would be laden with food that our mothers had prepared. We would play softball, run, and laugh until we were hungry again. Then we would have triple-decker ice cream cone eating contests.

Summer was free and fanciful in between helping Mom with the garden, and doing chores or helping in the hayfield when I became old enough. Imagination was the game we played, be it cowboys and Indians, making mud pies, or being a bride with a white towel or pillowcase veil.

In the winter when we were snowed in and couldn't get to school, we played "Hide the Thimble," "Button, Button," or made trains by turning the chairs over. As we got a little older we played cards, checkers, and Chinese checkers by the hour.

Memories can be vivid images or fleeting flashes. When I reflect on that time past I have to admit that we were poor, but I never knew it because we grew up surrounded by the love of our parents and the outdoors created by a God who made His presence known in the land and the living things that surrounded and sustained us.

Jason Elznic Wayne County Done by a French Impressionist

I want to see the massive plow
    a splotch of red
    splitting the land
    like so many carcasses
    going down the line,
The live electric green
    of five-legged frogs
    squirting out of the blades furrow
    living off the heroin
    injected in natures vein.

I want to see the rough-hewn horror
    that is cottonwood trees,

45

A vacuum at the bottom
        that used to be
dirt and water,
The transplanted behemoths
        sucking the last out of mother
their roots tearing at
        her very breast.

I want to hear the roar.
One Thousand Snapper-Baggers
        tearing the canvas
        in an ocean of sickly bluegrass.
All done in perfect pointillism
        the monster of summer
        reduced in the mind
        to a quarter-inch
        of the hundred foot canvas.

I want to see the artist
        fat on his commissions
        dancing here...
        dancing there...
With a paint-pail on his head.
The Don Quixote of High Art
        dashing at windmills
        with a Number Two Camel Hair,
Thinking justice is done.

Algene Stohl The Old Farmhouse

As you turn in the driveway, the first thing you see
Is a broken old mailbox, forlorn by a tree.
The driveway was graveled and traveled so much;
But now the weeds grow in one endless bunch!
Where are the people who loved this dear place?
I look with excitement, but can't see a face.
The gate is hanging by hinges of rust,
The fence is sagging beneath huge mounds of dust.
The sidewalk lies buried, half under the sod,
I stumble as I walk – between every clod.
No flowers are blooming, just thistles and vine.
The wires are hanging from the broken clothes line.
The roof of the house is caving in I see
If I'm not careful it could fall on me!

My knock at the entrance sends the door crashing down,
And I gaze in the kitchen, which I view with a frown.
The linoleum is torn and covered with tracks,
And field mice are running to their home in the cracks!
I don't see a dog or one friendly cat,
Just look at the chair where the old farmer sat!
The legs are so spread, the seat's on the floor,
As I gaze very quickly through the dining room door,
Where threshers once gathered and all ate their fill,
The birds fly from nests they have built on the sill.
Window panes are shattered, the curtains are shreds,
The rooms are empty where once there were beds.
A picture on the wall is missing the frame,
And it seems to look down in pity and shame.
I step ever so lightly, but my foot still goes through
When I walk on the floors that once were so new.
Where is the Maiden with her hand on the broom
That used to be sweeping the floors of each room?
The small farm was sold at an auction one day
And "The Farmer and Wife" have both moved away,
Leaving the farm in utter despair.
To "The Farmer and Wife," it doesn't seem fair!
One day in the future, I'm afraid "I" will see
That this will happen, to my "Husband and Me" –
But we hope we can preserve our humble farm house
And keep out the birds and the furry field mouse!
We're constantly fixing the windows and doors
We shingle the roof and carpet the floors.
We use paint by the gallon and nails by the sack,
Putty by the pound to caulk every crack!
The fences are white, the mailbox stands straight
Flowers cling to the trellis as you enter the gate.
We do our best with one old farm place
And we keep a smile upon our face,
But I've painted in rhyme about one vacant home
As I send you a picture – in the form of a poem!

Stacy Wegener   The Truth of the Matter

A drought has come to the Plains.
Less than one-half inch of rain in two months.
This ought to fix the farm crisis,
some stuffed-shirt economic researcher says.
The surplus will go down
and prices will rise.

Maybe this is true,
but farmers here know the true outcome-
it's trading one calamity for another.

Cathy Wilken   **One Hundred Twenty Acres of Heaven**

After much haranguing, whining and complaining, I'm
finally carrying a cell phone in my purse. I didn't ask for a cell
phone. I don't need a cell phone. I don't want a cell phone.
But, my husband bought it, so now I'm stuck. He says I have
to have it for safety reasons so he and the kids can reach me
anytime, like when I sneak out to Target for an hour on a
Saturday afternoon. However, the last thing I want is to be
interrupted in the home furnishings aisle by a phone ringing in
my purse and my son asking if he can use the last of the frozen
pizzas to feed seven friends who just happened to stop by, or
my daughter calling to tattle on her brother who's threatening
to kill her with a frozen popsicle. Call me a dinosaur (not to my
face), but I'm not a fan of our new technological age.

I grew up on my grandparent's farm where, when we
finally got a telephone, I could never remember if we were two
longs and a short, or three longs. It didn't really matter
because Grandma picked it up and listened in on the party line
every time it rang. We didn't get indoor plumbing until I was
three. We used a chamber pot in the middle of the night and
the outhouse during the day. Grandpa was the first one up in
the winter to stoke the fire in the kitchen so Grandma could
make breakfast. When we finally got electricity, it went out
more than we did. Even today, when a storm looms on the
horizon, I instinctively gather candles, matches and flashlights,
armed and ready for the inevitable.

I can still see Grandpa carrying sloshing buckets of
water up the hill from the well to our kitchen until he installed
the electric pump. Grandma did our laundry using a wringer
washer. In summer, clothes hung outside on the line. My
favorite smell is still a hot iron touching a fresh white shirt.
There was no air conditioning. We were always hot. During
winter, clothes hung on the sun porch, the house was heated
from a wood stove in the kitchen and a coal stove in the living
room, but we were always cold.

Grandma planted a huge vegetable garden and filled the
fruit cellar with a rainbow assortment of green beans and peas,
burgundy beets, yellow corn and peach-colored, well, peaches.
Grandpa fished for catfish and bullheads. He hunted for

squirrel, rabbit, pheasant and quail. I shared breakfasts in the kitchen with calves born in blizzards; a cat's main job was catching mice in the barn; and dogs were used as a warning system when someone pulled in the drive.

We never locked our doors. The neighborhood code for an emergency was not 911. Rather, you went outside and fired your shotgun in the air three times. It was Grandpa's nightly ritual to survey the land as far as he could see, making sure all neighbors' yard lights were burning.

We survived crop failures, droughts, prairie fires, a tornado, blizzards, floods, horses running wild, cows wandering outside the fence, arrogant bulls, angry bees, hostile hornets, greedy grasshoppers, badgers burrowing in the dam, bull snakes in the basement, the occasional rattler in the rock pile, and roosters as scary as any monsters in a dime-store novel. And we endured all this without a cell phone.

Five miles south of Palmyra, Nebraska, Grandpa christened our land the "Lazy J Ranch," but at 120 acres, it hardly lived up to the term. Dotted with fields of corn, milo, alfalfa; populated by a small herd of cows, three pigs, two dogs, and a motley crew of cats, it was my universe. Grandpa was always going to make one of those signs that arched over the gravel driveway but never quite got around to it. He sketched it, over and over again, on white paper napkins while drinking Sanka at the tiny kitchen table.

Looking back, I now realize we were just poor dirt farmers, but I think I had a childhood far richer than my own children are experiencing today and this makes me very sad. The family, our neighbors, the land, meant everything. The land sustained us, nurtured us, gave us gifts and occasionally reclaimed something for itself. Mother Nature ruled and demanded respect. No one sat and watched TV. There were no videos, computers, or microwave ovens. No one was bored. There was too much work to do. Even as a little girl I was expected to do my fair share, helping with housework, setting the table, washing dishes, hanging clothes on the line, picking vegetables from the garden, feeding cats warm powdered milk, carrying slop buckets to the pigs. I had few toys, some books, a teddy bear, wooden blocks, three dolls and a sock for money. That was enough. There was always a kitty to drag around. I searched for four-leaf clovers, gathered gooseberries, mulberries and wild roses from the side of the road or spent lazy afternoons in a rope swing hung from the tallest tree north of the house. I languished under sheet tents hung from the clothesline. I spent hours building snowmen.

Grandma sewed school clothes on a pedal sewing machine, taught me to embroider tea towels, mixed home-made cocoa from scratch in a graniteware saucepan and sang, "Oh What a Beautiful Morning" to no one in particular. She quoted from scripture, rocked me in her arms when I was sick, and, when I was naughty, made me cut my own switch from the lilac bush next to the sandbox. Grandpa took me hunting and fishing and fashioned a chair from a tree stump so I could sit next to him on the tractor while he plowed and planted. I sat on his lap while he read the evening paper and watched "Gunsmoke." We ate chocolate stars in delicious silence. He taught me the delicate art of dunking cake donuts in black coffee so they wouldn't fall into the mug. It requires an intricate twist of the wrist at just the right moment. Not everyone can master that. When he was feeling particularly jovial, he grabbed his fiddle and played a tune, an art learned from his father, neither one having taken a lesson in their life.

The world's going much too fast. I yearn to take my children back in time to spend a day on our farm—a day stretching on forever. We'd awake after a dreamy night's sleep, comfortable on clean sheets smelling of sunshine and fresh air, cozy and warm under hand-sewn quilt patterns of Sunbonnet Sue, Wedding Rings or Cathedral Windows. We never once were awakened in the night by pulsating car stereos, honking horns or screeching tires. We'd gather around the clean kitchen table and devour stacks of hot griddle cakes and drink fresh-squeezed orange juice. After breakfast, we'd venture out with Grandpa to count the cows and check the fence. We'd gather vegetables in a basket, delight in snatching tadpoles and minnows from the pond, bring up wheelbarrows of rocks to line Grandma's flower garden. And not once during that magical day would a cell phone ring to break the spell.

Although my grandparents have been gone nearly 20 years and my own family's income is not derived from farming, being raised on a farm is woven into my very soul. It's the cloth from which I was cut. The threads are strong and the material has yet to wear because it is good, sturdy fabric. Practical. Dependable. Made to endure. It is the bedrock foundation on which my life was built and my rural heart will forever be attached to this land.

Andy Raun   Non-Denominational Service of Renewal For a Fine Sunday Afternoon in December

First, take a nap.
Don't use an alarm clock;
Get up when you're good and ready.
Then, throw on an old coat
And take a walk.

With your farm cats for acolytes,
Make your way across the harvested fields,
Walking down the rows you irrigated in summer,
Rows you cursed so often in heat and drought —
Rows that yielded you survival.

Find yourself a remote corner:
One to which you will be the sole pilgrims;
A corner unpolluted by your neighbor's noise.
There, mimicking your attendants,
Flop down in the dirt and dry leaves.

With a cat on either side,
Lean back on your elbows. Survey your farm,
Looking across rows and rows of golden stubble
Toward the mighty bins — vaults for hybrid treasure;
Toward your house — a treasure called "home."

With visions of harvest in your mind,
Turn your face to the sun in the western sky.
Then, closing your eyes, feel your face warm and aglow
As a breeze, like fingers, ruffles your hair.
Feel — be part of — the goodness of God.

You'll know to leave
When the cats get restless.
Get up then — go back to mankind.
Recall the Rite of Fields
When the snows come.

Katie Deerson   Nature's Rest

The leaves of the trees fall down.
The petals of the flowers wilt.
As they fall to the ground,

They become a sheet,
Soon to be quilted with snow,
Comforting the earth for its long
Winter rest.

Jill Burkey   Pepper Creek Ranch

It rained so hard one year
that the old creek bed ran again
flowing through a land
wild and uninhibited by time

where the wind
plays and teases the golden stalks
of a wheat field whose
lush livelihood is deeply rooted
to the ground
you call home

where you can feel the dirt
grind against your teeth
and know everything you see is real

where you watch the persistence
of life over death
in the wisdom of the seasons
and know you are becoming more like the land
you stand on

and where silence somehow envelops
it all as the sun
sinks behind the vast familiarity of
the last cottonwood

Mary Ruff   Little Life

Tap root going deep, sap rising high.
Under new moon
I turn thawing ground
Like a pancake.
I smell it,
bend down,
sift earth between thumb and fingerprints
the way my mother, grandmothers,
theirs before me did.

In the distance, train whistles call,
answer each other.
zephyrs blow free,
hoofprints vanish.
I plant beans and cabbage at night,
flowers in the morning.

I stand bent over
in my sweet corn patch
fashioned in the shape of spider.
Rows irrigated by matrix ditch.
Under a chime clear sky,
insignificant on the one hand,
inseparable from dirt,
I join the little life,
smell it, bend down, whistle.

Hilton Stedman   Untitled

I was born Aug. 4, 1920 in Otoe County, Nebraska. My earliest memory of an event was the stock market crash of 1929. Prices for farm products also crashed. Farmers were having difficulty paying their grocery bills. Some of us even had our telephones taken out. The owners of a local grocery store paid farmers ten cents a bushel for corn in payment of their grocery bills. The owners of the store built a huge temporary corn-crib to hold this corn. They made a good profit on this corn when they sold it later. Corn was so cheap that it was sometimes burned in stoves to heat the flame.

Dad always had the 1923 Ford car cleaned up to go to church and Sunday school. This car seated five people. There were three windows on each side of the car. I believe the door was in the center of the car on the left side.

1933 was the beginning of the drought years and chinch bug problems. Our family had a cornfield next to a neighbor's wheat field. Chinch bugs moved from the wheat into our corn. To help stop the migration of the bugs we made a shallow furrow across the rows of corn. We then dug shallow post holes in the furrow and poured a narrow barrier strip of creosote in the furrow. The bugs would not cross this barrier and would eventually fall into the post holes. We would pour kerosene in the hole several times a day to kill the bugs. This was the time that farmers in the area dug trench silos and filled them with chopped cornstalks for winter feed for the cattle.

1934 was the year of severe drought and dust storms. On July 4 my brother Wyman and I were cultivating corn. We were each using a single row riding cultivator pulled by a team of horses. The corn was only three feet tall. A few weeks later when the corn was chopped for silage it had deteriorated to about eighteen inches high. Farmers used several methods to salvage the corn stalks. Dad had a stationary silage chopper next to the trench silo. Various methods of getting the stalks from the field were used. One method was to remove the reel and canvasses from a grain binder and just run the cutting sickle. Two men would ride on the platform and grab the stalks as they were cut off. When they had an armful of stalks, the binder was stopped and the stalks were piled on the ground. This was very dangerous as two young men in our area each lost the tip off of a finger when they were reaching for a stalk. The piles were then loaded on a hayrack and hauled to the chopper. We also used corn knives to cut and then pile the corn. After the stalks had cured, some farmers would put them in the barn for later feeding. This was a time of neighbor helping neighbor.

It was a very difficult time for farmers who had cattle. Some pastures died and alfalfa and clover produced very little hay. The government helped by buying cattle for $27 a head. We discovered that cattle would eat the leaves and small branches of box elder trees. We had many of these trees on our farmstead and in the timberland. We would cut these trees and drag them into the cattle yard as they had need for feed. We also would herd the cattle on the roadside.

I started to high school in 1934. This was an entirely new experience coming from a rural school and now in a class of thirty strangers. I rode my pony to school until the weather got cold and then I rode with a neighbor family who drove a car. In 1935 Wyman started to high school. Dad bought us a Model T touring car to drive to school for $15. I had a school permit to drive. We soon found out the side curtains on the car would not give much protection from the cold. Dad was a good mechanic so he found a used two door coupe body and used it to replace the touring body.

That spring Dad purchased his first two bushels of hybrid corn for $8 per bushel. The salesman said to plant it in April on the best ground. He planted it on some low bottom ground. It rained all during the month of May. It was too wet to cultivate the corn. Since that was before chemicals for weed control the weeds destroyed the corn.

1936 was a year of temperature extremes. During the month of February the temperature never got above 0°. There were heavy snows and blizzard conditions. Snowplows lacked power enough to get some of the roads opened. That summer was very hot and dry. On a day in July we were threshing oats and our thermometers showed 117°. Lincoln had a record 115°. It did not cool much at night so people slept out on the Capitol lawn.

In the fall of 1937, Wyman and I had a 1929 Ford two door sedan to drive to high school. Neighbor kids rode to school with us. I eventually owned this car.

I graduated from Bennet High School in 1938. I played baseball all four years. I don't think I had much ability as a ball player. Since I was only five feet tall, the coach would have me lean over while at bat, thus presenting a very small strike zone for the pitcher. I was lead off batter. I didn't get many hits but I sure got lots of walks. On our sneak day, we went to Omaha in a truck with a tarp over the stock racks. There were benches to sit on.

After graduation, I was ready to pursue my passion for farming. I worked for neighbors doing chores, cutting wood, shucking corn and anything else they needed. Usually I received $.75 of $1 a day for my work.

Eventually, I purchased a used Regular Farmall tractor. I equipped it with rubber tires and acquired a few pieces of machinery. I rented some farm ground. I now needed a plow but was getting low on cash. Louie, the John Deere dealer in Syracuse, wanted $30 for a used plow. Henry, a used car dealer, offered me $25 for my 1929 Ford car. I told Henry I needed enough money for my car to buy the plow. He walked across the alley to talk to Louie. When he came back he said Louie would sell me the plow for $27.50 and he would give me the like amount for my car. I now had a deal.

In January of 1942, I purchased a new I.H. Farmall H tractor and a mounted lister and cultivator.

In August of 1942 I entered the Army and was assigned to the Air Force. I spent considerably more than half of that time in the China-Burma-India Theater of Operations as crew chief on a transport aircraft hauling various supplies. Most of the time the load was 100 octane aircraft fuel in fifty gallon drums. I was discharged in February of 1946.

After I came home I had no problem renting 280 acres of farm land near where I lived. It was surprising that so many farm boys, after returning from the service, decided to stay in farming. I suppose we thought the depression and droughts that we witnessed in our youth were in the past and conditions would improve. And they did.

In September 1958 Mary Jo Sandsted, a Methodist minister's daughter and I were married at Friend, NE. We had three daughters. Mary Jo and the girls were terrific help in the farm operation. Mary Jo would go for repairs, raise a large garden, furnish lunch for helpers and do the bookkeeping. The girls were steady helpers in caring for the livestock. They went to the Otoe County Fair, Nebraska State Fair, and Ak-Sar-Ben. We also went to shows sponsored by various pork organizations.

Our family was one of the first in the area to build terraces and waterways. On many farms most of the better top soil had been depleted by soil erosion. In recent years, I have been practicing no till and minimum till farming. The residue left on top of the soil helps slow water and soil loss after a rain. A corn and soybean crop rotation has become quite popular in this area. Some milo is still planted and so is a small amount of wheat compared to other years.

I also had a livestock operation of cattle and hogs. I would buy seventy to eighty calves in the fall. After they had been confined in a dry lot for a few weeks, I would move them to winter pasture. This pasture had after-growth brome grass, a heavy timber and a creek with running water. I would move two 100 bushel self-feeders into this pasture. A ration was fed containing ground corn or milo and a protein supplement. A certain amount of salt would be added to limit the consumption of grain. During cold and snowy weather, big round bales of hay and bale feeders would be moved to the southeast side of the timber. Most of the time, running water in the creek prevented much ice buildup. The timber provided good protection for the calves regardless of the wind direction.

In the spring when the brome grass had reached a desired height, the calves and self feeders would be moved to the summer pasture. This pasture also had running creek water and some shade trees. The salt in the ration was gradually removed and the cattle were on full feed. In late summer the cattle were sent to market. I was very comfortable with this way of handling my cattle. It was not very labor intensive.

For my hog operation, I converted a barn into a farrowing house and grower building. Later the pigs were moved to an outside lot with several moveable buildings, automatic waterers and self feeders. This was a very labor intensive operation especially in bad winter weather. About this time, I had to repopulate my swine herd with SPF origin stock.

In 1979, I built a modified open front hog house. It would handle 250 -300 plus head, depending on the size of the hogs. When the weather was below zero it was nice and cozy inside the house. What a difference from raising hogs in outside lots. I usually had a market for bred gilts in late winter and early spring. Therefore, I would keep more bred sows and gilts than I could handle at farrowing time. After fall harvesting was finished, I would put up electric fences around various fields and run my breeding stock in these fields. They would do a good job salvaging grain left in the fields, thereby saving me nearly half of the grain normally fed during gestation. I fed sow cubes every second day.

I think most farmers observe some things in an operation that causes changes in their thinking. My example: I had a mounted two row lister on an H Farmall tractor. When the slope of the ground changed, one side of the lister would stay at normal depth and the other side would plant at a shallow depth in the mellow soil. The corn in the shallow row would emerge sooner and grow faster. I reasoned that a corn planter would plant on the soil surface and get the same results. I then purchased a new fully equipped John Deere corn planter. An older neighbor stopped to view the new planter and his response was "it will never work." In a few years listers were abandoned and surface planters of all descriptions have been used since!

I purchased my first self-propelled combine in 1958. I kept trading for a new one every few years until 1976 when I bought my last new one. Before I quit farming, I purchased a used Axial Flow combine. I could harvest more corn in several minutes than I could harvest all day when I was a kid and with a lot more comfort.

I had an automatic grain drying system. It was set up to transfer dried grain to three different bins for cooling and storage.

1998 was my last year of farming. Our farm equipment sale was in March of 1999. A neighbor now farms the land.

In early June
Along the creek of my father's farm
Armed with a spade
I attack musk thistles
With a vigor only things like
Spring and war bring to the middle-aged.

I relish the fight.
It's hand-to-hand combat
Against foreign invaders.
The spade slices even the biggest.
I dodge falling thorns and watch
Blood pour from severed torsos.

I hate the thistles
And the hordes of buffalo gnats.
They don't belong. They weren't here
When I was a kid. Nor were the bleached bones
Of all the elm trees.

In August I return for those I missed.
They're always there where
I expect them to be,
Gone to seed already,
But I hack them down anyway,
Ten-foot monsters sticking
Their virile shafts to the sun
From twisted patches of thorny
Gooseberry bushes or from
Tumbled piles of dead elm
Where they had hidden in June.
The gnats and mosquitoes are gone,
But the thistles and gooseberries
Put up a hell of a fight.
My hands and arms are a mess
Before I'm done.

I know it's futile.
I'm just sowing seed
Which floats in the wind.
Wild oats penetrate my socks
And mock my own feeble
Penetrative and regenerative powers.

I enjoy the fight I'll never win.
Though things aren't as good
As when the elms kept the sun from
Enticing the gooseberries and
The gnats and thistles had not invaded,
There is improvement—
Ash, hackberry and cottonwoods,
Buffalo, brome and even bluegrasses
Are taking over as sprayers
And chain saws have killed
The marijuana and removed debris.
I've had powerful allies.

In fact, I'm not really needed.
It's just an excuse to walk the pasture
That nourished me, that grew my roots,
To revisit the ancient camp ground
Where we found pottery shards,
Flint arrowheads, and our imaginations,
To realize once again I would never
Put the plow to this bit of twisting
Scrubby creek bottom.

No, I'm breaking no new ground here
But I want to leave my mark,
Unobtrusively, like buried flint.
Maybe fewer thistles,
Or less trash--old fence posts,
Barbed wire, dead trees--
Or poetry
Will do.

Faye Tanner Cool   Fantasy During a Full Moon

Sleepless
at midnight,
I watch from my window.
Watch the rooftops
turn luminous,
the bushes silvery,
the fenceposts
pewterized.
A shadow crosses
our pearl-gray lane
and I catch my breath.

59

I know I am seeing
the neighbor's
horned bull roaming free,
but by moonlight,
it is a unicorn
in disguise.

Elaine Phillips   Blackberries

I've been blackberrying this week. Does that conjure up
an image of rosy cheeked pioneer children scampering down a
creek bank to fill their pails and mouths with juicy, sweet
blackberries? You've been reading too much Laura Ingalls
Wilder. Imagine instead a sweaty browed woman, gingerly
reaching into treacherous brambles, swatting at biting flies and
yelling at the dog. That is real life in Nebraska, my friends.

I shouldn't complain; I'm the one who planted them. I
got the starts from a friend after she brought me a bowl full of
berries when I was sick one summer. Had I known what she
had gone through to pick them, I would have appreciated them
even more.

They are a vicious plant. We call them "Attackberries".
They will reach out and grab an innocent passerby and readily
deposit thorns in any exposed body part. They grow
uninhibitedly, under the wall of the shop into its dark interior
to wrap the unsuspecting combine head with pale thorny vines-
-probably one of the reasons we haven't used the small grain
platform in years. My father-in-law hates these vines and
declares he needs a machete to get in and out the shop's south
door.

Late winter, every year, I prune them. Wearing heavy
leather gloves and several layers of long sleeves, I take out the
old canes and shorten the ones I want to keep. I never emerge
unscathed. Weeds seem to escape the heaviest mulch, so
whenever I work up enough courage, I go out there to reach in
and pull them out. A bloody business. Then, of course, they
should be watered and so on. Always painful.

I bet you are wondering why I would bother with a fruit
for which the most suitable picking attire is medieval armor and
a pikestaff. THE BERRIES!!! A proper blackberry is over 1 inch
long and about 1/2 inch wide, sweet and good. The dog knows
this and will risk her tender nose and me yelling at her, to eat
them. If you ever accumulate enough of them (they have

trouble making it to the house), they make wonderful jam (seedy), pie and coffeecake, or are delicious plain with cream. So, that is why I continue to do battle with the "Attackberries". Sometimes I win. Don't tell my father-in-law, but I even FERTILIZED them this year!

Mickee Cheek   **Sandhills Seasons**

I don't have to wear a watch
To know the time of day
Or have a calendar at hand
To guide me on my way.

Here in cattle country
If you learn to read the signs
Everything has its own way
And gets done in its own time.

Early in the year
Before the grass is green
The cows know when it's time for them
and the calves show you it's Spring.

About the time things settle down
Branding rolls around
Get the irons heated up
The last pair has been found.

Then it's practice, practice, practice
For the rodeo's in town
And don't forget the hay crews
Working sunup to sundown.

Weaning time comes after that
Just hear those cattle bawl
It's payday for the ranchers
And that's how you know it's Fall.

The pace slows down, the bills get paid
The ranchers check their debt
Another year is winding down
Winter's nearly here and yet

Here in the Sandhills of Nebraska
We have learned to know the reasons
That work gets done when it gets done
With the changing of the seasons.

Sandy Straus   **Green Acres**

In October 1913, my mom, Ruth Bordy, was born in
Walthill, Nebraska. At the time, the media hype for that town
was: "Move to a thriving prairie metropolis!" Walthill never did
became a city. In fact, it wasn't even on the prairie.

Here's the story. The U.S. Railroad magnate, Jim Hill,
built a line on the west side of the Missouri River. His son
Walter came to the foothills to purchase land for the project. In
1906 he selected a site for a station stop. That site became
Walthill. There is some local controversy as to whether the
town was named for him or for a local farmer with the same
first name. At any rate, it was and still is a small rural farming
community on the banks of the Missouri.

Back to my family. My grandfather, Reuben Bordy,
owned a dry goods and grocery store on main street. He served
a term as village mayor. By 1926 he was successful enough to
retire and to move his family to Omaha. My mother, the oldest
of his six children, became a "thoroughly modern Millie." She
enjoyed all of the sophisticated pleasures Omaha had to offer.
She thought of Walthill as a hick town and never looked back.
That is why the place was for years a big mystery to me.

I was Grandpa Bordy's first grandchild. He had
fourteen. I too was a "modern" woman. Like my mom, I really
enjoyed cities. But not Omaha. First, I moved to Chicago and
then to New York City. A painter, I even managed to achieve my
fifteen minutes of fame in the art world. A friend invited me to
the country for a weekend. The visit changed my life. I met a
fruit farmer and fell in love.

David was from a prestigious family that claimed
descent from Charlemagne. He was steward of land that had
been worked by his family for three generations. His farm was
on the edge of Schuylerville, an upstate New York village
situated on the banks of the magnificent Hudson River.

My sweetheart was exotic. He was romantic. So was
farm life. I moved to the farm. My interests turned to hail
storms, winds, pests, scab, rainfall, and ripening. Always
something! Near dawn, checking the orchard for insects erased
all desire for breakfast at Tiffany's. Riding on the tractor with

62

my beloved became far more appealing than dancing at the Waldorf. Listening to the birds and the wind became more melodic than opera at the Met.

The romance with David was a dream. The romance of farm life, however, was tested by an unpleasant concern—the farm's growing indebtedness. Creditors, including the Farmers Home Administration, breathed down our necks. They competed with current operating expenses. Tough times. No profit.

We worked very hard to make it go. We borrowed money. I lent money. We presold the crops. We sold land and mining rights. Finally, we borrowed from a family trust. Not my idea.

I tried to be innovative. I opened a cafe in the farm stand and organized events to attract crowds. I started a bed and breakfast in the lovely 18th century family farmhouse. We managed to keep all of the balls in the air until brothers and cousins wondered where the trust money had gone. We fought hard. We lost the battle. The farm was foreclosed.

Suddenly, we had lots of time on our hands. I started painting and selling my work again. David started a new business, and we began to travel. One of our trips took us back to Walthill. It was my first trip. We were warmly received, and I fell in love with the landscape.

In August, 1996 mother died. The farm was gone, and I was in New York City. But over the last few years, my love for a special, misnamed prairie keeps pulling me back to Nebraska. Smiling, I tease the title of an old song "How you gonna keep them up in Paree after they've seen Walthill?"

Fredrick Zydek   A Brunswick Autumn

Here on the plains near the Elkhorn,
the season's talents smolder
in what the wind knows.

The seeds of drying things
crack open easily as sparrow eggs.
I've seen the color of the dead

move out into the fields
and learned that it too is beautiful.
Soon the green gods of summer

63

will wear a pumpkin flush on their
faces, and the sky will become
a thing of wings unending.

Yasmin McEwen   Gone Country

Roger Sluka used to clean your stalls for $5 dollars
each, and as I remember it, didn't you have a crush on him too?
I knew I was hooked though. Once I got a whiff of that new
fresh sawdust, loose pine shavings, your mother's fudge
brownies, felt the horses gallop from under my legs. There were
those nights in the summertime when we couldn't sleep, and
you let me get Ben out and we'd ride him around in between the
Pine trees. Wishing and dreaming of boys, boys, boys.

I remember all the times I laced up your curly cued red
headed sisters brown muckety muck boots and shoved my cold
mismatched socks into the frozen soles. Splinters of straw and
wild grass stuck out. Their stems woven permanently inside
the hem. I went running down the hill with Sissy ahead of us,
her Australian Shepherd blue and green eyes searching out wild
rabbits. Her quick bark to let them know that she was coming.
First Skip, then Missy would start to jump and slam their
butterscotch gnarled tufted thick muscled bodies against their
kennels. Tails wagged once and we scooped then poured
generic dog food over the chain link. Growls became humming
vacuums as their snouts sniffed out and sucked up the pellets
from the cool concrete floor.

We lifted and slid that big slate gray metal barn door
aside, and you hooked up the radio to the extension cord that
hung down from the rafters. Keith Whitley's voice crooned, our
voices crooned too in unison sing- song contralto. Sending
waves of sound that sighed and slid out into the still crispy cool
fresh of the night. Navy black sky whetting and quenching any
longing for love that lingered on in our young hearts. White
cottony stars look in at us. As the scene inside the barn
became a miniature dollhouse illuminated to the quiet universe.
Framed by the outline of the big boxy door in three-D form
dimensions; clean stalls, stacks of hay, fly tape hanging from
the ceiling, wooden plank floors, and dusty lights. Ben and
Scarface whinnied as we worked fast filling old red and black
Folgers coffee tins with sweet smelling grain. Then outside I ran
to kink the hose that snaked along the barn, fastened to the old
pump with the bright red handle. I remember you had to lift it
a certain way to get the water to come out. My hands would get
so cold from the icy water that flowed through the metal pipe.

Splish splash it guzzled and gurgled into matching black buckets. Back to the barn I stumbled in shoes too big trying not to spill the water. Big round belly's hungry for more. I remember the feel of their soft black muzzles searching around in the bottom of the bucket hungry for more. Like furry peach fuzz. The spray of their warm breathe through cavernous nostrils on my frozen hands.

I still remember waking up in the middle of the night thinking a spotlight had been shone into the window only to find the moon peering in at me as I lay still. Then of course your Peacock would make his blood curling call out to who knows what kind of a mate. We would wake to corn break muffins baking and eat warm oatmeal as we flipped through new Quarter-Horse Quarterly Issues and you showed me horses you wanted and I just wished for a horse period. Your big brother would come walking through the kitchen all decked out in his camouflage with his bow and arrow. On his way to hunt deer. We would snicker and laugh at him. Your sister would come in with her mail order catalogs, sale ads, and car keys. She would ask your mother for shopping money, and they would haggle over which one of them owed the other for the new coat bought last week or the new pair of boots. Your mother would say, "well, I bought the grain last week and you still owe me for the watch I put on lay-a-way for your father's Christmas present." You would kick me under the table. We would get up and take our bowls into the t.v. room. Where we would branch out on the wide couch wrapping blankets around ourselves. We would re-watch reigning videos and the World Horse show that you went to every year in Oklahoma. Where cowboys smiled and winked at the camera just before the shoot opened up.

It wasn't long before your mother came back into the kitchen and said, "Amy!" In her high pitched loving voice, "get off that couch and help me fold those clothes over on the chair.

And don't forget when you go into town bring back a gallon of milk and pick up a box of that Bakers' Chocolate for my cheesecake."

Off to town my little Fiero raced down Saltillo Road then careened off of the gravel spraying loose sediment onto a paved highway. We hydroplaned going well over the limit and always skipped the interstate cuz the fuzz might be waiting for us there. I could do eighty on South 14th street all the way into Lincoln's city limits. Most days you would still be putting on your make-up trying to balance your mascara wand as my little car went up and over bumps in the road. Some days we'd both yell "train!" And have to stop and wait while we sang along to country music on the radio. Looking back in the rear view mirror I saw yellow fields and wild trees. Their golden green autumn leaves winking back at me. The train would trail away and we were off again heading into town leaving all that I loved behind.

M.J. Anthony   Storms

Thunder crashed, the lightning slashed
The rolling clouds so drear.
She looked across the tall cornfields
And felt consumed by fear.
"That lush green crop's our livelihood
A way to pay the bills,
Our children's education,
Our way to fight life's ills.
Please, God, don't let the hail come,
Preserve our chance to stay,
To continue in this way of life,
A challenge day by day."
She slept, and when the morning came
And the crop was safe and strong,
She looked around her at this land
She'd loved for, oh, so long.
Raising her eyes to clear blue skies,
She whispered, "Thank you, God!"
A grateful farm wife's partnership
With Lord, and sky, and sod.

When I was a child the Alexandria State Lakes had giant turtles living in and around them, with shells two feet across. My parents claim we rode on them when we were small. I have only a vague memory of the few that were left lying dead on the roads around the lakes, shells split and ugly flies buzzing over them. Now this memory seems more like a dream, but my parents have verified it is true.

We often drive the few miles from our farm house west of Fairbury, Nebraska to the Alexandria State Lakes in western Jefferson County. We walk around the spring fed lakes on the narrow gravel roads, fishing with artificial lures and spinners as we go. To the south of the lakes is a swamp at the bottom of a steep bank. Muskrats live there and turtles sunbathe on logs, lined up overlapping in a neat row.

Our youngest daughter, Dusk, had wanted a pet turtle for years. Her older brother, Marc, had told her about "Mr. and Mrs. Cornelius", the pet turtles he had before she was born. At the time Marc was five-years-old and we lived in Grand Island, Nebraska. Mr. and Mrs. Cornelius lived in an oval, clear, plastic pool with a tiny island in the center. The island came equipped with a plastic palm tree, state of the art "digs" for pet turtles at that time. By the time Dusk was born in 1973 we had let Mr. and Mrs. Cornelius go somewhere along the Platte River.

This trip to "Alec" we were fishing in Lake #3 without much luck. My husband had moved over to Lake #2 and I chose the swamp as my next fishing location. I started down the very steep path of soft dirt towards a spot near the overflow tube coming from Lake #3. As I approached it carefully I caught my foot in a tangle of roots and pitched forward, falling. I landed with my face and head totally submerged in the swamp. I used my hands to surface for air and remove myself from the stinky muck. Sitting upright on the edge of the swamp, and not very happy about the whole experience, I realized my glasses had been sucked off of my face into the murky water. On top of the basic indignity I felt and the new hairdo I hadn't planned on, I now was blind as a bat. This is when I chose to yell for my husband. He assumed I had lost my lure (a frequent happening) or had caught a fish (a not so frequent occurrence).

He showed up in due time and I explained the situation. He calmly offered to dig with his hands into the swamp muck to find my glasses. He found a broken beer bottle in the spot my face had just vacated and then my glasses. We were both

67

fortunate not to have been cut.

My husband assisted me up the steep bank while carrying my muddy glasses. We called for the children to gather to head home. All I wanted was a nice clean shower and soon! I was watching each step through my blurry vision as we walked down the road along the swamp edge towards our truck. In my path on the gravel was a very tiny, round, dark green thing, barely visible to me. I asked my husband, "Is that a turtle? Is it alive?" That is how "Clyde" came to live with us.

Clyde grew for many years in a very large, clear plastic Rubbermaid storage box. It was filled with water had a rock island and a tree branch log. Dusk would feed Clyde sticks of floating turtle food. He would swim up and attack each stick as it hit the water like it was alive. When Clyde had more than doubled in size we all agreed that he should have a chance to marry and produce more tiny "Clydes". We set him free in the swamp by Fairbury, near Crystal Springs.

Dusk has since grown up, married, graduated college, and given birth to her own baby boy. She reminds me each spring that Clyde was her favorite pet ever! And if I should happen to stumble blindly upon a tiny, little turtle I am to capture him for her.

Mae Hiatt   It Rained Last Night

There's a tiny sparkling diamond
On every blade of grass;
And the trees are dripping jewels
On the people as they pass.

IT RAINED LAST NIGHT

The birds are singing praises;
Each flower lifts up its head;
The drowsy bees have wakened;
The summer drought has fled.

IT RAINED LAST NIGHT

I stand beside my sun-scorched field,
Within my heart a thrill;
For the rainbow is a promise
There's a God who loves us still.

IT RAINED LAST NIGHT

Anita Wells   Before a Thunderstorm in the Nebraska Sandhills

Thick, gray bouquets of clouds
hover over the horizon
caressing the grassy knolls.
Cattle huddle in the ravines
their backs to the hillside.

Among the mounds of hay
stacked like bread loaves,
sunflowers stiffen their golden heads
and the scattering of trees
stands in reverent silence.

Like a church choir on Easter morning
the sky unleashes a peal of thunder
that resonates across the landscape.

The sandy soil drinks the rain
pouring like wine
into the mouths of its disciples.

Norman Gustafson   The Pond

The rolling hills of Eastern Nebraska do not own many naturally formed bodies of water that could be called lakes. Old buffalo wallows or natural basins, often called ponds or sloughs form after heavy rains but they soon dry and the mud turns into a crumbly flat of soil.

However, man has intervened and made small changes in God's creation which have turned areas of waste land into places where wild life and plant life coexist, nurtured by rains and spring fed water, thus the birth of a pond.

The years 1954, 55, and 56 were dry years. Crops were poor with yields of one half to none. Farmers were eligible for crop payments if they mowed, plowed or harrowed their fields to destroy what little grain was there.

There was a flip side to these dry years: it provided the opportunity to complete many projects of public works where dirt moving was involved. An innovative plan was initiated to replace aging road bridges with earthen dams. Drop outlet tubes allowed heavy rain runoff to slowly drain down stream. These small dams together provided a measure of flood relief

69

along the creeks and streams below.

Such a dam was built on my farm on the upper reaches of Clear Creek in Northeast Saunders County in 1956. Soil moved for building the dam created the depression for the pond. The rains came soon after the dam was completed forming a body of water one-acre in size and fourteen feet deep.

The pond, now with a life of its own, waited patiently for its waters to clear so that it could nurture the life around and within it. The warm breezes of spring brought blue winged teal ducks to rest a few days on their journey north. Mallard ducks and Canada geese feeding in the surrounding cornfields dropped in for short visits in the fall.

As yet, the pond had only transients to use its waters. One day this changed. Fingerling blue gills and large mouth bass, placed in its body to be nourished by the algae and plankton which nature had provided, grew to "keeper" size.

How has this man-made pond enhanced the lives of those who have experienced its presence? A neighbor, now 50 years old, remembers his kindergarten class coming to watch the big dirt-moving machine dig the lakebed and build the dam. A visitor from Tennessee who wrote a weekly newspaper column about fishing asked permission to fish the pond. A couple of hours later he said it was the best fishing he had ever experienced, having caught and released over 50 bass in an hour and a half. A father and son built a diving board and enjoyed the cool of the evenings, diving and swimming in its temperate waters. Who would have guessed that two young girls, riding their horses bareback, would be seen swimming their horses across the pond? Hours spent with grandchildren snagging tree branches while casting for blue gill. A mallard duck nesting along the edge of the water. The ice of winter attracting people who loved to skate. The pond was providing a variety of recreation for many people.

Seasons have followed seasons and the pond has matured. Silting has decreased its depth and water weeds have increased. A family of beavers, wanting to preserve the pond, has plugged its outlet.

The pond has provided a small sanctuary for wildlife and a recreation area for family and friends for over fifty years. The enjoyment from these activities has far outweighed the loss of production from the small tract of land.

Now the pond is old and shallow, becoming more marsh-like each year. To save the pond man must intervene by finding a new home for the beavers and clearing the outlet for the flow of excess water. Dredging the silt to restore the depth of the pond may be necessary in time. Careful management of the watershed to limit erosion of soil into the pond must be continued. Caretakers of the pond will determine its future. The passage of time will provide the answer to the question "Will the pond be there for future generations to enjoy?"

Effie Thompson   The Home Place

120 acres of hills, gullies and a creek. No one knew the hell of working from dawn to dark and putting what little we could make back into the farm.

I met Pete because my sister was married to his brother, Joe. She wasn't well and needed help while having their son Mike. I was seventeen years old and spent the summer there with her on a farm owned by Storz Brewery. I went back up to North Dakota after Mike was born.

Along came the war, the two younger boys went into the service so Pete and I farmed on the home place as Mike and Lil (his parents) were too old by then to take care of it. Our two sons were born and died soon after birth so I was alone a lot as Pete liked nothing better than going into town to play cards and drink beer with the guys.

The war was over and the guys came home. As soon as B.J. got back to Blair, his girlfriend, and my pal and shirt-tail relative, June, says "Let's go out to Pete & Ef's" He says, "Who the sam hill are they?" and she tells him "You will see." So out they came.

I was in the kitchen getting supper and Pete was out in the machine shed changing the wheels on the tractor (good old John Deere) so I say "Pete's out back" and he went to find Pete; and June pitched in to help me.

B.J. says he walked up to this farmer in dirty overalls and rolled up shirt sleeves, who looked up and said "Hand me that wrench." So he helped him and they hit it off right fine.

As soon as supper was over and dishes washed, Pete goes into the cellar, brings out a tub, puts a chunk of ice in it and of course bottles of beer. Out came chairs onto the porch and kerosene lamps onto an upturned box. We proceeded to visit and get acquainted with B.J.

Pete and June would howl with laughter every so often. B.J. and I looked at each other and wondered what was so funny until we heard this thump, thump, thump on the porch floor.

We realized every time old Herman (the ancient dog) scratched his fleas, his male organs hit the floor and bounced.

71

B.J. said he never forgot our first meeting as it was a fun time.

The Thompsons were a close-knit family and were pretty much ruled by Lil, their mom. Old Mike just sort of looked on. Pete loved his Mom and told me of the times they worked together while he grew up. Pete didn't get along that well with his Dad. I guess they were too much alike, both stubborn Pollocks.

Dolly Eledge lived close to sister, Mary, and her husband Vince. He stayed with them for awhile after he got out of the Army. Pete and I promised Paul he could come on the farm so we sold out and went down to Omaha and each got jobs and for a while lived in the apartment on St. Mary' Ave. that had been Paul and Dolly's. They were the last ones to live on the farm there and my dear sister-in-law that I think a lot can tell you much more. The tears that fell unheeded, the laughter and footsteps that sounded through those buildings are all forgotten. Still words spoken by those long gone, stay in our thoughts.

Pete sent a load of hogs to be sold and got top price one year but he didn't get to send Squee my pet pig. I made a pet out of her as her mother had a big litter and couldn't take care of all of them. She slept on an old coat behind the heater. In the morning she woke up and came to find me and would root around the covers until she found my face and put her cold nose on me.

Her favorite breakfast was half an orange and a soft cooked egg in milk. She didn't know she was a pig, and if I put her in the pen with the others she would cry pitifully until I lifted her back out. If I sat down to read she would lay on my lap, put her snout in the crook of my arm and suck her tongue loudly. That was her pacifier until she got so big her back end hung over and she couldn't fit anymore. She talked to me with a Rhu Rhu Rhu if she was satisfied and a Ree Ree Ree if something was wrong, like the time she crawled into the sleeve of her coat-bed and couldn't get out until I got a hold of her back legs and pulled her out.

One day a salesman for a farm paper came to try to sell me a subscription. He was talking to me in the kitchen when Squee rooted the door open and came in. He couldn't believe what he saw and wanted to buy her. Of course, I wouldn't sell her. It would be like selling a member of the family.

One hot day Squee came crying and I said to her "Squee, go lay on the porch; it's too hot for you." So she did, took a couple of breaths, looked at me with her little beady eyes and quit. I buried her beneath one of the Chinese Elm trees Mom and Dad had planted along the cellar hill. I never forgot her; or the many ducks and geese I raised and talked to. Animal friends are almost as good as people friends.

I can still hear the creaking of the old windmill as it pumped water through the pipes up the stock tank for the cattle and the hog house and to the cistern so we could pump water for use in the house.

How lucky I felt if I could get into the house with two pails of water before that mean white rock rooster jumped on the back of my legs. I fooled him though, when I heard him stomping behind me, I called Hank (the dog). Until one morning Hank watched with a mouth full of feathers and I put the pails down long enough to watch Pete grab him (the rooster) by the legs, lay his neck across the chopping block and chop off his head. I don't recall if we enjoyed the chicken meat but I do know he made real good broth for noodles.

Mother Thompson made the best home-made noodles I ever ate and she taught me how. She also taught me how to fry down pork; cover it with lard in jars and store it in the cellar where it kept reasonably cool until reheated to eat.

Two good sized mulberry bushes grew along one ditch and were ready to pick about the same time the rhubarb came on. Sure made good sauce, always canned a few jars for later. Fall was the busy time; the apples and potatoes were put in the cellar in bins.

One Sunday, the whole family was working making apple cider. The big crock wasn't quite full so Paul thought he would help; spying the kerosene can he proceeded to fill it to the brim. That day's work was done.

Pete always expected me to work with him. Oat planting time he filled the wagon full of seed oats, put the end gate seeder on, hitched up Lanky and Dick and drove them back and forth while I stood in the back and kept the seeder full. I had to be careful, though, or when he crossed a ditch and the wagon lurched, I would lose my footing and fall into the beds of oats.

One morning right beside us in a ditch we spied a whole bunch of mushrooms. Pete jumped down and filled his denim cap and we had mushrooms fried in butter for supper.

Winter time was bad. We had a radio but having no electricity the batteries ran down. It was so darn cold you couldn't put enough blankets on the bed to keep warm.

Dick was a good horse. He could outwork three other horses and wouldn't even be puffing, but watch out for his hind hoofs. One day I was shucking corn by myself, taking two rows through the field and hitting the bang board as the ears went in the wagon. I said "move up Dick" but he was busy eating so I gave him a whack with an ear of corn. Wham! Just that fast I felt a breeze as his hind hoofs went by my head. I didn't do that again.

One day Pete was bringing in hay from the field to put it in the barn loft. Mickey was staying with us and it was his joy to be right in there helping. He crawled too high on the front of the hayrack and fell down right behind Dick. To our horror he took hold of Dick's tail and hind leg and pulled himself up and under the tugs to get out. Pete spoke to him "Whoa Dick" and he never moved a muscle. He wouldn't hurt the boy, but oh, he got Pete.

The horse and dog had a running battle as Hank would sneak in the barn ahead of the manger and when Dick reached down for a mouthful of hay, Hank would jump up and bite his nose. One evening, Pete was doing chores late and as he bent over in front of Dick's stall, Dick, thinking it was Hank, got a big bite of his back. Of course, as soon as Pete yelled Dick let go but it left a scar for a long time. There were big teeth marks, even through his jacket.

Even so, it was hard leaving the old place. Hank followed us around and couldn't know why we were loading so many boxes of stuff in the old Ford.

He didn't know he wouldn't have to go in the cellar and bring out a snake that had curled around a fruit jar and I was afraid to get it to leave. He would calmly get it in his mouth and bring it to me with me yelling all the time "No! No! Hank take it away." We humans are a sorry lot.

The mama cat came up to the house to see what was going on, so I told her goodbye, and to be a good cat and go down by the corn crib and see if she could catch some of those mice and rats and wait for Paul and Dolly to get there and everything would be O.K.

But as I got into the car, Hank looked sad, I went back in the house and got the remains of a pork roast and gave him the whole thing. He was so content chewing on it that that he didn't even look as we drove away.

I didn't look back. The only thing Pete ever said to me months later was "why didn't you make me do this sooner?" Of course it always had to be my fault. OK.

When Pete reached the age of sixty-one, he got sick; emphysema, an enlarged heart and of course, poor circulation, and had to quit work. I kept on working for Campbell Soup Co. and he stayed home until he had a stroke. He was hospitalized for six weeks and had to go into a convalescent home, but it proved to be too much for me to handle everything.

So when I was sixty-two, Campbell Soup was good to me and let me retire. I had been with them for 33½ years so I had all my benefits up to par. Pete made it until he was seventy-six years old. I got up one morning to find he had died in his sleep.

I didn't like living in the house alone so I sold it and came back to Blair. I couldn't find a house I liked so I decided to rent an apartment. I am quite content and can drive out to the Blair Cemetery often and visit Pete and my babes' graves. Some of our old friends remember me and it's good to talk to them and think about the old times. Blair has changed much since we farmed the home place but I feel I am home.

Carol Beins   My "Somewhere Real" Is Right Here

I don't remember exactly when I decided I wasn't going to leave Nebraska after all. It wasn't a conscious decision, really. Growing up there was always this assumption in my own mind that when I was old enough to go somewhere else, anywhere else, I would. Friends voicing their aspirations to go "somewhere real" didn't help matters any.

Yes, I'm afraid I did see being from Nebraska as ripe with embarrassment. I used to complain that there was nothing to do. Now each March I am awestruck by all the migrating feathered beings, and there are times when our star-lit sky is so bright and clear that it makes my eyes water. Where else could my small son insist he can touch the moon because it seems so close and clear and friendly looking? These are experiences that easily outshine the offerings of so-called "cultured" locales.

Once upon a time even the people who live here made me nearly squirm with shame. Where else do you see old men in washed out overalls which have given up all hope of ever buttoning on the sides, for crying out loud? And how many different seed caps does a person need in one lifetime? But for all the "local yokels" which abound, there are far more good, solid people who bother to wave at strangers, still know a large percentage of people they graduated from high school with, and can tell you precisely where their grandparents lived as honeymooners. (Back when people still had the modesty to be a little red-faced from the wedding trip.)

And so the years have passed and with them my wanderlust. At some point, I realized that it just doesn't get any better than this "no-where" state. This is not just a case of inertia or complacency. I have genuinely grown to savor the bone-deep sense of home that this so-called backwater has afforded me.

When I was young and admittedly shortsighted, I swore I wanted nothing more than to be free of this place. But now it feels like Nebraska and I have made peace with each other. Sometimes it is good to be wrong about something.

Fredrick Zydek   **Thunderstorm: Great Plains**

The trees hiss with starlings.
It is the first hint
that the wicked wind is coming.
In the distance drums begin
their deep and low-pitched lowing.

Deep into the cedar boughs,
things of feather and fur
wait out the coming squall.
Gossip of the thunder's coming
moves among them like a chill.

Out west the sky is at war.
Darkness rides the wind
like a fallen angel.
Soon the green air will fill
with hail stones large as fists.

It is then the frantic clawing
of jagged and dreadful light
will snap its awful secrets
until leaves scatter like bees
swarming for the kill.

Great trees, lifting their arms
in twists of light, will snap
like celery. We become motherless
things, candle burners huddling
like preserves in the cellar.

Becky Faber   I Spent the Night in Custer County

I spent the night in Custer County
Driving through canyons
Searching for a way out
A road that would lead to somewhere

76

But none exists,
Only cattle grazing
On hills as steep as life
On grass as sparse as hope
Planted in soil as dry as my skull.

Merna will never reach Milburn
Arnold won't come near Berwyn
And I won't ever touch the world.

Somewhere south of the South Loup
Lies Eden
Where people dance in the rain
Watch plants sprout
And practice fertility.

But I'll spend another night in Custer County
Counting rocks and dry gullies
Cloudless skies and yellow stars

And mark off the number of nights
That I have yet to spend
In Custer County.

The Sky

J.V. Brummels — Teaching the Dawn

All of this is. A ridge
running through the dark
half a mile away, the wind
blowing faster and faster.

There are people who believe
the sun won't rise if they're
 not there to witness the dawn.

The moon setting behind me
could be a madwoman,
her jealous fit waning,
but she is only the moon.

But the little stars are
all the grandparents
of all the generations
witnessing what we do.

That first vermillion glow
above the ridge is tradition
slashing above a black rock.

Faith is an old trick
I'm teaching a new dog.

Marjorie Saiser — Not So Much Bottom Line As Bluestem

I saw a man hugging his son; he took him in,
rubbed his back, folded him to his own body
in the manner I have seen one person
hold another in dreams,
and I was ashamed how I had a moment before
been promoting myself, trying to get ahead, selling myself when
what
really matters is so fragrant and loyal, so close against the ribs
and next to the beating noise of the heart that I

longed to be there in that space between people.
I wanted to be worthy so that my father would

rise up and cross a distance
quickly to hold me,
hold me first with his eyes across the space of the room,
then the smell of the skin of his neck
and the soap in his shirt
would hold me softly not so much to crush as to join.

In that warm and loyal space I wanted to learn
not so much profit as mystery
not so much increase as Elkhorn
not so much to envy as to bud
not so much to advance as to seed.

Today my friend told me he is wearing
his dead friend's reading glasses,
taking up her glasses out of his pocket and putting them
on his face, wearing something she had held
and lifted toward her eyes many times
without thinking, glasses she laid on the pages
of her book, glasses she chose and cursed and
looked for when they were lost,
folded like a tidy bundle of twigs on the table,
glasses her eyes looked devilishly over
when she cracked a joke. He said

when he took her to the hospital
that last time, she wanted him to gather up this and that,
and after she had died, there were her reading glasses
in his shirt pocket
as if she herself had tapped them in, saying, *Here, Babe, it ain't
Scotch
but these will definitely last longer.*
My friend is wearing his dead friend's reading glasses and

I want to do that, too, to take up what someone has accidentally
or purposely left me. My friends are
helping me get a little closer,
not so much to conquer as to leaf out
not so much to own as coyote, badger, deer
not so much critic as Niobrara, Missouri, Platte
not so much one-up as switchgrass, sumac,
bluegill, catfish, wolf.

Back and forth they rocked in the room,
the man holding a child grown,

79

a child grown holding his father,
rocking one another in time,

Oh Papa I'm sorry each come home to this neck and
shoulders, spine and arms
and hand in the hair, rocking
slow as midnight rain.

I saw once on a wide plain a cloud of geese
rising, a spiral in the light,
the geese like hundreds of papers
in a whirlwind, rising, rising
and I wanted to whirl in that column. I held out my
arms, raised my face
not so much the power as the trail
not so much to garner as to free

and I rock with my father *Papa, oh Papa*

I hold out my arms to the column of birds,

I rock back and forth
my mother father friends daughters sons arms hold me,
hold me: not so much the market as the daybreak
not the rush but the lake
not so much resume but to live
not so much promote as bison, elk
aquifer, sandhills, blowout, plum brush.

My friend is wearing his dead friend's reading glasses;
I, too, want to take up something of hers, of yours
something that rested on your skin or hair
something your hand touched.
I want to extend my hand, want you to reach with yours,

as if I can stand close enough to matter
in that radius where we are separate together
not so much impress as honest
not so much merge as search
not so much first as true
not so much to grasp as to fly.

Fearless as a queen,
the bald eagle
is perched on a tree limb
overlooking the river.

She, like the sun, is the supervisor of all acts
her tail white like the snow geese,
her prowess that of the great hunter.

Vigorous as a thunderbolt
she soars above the waters.
Dexterous, she combs the river for its fish
shad carp catfish
dipping
    her talons
            below the water's surface.

Sagacious,
conqueror of wealth,
her wings
speedy for exhilaration and protection.

She has returned to the Loup and Platte rivers
in the plains of Nebraska,
unwearied,
flashing out brilliance as of old.

When the earliest days of spring arrive,
she disappears northward
to the northern prairie provinces
of Canada,
to the timber-fringed lakes,
nesting grounds
for the pious worshiper.

Twyla Hansen   What I Did

What I did I did because of the dirt,
the cattle and the moonless nights.
Because of the open breathing cornfield
and the sounds of roosting hens in the brooder house.
Pears hanging in the pear tree, ripening,
bees drunk and tainted with pollen.
Because of snow storms and power failures
and standing on top of ten-foot drifts.
Because of manure and rutted mud roads
and a dozen mewing kittens, eyes wide,
hungry for the teat. I did what I did
because of a hot breeze on a hot night
when the house wouldn't cool down,
because of home-canned peaches
and a '39 International rusting
in the grove. Because I was alone,
walking in the pasture alone,
studying the creek for anything alive.
Because of the corn crib with its ladder
and heavenly mystery, its unshelled ears,
all listening. Dust and diesel fuel and dumb
lazy afternoons. I did it because of pine needles
and columbines and tiger lilies, because
my grandmother came to this treeless land and lived.
I was alone in the brome, in the ditches and high up in the
maple.
I stayed there until I was called in, stayed there
where the branches held me, stayed there
and stayed to hear the wind talk back to me.
I did what I did because I thought everybody did,
counting the large coins in my father's drawer,
standing in the dark closet to smell mothballs.
I didn't know. I didn't know what any other child knew.
I knew the claw-foot bathtub and the one glass
at the sink we all used. I knew the creak of each step
on the staircase and where to step so it wouldn't.
I was awake when I should have been napping,
up in my room instead of lying down,
looking around during the Sunday prayer.
I played with the cats, an old deck of cards,
with the unmatched unfinished blocks of wood.
The nights held eyes though no one was around.

The dreams were nightmares even though I was loved.
The hay grew tall and we always had enough to eat.
I did what I did because my father loved me, my mother
was occupied and my brothers didn't want me around.
Because of Brown Swiss and John Deere and Hampshires,
neighbors down the road and a one-room country school.
Because of ice cream and watermelon and green apples,
because of fudge and popcorn and wax paper.
I played alone in the silo, in the cellar and on the screen porch.
There were comic books and Lincoln Logs and rollerskates,
bicycles and sand piles and Tinker toys.
What I did was simple and dirty, requiring time alone.
There was no one to talk to, no one to listen, no one to ask.
I wore hand-me-downs and five-buckle overboots,
dresses and saddle shoes, barrettes and anklets.
We ate potatoes and beef, tomatoes and pork,
chicken and dumplings. We went to church. I studied the
Bible.
I studied my numbers, my alphabet, my spelling.
My teachers said I daydreamed, wouldn't pay attention.
Alone in my bedroom, in my parents', in the barn.
They hoped I would never know.
Because I wanted, it happened. I did what I did
when it was time, I put in my time when I had to,
I lived through it.

Anneke Gustafson   Lost in the Maize

I looked up at the sky but saw only slivers of blue. The
big, scratchy corn leaves formed a canopy above my head. I
was in a sea of green. My parents had warned me repeatedly of
staying away from the cornfield. I always assumed they must
be hiding something from me, a stash of toys or a swimming
pool, perhaps. Their warnings were really just excuses to keep
me from finding the fun.

At first I played contentedly with my doll, building
castles out of corn and dirt. The field was our kingdom. Soon I
grew bored and decided to find my way back home. Everything
I attempted failed. I tried climbing a cornstalk, but it collapsed
under my weight. I followed the rows but got nowhere. I never
thought I would have any problem getting out. I'd seen my dog
go in and out of the corn millions of times. Finally, I realized I
was lost. Never again would I doubt my parents' word. I got
scared, wondering if I would ever escape from the cornfield. I

screamed, hoping someone would hear my cries for help. My voice grew hoarse, and my screams turned to sobs. The tears rolled down my face and fell onto the ground.

The sky was getting dark, and I was cold. I'd been playing in the sprinkler when I decided to find the treasurers hidden in the field. I was wearing just my swimsuit and a t-shirt I'd put on to keep my shoulders from being scratched by the corn leaves. I grew hungry, not having eaten since the early lunch my mom had prepared. I hoped my parents would soon realize I was missing and come look for me. It was nearly dinnertime, and they would surely notice my absence.

I lay on the muddy ground clutching my doll. The night noises sounded eerie in the dark cornfield. When I was in my house, they seemed peaceful, even relaxing. Exhausted from crying, I eventually drifted off to sleep. I dreamed of being at home in my own bed surrounded by my stuffed animals and my family close by.

Later, I awoke hearing sounds in the field. Thoughts of wolves, coyotes, and worse crossed my mind. I crouched in the row hoping to hide myself. Leaves were rustling, something was moving towards me. A bright light swung through the rows and in the distance I heard people calling my name. I jumped off the ground and ran towards the light, stumbling through rows in my excitement. My parents rushed towards me as they heard my cries of relief and joy. Finally, I was safe in my father's arms as he carried me home.

Claudia Loomis   **For Jess**

Between dirt road and cornfield
we swim in a mud-water ditch.
We know we're too old,
but we bring our skin to water
and recline against a soft bank
letting only chocolate water
(moving remnants of river and tree)
divide us.

This water our connection,
our realization of things
we don't know,
of oceans, and rivers.
And rain that falls on ground
we'll never see.

Kathy Disney   **Memorial Day 1998**

Today I help you with flowers for the cemeteries,
twenty-three stops in three towns.
Some gone before you were born:
great-grandparents, distant uncles and aunts.
Some recent: mother, father, husband, daughter.

Mid-afternoon in Blue Springs, the threatening clouds
finally open up. "It's raining", I say from the car. You,
grinning as you open the door, reply "We're wash and wear".

Arranging the flowers on the graves, I realize
that all those we visit today were wash and wear people.
Not "delicate", not "fluff only", sometimes not even "normal".
And as I watch you, daughter of these ancestors,
smiling in the rain, my heart is grateful to be counted
among the wash and wear.

Linn Hamilton   **Heartland**

America, America.
The land we learned to love.
No longer can we hold thee,
As our fathers did in love.

Your land is fast becoming
A rich man's paradise.
Your folk are no longer tending
Your fields of corn and rice.

Your sons of the sod are fading
From the sweetness of your side.
And no longer are they singing
In your majestic countryside.

When the few own and possess you
And turn you into gold,
Remember how we loved you
When you were ours to hold.

The rich will now exploit thee,
Take your beauty and your pride.
We will mourn to see thee
As they take you for a ride.

We have no way to love thee,
To hold you in our embrace.
The forces of the market
Have all but won the race.

Our divorce will be in agony,
Our tears will hotly flow.
Each time you haunt our memory
We see your beauty go.

Down the muddy river,
Or over the railroad line.
You were once our country,
But now have ceased to shine.

As they cart you off to market,
For all the world to share.
Don't forget that we love thee
From our city plot and lair.

Randall Dunn   Return of the Wolf

From the dawn of time, they roamed the land
From the dense forest to the prairie sand
Keeper of health, the Tribes say
As the sick and weak were usually their prey
They culled the herds, leaving only the strong
Thus the future for all would be long
As the Europeans moved their way
Working for the end of their existence one day
With poison, traps, and guns
An effort to exterminate had begun
But high in the mountains, and deep in the forest
One can still hear their enchanting chorus
As they move in the shadows of the night
No sound do they make, their steps are so light
Slowly they're drifting back to their homes of old
Like ghosts from the past, so fearless and bold

Paul Timm   Father Farmer

The endless strain and toil the Father Farmer endures for His children has no bounds. He begins the season by planting the seed within a nurturing Mother earth. He knows all the risks that come with this act of affection: weeds that try to choke away the Living Water that the seed requires for life, drought that withers, hail and wind that attempt to tear at every fiber of the plant's being. He releases that not every plant will survive long enough to bear fruit of his or her own. None the less, this does not faze the Father Farmer because He is there to watch over His crops with love that withstands even the worst of afflictions imposed on his fields. Pride is displayed across His face as the morning sun emerges to reveal the golden silks covering the ears that were formed out of His compassion. And when the proper day comes, the Father Farmer will go forth atop His brightly shining combine to reap the Harvest that yields the bounty of his labor. May every person experience the joy that comes with bearing the love of the Father Farmer.

Izma Buethe Seeba   I Saw His Faith

I saw his faith at work today
    As slowly o'er the field, bethinking snail at likely pace,
Amid the blowing dust, he'd wend his way,
    Knowing not the future he's to face.

With diligence, he guides his tractor o'er the field
    A lone bucolic creature, close to God:
As tho with pact, he and the Lord have sealed,
    He tries once more, despite the odds.

I saw his faith—beneath his dark tenacious brow
    Where myriads of dust and dirt have settled deep:
In lines ingrained upon his face,
    The mirrored cares, time and eternity cannot erase.

No occult here, nor mystic power
    But faith that in another year,
The Lord will send the blessings of His rain,
    To sprout, to grow and yield the hidden grain.

Thy hand with raindrops tender touch
        Caresses the land, and small seeds lying there,
Vouchsafed by God's unfailing love,
        Small blades of green appear!

Mark Gustafson   The Sky

The sky is large, larger than yesterday.
        It's a Yankee sky today, blue and not gray.
Contrails have multiplied over the years.
        Some days you can see a dozen or more at a glance
Some go East. Some go West.

A hundred & fifty years after the pioneers headed to Oregon
        you can still see the ruts of their wagons in places on
the prairie.
Now the wispy ruts last only minutes
        before jet streams blow them to nothingness

Max Malone   The Abandoned Farmstead

Alone and neglected, the old house stands,
On a lot grown to weeds and trees.
The rain pours in through the leaking roof,
And the old porch sags to its knees.

The glass is gone from the window panes,
And the wind swings the broken door.
The paint on the walls has faded.
Time and weather have wrecked the floor.

The old barn leans from the gusting winds.
The door hinges are stiff with rust.
The straw, in stalls where the horses stood,
Has long ago, been changed to dust.

A rusting pump still stands by the tank,
Where cows, once, drank their fill.
But the water trough is rotted and cracked.
There's no wheel on the old windmill.

The plot that was the garden patch,
In which the farm wife took such pride,
Is a thicket of plum and sumac,
Where flocks of squirrels and rabbits hide.

88

The place was once a family's home,
Folks with their joys and their cares,
With children walking home from school,
The sound of footsteps on the stairs.

But years and progress took their toll.
The old time family farm's no more.
In fields, where horses pulled the plows,
Now mighty diesel tractors roar.

The people, who where children then,
Have gone on to life's new roles.
But memories of the old farmstead,
Remain deep rooted in their souls.

3/26/85

Jack Ostergard   A Few Words for Motherhood

The inspiration for this poem came from "The Gift of Good
Land" by Wendell Berry.

It is the season of motherhood, on the ranch a special time,
Where we are preoccupied with the pregnant and unborn and
I'm
On the last round before bed, to the barn and around the
corral,
To check expectant mothers for some sign that might tell
If birth is imminent, if tonight might be the night,
And if problems should occur, I should be there to make them
right,
We joke about how seldom things are born between two and
three.
Yet the conscientious rancher will get out of bed to see.
He will wake before the alarm goes off and ponder on the need
But he knows he will go and check them, so he dresses with
some speed,
Driven not only by concern & anxiousness but curiosity
Because new birth is surveyed with joy and responsibility.
Thoreau was very possibly the first person to mull
The idea human beings should not belong to an animal.
While I will never be a mother, all my adult life
Has been used up by motherhood; foalings, calvings, even
birthings with my wife.

There are good arguments against female animals that need help,
Including cows, ewes, mares and animals that whelp.
But I'm always grateful if I've been there to fill their need.
Possibly that's why I'm here, plus I've an ego I must feed.
Now that heifer, she's laid down and strained, then got up and smelled around,
She's a heifer, so how does she know something should be there on the ground.
But she has worked awhile, and all there is to show
For all her work and time she's spent, she's given birth to just one toe.
So we help her and as she strains I pull—
First the front feet, then the head. I'll bet this calf's a bull.
And now, more easily the rest,
He shakes his head and a gasp expands his chest.
We clean his nose and help him breathe; his mother's just a heifer
But instinctively she licks and dries her newborn baby's fur.
Though she's never seen a calving, or at least paid little or no attention,
She knows the calf is hers and her job has just begun.
And all the while she talks to him, a soft and gentle moan,
Meant I think to comfort, encourage, and reassure her own.
How does she know so much, how does this come about?
Instinct, survival of the fittest there's no doubt.
I understand survival of the fittest, good mothering instincts survive.
While lesser mothers lose their calves, the good keep theirs alive.
What prepared the mind of the first cow or ewe or mare,
For this careful passionate welcome, now within her care.
We call them dumb, dumb animals and most times I will concur
That they are devoid of reasoning ability, yet one must look at her
To see they're allied with intelligence more articulate and refined
Than is in any obstetrics textbooks you can find.
When I see this heifer standing in the straw and dung, licking her calf,
My chest swells up with feeling, and I can't suppress a laugh.
She's up and the calf is wobbling on his hind feet and his knees.
As you watch in frustration and silently pray, "Please."
Because time is passing fast, I will lend a helping hand.

So I take his tail and carefully I help him stand.
Slowly I maneuver him over to his mother's flank,
She doesn't move away, but stands as if to thank
Me for the help I've given and though I should not be there
She permits me, tolerates me to assist her in her care.
When I hear the first smackings as he takes hold of a tit,
Pressure builds against my ribs and laughter releases it.
I don't know what this means but it certainly does affirm
That saved money value of the calf was not our most concern.
I look at both cow and calf, then grin with relief,
And I exult because tonight has renewed my belief.

Carole Tharnish   The Church Stands Alone

It is a small green sign that appears just before the large
Nebraska hill marking the separation of Boone and Antelope
counties on Highway 14: "Raeville 2: via county road." I stop,
not for the sign, but for the view I know that comes at the top of
the hill. A stranger might not know to stop, but would suddenly
notice on the right a sight seemingly out of place—a huge
church in the middle of nowhere.

The Romanesque-style church rises from the rolling
valley like a monument magically appearing from a distant
European city. The austere church is flanked by one-hundred
foot tall twin towers. In the middle of the double spires is a
gable which houses a white statue of St. Bonaventure. Below
the saint is a daisy-shaped stained glass window, and on top of
the gable, as well as on each tower, is a barely discernible
simple white cross. St. Bonaventure Church, with a seating
capacity of 600, seems to survey the surrounding farmland
approving of its richness by reflecting its own grandeur with its
light tan-colored impervious clay brick. The red roof of real
Ludivici tile is gone now—replaced dutifully with more fire-
resistant brown asphalt shingles. If one flew over it, the church
would appear adorning the populated prairie with a dark
cross—the body of the church intersected by the flanked
appendages housing the holy altar and sacristy. Oh, how
strangers must look wondering how a church came to be all
alone and whether the small green sign passed on the road was
part of the story.

This church is the lasting emblem for the barely
breathing borough of Raeville, Nebraska. Now an
unincorporated village, Raeville had at one time a crowning
population of 100 residents. Raeville, a name contrived by the
United States Post Office, was established before the church

91

came, but was never really meant to be a town. It started as a way for two Canadian settlers, the brothers Rae, to get their mail. The "Rae Boys Post Office" was shortened to Raeville in 1874. The Rae brothers did not plan to settle in Boone county, but were guided by an immigration agent from Omaha to come to the county—"a land flowing with milk and honey"—because a railroad was to be built into the county seat and if they didn't hurry, the railroad would get there before them. As you'll find out the Raes need not have hurried; they definitely got to Raeville before the railroad ever did.

> "We [the Raes] ascended a high hill and saw what is now called Raeville stretched out before us . . . it was one of the most beautiful sights we had ever seen. So far as the eye could reach, for miles and miles were hills and valley covered with the most beautiful mantle of green. We decided then and there we had gone far enough; that this was the Promised Land for us."

In May, 1872, Thomas and James Rae staked claim to their "promised land," a tract of prairie four miles wide and ten miles long in northern Boone county, Nebraska.

In 1874 great masses of grasshoppers congregated on Nebraska plains. Just one year later came the start of the Raeville congregation. Three German-Catholic families settled to the west of the Rae brothers in August, 1875. Like the Raes, these early settlers did not set out for this little valley. They came from Dubuque, Iowa after the Rt. Rev. Bishop J. O'Conner encouraged Catholic immigration to Nebraska. The Catholic church was seeking to expand their membership across the plains. During the late 1880s, the Catholic church was racing against itself to create ethnic-based church settlements—Irish and German were the two most predominant. Establishing settlements was imperative to gain a stronghold on the newly staked American prairies to provide an ethnic and religious community for immigrants to gravitate to.

After those first Raeville settlers got off the train in Columbus, they were ready to make their settlement. But, they were told cheap and good homestead land was still available in the vicinity of Raeville. These devout German-Catholics headed for Raeville, settled in their dugout soddies, traversed long distances to Columbus to market their produce, and endured severe winters. Homesteaders felt great desolation in the winters and maybe as those early Raeville settlers sat twisting the tall prairie grass into compact bundles, burning them as fuel, they thought the overly enthusiastic Bishop exaggerated the description of the living conditions at their new settlement. Yet, the settlers stayed, and in this small valley nestled next to nowhere, masses of other German-Catholics continued to come.

What led them to Raeville was the Church—the church that remained unbuilt and silent for the first six years of Catholic settlement. In 1881, a priest came celebrating the first church service. The Catholic settlers were thrilled to have Rev. Wunibald Wolf from Crete, Nebraska visit their colony, even if the church services were in the Bremer sod house and were only performed three times during the Summer of 1881. Visits from the priests were cherished. Churches, whether sod, wood, or brick, filled an important social and cultural role in these budding Nebraska communities. Soon Raeville became a mission parish and a small church was built early in 1882.

Raeville's pastoral needs were neglected for a time in 1884 when the forty families of St. Bonaventure had no mass all summer. This German-Catholic settlement was based on a common heritage, religious affiliation, and foreign language, so the tendency was to isolate themselves from other foreign and American influences. When the church was not there during 1884, an impassioned letter was sent by parishioner, Mr. Schlipf, to the Bishop. The Catholics were becoming careless in religious matters and, like their *Protestant* neighbors, began working on Sundays. The German homesteaders were uprooting their Faith—letting America soak into them. Mr. Schipf entreated, "For the sake of religion, send a priest in our midst."

My first church experiences were at Raeville, but I perceived church services very differently from those early settlers. I went to St. Bonaventure Church *every* Sunday and was not always thrilled to search my soul even if it was to be done inside the living, breathing bible of a church that is St. Bonaventure.

The large church with its imposing grandiosity is filled with hard-earned and donated decor brimming with symbolism. I remember sitting in the rich mahogany-stained pew marked with the gold-plated number 38—our family pew—studying the lavish interior, thinking it must have been created somewhere else, certainly not from nowhere Nebraska. Indeed the large paintings were completed at a Studio in Milwaukee, Wisconsin. The stained-glass windows were miraculously imported from Germany sometime during the First World War. These precious imports symbolize a living liturgy surrounding the church. The large center window is set in the East bringing in the bright

93

Sunday morning light onto the altar and shining through the Jesus image onto all who come to the church. Two large windows on either side give multicolored images reflected up upon God's table. One of those windows illustrates the Good Samaritan parable and the other the Prodigal Son; each is capped by a daisy design, Jesus shown in the center of the flower. Eight other windows (four on each side) are inscribed with the names of various benefactors. Each side window carries a message too.

For a youngster attending church each Sunday, there was a lot to look at and even more to wonder about. The side windows to the left, the ones closest to my parents' pew never held my attention long—I knew the school was behind those north windows. It was the one window to the south, the one with Jesus beckoning all of mankind to "Come unto Me, all ye that labor and are heavy laden, and I will give you rest," that kept me puzzled. At a time when a second-grader should be reflecting on the stained-glass images of corporal mercies—the importance of feeding the hungry, giving drink to the thirsty, sheltering the homeless, clothing the naked, caring for the sick, visiting the imprisoned, and burying the dead—I was wondering why I could not see, clearly, the outside.

Beyond that stained window was a mystery. I spent most of mass time contemplating the contents beyond Jesus's window. For some reason I kept seeing a junkyard. Looking back I wonder why I just didn't look to see what was on the other side of that window. In fact, I'm sure there were times during school recess that I ran around the church, quickly so as not to get caught off "official school grounds," and indeed I knew what was there. Yet, when I closed my eyes during mass, I saw a very clear cluttered junkyard beyond Jesus's window. It was a collection of items that someone just threw away having no value to them, or perhaps, things that just were not good enough to be in this church.

Could it be that I, at the age of seven, already knew the symbolic story of the town that housed this Church? Raeville, it is said, could have been a great town. It could have grown to 500, 800, or 1,000 people. It could have had a high school for longer than only 25 years. It could have kept a post office. It could have had a doctor's office. It could have had a gas station for longer than 30 years. It could have had a real grocery store. It could have had a cafe. It could of have had a bar. And, *it could have had*, of course, Mennonite, Methodist, and Lutheran churches. All this could have come with the railroad. It didn't.

The engine that could have was turned away because Raeville refused the railroad.

When the Northwestern railroad was extended through Boone county in 1886 (just as the Rae brothers were told it would be), three stops were planned between Albion and Oakdale: Loretto, Raeville, and Elgin. These Catholic settlers, guided by their traveling pastor, the Rev. Bonaventure Faulhaber, who had been assigned to Raeville just a few short months—voted against a station. It was rare for towns to refuse the railroad. Settlers usually saw the railroad as bringing great opportunity, but the reason cited in all the written history and in everything I ever heard is that the settlers "feared the demoralizing element of the railroad" (not to mention Methodists, Lutherans, or so I thought). Perhaps all that "junk" outside the south window was not good enough for St. Bonaventure Church.

Indeed all that "junk" did end up south of Raeville, beyond Jesus's window, at the birth of a new town, Petersburg. John Peters, the county clerk, happened to own the land west of the Rae Valley. As the railroad was left scrambling for its third station, Mr. Peters offered his land and created his own town named Petersburg. The first church the railroad brought to Petersburg was Mennonite. The second church, Methodist, was purchased by Petersburg-Catholics, in 1896.

After refusing the railroad, St. Bonaventure parish continued to grow even if the town of Raeville did not. St. Bonaventure received a resident priest, erected a second, larger church in 1888, and established a mission parish at Petersburg's transformed Methodist church. Raeville's church grew to about ninety families at the turn of the century and rather than build a bigger church, Fr. Mueller, the first resident pastor, organized an Elgin church, St. Boniface, and assigned his assistant priest to take it over in 1900.

While the surrounding railroad towns were hauling harvests, building bars, laying brick, and staying store fronts, Raeville was on its way to securing non-secular schools and cementing a church. The settlers were willing to give themselves, their land, and their money to the church—it was their mainstay. The Church was something that came from the old country, something to cling to, something from their past. They were less willing to give their money (and perhaps their souls) to the railroads—who charged too much, who subjected their community to diversity beyond their intentions, and who were a part of this still foreign land—America.

Raeville by refusing the railroad station remained true to their German-Catholic heritage; however, a later generation questioned the wisdom of that refusal. After twenty-four years of hauling crops and supplies to and from Petersburg—five miles away—the faith-inspired refusal tasted sour in the mouths of homesteaders struggling to sustain their growing fields and families.

In 1902, Fr. Frigge came to Raeville and did more than question; he made it his personal mission to reverse Raeville's fate by building a bigger school, establishing a classical-oriented high school, erecting the magnificent church, constructing a pastoral home (complete with large Grecian-style columns), creating a parish hall, organizing a cornet band ensemble, and, not the least of which, finally securing a railroad station for Raeville. And, certainly parishioners, who brought building materials by horse and wagon to and from the railroad in Petersburg, questioned the 1886 refusal over a thousand times—with each of the 1,375 trips made in 1910 when building the parochial school.

When the seventy foot by one hundred and fifty foot church was constructed during the first World War from 1917 through 1919, the railroad was there to help. Fr. Frigge got the railroad to establish a station at Raeville in 1917. The priest house constructed in 1923, appears lavish, grandiose, and almost too extravagant, but it was made from the lumber left over from the old church. One old parishioner explained the reason for the large structure, "they didn't have heavy enough saws to saw the lumber [from the old church] so they made it [the priest house] fit the lumber." They made it work.

When I was a child, a small farm girl in second grade, I didn't know the reason why the priest house was so big, I just knew that everything in Raeville seemed enormous. Walking from school to the one place of business, Bode's store, was a long walk back in 1970. I remember buying a ten cent "Chick-o-Stick" with only a dime in my pocket. I didn't know about the one cent tax, but ol' Sis Bode told me I could return to pay the penny. The walk to the store on the next day was even longer when I realized the embarrassment I brought to my father with that one-cent debt. I learned early in life that the religious German heritage surrounding me had another common trait. Germans despised debt.

Considering all of Fr. Frigge's constructions, about $140,000 (millions in today's dollars) was spent and many more thousands in furnishings, materials and labor were donated.

During the worst crop years, the thirties, Raeville continued to repay its debt. When the 1940's brought bountiful crops, Fr. Kluthe asked all ninety parish families to plant an acre for God. The families—without question—planted God's Acre and successfully repaid their debt in 1949.

I think about all the sacrifice endured by the St. Bonaventure parishioners and I wonder, with all this dedication, hard work, and faith, why did this village and parish die? Many would say the early settlers doomed the town by giving up the railroad, but maybe that's too simple of an answer. The tough times of the thirties forced some families off the farm, leaving others, like my grandfather, to buy up more "cheap" land. Farmers were able to farm more acres as machinery replaced the horse plow. The land just needed fewer families. Catholic families got smaller in the 1960s and 1970s—a dozen children per family became rarer. Looking at the Raeville cemetery one can see that some early settler families just died off. There were many reasons for Raeville's decline, but a compelling reason seems best described by my father when he explained why he left the Raeville high school after his freshman year: "St. John Berchman's School didn't have a basketball team and any good-looking Raeville girls were going to be nuns." Perhaps the secular influences which the original settlers avoided for awhile finally made their way to Raeville.

From the mid-twentieth century to now, Raeville and St. Bonaventure parish has celebrated a series of ends. The end of the Catholic high school; the end of nuns teaching school; the end of the post office, general store, gas station, and the late-acquired railroad; the end of the school itself; and finally in 1994 the end of a priest living in the pastoral home. Raeville still has mass on Sunday, though. St. Bonaventure's parish is now a mission parish of Petersburg. Now, the still dedicated parish rents out the priest house as a place to hold parties, house funeral travelers, and lodge wedding guests.

When I was young it was easy to think that the original settlers were narrow-minded isolationists who doomed the budding community by denouncing the rails; who were too pious to accept others; who wanted to keep all that "junk" outside the church window. But, now I'm not so sure. Having a railroad was no guarantee for a prosperous, enduring town. After all, today on Highway 14, I pass Loretto, one town that did get the railroad in 1886, and I realized the only thing it is now known for is the reduced speed of 50 miles an hour which one

97

must endure as one passes that unincorporated village. It doesn't even have much of a church.

Looking out at the valley, which tossed the arrogant railroad off, I smile. One of the hardest things in life is to face opposition, steadfast in your beliefs, to endure the mocking of the majority, and to make a decision based on your faith. More than the railroads and horse-drawn wagons, faith brought the settlers to Raeville. The church, the lasting symbol of Raeville's faith, remains long after the railroad spikes are drawn up and the stores close their doors. And finally that same faith which built the church remains in me and hopefully my children. It's good that all that remains of Raeville is the Church. After all, the Church brought us here and wherever we choose to go, the Church should always stay, steadfast, silent, to stunningly survey the cornfields covering this small valley, standing alone, remembering that once it rose above it all.

Joan Hoffman   **Grass 1997**

In commonplace light
the befitting essence
of the sun leaves
a golden imprint upon
the hillside,
and when it is dark
and the air is chilled
and tranquil
bright stars pantomime
fireflies.
Nothing is immovable here.
Not even yucca or wild roses,
fierce remnants of the thirties drought,
nor buffalo or gamma grasses
lifting their slender banners,
nor coyotes lurking in the shadows
like two-faced heroes cum tricksters,
not even smooth stones which
stay warm well into the night.

Dick Schanou   **Dutch Elm and Cancer (In Memory of Mom)**

I go back . . . back to the elm tree,
One branch whose leaves trail the ground,
A tent of sun shafts and greenery.
Orioles above, flashing through
The branched sky.

We pretend . . . a fort . . . a house . . . a teepee--
The woods of early America
Resound with our war whoops,
Squaws bustle, buffalo pound,
Horses snort and stamp, as we charge
From the shelter, and with our
Guns, axes, knives, bows and arrows
We attack trees, bushes, hay piles . . .
We play and play, and Mom calls dinner,
We think, or was it a rooster crowing?

She left us pretty much alone
With our war games,
Except for a couple of times--once
When she found a bb under skin
While butchering a chicken . . .
(The cats ate the few who
Actually bought the farm
'Cause they were huddled in the trees
Planning some outrage, and she
Couldn't hear the twanging and the
Squawking from the kitchen window,
And we never showed her just how
Good our homemade bows really were--
No need to worry her, you know.)

But then there was that other time,
That time she caught Charlie
Laughing at a reeling, gurgling chicken
Staggering like old goat-faced
Willy used to do on Saturday nights.
We had seen the cartoon, the Stooges,
And the Western, and watch as he
Lifted first one foot, then the other, high
In the air over each of the eight UP tracks.

99

He was almost more fun than the movies.
So this chicken was really something . . .
Except it wasn't drunk. There was a
Homemade arrow sticking through its head.
"I shot up in the air," he lied.
"Yes," she said quietly, strangely,
"What if that chicken had been your brother?"
We shot no more chickens.
Charlie didn't play with his bow
For a whole week.

In those days of pure imagination
The whispering winds brushed
The cascading leaves
And caressed her flowing hair
Before the ravaging storms
Exposed a twisted and stark reality and
Uncovered the bald truth.

I go back under the screen of leaves,
Under the elm, under the swinging,
Woven nests, and I'm buried in a past
Which flutters and flashes
In a kind of flickering brightness,
But I see that it only briefly colors a
Blighted landscape . . .

There is a slight rise in the corner of the lawn,
Where one root escaped the chain-saw
And became a menace to mowers--a
Rut which jolts the stumbling mind
From its soaring, dappled dreams
To the Shade which lies
Under the grass.

Don Welch   Funeral at Ansley

I write of a cemetery,
of the perpetual care of buffalo grass,
of kingbirds, catbirds, and cottonwoods;

of wild roses around headstones,
with their high thin stems
and their tight tines, and their blooms
pursed in the morning.

I write of old faces,
of cotton hose and flowered dresses
and mouths which have grown up
on the weather.

And I write of one woman
who lies a last time in the long sun
of August, uncramped by the wind
which autumns each one of us

under catbirds and kingbirds
and cottonwoods, and the gray-green leaves
of the buffalo grass.

Elaine Frasier   Scrapbags

The quilt is a piece of my past. When I first fashioned it
in my mind, I saw it as a patchwork of multicolored, various
patterned pieces of material. As I gathered these scraps from
the scrapbag, it seemed that so many were from projects that I
had completed years before...this white eyelet became a sunsuit
for my dark haired baby girl; the lady bug print, another
sunsuit; the mouse print an outfit for her first day of school.
The theme of the quilt was destined to be the fabrics of my
daughter's childhood wardrobe. It became hers and my shared
experience of "Remember this?"
       I also have a scrapbag of memories made up of snippets
of time from my childhood.
I can describe the memory of sitting on my mother's lap as she
rocks me one winter evening. We four are listening to a favorite
Saturday night radio program. Though I know it is cold outside
our little circle, I am warm in my flannel sleepers and confident
of the warmth of my mother's arms.
       When I close my eyes and listen, I hear the
meadowlark's throaty warble announcing the arrival of spring.
The air is just warm enough this afternoon that a jacket isn't
needed. I inhale the pungent aroma of burning dried thistles
that my dad is removing from the fence-line behind the house
as he readies the field for planting. It seems that all is right
with God's World this day.
       It is during a late afternoon summer thunderstorm that
we four sit on the porch watching sheets of rain coursing across
the driveway. Lightning slashes the skies and we expectantly
wait for the ensuing rumble of thunder so we can shout, "Tater

101

wagon!" (In later years I would learn that this was a rare glimpse of my dad's German heritage).

Both of these endeavors—piecing together bits of cloth into a colorful quilt and piecing snippets of memories into a written piece of prose—yield a uniquely personal product. Something to treasure and something to share.

James Magorian   Imperfect Bounty

The curved sidewalk takes the cedars by surprise,
new snow drops from their branches.
At midwinter the farmhouse breaks its vows,
drinks watered-down light, sings,
extends bare shoulders above collapsed vines.
the season is celebrated for its flaws:
the fallen snow-fence,
the steel ruts in the road,
the frozen windmill,
the sloppy harvest that left clasps
of yellow in the cornfield,
the dead sparrow by the porch,
the jars of fruit gone bad in the cellar.
It is this imperfect bounty,
the sad amazements,
the dark mystical beauty of doubt
that is commemorated by the long shadows
and the earth's dance through space.

R.F. McEwen Coyote's Cry Dawes Co., Nebraska, 1996

Sharp against the sandstone bluff
I heard a coyote's cry.
No wind could sound as desolate
that morning, with the sky's

unwillingness to show the sun,
and fog like shoulders
bowed and gray and settled in a shroud
upon the boulders

of the bluff. They set out bait,
the ranchers hereabouts,
strychnine, I think, and things go hard
for coyotes and stray dogs

not practiced in efficiency
of modern management.
It's not malicious, mind. If you
kept lambing ewes, or sent

cows off to market every year,
depended on each birth
to hold your place, you'd do it, too.
You'd measure your own worth

against a howling at the bluff,
(flint sharp beneath the fog)
against the nasty dying of
a wild, untutored dog.

Mary Ruff   Washday

Our rooster
chased my mother
until she
trapped him
underneath
her bushel basket.

She was eight months
pregnant,
sat her egg-full
shape over the basket
to capture him,
save herself.

Shell white sheets
flapped on the line,
her scream
subdued by the wash,
south wind.
My brother and I

stood in the safety
of the shed outback.
Our father came,
clasped our hands,
we all ran breathless
to help Mother.

103

The basket,
our circle
round a rooster,
the past, present, and future
indelibly
etched beneath
one summer's sheath.

Mary Maas   Riding Between Life and Death

A person would think that riding around in a pasture or pen riding should be just a simple task. That this task would be just a normal part of a daily routine, not particularly exciting, but certainly electrifying as the event unfolded. This cowboy found out that daily routines could turn deadly in a split second.

LeRoy Daniel, of Stanton, NE shared his story about his close encounter with death on a crisp autumn day about fifteen years ago. He was riding pens to check on cattle at the feedlot when he noticed four critters were down on the ground near a water tank.

"I knew they weren't down when I checked the pen on noon rounds, so I knew something was wrong," Daniel said.

He opened the gate and rode into the pen. As he approached the area of the tank he said he felt his mount, Queenie, take a jolt and the horse started going down.

Daniel said he yanked hard on the reins to get the horse's head up. That reflex action helped give them a couple extra seconds of momentum and the horse stumbled forward a few extra feet, away from the dead cattle, before falling to the ground. Daniel said his leg was pinned against a bull fence panel by the weight of the dead horse.

They went down only a short way from the area of the tank where the dead cattle were lying in puddles of water that had overflowed from the tank. Daniel said he started hollering for help as he struggle to stay up on the saddle leather.

"Every time I tried to get my leg free by pushing on the bull panel, or on the horse, I could feel electricity tingle through me."

Then he saw the electrical wire, which had fallen to the ground from off a pole, coiled on the wet ground near the tank. While Daniel was pinned under his horse, another calf walked toward the tank and he said it, too, fell dead to the ground.

Daniel said he figured he was in the pen for about twenty minutes before rescue help arrived.

"I just kept hollering for help until someone from the crew heard me and came looking, because I knew they couldn't see me where I was down."

When the rest of the cowboys finally heard him and found out what happened, Daniel had to keep telling them to stay out of the pen and get someone to shut off the power to the wire. An older fellow, who occasionally helped out with odd jobs at the feedlot, was a retired electrician. Fortunately, the electrician happened to be at the feedlot that day and he knew how to safely cut the wire.

Even after the power to the pole and the fallen wire was cut, the electrician warned every one that the electricity was still built up in the ground and would be dangerous for another half an hour. So, Daniel said, he had to remain where he was for what seemed to him to be a very long time. The electrician told them because the 110-volt wire was coiled around about four times, and was in water, that it produced a more deadly level of electrical power. He said that it would take extra time for the electrical current to drain out of the ground.

After the danger of electrocution passed, Daniel said he was able to get his leg out from between the horse and the fencing with out any broken bones or electrical burns. He said his leather saddle, gloves, chaps and rubber boots must have been what saved his life. He found that the buckles on his boots had left burned blackened holes all the way through his chaps. He figured that the metal horseshoes probably conducted the electricity from the ground and that is what killed the horse.

Daniel said he just was really lucky that he was able to keep from touching the ground and stayed up on the saddle leather. He said the hardest part was to keep his foot, on the leg that was pinned, raised off the ground. If he let his spur drop down and touch the ground he could feel little jolts in his foot.

When asked if the incident changed anything in his attitude or life, he said he guessed he was sure lucky and it just wasn't his time to go.

The one bad thing he said was that Queenie wasn't his horse. The horse belonged to another Stanton cowboy, Landon Hansen.

Daniel said he and one of his horses had survived an encounter with lightning about twenty years earlier. In the mid-60s, he was working as a cowboy on a ranch in western Nebraska. He was riding and checking the herd out on grass just south of Wood Lake. The day was cloudy and the weather started to get stormy with lightning flashing all around.

"I saw the bolt that hit my horse," Daniel said. "It was just a blinding flash of white that hit right in front of me and we both went down. I didn't feel anything. The lightning bolt didn't kill my horse that time, it just dazed him for a little bit."

Daniel said when the horse quit stumbling around they "got the hell out of there".

"I guess it just wasn't my time," Daniel said quietly, "neither time."

Fredrick Zydek   **Abandoned Church: Platte County, Nebraska**

- for Tom Greisen

There's a grove of young cottonwoods growing
through the sidewalk leading to the front steps.
They've broken the concrete like an iceberg
breaks through the hull of a ship. In this place
the great anchor did not hold. Captain, ship,
cargo and crew - all evaporated
as surely as the great sea that once swirled here.

We climb the steps to the big weathered doors,
avoid the cow patties and pigeon doo
as best we can and continue upwards
like prospectors or tourists great white bears
out to seek their fortunes in what is left
when the fire is taken from the hearth
and the cave is left to fend for itself.

We enter like wounded sheep. The place reeks.
There is bat dung everywhere; rows of them
cling like demons from the loft and belfry.
We go below them unnoticed. Stained glass,
broken and strange, is everywhere. We find
a saint's cracked eye near the high altar,
pieces of halo in the men's room,

a stained-glass thumb in the old sacristy,
the words *ora pro nobis* lost in the dust.

106

The floor sags. Its brokenness claims us.
We hear odd sounds hurry in the basement
and forgive our urges to go downstairs.
Something here is dying. It knows our names.
We leave its great silence almost ashamed.

Maxine Isackson   Rain

It is a day in late July. Bleak, hot, and oh, so dry. I
walk through a field where corn leaves hang limply on dusty
stalks rustling as I pass, telling me of their thirst. I whisper
back, "I know how it is." I reach out to stroke one of the
parched plants while across the valley the tormenting roar of an
irrigation motor assaults the ear, pumping liquid gold onto a
neighbor's field. Not for the first time and probably not the last,
I question our decision to stick with dryland and the ecosystem
of farming.

I trudge back to the house, dust coating my shoes,
studying the sky as I go. Far to the west, a thin line of dark
clouds edges the horizon. Dare we hope? The weatherman at
noon said only thirty percent chance of rain, but...there is that
dark, tenuous line in the west.

Night falls. The heat remains. Faintly, a rumble of
thunder is heard from the line of clouds emerging ghostlike,
encroaching slowly eastward. A quick, flickering flash marks
the blackness of the distant heavens...lightning. Our small,
drought-plagued world waits, hushed and longing ... will the
rain come our way or will it cut by to the north or south?

Ah, yes! It's coming. Straight for the valley! Praise God!
It's coming!

The thunder crashes and the lightning cracks. The rain
falls in gray sheets from the darkness, its sweet scent filling the
cooling air.

I cannot see the cornfields in the night, but I can
imagine them. The dust has been washed away. The green
leaves are lifting. They'll be crisp and bright in the morning,
jeweled with beads of moisture. Standing by the open window
in my nightgown, I smile as the breeze caresses my face.

I will walk in the fields again in the morning. I'll hear
the green leaves whisper joyfully and I'll answer, "Yes, I know.
It rained last night. Once more it rained!"

Frederick remembers as a boy
looking up as he worked
with his grandfather, saw

him climb the windmill
on the home place,
reach for a rung
only to find it rotted.
With his pull
it pulled away.

He grabbed for the next,
higher up,
hoped for something

solid, fixed.
But it gave way, too,
rotted through.

Grandfather felt himself
falling, kicked back
so he'd clear the stocktank,

aware of the nearness
of death, his body
obeying instinct.

Something fell away
in his brain
as if a million years

of evolution unraveled
a thin filament of DNA,
releasing him

into his reptile brain
a long leanness of muscle
in mid-air twist, a return

to an earlier life
in the crawl of centuries.
He flipped himself

over in the air
with an animal ease,
rode down on four legs

landed light upon
four feet, breaking
only the tip of his nose.

The boy saw him crawl
across the yard
on his knees, unable

to speak, a lizard-flicking
of his tongue
to spit out sand.

Bruce Stock   To Seek and Find After the Run

A lot of us wonder about and experience our lives from
stage to stage, seeking what seems to be the unknown.

As youngsters we run as hard as we can. We care not
about the finish line, for it is for the run we live.

As the simplicity of childhood and running gives way to
the teen years, the running continues, but now we begin to
seek. The lucky can visually see what they are beginning to
seek, but for some of us there is hardly a blur for us to see.

With incredible good fortune and someone watching over
us, we ran out of our teen years, went through the war and into
our early adult twenties. Still, some of us are more confused as
to what we are seeking than ever. We tried to mature beyond
our minds' and bodies' ability, not knowing what we would find
in our futures that we so desperately were seeking.

The path for many of us has been as rocky as a
mountain trail, a trail which we followed by running, walking,
and stumbling. For the lucky ones of us who have lived, we
have sought and found LOVE from another. For the blur and,
at times, darkness in front of us gives way to light, shown by
the love of another person.

As for myself, the ultimate mystery was unveiled when I
had my sons. All the stumbling and falling down, the cuts and
emotional bruises, all make sense with the love only a child can
give.

The running slows to a satisfactory or even comfortable pace. I now have an inner strength given by my sons which helps me cope daily.

I will probably continue to run, but now have a focus and I'm less confused and more content.

I thank my higher power for my sons. What a run it has been.

Gaylen Mosel   One Out of Two

I still remember when the two kids arrived from South Dakota
I'm not sure, but I think their tribe was Lakota

The boy was adopted by our white neighbors up the road
This must have been a large increase in their work load

The two were sister and brother
They seemed lost and scared when holding hands with one another

The girl couldn't adapt so she went back home
The boy was left to learn our ways: from using a knife and fork
        to parting his hair with a comb

He and I became best of friends
His name was Leslie

Sometimes I would learn from him
And sometime he would learn from me

He and I went through a ritual and became blood brothers one day
He said things would be different between us and we ran off to play

We rode horses together and tracked the little animals for fun
We played with bows and arrows awhile then off we would run

Things seemed just fine and we had a lotta fun for a few years
We talked of everything and at times we shed some tears

One time he went swimming and I wasn't there
He drowned that day: life just didn't seem fair

110

I can still walk the same little animal trail
Chasing up pheasant, deer, and sometimes quail

When I'm in the wild the memory of him is strong
I suppose I'll join him in the happy hunting ground before long

Jason Elznic Dead Cottonwood, Madison County

I
Late September

I sit here waiting
Waiting for permission
to haul your old bones down
Observing your gray arms
puncturing the blue sky
like a final answer--

Were you here long enough
to see horse give way to gas
Gas give way to diesel
corn picker give way to combine

Where did your affiliations lie
on this divide
separating Humphrey from Madison
Madison from Platte
Platte from Elkhorn

Was it change that brought you here
Was it you that created the earth
in which you now stand
or
Did change bring about the end
As irrigation sucked away life-giving water
until your old roots couldn't dig anymore

I ponder your solitary existence
Sticking out on the plain
A road mark for visitors,
like me

II
Early October

I hear a horn in the distance
The blustering wind
a rural delivery against time
And find myself counting it out
"Two miles north,
"a quarter west"
That's where the alien train emerges
out of brome and elm
Carrying not cattle
or corn
or anything else of this land
But scrap iron
Steel
Heading north to be made steel again

III
October

I pick road grit out of my ear
and watch the big Ford approach
in the rear view mirror
of the smaller Dodge

"Would you believe it,
that old guy won't let us touch that tree"

I laugh
and shake my head
But inside I sympathize with a man
desperately clinging
to the way things were
And feel somehow relieved
to let the sleeping giant stay

"We're heading north a ways"
And the Ford rolls on
kicking up pillows of dirt

I turn up the radio
Push the old Dodge through the gears
2...3...
Fourth gear rattles
as we crest a dusty hill
And my mind keeps time
Racing the train

Algene Stohl A Beatitude

A true account of my life as a child on the farm. In loving
memory of my parents--Ernest and Julia; sisters—Ina, Verna
(old-partner), Alvena and Hazel; brothers--Curtis, Carrol and
Vergil (prince charming). Only "I" remain. These are "Happy
Memories", one's we can wax-back to & remember - <u>our</u> -
LOVED ones and our YOUTH!!

BEATITUDE - (Webster's Dictionary Definition) A heavenly
happiness, a happiness of the highest kind; sayings of "Christ".

"A BEAUTITUDE"

Being the youngest of the family means you have a whole bevy
of Mothers and Fathers. You have your own preachers,
teachers and baby-sitters. You learn young, grow up fast, and
if you come along as a tail-ender, as I call myself...you
sometimes live and play in a happy, make-believe world.

You pretend you have someone with you, riding in a horseless
carriage out beside a house filled with busy, feathered friends.
They seem like little people as they scratch and peck, cackle
and crow! You learn the facts of life early on the farm. There's
nothing quite as cute and soft as a newborn chick! You learn
how each species protects and nurtures their young.

About now, you need to run over to a little-house! It's not any
bigger than a play-house but big enough for two or sometimes
three. Every farm had one of these for our comfort! It was quiet
and a neat place to read an old Catalog. We especially liked the
thin pages!

When your attention starts to wane, you run over and crawl up
onto the rooftop of a building, with a fence between you and
other friends, who are much bigger. They grunt and grovel in
the mud next to a water- hole so they can wallow away the day
while others play drop the handkerchief with a bright yellow
corn-ear; until just a rosy-red corncob is left, which you will
have to pick up in a bushel-basket to be used to heat water for
your Saturday night baths. After that-you are a Kin-to-Them.
You are covered with their scent!

113

Then it's time to sneak out...into the pasture...where thresher's have made you a special yellow, straw mountain, all your own! You slip and slide as you unsuccessfully try to climb it. Finally you're satisfied reaching a plateau, just high enough to watch a herd of mooing friends lazily-grazing on a carpet of green. Their tails switching...the ever present little nuisances, who insist on bothering them! It seems strange. Even though some are reclining over to one side, they continue to chew constantly, swallow, burp and chew again! On occasion, one heavy friend will move away by herself, go through a whole ritual and before your very eyes present you with a Living-example of 'herself'!!

Before long you're offered a ride on an old gray, reliable friend, named "Babe". You're hoisted into a leather seat, with an aroma all it's own, but just right for little girls. Your short legs don't reach the stirrups but, no mind, because Prince-Charming cradles you between his arms and you enjoy the ride. With a snort and a gallop, you're off to 'Never-Never-Land,' a grove of trees where all kinds of things grew! Come sundown you've seen it all and tasted more. Wild-Strawberries to tickle your tongue, an apron full of asparagus and sheep-showers. You stop by a fountain, flowing deep and wide. You can be sure for all my 'friends' are gathered there. It's so refreshing. Even the wind joins in to satisfy our needs, as the wheel turns in delight-to the rhythm of the breeze!

Now it's time to wash-up, sit-up to an oilcloth covered table where 'ten' pairs of shoes are placed neatly... under it! A quick "Blessing," and the breaking of fresh-baked-bread, Lemonade, with chunks or river ice to cool it, 'New'-potatoes, garden vegetables and a platter of My crisp, fried friends and even I understand... one is made for the other!

With dishes done, baths and such...I'm cuddled into 'slumberland', next to an old partner my big Sister... while she reads..."Blessed are the pure in heart for they shall see "God"!

(Matthew 5:8)

She KNOWS for SURE and although I'm seventy-eight, I haven't forgotten her words...By the way...there is only one pair of shoes...left...to place under that oilcloth-covered table...and "I"...too...shall see "God"!

Charles Fort   The Cranes (Once Removed) from the Platte River

They land between reef and hollow
the daredevil and dragonfly nightborn
a lifespan under a stone bridge
to breed in the skim and hum
given their mortal weeks to fly.
The land and sky underwater
a sordino and drunken waltz
tins of light tied to hollow bone
as shadows brood and horizons flare.
What has fallen over this world
a wingspan across the plains
between morning tide and half-moon
eclipsed by the dance and daredevil
covers us like a thousand nightborn.

Randall Dunn   The Roots of Our Future

Like a shot in the dark, I took a blast
And through her wisdom, sought my past
Our roots were common years ago
So I thought, perhaps she may know
Of the American blood that ran within
And could tell how thick, or ever so slim
Maybe she had stories passed down through the years
Some of glad times and some of tears
Perhaps some pictures, or keepsake treasure
Something with which our past we might measure
I hoped she might know the tribe of descent
But this knowledge wasn't hers to be lent
We did share stories and pictures of past
And her friendship for me will forever last
Perhaps one day I'll continue to seek
The blood within, however so weak
As the spirits I hear, every now and then
Stir a need to know, from deep within

Lora Stauffer   Worship

I can worship God in a sunlit field where
shadows seldom fall,
or in a deep and shady glen where the sun
doesn't shine at all.

115

I can worship Him in a silver plane
high in a sunlit sky,
or in a mine deep underground where
birds just never fly.
I can worship God in a country church
high on a little knoll,
and when I worship in His Church then
peace really fills my soul.

Alice Heller   Mother's Kitchen

The World's greatest cookies could be found
In my mother's kitchen on the farm.
The wood burning stove made a crackling sound.
Warmth and love sheltered us from harm.

The kitchen was narrow and long,
Wainscoted green and papered in flowers.
A radio often played a Christian song.
Times spent there were happy hours.

A bouquet of flowers in full bloom,
Sat on an oval drop leaf table.
Old wooden cupboards were in the room
And a refrigerator of the Hot Point label.

Peas in pods were quickly gleaned.
Delicious bushels of fruit we'd can.
Endless chickens were carefully cleaned
In heat of summer, cooled by a fan.

I wish we could go back again,
To my mother's kitchen on the farm.
Life was certainly simpler then.
Now with love we shelter her from harm.

Faye Tanner Cool   Harvest Squall

A storm of birds rains
from the sky
and drops down
on a road nearby

to glean and gorge
on harvest fare
spilled by
haulers unaware.
As other motors interrupt
their feeding, this cloud—
black—looms up,
its whirring growing
by degrees...then,
loud complaint pours
from the trees.

Elaine Phillips   **Harvest Literature**

Recently, I have had the occasion to ponder the relative
merits of Harvest Literature—i.e., what to read while waiting in
the truck or tractor to load-unload, weigh-reweigh, receive
instructions-transfer instructions and so forth. During these
times, there is ample opportunity to get a lot of reading done.
But what should you read? What is good Harvest Literature?

Escape literature like a good Gothic novel or Western
can whisk you away into a world of adventure, excitement, and
passion. You may become so enthralled that you miss your cue
in line or field and excitement and passion (of a sort) could
invade the adventure of real life.

This may be a good time to read self-improving or
morally uplifting books. By the time you have been interrupted
several times to do your assigned job, and subsequently re-read
the same passages several times, the message may sink in and
you might benefit from it.

Newspapers are good truck and tractor reading. You
might as well read them then because you won't have time
when you get home. You could emerge from the harvest season
better informed than you have ever been in your life! Don't save
old newspapers to read. You will become well-informed but
your information will be dated. Newspapers have the additional
advantage of being disposable. Harvest Literature gets dirty.

Now is a good time to dig out those magazines from
under the bed and couch and stash a few in every vehicle.
Then, whatever you are asked to drive will be equipped! In
addition to being disposable, magazine articles aren't as likely
to be out of date--unless they've been under the bed a long
time.

Poetry can be very good for the cab reader. It is condensed literature and benefits from multiple readings. Now is your chance to read all of EVANGELINE, HIAWATHA, THE WASTELAND, or lots and lots of Ogden Nash.

Farm magazines are mixed blessings. You can read them and make "after harvest" plans to emulate their well-organized shops, profitable marketing approaches, beautiful farmstead designs, efficient record keeping, etc. Or, you can become frustrated. These articles are about people of action, decision-makers. You, on the other hand, are trapped in enforced passivity, waiting on other people's decisions.

It is safe to take catalogues of all types in the truck and tractor. Removed from checkbook, charge card and phone, you can dream and select without paying the price. By the time you get home, it's too late to call, you've changed your mind, or you've lost the catalogue.

It is not a good idea to take cookbooks for study and menu planning. They get dirty, you get hungry, eat all your snacks and lunch too early and regret it the rest of the day. You may make a few plans or try a recipe or two later, but is it worth it?

At harvest time the "Reader's Digest", current and past, are removed from the bathroom and placed in all well-equipped truck and tractor cabs. It is really the ultimate of Harvest Literature. It contains humor, horror, adventure, excitement, self-improvement, simple poetry, and timely topics. The articles are short and to the point. The magazine is a handy size and is disposable. What more could one ask of Harvest Literature?

If you have not planned ahead, you may be forced to read the mouse-chewed operators manual (my husband thinks that idea has merit), or the ingredients list on your purchased snacks, or try to figure out the abbreviations on the scale tickets or on the dials and knobs of your vehicle's dash. It is better to be prepared.

Some may ask--Why not just sit and think and enjoy the beauty of a Nebraska Autumn? There is nothing wrong with that, but you wouldn't have a chance. If seen to be idly sitting, not involved with a book or magazine, you would probably be asked to grease something.

Andy Raun   Memorial Day Observances

His tractor sits, waiting, beyond the chain-link fence
While he kneels in the buffalo grass,

Tracing the etched letters of her name
With a grime-blackened finger.

A day's-last ray of sunlight
Touches the rose granite face of the marker.
A meadowlark serenade rides the air,
But he is weary, and he does not heed.

For a quiet moment, he forgets the seed bill,
His tractor payments, the price of corn.
He remembers the feel of her lap,
The smell of her kitchen,
The sound of her voice.

Then, as if awakening, he raises his head
And hears her love in the bird's song,
Feels it in the caress of prairie wind.
He sees the winking lights of yonder farm:
His farm. Her farm.

He remembers his place — next to her,
And the bird, and the grass, and all that lives.
Smiling gently, he returns to his work.
Silently, his lips form her name over and over:
Mother.

Renee Lanik   Two Poems

1
Our son was born as the sun rose blurred and red-hot to
straddle the horizon. When I finally slept I dreamed of soft
damp green fields where I lay with my son gazing upward to
drifting clouds, deep falling stars and the man in the moon. I
feel as if I am seeing all I have seen for the first time through his
eyes. Each star shines brighter than the other spilling over
embracing warmth. I forget everything I knew before and I drift.
"Hey Mom," my son says suddenly, and I wake. Look over at
him and see he is in a state of serious wonder and delight.
"We're alone together, aren't we Mom?" and I know there is
light.

2
Where deer tracks enter the corn field, the wind's erased them.
Silky milkweed seeds tag along on the shifting wind. It's fall and

everything is letting go. Even the bitterness of my childhood is leaving me. The acorns fall from the trees leaving their capped-hats behind. They hit and roll through the dry corn rows, eventually finding that perfect place in the ground to rest and go on. So will I.

Nancy Peters Hastings   **Windfalls**

In grass she works, unable to stand
up straight, bent from hoeing
her garden too many years.

She seems not to want to reach
high overhead, where sun shined
Jonathans weigh the branches down.

Instead, this is her duty
an inner nature decrees:
to keep windfalls from the worms.

She retrieves only those ripe and ready
Before they've crowded brown with ants.
She seems not to see the difference

between the apples dangling plump,
delicious, and those underfoot.
The bushels she takes glow in the grass.

She saves the best for someone else.

The Gift of Agriculture

Sarah Hilkemann   Lilly's Farm

Lilly stared out her bedroom window. The beautiful fall colors that she loved so much were beginning to creep into the leaves. I love the farm, she thought. If only Dad could make enough money to keep it.

"Lillian May, you get in here and finish these dishes! Your father will want those cows in, too, by the time he gets home," Lilly's mother called from the kitchen.

"Coming, Mother!" Lilly called back. She sighed and left her perch by the window.

The dishes didn't take long and she soon headed out to the north pasture for their dairy cows. As she walked, Lilly again went over their situation. No money left to pay bills, people coming out from the bank every month; she just couldn't understand why her dad had to give up the place they all loved so much. He had tried to explain it one night at supper.

"Lil, you know I love the farm, but I just can't keep up. The bills are piling up and the bank and stores aren't going to keep giving us credit. We'll have to sell."

Lilly had cried that night. She couldn't just give up the place that she loved.

"Come on, you old critters! Let's get to the barn!" she shouted as the cows poked along. Just then, she heard the familiar rattle of her father's pickup. "Let's get moving!" she shouted. Dad will probably change clothes and be out, she thought.

Finally, the cows were in the holding pen, and Lilly quickly fed the baby calves and their flock of chickens, then gathered the eggs. Her father still hadn't come out.

Lilly trudged up the house. Dad and Mother were probably discussing bills.

As she entered the small farmhouse, Lilly heard the muffled crying of her mother. "What's going on?" she asked, quietly entering their bedroom.

Lilly's father turned and said sadly, "I sold the farm, Lil. The milk cows, too. A guy's coming to look at most of the calves tomorrow." He paused at Lilly's horrified look and then added, "I'm sorry, Lilly. There wasn't any choice."

*   *   *

After the farm sale, Lilly's father took his wife and daughter into his arms. "Just think, ladies. We'll be ushering in the new millennium with a new place. I know, 1999 hasn't been the greatest year for us, but who knows what 2000 will bring?"

Mary Borm   Who Needs This?

I woke today, again convinced,
that I don't need this pain.
The price of beef, the cost to live,
the constant mental drain.
The weather's wet or much too dry,
or maybe it's too cold.
Our dollar just ain't worth a dime.
This gamble's gettin, old!

121

Those calves that die for nothin',
'fore they even learn to play.
You square your shoulders, lift your chin,
pretendin' you're blase'.
The grass is gone before it's time,
to take the calves to town.
The hayin's goin' much too smooth,
so everything breaks down!
We worry 'bout the neighbor's corn,
we can't afford to feed.
This ranchin's not for everyone,
it takes a special breed.
And it also takes a partner,
who wants the things you do.
You bow your neck, tighten your belt,
find reasons to pull through.
Those wet springs bring the ducks and geese.
Wild flowers thrive in heat.
In fall the wildlife all comes back,
just lookin', for a treat.
Then with winter, comes the terror,
of cold and drivin' snow.
Or, midnights, checkin', heifers,
dozin' in the full moons' glow.
The snow that squeals beneath my booth,
the night sounds in the trees,
the concert as the river,
tries to ward off this year's freeze.
Those babies, touched by magic,
though there stressed, they still survive.
The warmth of that man's gentle smile,
It's good to be alive!
I guess, I'm just a masochist,
I flourish in this strife.
So, maybe that's why God chose me,
as this poor rancher's wife?
It seems, I've changed my mind again,
now that I thought it through.
When my brain screams, "Who needs this pain?"
My heart answers, "I do!"

Second week at the place
And I haven't planted a damn thing.
Got stuck up on this roof
Tearing off shingles so they can be
Replaced with tin.
Everything's tin now. Easier to burn the barn
And build a machine shed than
Fix her up. Windmills without wings,
Their blades building equity
In all the backyards in town.

They won't give me rein
To buck out these John Deere's either.
Gotta fill the loader bucket up,
Inch off this roof and walk out in the beans
To flag one of 'em down.
Waste of time and 109 is too damn hot
To be walking out in this field
So they can dump the load
On the burn pile themselves.
Can't be that hard to run this rig.
Only problem is its old,
Like the rest of the stuff here.
Gear-shift directions gone to
Rain and rust. Should have bought
International Red.

What I figure is reverse is back and
Drive is forward—simple enough.
They'll know it too,
When I start it up—black cloud be pouring
From this erected muffler.
Just let off this clutch here
And be on my way.

****

I waited half an hour
Before I walked a line of beans to tell 'em
Their tractor had gone awry.
No sense in waiting for them to see
For themselves. JD 3020 Standard
Now wedged between the frame and plywood.

The shingles strewn on top of the roof
Had re-glued themselves. Belly Mower,
Blading concrete.
An empty fuel tank smashed between a tire
And new hole in the garage—loader bucket
Gone full tilt on it's own,
Leaving me to take
The blame.

Mark Gustafson   The Barn

The old barns around Nebraska are going, replaced by
modern machine sheds or specialized buildings: finishing
sheds, farrowing houses, milking parlors, loafing sheds, broiler
houses, etc. Today, farm animals have buildings designed
especially for them. These buildings are large, well made,
modern in design but not nearly as appealing to the eye as a
good old barn.

Our barn stands just to the west of the house. It's a
good-sized barn, latex white now, but when scraped you can see
that it was once oiled red. Although today it appears to serve
primarily as a home for cats and a storage shed for odd pieces
of equipment and the household over-runs, it is actually much
more. To begin with, it is the signature structure of our
farmstead. It is the first thing you see when you crest the hill
beyond the pond to the west. It stands surrounded by the old
corral in need of paint and repair. It is also an important
depository of memories. Memories that are important enough
that the barn may need to stay for no other reason than to serve
as a memorial to them.

I'm not sure what my earliest memories of our barn are.
The years have treated my childhood memories no better than
they have treated the barn itself. Both memories and barn have
missing pieces and are not as structurally sound as they
probably should be. Both are covered in cobwebs and layers of
dust. The recesses of my brain contain a varied collection of
odds and ends, as does the barn. Almost all of my memories of
the barn are good. Some painful, some exhausting, most
involving work, but not all.

When I was a kid, our barn was an important part of the
farm. In the fifties, at various times, our farm had chickens,
turkeys, cattle, pigs and sheep. Cattle, pigs and chickens
seemed to be there most of the time. We also had workhorses
when I was very young and riding horses as my sisters and I
grew older. The barn was home to the cattle, pigs and horses.

The chickens and the turkeys had less grand accommodations. The sheep were consigned to the chicken house after it was decided we could live without our feathered friends. We soon learned we could also live without the sheep.

Today, surprisingly, the barn still appears to be big. Not as big as when we were young, but still big. It measures forty feet by forty feet and stands close to thirty feet tall. At one time, it had a cupola in the center of the roof, but that was removed forty-five years ago by our father to keep moisture and sparrows out of the hay. It still has two decorative lightning rods with blue glass balls pierced by arrows pointing to the sky, almost daring the clouds to give them their best shot. The mow runs the full length and width of the barn and when filled would hold hay twenty feet deep at the centerline.

Downstairs a central alley runs from east to west dividing the barn. The south space was adapted to farrow pigs. Originally, this side of the barn was for milking cows. Milk cows were some of the first farm animals to leave our farm when the folks discovered that their finicky kids wouldn't drink un-homogenized milk. Forty years ago nine sows could be farrowed in this space at a time. The farrowing crates designed and built by our father were removable to facilitate the cleaning process between litters. The crates, floors, and walls were scoured with hot water and lye to eliminate any diseases that might linger and affect the next batch of baby pigs. Once the pigs were old enough, they ventured outside summer and winter onto the cement pad poured on the south side of the barn. The pad was the same length as the barn and was anchored in the south east by the old cement stock tank. A reporter for the Omaha newspaper once came out and took a picture of a particular sow who had learned to throw her front legs over the tank's edge so she could share a drink with the cows rather than drink from the lowly pig waterers.

The west half of the north side was a place for cattle. Births, castrations, bottle-feeding, treating ailments, and the training of 4-H calves took place here. Kicks, toe stompings, body slams, and head butts also happened here. At the west end of the central alley was the mow door where hay was dropped from the mow to be fed in the mangers on the north side or out into the rack that ran along the west side of the barn. The east half of the north side consisted of two small rooms which were originally used to store grain. The rooms or bins were filled either through windows on the east and north side or through two small doors in the floor of the mow. In the alley along the bin walls, hooks held calf halters, lariats,

125

bridles, and prods. An old medicine cabinet had been nailed just inside the east door for animal medicines and syringes.

My memories of the barn are divided in the same way the barn was divided. I have memories of working with pigs (south side memories); memories of feeding the cows (north side memories); memories of putting hay in and taking hay out (haymow memories); and memories of scooping oats into the bin rooms (itchy, sweaty memories). Like the purity of some bottled spring waters, my barn memories are 99.9% good.

Most farm kids of my generation had livestock chores. We were no exception. The first chore I remember was shutting the small door to the chicken house after they had returned to roost. Since chickens seem to linger outside until long after the sun sets, this chore was done in the dark. I did not like this job. It didn't take much time but it took an enormous amount of courage. I don't know if I had an overdeveloped imagination for an eight year old, but I always expected some wild animal to grab my arm and devour me as I bent over and reached up into the chicken house to release the small door. The walk to the chicken house was slow and filled with fear. After the door slammed shut, a professional sprinter would have been hard pressed to cover the distance between chicken house and our house quicker than I did. My worst fears were realized one night when bent over in the most vulnerable of positions I shined the flashlight into the house and two eyes, large enough to belong to a mountain lion or small bear, glowed menacingly back at me. In less time than it takes to say boo, I was in the house alarming the family. Shortly after, I accompanied my father back to the chickenhouse where a rather small opossum was dispatched.

Later, I graduated to chores of more responsibility. Early adolescent chores were feeding cattle hay before and after school during the winter months when they couldn't find leftovers among the cornstalks. Again, the chores experienced were not all that pleasant, but over time they have evolved into good memories.

The days I remember most were bitterly cold with the normal Nebraska wind blowing hard out of the north. Pushing hay down from the mow into the alley wasn't so bad but trying to fork it out to the rack in the face of the wind was nasty. The freezing cold soon found its way in and around the ill-fitted cotton work gloves we used. Small stems and leaves blew back into my eyes and nostrils and down my neck. During a couple of very dry years in the mid-fifties, dad cut the corn for silage since the ears were very small anyway. The silage pile sat outside the corral next to the barn, and feeding our twenty cows silage became one of my winter chores. The first silage forked in the crisp cold air exposed the warm interior of the pile, releasing a cloud of steam and the sweet/sour smell of the silage. The heat from the fermenting silage took the edge off the winter's cold. The warmth and smell of the pile combined with the rack being south and down wind of the pile made forking the cows silage rather than hay a much preferred experience.

Many of the barn work experiences weren't chores but seasonal jobs that were done in a day or two. Whereas chores were great teachers of day to day responsibilities which must be met no matter the weather, personal health, or competing activities, the seasonal tasks taught other important lessons.

Twice a year, baby pigs needed to be prepared for their life as feeder pigs. Shots were given, teeth clipped, and castrations were performed all at the same time. The first thing in the morning my father and I would get ready by dressing in our oldest work clothes and having a good breakfast. Syringes, knives, and clippers were sterilized and laid out. The vaccines were retrieved from the refrigerator and everything was taken to the barn. A small worktable was set up for the equipment and the process began.

My job was to catch and hold the pigs while my father shot, clipped and cut their most tender parts. The pigs were herded into the west half of their part of the barn and barricaded with a couple of low boards temporarily nailed to each wall. Too high for the pigs to scale but low enough so that I could step in and out and carry the unlucky victims to the worktable. The pigs were held with their front legs spread apart while my father gave them a shot. He then clipped their eye teeth. After these operations, the females were released to run outside. The males had one more greater indignation to suffer. Shifting my hold, I also grabbing their rear legs, exposing their testicles. My Dad put down the clippers and took up the razor sharp knife. With a squeeze and a cut, he changed their position in life from boar to barrow.

In the beginning, I did not like this job as it was smelly and dirty, with the pigs often relieving themselves on my pants as I held them. But the worst was the noise. From the time they were grabbed until they were released they squealed their protest. They did it with gusto. High pitched and loud, the pig squeal is designed to bring a mother sow charging from three miles and every other hearing life form running in the opposite direction. Whether standing or sitting, the holding position I had to use placed their head about two inches from my right ear. The volume was excruciating and the pitch unnerving. It was before we were aware of earplugs on our farm, and I sometimes tried yelling back in a vain effort to counter balance the noise. I doubt it worked, but in some way it did make it more bearable. At least for me, perhaps not for my father.

Over the years, my experience of this job became more enjoyable. Not because the work changed but because of the satisfaction I got from completing an unpleasant but necessary task. If part of life's purpose is to collect interesting memories during that time when we are too frail to do anything but remember, then, based on my "barn memories," perhaps we ought to be looking for uncomfortable challenges to put ourselves through. These challenges and the odd, unplannable experience seem to make up the most vivid and amusing memories.

A more pleasant seasonal job was riding the racks as we baled hay and then put it into the haymow. Part of the enjoyment came from the camaraderie of the people involved. Whereas the working of pigs involved just two of us, baling involved four to six and included friends and relatives. It was a kind of a working party with a certain amount of horseplay allowed. It took place in the Nebraska summer, so it was always hot, always humid, and by the end always exhausting.

When I was too young to be of much help, hay was put into the barn by taking each bale off of the rack and placing it just so in a grain elevator. It was carried up through a floor level door where a person took it off with a hay hook and dragged it to where it was stacked. This got increasingly difficult as the stack grew higher. Theoretically, you could get a lot more hay in the barn stacking it but in practice it was a heck of a lot of work, and I don't remember ever seeing the mow full of stacked hay.

Later, we put hay in the barn in an easier, more exciting way. The large mow door that extended to the peak was opened and grappling hooks lowered to the rack. Eight or ten bales were arranged so that the four hooks of the grapple were stabbed, one to each side. When ready, the hook setters on the rack stepped aside and someone running the "gizmo" pushed a button and the bales rose slowly to the peak where a lever was tripped and they lurched into the barn on the overhead rail. Once inside a hook setter pulled a small trailing rope. This yanked the hooks loose and the hay tumbled to the top of the pile. Holding onto the tripping rope the setter would jump off the rack and pull the grapple out and down to begin the process

128

again.

To run this setup, my dad cobbled together "the gizmo" by taking a transmission from an old Model A and hooking it up to an electrical motor and a large spool. A rope of one and a half or two inches in diameter was attached to the grappling arms that ran up to the barn peak, through the large door, along the overhead rail to the west side of the barn, through a pulley, down through the mow door, through another pulley and along the alley floor to the "gizmo" which was anchored to the sill of the alley door.

A loaded hayrack was brought in from the fields and parked as close to the barn as possible. The grapples were lowered and set in the hay for the trip to the mow. Everything worked fine if the hay was in good condition and the bales were of uniform size and tightly tied. When this was not the case, one or two bales and sometimes the entire stack would slip free and tumble back onto the rack. The setters had to be attentive and quick to leap out of harm's way. This element of danger somehow made the job more exciting and the sense of accomplishment even greater for a teenaged boy. It also provide some entertainment as dignity was abandoned in the mad scramble to get out of the way of the falling bales.

This method of putting the hay in the barn resulted in a disorderly pile that extended the length of the barn. The pile peaked under the overhead rail and sloped steeply to the sides. It became a mountain to be explored. It had crevices for cats to have their litters and chickens to lay their eggs. By rearranging a few bales, small caves were created to play in. It was a great place for playing "hide and seek" and "king of the mountain". I especially remember a vigorous game of "king of the mountain" played with a friend who was also a halfback for the Cornhusker football team. His high-stepping running style caught me under the chin as he re-took the top of the "mountain". I still have the chipped front tooth to prove it. I must have been twenty-two years old at the time. A mountain of hay can bring out the kid in anyone.

When the barn was relatively empty, the great rope was lowered and it became a swing. Better yet, a couple of friends could hoist you the twenty-five feet to the peak of the roof as you hung on for dear life. In the summer when the large door was open, we would use an empty rack below as a stage to put on our amateur plays. The open door was used for special effects from the sky. Mothers and fathers, aunts and uncles sat on make shift benches in the gravel yard in the warm evening.

After the "show" homemade ice cream was added to A & W rootbeer and performers and audience enjoyed a float as the dusk deepened into night.

The hard work and imaginative play in the barn tested our mettle and expanded our youthful minds. It showed us that you could work hard, have fun, and at the end of the day have a sense of having accomplished something.

The modern single purpose farm buildings do not seem to provide the same opportunities for farm kids today as the old barns did a generation ago. Certainly, there is work to be done in them and a basketball hoop may be raised and the cement floor swept for a father and son pickup game. But looking at a cement floor and thinking "let's play" somehow seems different than looking at a large tumble of hay bales and thinking "let's play". The basketball game is great fun and provides an important bonding experience with my children that I wouldn't miss for the world. Yet, I wonder if the activities have engaged my kid's imagination as the barn activities did for my generation. The same holds true in our work world. Tools and equipment are more often bought than built like the "gizmo". The work is most often done alone. If two are working in the same place at the same time it is often on separate tasks. I can't remember the last time there was a group of four or five farmers, family members, or friends working together as we often did putting up hay or shelling corn out of the corn crib when we were kids. Those experiences seem to be gone for now.

Our barn is in need of a paint job and part of the roof was severely damaged a couple of years ago. Given the farm economy we wonder if we can afford to fix up a building that has little value to our farm business. But I'm betting we'll make the investment.

In the next year or so, the fully extended ladder will be sitting on a makeshift platform on top of the truck. As I'm reaching above my head to paint the very top of the peak, I'll still be glad that we have a big barn. It needs to be big. It has a lot of memories to hold.

Lyn DeNaeyer   Dispersion

"What am I bid boys, what'll you give
For a hunk of heritage and pride?
Reputation follows this offerin',
Years of hope wrapped in horsehair and hide.
It's a legend built on dreams and such
But them ain't things a man mentions much.

The breedin' runs strong in these ponies,
Disposition and heart, don't you know?
The best teacher your youngster could have.
Here's geldings, ranch broke, and ready to go.
The end result of a lifetime plan,
Common sense, from an uncommon man."

"Let's go fellers," the auctioneer cried.
"This here's a winnin' proposition.
It's just between you and your conscience
To put a fair price on tradition.
But handle 'em gentle when you do,
'Cause an old cowboy's heart goes with you.

For Bob Tinant, and "Pete"

Mae Hiatt   Victory or Defeat

The young man plucked at the sodden straw
As he gazed at the battered field.
Heart-sick at the waste of a whole year's work
And the loss of the promised yield.

The old man saw the sky beyond
And a few brave stalks of wheat
Like flags, that beckoned amid the wreck
And promised victory through defeat.

Jack Ostergard   Corporations

I believe in Divine Creation; however, some things do evolve
And watching things transpire has only strengthened my
resolve
To speak out against some happenings that don't appear to me
To be in the best interest of our great country.

Through all the years I've watched it, and there have been quite
a few
And the history I've read about, in this land where dreams come
true.
The thing that made it really great, a place beyond compare,
Was the work of individuals, the desires and goals they share.

Now it wasn't corporations whose only goal is money.
Control and wealth is their desire in this land of milk and
honey.
They would have us all work for them, punch a clock from nine
to five,
And cash a guaranteed monthly check as long as they survive.

Corporations are taking over as far as we can see
In almost every facet of our economy.
Small towns are drying up as the financial base gets thin,
Because a corporation operates the land that once took ten.

Ten families that bought their needs from local folks like you
Instead of buying direct or fleet like corporations do.
We have seen other countries who could not compete with ours
Because with individual ownership people count the job, not
hours.

I don't say that we don't need them because some things are too
large
But is it necessary they be the entire entourage?
Take the cattle business it all started at the end
With the retailers and chain stores who compete for what you
spend.

No more mom and pop stores because they have been replaced
By a super duper super market which is corporate based
Then we back up to the packers whose numbers now are few.
In fact three now handle everything that hundreds used to do.

And they will finance cattle feeding to guarantee supply
Actually you work for them, so much for your share of pie.
This brings us to the feedlots whose numbers still decline
Just 200 fed over half the cattle in 1989.

They encourage retained ownership because you will be missed
If they have to buy the cattle and thereby assume the risk.
They will background all your cattle, furnish all the feed
And send a bill bimonthly, a blank check is all you need.

When it comes to raising cows and calves ingression has been
slow.
It's hard to hire a man who cares like the owner would you
know.

So any one can be a cattleman, and this is not meant to be
funny,
Because you can hire everything, all you need is corporate
money!

Kevin Meyer Threshing

Grandpa stands by the machine, but his eyes are
looking to the west northwest. A long, low, blue line is getting
closer. Thunderstorms. He has been watching all day. It's now
about 1:30 in the afternoon. It is a late July day. Hot and
humid already at 7:00 in the morning when the threshing
started.

It was hot. You walked two steps and the sweat broke
out, running into your eyes, burning. Grandpa takes another
glance at the thresher, then walks back to the Farmall Regular.
The power is the long belt to run the machine. Grandpa checks
the belt as he walks along it.

A rain would be good. The corn was tasseling and needs
it. Rain would make a good third cutting hay, and the pastures
were getting dry. Yes, it was going to rain. Even Louie
Slaybough, the weatherman at station WJAG, had said so. He
was the most listened to man in Northeast Nebraska.

Yes, a rain would be good. But first we needed to finish
threshing the oats. We were at Grandpa's nephew, Ervin Bos.
His was the last farm to be threshed this year. We had arrived
at to his farm yesterday after dinner, set the machine on the
edge of the oats field next to the farmstead and were threshing
by 3:00. We ran until 7:30 at night so we'd have a chance to
finish today, Friday.

Grandpa checks the gauges on the Regular and looks to
the west again. Yes, there was a chance. We could get done if
nothing broke and the crew didn't wear out. It was the early
'60s and this was one of the last threshing crews left. Most
farmers now had their own combines.

But Grandpa's crew were almost all in their '60s, about
ready to retire. They figured they'd just keep threshing until
they quit. You don't easily change 60 years of ritual.

It wasn't a large crew. Jim Spale and his teenage son,
Doug, and Joe Bridicko were the only two not related. They
were in the crew as neighbors, and they all farmed Novotny
land. And of course, Polanske, the faithful Novotny hired man
who started working for B.J.'s dad when he came over from
Bohemia in 1898 when he was 14. Now it's over 60 years later

133

and he's still there. Living in the barn. Now because of his age, they let him sleep in the house basement during the winter. But he's happy. This is all he knows.

Grandpa's cousin, Joe P. and his son, Wayne, are in the crew, as are his brother, Tom, and nephew, Ervin. Today to try to finish, brother Jerry has been brought out from town for the final push to finish.

The crew was a well-oiled machine. They had worked together for 50 years. Tom hauled the threshed grain. Polanske stacked the straw. All the rest but Grandpa were bundle haulers. When it came to threshing, Grandpa was King of the Realm. He owned the Farmall Regular that ran the machine. The machine was owned by the company, but Grandpa was in charge. He checked the machine, ordered the repairs, decided where to set, when to start, when to stop, kept all the records, settled all disputes, and made sure of the rotation of who was first and in what order they went. His word was the final word.

He'd earned this position by working on big steam outfits as a young man, but mainly due to his reputation as being someone who never lost his temper easily, being someone who kept a cool head in every emergency, and being as fair and honest as anyone who ever walked the earth.

This summer Grandpa and crew was bigger by two. The Old Man (me) and brother Keenan (Squirt) were drafted to help because, as Grandpa said, we had young legs and he didn't. Because he broke his knee as a boy from being run into by the snoot of a cornpicker, Grandpa's legs were shot. His legs so bowed out, he could walk over a 15-gallon drum and never touch it. But with the aid of his walking stick he never gave up.

Today, the crew was even bigger because Ervin's boys, Tom and Ron, were there to help. Any other year, Jo would have also been there. We'd played together many summers, but this summer, much to our surprise (Squirt's and mine) we found out Jo was JoAnn, a girl, and now she was considered too old to play. But old enough at nine to wear dresses and work in the kitchen with her Mom, Mary Ann, and Grandma Anna, Tom's wife, cooking for the crew.

It has long been debated who did more work--the men threshing or the women, cooking and serving a morning lunch, noon meal, afternoon lunch and often a supper (leftovers were permitted here) to a crew of 10-15 men and boys. In those days there were no convenience foods, running water, air conditioning, automatic washers, or dishwashers. Mostly, a small fridge, wood stove bringing the temperature in most farm kitchens up to about a steady 110 degrees, chicken on the hoof, baking supplies in the pantry, veggies in the garden and fruit on the trees.

The only thing else the women had to do were their regular duties of cleaning house, sewing, washing clothes, the garden, flowers, mowing the lawn, taking care of the chickens, ducks and geese, milking the cows, and carrying in water, wood and cobs. And carrying ashes and dirty water out. And incidentally raising 3-9 children. In their spare time they could pretty much do as they pleased. Who did more work I leave everyone to decide on their own.

Due to the expanded crew, Grandpa had one eye on the Regular, one on the belts, gears and chains of the thresher, one eye on the clean grain, one on the strawpile, one eye on the bundle haulers, and one eye on the weather. In his spare time he watched Tom, Ron, Squirt and I, having us bring water, hook up wagons, level the oats wagon, bring him one of the dozen oil cans or grease guns or belt dressing bars from the orange crate strapped to the Regular or from the trunk of the Chevy parked strategically close. All of this Grandpa handled with ease, giving his Grandpa grin and wink, and telling us to be careful. For some strange reason, I think, besides our younger legs, Grandpa just like having us around, but he didn't want any accidents where we had to explain things to Grandma which could provoke a sharp, quick stream of Bohemian. "So," as Grandpa would say, "as long as everything turns out OK, Mama doesn't need to know everything."

After the machine was shut down for the evening, it was decided we would start at 7:00 this morning and to try and finish for the season and beat the rain. We wouldn't stop for dinner (a highly unusual decision) but Mary Ann would bring out a lunch at 9:30 and 12:30. Us kids would pass it out to the men and we'd keep going.

It's 3:00. The last bundles are on the rack and next to the feeder. Grandpa opens the Regular, full bore, trying to speed things up. Two more men climb on the rack to pitch in more bundles. We get in an empty wagon to hold the last of the grain. Tom has all the other loads in the granary. Grandpa has one eye on the threshing, the other on the weather. The long, blue line has turned to high thunderheads all over the west and northwest, as high as you can see. Gray, black, purple and green. It's going to be close. The last bundle is in the feeder. The knives cut it up. The last oats go in the wagon. Tom takes off for the shed. The last straw is out of the blower. Grandpa shuts down the belt pulley on the Regular. Instead of waiting for it to stop, he takes his walking stick and throws the belt. Dangerous business. We kids know this is serious. We run to roll up the belt. Grandpa backs the Regular to the thresher tongue. We hook him up. The men have folded the feeder. One eye on the weather, Grandpa sees the first lightning. He hollers, "Everybody to the place. In the barn."

We all take off--racks, tractors, horses, and Grandpa with the machine. Someone drives the old Chevy in. We can hear the thunder. There's more lightning. We're on the place. The tractor's are shut off. Grandpa, in charge to the end, hollers, "Horses and everyone to the barn."

We head in. Ervin and the boys come from the house. He's carrying a case of beer. The boys, pop. We're all in the barn. Cleaner than a lot of people's houses. We spread out, sitting on bales, buckets and an old bench. Ervin says lunch will be ready in about 40 minutes. We'll wait in the barn.

The lightning flashes. Thunder claps. The first rain is hitting the roof. Everyone relaxes. Ervin looks at Grandpa, still in charge.

"Yes," he nods, "give them *pivo.*" (After seeing an alcohol-related bad accident when he was working with the steamers, Grandpa allows no booze for his crew if the machine is running or is going to run.) The men take *pivo.* We boys are offered pop, the usual Bos short 7-ups and Dodger grape.

But Ervin is of a younger generation. There's also root beer, creme soda, orange and strawberry. Everyone is relaxed. Some of the men take a second beer. They start telling stories in Bohemian. Of course, we listen but don't understand it all. We have another pop, play with the horses and cats. Hear a few more stories. The rain lets up. Mary Ann hollers, "Lunch is ready. Boys, run get it."

We do. Mary Ann brings the coffee. Everyone eats, but the exhaustion and pressure of the race with the weather is starting to tell. Everyone is tired, ready to go home with the rain, and tomorrow being Saturday, we can rest Saturday and Sunday.

In between rains, Grandpa checks the Regular and thresher. It's all okay. If it's dry tomorrow, we'll come take it home. For now everything can sit here.

We pile into the Chevy and head home, and put the car in the garage. We'll unload it tomorrow. We head for the house. Grandma caught rain water and is heating it for baths.

Nothing like a bath after threshing. We go in the house.

"Oh," says Grandma, "I heard you'd gotten done."

Grandpa says, "We did."

She replies, "You still have your hat." In all the rush, we'd forgotten the old tradition that at the end of the last job all the straw hats went into the machine. This year Grandpa gets to save his sweat-stained hat with the green plastic visor. First time in years.

Grandma has the chores done. Squirt, Grandpa and I each take a bath and put on clean clothes. Grandma puts Squirt and my clothes in a tub of rain water to soak. Grandpa's, as every year, she throws in a pile to burn.

We sit down for supper. Now Grandma's all questions. What did you have to eat? Who all was there? Any news from town? How was the oats? You really ate in the barn? Did anything break? How far ahead of the rain did you get finished?

Grandpa eats in silence. Squirt and I answer the questions. We start telling her about being in the barn. It starts to rain again. Grandpa gets interested looking out the window. We tell Grandma more about the time in the barn. It's raining harder. Grandpa's looking out the window, interested in something. We tell Grandma more about the barn, some of the Bohemian phrases we've heard and committed to memory. Grandma gets quiet, lays down her fork and looks at Grandpa.

By now, Grandpa's really interested in looking outside and watching the rain. Squirt and I tell Grandma a few more choice Bohemian phrases we've learned in the barn. Squirt and I stop talking. Grandma clears her throat and says something to Grandpa in Bohemian.

Grandpa's really interested in watching out the window and doesn't hear her. She speaks up. He still doesn't hear. Squirt and I look out the window. What is so fascinating that Grandpa sees and we don't?

Grandma speaks up louder, all in Bohemian. We don't understand it all but catch some words. Little pitchers have big ears, something about Mary Ann should have washed everybody's mouth out with soap, something about *pivo* loosening up tongues, and something about--is that all you men can think and talk about? She gets up and goes to the parlor.

Whatever Grandpa saw outside must be gone. He finishes supper and goes to read the paper in his rocker. Next day things are kind of quiet and when we go to town Saturday night, Grandma warns Grandpa and Squirt and I about going into the tavern, suggests the cafe might be better and church on Sunday morning wouldn't hurt. Grandpa still doesn't seem to hear.

On Sunday, Dad, Mom and Potato come to Grandpa and Grandma's to check on us and to see if we're ready to go home. (We're not.) Mom, Potato and Grandma are in the kitchen. Grandma's telling Mom something in Bohemian, whispering. Squirt and I aren't supposed to hear, but they're both shaking their heads.

We wander out to the porch where Grandpa and Dad are. Dad asks if we were any help.

Grandpa says, "Yes, lots."

Dad asks if we learned anything.

Grandpa says, "Yes, lots." He starts grinning, his eyes twinkle, he leans over and whispers something to Dad. They both laugh.

From the kitchen comes a disgusted *"Humph,"* from Grandma.

Grandpa winks at us and gives us his Grandpa grin, leans over and whispers, "Mama don't need to know everything."

J.V. Brummels   Irons in the Fire

He drove an old two-tone Chevy wagon,
so under-powered he called it Moby Dickless,
but then we all ride those older horses,
pick those gentler colts later on.

A branding fire: gray ash and red coals,
blue flame, charred chunks of wood
and the heads of a dozen irons lying
in the fire, their long shafts going soft.

Each year but the last he stamped calves,
so proud of his work that at Roeder's Fork
he brought a friend, a dude, a sort of
personal photographer to record each brand.

He missed last year down on the river
at Wood Duck, though he was just a town
up the line that day. Just too busy
with some domestic chores, I guess he said,

138

but maybe he'd seen enough, smelled enough
burning hair, heard enough calves bleating
and cows bellowing, felt enough of that heat.
Funny he didn't see the flashing warning,

feel the rumble bars. A car so dickless
doing sixty when he barreled through the junction.
Certainly, he didn't see the van that broad-sided
him before he rode on ahead, dead before the end

of that rolling, pitching, wild ride.

Betty Chittenden   Ode to a Fallen Shrine

The barn brings back those memories that keep the "cockles"
warm
The reminiscence of our youth and cob tag on the farm.

The running leaps we took, unmindful of the danger.
And Bill's bare facts revealed when he didn't clear the manger.

The powers that be protected us from the vast expanse below
While inching on the hay rope track to reach the cupola.

My brother Tony by tinkering kept his motorcycle hopping.
His genius got it running, his problem was in stopping.

Expedience decreed that day—an observation candid,
The manure piled around the barn was the softest spot he
landed.

As for my brother, William, whose performance was reknowned,
The roof was an inviting slope he'd use for sliding down.

The memories of his escapade sear the reaches of the mind.
It also seared his britches and splintered his behind.

Once as Dad strolled into the barn (it was his lucky day),
He sneezed his memorable sneeze and his teeth lit in the hay.

The timbers of that mighty shrine have sheltered kith and kin.
The fowl and furry knew its warmth and tramps that slept
within.

We mourn this structure's brash demise where the ghosts of childhood walk.
This salient fact consoles us--Thank God the thing can't talk!

Janet Eckmann   Summertime and the Living's Easy

"Summertime and the living is easy" so goes the words to an old tune from the musical Porgy and Bess.

Such nonsense must have gone out with manual typewriters and eight track tapes. There doesn't seem to be much easy living around the country these days. Everyone has someplace to go and two or three places they should have been. Time is at an essence and there is not nearly enough of it to go around.

"The Lazy Hazy Crazy Days of Summer," words from another old song ring loudly in the memories of my mind. Perhaps if you are a child under the age of 10, swimming, watching TV, sleeping in, a week of Bible School and going to the park is what summer is all about. For kids, as it should be, it is the same song, second verse. But to most everyone else, we move to a different beat of a much faster drummer.

Experience has proven to me that summer can be just as busy and hectic, if not worse than the nine months in between Memorial Day and Labor Day.

Crops went in the ground fairly early this spring, giving the farmers here just enough time to get the first cutting of hay put up before the sporadic rains of June. Others were not quite as lucky and getting that first crop of alfalfa harvested was a real headache.

That is how the pattern will go for most farmers the rest of the summer. Most years farmers are lucky if they get the corn laid by before the second hay crop is ready to cut down, or the oats are ready for silage.

Each summer is a challenge to get the oats in windrows before the last big rain of July beats it to death (We didn't this year as strong winds and 1.6 inches of rain came in torrents late Monday afternoon.)

This was followed by several weeks of oats combining, waiting until the morning dew was off the field before the 10-hour days of harvest began. Climaxing the oats harvest is the day-long ritual of making small square straw bales and packing them tightly in the corn crib. It was always a goal to get that nasty job done before the pre-fair 4-H activities started.

Of course, summer wouldn't be much fun if you didn't have several major or minor breakdowns of farm equipment.

The battle between the weeds and the farmer is ongoing. Many hours are spent checking fences and draws for the pesky thistles that thrive in the heat of summer.

I try not to let the demands of lawn mowing and gardening control my life during the summer. I enjoy my flowers and garden but not in the heat of the day.

Regg, 19, manages to keep us guessing if he is going to work or come home. If not at work, he is either in bed, in the refrigerator, or under the hood or trunk of his car.

He often stops off at his friends on the way home from work or takes in ball practice at Jessen's field on Thursday night.

Riley, 15, manages to get her clothes unpacked from her well-traveled bag and throw them on the laundry pile with the assumption that they will appear clean and ready to go to the next practice or camp she has scheduled.

She has been a busy teenager this summer, helping out in West Point with our grandkids and all. The West Point Eckmanns are expecting a new baby soon and Riley is good help to have around with the other three little ones.

Julia is often able to meet me halfway in Norfolk and we ferry Riley back and forth between here and there. We kept the three kids at the farm for eight days in June while their Mom and Dad went to a medical convention/vacation in California. That is another whole story.......

With all the preparations for Lindy's July 4th celebration and the recent cleanup from the storm, and the not forgotten columns and news stories, meetings, weddings, showers, and chores, our summers definitely fall into the Hazy Crazy Days of Summer pattern.

The last line of that song is "We wish that summer would always be here." Personally I dislike the hot, hot days of summer.

I detest the freakish lightning and hail storms that often accompany several days of soaring high humidity. This week of July 1998 we give thanks to God that the storm's damage wasn't worse. And we give thanks that he spared the life of Todd Edwards, who was in a serious car accident. He's my brother Ray and his wife Twila's adopted grandson.

We have the "Crazy, Hazy Days" where are the "Lazy Days of Summer?"

141

Diana Lambson   Crisis by Design

Gavel buzzards picked
the bones of Hanlon's farm Saturday;
picked them bare-dirt clean,
not even coffee cans of nails and bolts left
to catch Sunday's too-late rain,
hold it to brood new crops of mosquitoes.

June Hanlon moved the kids to town.
She's clerking at the county courthouse.
Des Hanlon's just gone;
sucked away
by no-parity-corporate world-economy.

Not by design are cornfields
no-till this season,
even though local conservationists promote
the idea for water and soil's sake.

Dillon Emmett from Farmer's Bank and Trust
in Brakerville,
called the pivot company
to set an appointment with a salesman.
Wants a price quote
for Des's north two quarter sections.

Their cattle and hogs
got sold just before the
county livestock sale barn went broke.
Didn't bring enough to settle feed store and vet bills.
June used the kid's college fund to pay
Presler's Trucking to haul off the livestock.

She didn't show up to hear
their dreams called away
by the auctioneer from McFarland.
She drove the `76 Chevy van out
the gate last month, kids crying,
holding on to the dog,
never looking back;
the van's radio touting rebounding
commodity prices and an end to the crisis.

Now their half-mile driveway safety zone
points a finger at an orphaned house.

Joyce Maser The Farmer

He feeds the world
and tills the land.
From dawn to dusk
He'll lend a hand,
To stranger, neighbor, friend-in-need.
What 'ere the task,
He'll take the lead.

The times are tough
Expenses high.
His crop at market
He asks, "Why--
Are prices low
When things I need
Like trucks & fuel, and feed & seed
Get more expensive every year.
I'll lose the land--
This is my fear."

He'll watch the sky
And hope & pray,
That God will keep the storms away.

A special breed it takes to be
A farmer, and you'll know that he
Will feed the world
As long as we
Keep him in farming -- You will see.
But if we lose this special man
What will happen to the land?
Who will want to feed the world?

No one left to feed the world.

Vesta Linderman   Life on a Dairy Farm, 1916 to 1943

Five years before I was born, my father had established
a milk route in Falls City, Nebraska. He and mother milked a
few cows, bottled the milk, and delivered it door to door to their
customers. Barney and Sox, the farm horses, furnished

transportation for the six mile trip to town. To support a family of seven required intense activity, spelled W-O-R-K, on the part of everyone. It was customary to drink whole milk, so we tried to breed cows whose milk was at least 4% butterfat. Skim milk was feed to the cats, pigs, and calves. It also made good cottage cheese. No person would drink skim milk. Since we were a dairy family, we had one or two quart bottles of milk on the table at every meal. Also, there was a half-pint bottle of cream to enhance the flavor of oatmeal, strawberries, and many similar foods. You see, cholesterol had not yet been invented.

In a few years, Papa bought a Model T Ford to deliver milk. How thrilled my three brothers were when Papa brought home a car. But the thrill turned to bitter disappointment the next day when the car would not start. Barney and Sox were hitched to the car and my 10 year old brother had to steer while it was towed back to town. My father got his money back, but it was another year before he bought a new Ford with happier results. Now, the 5 a.m. trip to town went much quicker.

In 1921, when I was born, there were three brothers and a sister to welcome me. When I was older, my mother told me she always hoped for about six children. I am six years younger than my nearest sibling, so they were all happy about my arrival. My brothers and sister were always a joy and inspiration to me. Probably, I was spoiled, but it didn't prevent me from doing my share of the work. No one said, "I love you." That just wasn't done in rural Nebraska in those days. But we knew.

As the kids grew, so did the milk route. It become a daily trip instead of three times a week, as at first. As the boys became older teens, they took over the delivery job. In warm weather, they brought 100 pound blocks of ice on the return trip, because the bottled milk had to be kept cold from evening chore time until morning delivery. The ice was manufactured in Falls City. As soon as the milk truck returned home, someone had to wash and sterilize all the bottles. In the milk house was a boiler which produced steam to the radiators in the house. Also, steam was used to heat the water in the milk house for washing all the equipment. A small turbine turned the brush of the bottle washer. There was a steam engine to run the buzz saw. Of course wood from the farm timber was our fuel.

The dairy farm was such a fun and exciting place to grow up. I thought a baby Holstein calf was the nicest thing to see and feed. The first thing for a calf to learn was to drink milk from a bucket. Nature told him to reach up for food, but we forced his head down into the bucket. Such sputtering and pushing that produced. It was pretty frustrating for calf and handler the first few times. You only milk a cow about ten months; then she needs to go dry for a couple months so she can rest and produce another calf. So with 15 or more cows, each having a calf every year, there were plenty of cute babies to enjoy. We were always glad for a heifer because she was needed to replace cows in the milk herd who had to be sold for some reason. The bull calves were mostly sold when a few days old to someone who wanted a beef animal. When I was five, a man came with his wagon to get a baby bull calf. As the men were lifting "him" onto the wagon, I said, "Hey, that's not a bull; it's a heifer." So the man went home with an empty wagon. Sex Education on a dairy farm was not taught, but learned by osmosis.

Recently, when I saw a young man with a ring in his nose, I thought of the bull on the farm. Holstein male cows are typically very mean and strong. The only safe way to handle one is to lead him by a ring in his nose. Noses are tender and he won't pull very hard by a chain on that ring. My worst nightmares were of a bellering, pawing bull. One neighbor had been killed by a Holstein bull.

Each year, one or two steers were kept to be fattened for the family's meat supply. We also butchered chickens and ducks. Another source of meat was rabbits. When alfalfa was mowed for hay, they started around the outside of the rectangular field, going all the way around the perimeter. As the strip of alfalfa became narrow the rabbits ran out and sought another place to hide. One boy would carry Blitz, the rat terrier. When a bunny came running out, the mower was stopped, the dog was released and the race was on. Such excitement, with the dog yapping, the boy yelling and the rabbit darting around looking for safety. Usually, the dog won and we had fried rabbit. We were kind to the animals and fowls while they lived, but when it was time for a chicken to die for our dinner, out came the ax. I don't remember any great trauma about it. It was a way of life; their life versus ours.

With daily milking, feeding the animals, and keeping the house going, everyone was busy. So, as I watched all the other workers, I wanted to help. My first paying job was trapping mice. Even three or four cats and Blitz couldn't get rid of all the mice around the barn. I would set a trap in the bin where the ground feed was kept for the cows. However, I was too small to set the trap with the strong spring so someone else had to do that. All I did was check everyday to see if a mouse was caught. If so, I dumped it out and asked someone to reset the trap. For

145

that, I received a penny. Rats were worth a nickel, but a rat trap was too dangerous for me. The barn had a cement floor and, behind the cows, was the gutter. It was 6 or 8 inches deep and as wide as a scoop shovel. Everyday, it had to be scooped out and carried to the manure pile in the barnyard. Periodically, it was hauled to the fields for fertilizer. The fields consisted mostly of pasture and hay, with about 20 acres of corn to be ground for feed. A yield of 50 bushels per acre of corn was considered pretty good in the days before hybrid seed corn. One rainy fall evening, I was hanging around the barn, as usual, watching the others work. While climbing around behind the cows, I fell and landed in the stuff behind the cows. I went crying to the house to get cleaned up.

One brother used to let me stand by him while he milked, and try to get some out of the teat. One needs to squeeze from the top down and have a good grip. By the time I was six, I had learned well enough that they gave me a bucket and a one-legged stool and I sat down to milk Red Clover. I milked Red Clover because she was gentle and very easy to milk. The milk almost ran out by itself. Each cow had a name and a personality. Queen was blind and had trouble finding her stall. Each had the same place to be tied up twice a day. Blackie was mean and would shake her head at me if I would walk in front of her stall. So I stood at a distance and made faces at her. Star didn't want to be milked, and kicked, so she had to have her right leg tied back with a rope. Then there was Omaha with a short stubby tail. Her tail was tied to the wall so she would not switch the face of the boy who was milking her. When he untied her neck, he forgot the tail. She pulled until the end of her tail came off.

When I got older, I milked before and after school. We lived in a large district so there were from 35 to 40 children in the one room school. Every family had a mother and a father at home. There were no single parent families. The word divorce was probably not even in my vocabulary. We walked to school, of course, but sometimes a car would stop and the driver said, "Want a ride?" We hopped right in, even if we didn't know them. Usually, it was a neighbor; we pretty much trusted everyone. It was kind of a culture shock when I started to high school in Falls City. I walked only 1/4 mile to the main highway, where a neighbor boy picked me up. By the time we got to town, he had picked up five kids. Until then, my friends were all country kids. Now, I met girls who wore ready made dresses. Some even went to the beauty shop to get their hair done. They went to the movies and dances. Some families did not attend church. The businesses in town were all located on two or three streets in the middle of town. There was no urban sprawl encroaching on the nearby farm lands.

Most of the animal ailments were taken care of without the help of a veterinarian. Occasionally, a valued cow or horse needed the help of a vet. Dogs and cats were hearty, and they either lived or died. No vet was called for them. I liked our vet, Dr. Wise, because he took time to talk to a little girl. Once after he finished his work in the barn, he showed us how to hypnotize a chicken. After that it was a fun thing for us to do. First, we caught a chicken and held her down, stretched out on the ground. After she quieted down, we slowly drew a line in the dust from her beak out about eight inches. Over and over we quietly drew the line. After a couple of minutes we carefully let go and walked away. She would just lie there a few minutes, then get up, look confused, and go back to her business of finding something to eat. Mother once saved the life of a duck. When the flock came up from the pond one evening to sleep in the shed, she noticed one young duck had a hole in its craw. Probably a turtle or muskrat almost caught it. So she took a needle and thread and sewed up the wound. The duck lived until Thanksgiving.

There was not the problem of a power failure. The REA did not bring electricity to our area until about 1940. Before that, cranks were important. A man or woman cranked the separator at the rate of 60rpm to separate the cream from the skim milk. The churn and ice cream freezer were cranked. One of our culture things was the Victrola, which was cranked up and then played Sousa Marches or the beautiful tenor voice of Caruso. The big grindstone stood in its framework in the yard. One person turned the crank while another held the scythe, ax or whatever tool needed to be sharpened. And of course, the Ford had no self starter, so it had to be cranked to get the engine started. A few people suffered broken arms or thumbs in the old days when a car would kick, or backfire.

Maybe things were not better than now, but they were simpler. Our telephone number only had four digits. Our address was Falls City, Nebraska. That's all. Letters from my grandparents near Chicago came in one day, by train and the rural route. Maybe time has erased the unpleasant events, but I remember my childhood as a happy time. We had time to play too, croquet was a favorite summer game, as well as ball. The pond provided summer and winter fun. There were wiener roasts in the timber and table games like checkers and tiddly winks. Since I was the youngest, I didn't often win these

147

games, so I cried. At least I learned that in life one doesn't always win. There was time for church every Sunday morning and evening. We never took family vacation because we couldn't leave the cows and the milk route. But almost every summer Papa and one or two others went on a trip. Some places visited were Yellowstone Park and Mammoth Cave. And, of course, trips to the grandparents in Illinois and Kansas.

The dairy was upgraded to include an automatic bottling machine and pasteurizer. About the time I went to college, electricity came to the farm and the first electrical thing bought was a milking machine. In 1943, brother number two bought the cattle herd and another farm. When he moved that was the end of the milk route as he then sold bulk milk to a big creamery. In 1946, when brother number one returned from the army, he bought the family farm.

Stacy Wegener   Worst in a Decade

My father is nervous.
The spring planting is a little behind
due to all the rain.

In my class,
the teacher says farmers who can't make it
go into the fields in their tractors
and end it all.

TV anchors interview small town farmers.
It's the worst I've seen it in a decade, they say.
The government needs to help.
It's hard living this way.

Other people have signs
their businesses are failing.
Farmers get the warnings
a few hours ahead of time
from the "guaranteed forecast"
on the local news or beeping messages
flowing across the bottom of the screen.

After the corn is two inches tall,
flashes of lightening reveal
the river running through the field across the lane
and Dad stays up all night
wondering if he'll have to replant.

If it's not too much rain,
it's too little.
So we pray.
Dad says you'd have to be crazy to farm.

Prices are low.
It's the worst I've seen it in a decade, he says

Mel Krutz   Winter Wheat

The cold, brown earth, the gray, the tan,
laid out on farmland all around,
awaits the snow of wintertime.

Amidst these fallowed fields
and up-turned rows,
defiant of the ice to come
springs up a sprightly virile green.

In welcome of the winter wind
it grows toward promise of the coming spring.

My neighbor oversees its care,
his form arthritic, bent,
shaped to fit his aged tractor's seat,
and leaned toward oft repeated tasks,
the hoists of bales,
the scoops of grain,
the tests of sod,
and slop to hogs.

With courage of the winter wheat
in his aging veins,
his back is further hunched
to steep itself
against the deepening frost.

The contoured plow lines on his face
are seasoned evidence that
deep within
new grain begins its budding into beard
readying for spring's
new energy and hope,
the visceral power of
the man and of the crop.

149

Deb Carpenter   Suffering

The piglet was emaciated, spine and ribs poking through thin pink flesh. He ate, yes, drank milk from a bowl, but only enough to keep him alive for another day. He soon slept with his head on the edge of the bowl, tongue hanging, flies buzzing, feet twitching. I wanted to put him out of his misery.
"He might make it," my husband told me. "Just give him time."
So I gave him time: three sweltering days of suffering with his head on the edge of the bowl.
I finally put on my garden gloves, dug a hole in the corn patch, and got the hammer from the house. I carried his listless form to the hole and laid him in it.
Whack. Right between the eyes. He squealed and sat up. Whack. Another blow between the eyes. It was beginning to hurt me more than him, I thought. He let out another squeal and began struggling. I chose a spot on the top of his head, directly between his ears. I hammered with all my strength, then began piling the dirt on, hoping he was dead and that he wouldn't struggle from his grave or suffer from claustrophobia more than he had already endured from the pressure of living.

M.J. Anthony   The Rancher

The man's a workaholic in a cowboy hat and boots.
His philosophy can be summed up like going through a chute.

"You must be moving forward or you'll surely slip on back.
Keep your mind on what you're doing or you'll slide out of the track.

Feed the best and sell the rest is the way you handle hay.
The livestock must be cared for in the best way every day.

Six days you do hard labor and on the Sabbath rest and pray.
There's time to play and visit at the end of some good days.

When you're working, do the job well; have no reason for disgrace.
Good work is just the rent you pay for taking up earth's space."

His family works right with him, and he knows just where they're at.
God's blessed the workaholic in the cowboy boots and hat.

150

Kurt Lewis   The Marketing Blues

Oh, those marketing blues,
I sold a bit a' corn for nothin,'
Gave away the milo.
They cheated us on the beans.
Oh, I got those marketing blues.

Oh, those marketing blues,
The Pappy--he say I done wrong,
But I know better,
The kids, they in rags,
On Christmas Day,
Oh, I got those marketing blues.

Don't worry none about those marketing blues
Cause money ain't the goal,
And the kids, they can read a ragged book
Rather than play Nintendo,
And when you look at the Farm,
You know
You can always grow
Some more corn, beans and milo
Cause the land--its still there,
So I don't worry none no more about those marketing blues.

Bruce Messersmith   Stockyard Journal

I'm stopped here at Crawford, waiting for help
To horse this ol' coal train over the hill.
Pulled down to the crossing, down by the stockyards
They're working cattle, I get an old familiar chill.

On one side, I see trains goin' by,
Smell the diesel and heated brake shoes,
On the other, cowboys are workin' cows in spring slime,
Some relaxed and workin' a chew.

My attention is drawn to sights and smells of days past,
Memories of workin' cows in the spring,
But I'm jerked back aware of reality's stare
By a horn blast and an engine bell's ring.

Well, there's numerous reasons that I had to leave
The cattleman's life that so beckons me,

151

Like the size of the place that couldn't support
Dad, Mom, my brother, and me.

Fact is, it was found, it could only support two,
And my brother, in turn moved away.
Though Dad's now retired, I've committed myself
To this railroad that occupies each day.

What is it 'bout bovines that draws us back
To memories we might have lost?
Or, makes us dedicate our lives to them
Regardless of the cost?

Perhaps it's not the cows themselves,
Belchin' and rollin' their eyes.
Maybe they're just one of myriad things
Their existence signifies.

Like cool, moist air behind a spring rain,
Or swirling mists on a summer morn,
The electric chill of a winter wind,
Fall frost, weeds and trees to adorn.

It's the alfalfa smell of new cut hay,
Sweet clover smell of July.
Or Ivory snow in the calf-pull water,
Ozone smell of lightning nearby.

Maybe, watchin' that youngin' take his first steps,
Or the stallion prance 'round his herd.
The rose-red brilliance of an autumn sunrise,
Graceful circles of the national bird.

It's the creak of dry leather on a hot summer day,
The chirp of a ledger plate just about gone,
Coyote pups yippin' just over the hill,
Weaned calves bawlin' and carryin' on.

The taste of clear water from an artesian well,
Tracks of the milk cow's tail 'cross your face,
The alkali dust from the dried lake bed,
Steak and eggs at the old home place.

I'm sure my memories could go on and on
And never risk scratching the crust

152

Uf experience I lived in my younger days,
Workin' cattle and eatin' corral dust.

Maybe someday I'll make my way back
To that little place under the hill.
Once again I might live, not just remember,
The experience that gives me this chill.

But until then, I'll just have to get by
With memories while out ridin' trains.
Hopin' to wait at Crawford for helpers
To hear the cry of the auction refrain.

Fredrick Zydek   Combine

Morning scratches at the icy window,
chisels pristine and crystal reminders
that the harvest hasn't ended unless
the workers have gathered in all the sheaves.
We, armed with thermoses of black coffee,
tapes of Beethoven, Bach and Aretha,
mount the great harvester-beast two by two.

We look more like pilots in a cockpit
than dirt farmers about to tame the land.
We perch in the cab like captains guiding
an enormous ship safely out to sea.
Great crows, sea gulls of the fields, lead the way.
The air is laced with smells of ripe sorghum,
the brittle sounds of cornstalks snapping in the wind.

We bring the fields to their knees, move through
the long rows like some giant sloth inching
its way belly-deep through the ornaments
of corn and barley, wheat and sunflower,
all the weighty symbols of bread and wine
waiting to be harvested for them that sing.
We do not go among them unnoticed.

We leave nothing in our wake but stubble.
Even the crows will not have it. The fields
look gaunt and hungry, lean as death itself.
What once bloomed with honey has paled white,
dusty as the dry ferns crumbling along the Platte.
But in the silos outside town there are seeds

153

enough to reach from here to the moon.

Carlene Bodlak   The Gift of Agriculture

Farming is a way of living, a life that is precious to so
many of us who are involved with agriculture. God gives us
each different blessings in life, and agriculture is one of our
gifts.

In agriculture, there is the land itself. The land gives us
a sense of belonging, a connection to the people who have gone
before. For many families, the land has passed from one
generation to another. The love of that land has become part of
a family's heritage, as with the Bodlak family. Today, my
husband farms the same land, plus more, that his grandfather
purchased after emigrating from Czechoslovakia in the early
1900's. Although raised as a town girl in the heart of
Nebraska's ranch land, I have also come to love this farm in
Eastern Nebraska. And this farming heritage will be a part of
each of our children's lives, wherever life may take them.

We do not live by majestic mountains or awesome
oceans, but the land we farm provides simple beauty. We
watch the seasons grow in the land. The bleak winter
landscape, sometimes brown and sometimes white, melts into
the delicate greens of spring. Those greens emerge into the
dark and lighter greens of the growing soybeans and corn. The
shimmer of tassels is the first sign that autumn approaches.
Then fall comes with an explosion, or sometimes just a slow
changing of foliage in crops, pastures, and bordering trees.
Each year is different, but each year the seasons of the land
come and go with grace.

Work is wrapped up in the gift of agriculture. The long
hours of hard labor on the land can be very fulfilling. The
greatest noise is the sound of machinery in use; the only traffic
jam is the seasonal rush to the grain terminals in town or city.
A farmer can stop for a nap under his tractor or take a lunch
break beside a haystack with his children on a hot summer's
day. A cold winter's week may provide the excuse to stay in the
house and work on that (sometimes) neglected paperwork that
has been piling up for months. For better or for worse, the
farmer is his own boss.

Agriculture is indeed a gift, but not one without its
challenges. The unstable prices of commodities can be very
frustrating. The high cost of equipment makes us hang onto
that old piece of machinery, held together only by the
mechanical skills of my farmer husband. We live without cable

TV or satellite dish. We usually forego vacations, though last year we did get away to a state park for two days. Meals eaten out are a rarity. Going to the movies is almost non-existent. But our daughter is in dance and piano lessons and our sons play a sport or two a year. We are by no means destitute, but farming does limit our financial resources. I think this helps us to appreciate what we have more than we might otherwise; I am content as long as we can pay the bills.

Another major challenge of farming is the weather. Each year is unpredictable. Occasionally, irrigation (when available) is beneficial as soon as the seeds are in the ground. Some years it is too wet to plant and getting the crops into the ground is a major challenge; then the clouds dry up when we really could use the moisture in summer's heat. Probably only the farmer stops to thank God for the oppressive humidity during a hot, rain-starved July; that moisture in the air is the only thing saving the corn. Hail is a dreaded threat of spring and summer. Autumn can come with its own set of weather related problems, from an early killing frost, to a rain-delayed harvest, to a heavy snow on unharvested soybean fields. Despite its uncertain outcome at times, the weather adds challenge and excitement to farming. I especially love to watch a thunderstorm in the country. The beauty and power are awesome; an iridescent rainbow or a gorgeous sunset provides a special treat.

I have been on the farm for a decade and a half. I love living in the country, being part of agriculture. I am not an active participant of farming; I leave the tractor work to my husband. But I am a supportive one, running errands, taking lunches to the field, giving rides from one plot of ground to another when equipment is being moved. During last summer's drought I even got in on fighting a couple of minor field fires set by the combine. Raising our four children is my priority, and there is no better place I would rather raise them than on our farm.

Life is full of challenges, wherever we live. It is also full of blessings. I am so thankful that the gift of agriculture is ours.

Claudia Loomis   **Surviving**

For Dad

How many pencils
did you wear out

155

figuring our way out?
There were 200 heifers, 7,000 acres,
one blistered house inside 100 dying trees
and 17 nameless horses.

How many Old Milwalkee cans
did we smash with dead-skin feet in
the dead smelling separator room
(gasping for air as though our heads
were gunny sacks) only to sell in shame
on Sunday to greasy men at conveyor belts?
Ride your bike down dirt, keep
an eye pealed for ditched cans. 19 cents a pound.

The night before you got us out,
you lay in your drunk chair
a dust-covered face, filmy hair, taped-together glasses,
making me start the Marty Robbins record over and over:
"I'm as sad as the willows that weep in the valley"
and you wept too.
And that was the second time
You said you loved me.

How many people stood round the tire swing,
drank coffee and ate church-lady sandwiches
to the sound of auctioneers' voices
or just stopped by to croon, "How brave
you are for getting out"?
And that night you walked for hours.
I went to the barn to see
if you'd blown your brains out
Like Old Floyd did last month...

Suzanne Glendy   Untitled

The peace at two o'clock in the morning surrounded my
inner self and my body completely. The lullaby of the steady,
spring breeze put me in a transcendental state of mind. My
mind was clear and my body alive, a feeling I haven't felt for so
long.
Ranching has taken its toll on my family this year. My
husband's exhausted sunburned body rests beside me. His
breaths are so light I almost wonder if he's even breathing. He
has been on a tractor all day and his humor tonight was
irritable. He was restless and his frustration with the heat, the

bank, his family, and farming made this cowboy tired.

Eight years ago his impeccable smile, body, and heart captured me. He gets this grin on his face and a boyish look in his eyes that make me melt. I met him in college 11 years ago and I have been with him ever since. He was with me when my cherished mother died; he was a rock for my sister and I. He drove us there in a blizzard aftermath that left behind snow and treacherous icy roads. He didn't complain, ever. He still has the same place in my heart now that he did years ago.

Ranching doesn't come easy for anyone. If you want instantaneous results for your work and benefits paid yearly or scheduled time off, this business is not for you. I get damn mad when over-privileged Americans make uneducated criticisms about the product we raise. Beef cattle are as important to me as my children. We vaccinate the baby calves for diseases the same as human babies are vaccinated against their childhood diseases. I would never feed an unhealthy product to my family, and I am instantly sparked by comments that beef is unhealthy to our diets. Furthermore, it is neither economical nor beneficial to give our cattle unnecessary antibiotics, rotten feed, or bad water. Our water is pure and our environment wins hands down with no pollution. I plan on living on this ranch for the rest of my life, and I know Brian would never move to town so keeping care of our natural resources and livestock would hurt no one but ourselves. There, enough of me on my soapbox!

The industry we are trying to make our living from of is not always profitable. We have to have the knowledge of a veterinarian, lawyer, financial advisor, weatherman, and the faith of a preacher. My husband does a good job at "keeping the faith." He somehow manages to stay on an even keel. I have been known to blow up and talk later but he is always there showing not much emotion either way. I have seen him worry and get discouraged, but he does it with dignity and I am always impressed. The ranching profession is in our blood, especially Brian's. Blood, sweat, and tears are put into this operation. This is more than a job; it's a way of life. Can you really put a price on your happiness?

The hills that surround us have been in the Glendy family going on 90 years. Spacious countryside dotted with horned Hereford cattle, gravel roads that take you back into the hills, rivers that wind and wither their way through the land, and many cow trails and autogates are some of the things I see when I drive through our land. My sister laughs when I tell her this cow or that cow is pretty. She says, "How can a cow be pretty?" I can't explain it very well but I try. I tell her you have to look at how they're made. Sure on the outside they appear to be horns, hooves, and hide but there is much more to it. They can have a feminine look to them. You want your cows to look like girls, not linebackers! Breeding stock shouldn't be fat, blocky looking or rigid. They need to have girlish curves, good feet, udders, and a good background. The hills that have the beauties scattered on them are picturebook like. I can drive to the top of this one hill at the ranch, park the pickup, roll the window down and imagine what God must feel like when he's looking down over His creations. What a sense of pride I feel. Sometimes we are criticized for not making it to church. The boys go every week, but Brian and I just can't always make it. Brian sums it up best when he says, "when I ride my horse checking baby calves and I sense what God has created I don't need anyone preaching at me as to what is good and right –I see it here in these hills when I ride."

The native grasses of Central Nebraska this time of year are growing everyday, making the hills look like endless miles of a tranquil green sea. Tranquility is a big issue with me. I absolutely love the environment here. We are fortunate enough to have ample trees and wild plum bushes. The sumac is pretty in late summer but is such a waste of pasture space that it is often considered a noxious weed. Hues of purple, reds, oranges, yellows, and blues make watercolor paint brushstrokes across the prairie.

Brian dreams of life in the 1800's. I have even imagined traveling across the country hearing the birds sing, and the prairie orchestra playing sweet music to me as Brian drives us under a blanket of stars in his surrey. I can hear the jingling of the bells on the horses and I swear I smell sweaty horses and leather. I am grateful for modern day conveniences, laws, fences, and the effervescent chance of peace, but I can't help but think once in a while about having my own "little house on the prairie."

I have heard that some people in large metropolitan areas have never seen the wondrous beauty of a good old-fashioned thunderstorm. I have seen them pop up without warning and disappear like a circus trick. They are truly a marvel. It's a wonder that these old trees don't break in two and it's a miracle this old house withstands the beating it gets from the ruthless Nebraska winds. Trees surround our house but out at the mailbox you can look down highway 40 and see the dirt blow. I remember once Brian sent the boys and I to the basement and we thought he nearly blew away with the dirt.

We were at rodeo one time and Brian and his partner Doug Rohde just got done roping when a tornado came through. As we were running to the pickup and horse trailer, garbage cans, mailboxes, and other debris were flying through the air. People on a desperate attempt to get to safety were blindly running their horses through the night. When the guys finally made it to the rig the rain was pounding and we decided if we stayed where we were we might be OK. When the storm finally died down we headed into town and as we were crossing the rail road tracks we noticed the cross arms on the tracks were bent and twisted around like they were a bread sack twisty tie. That's how bad the wind was.

Another weather story to share with you is the time we were at a rodeo in Norfolk, NE. The lightening was really sharp and I headed back to the vehicle with the boys. Brian and Doug just got the horses loaded when we heard this mighty crack in the sky and everything went black. People were screaming and we saw people standing about 4 feet from Doug's trailer. We jumped out of the vehicle to see on the other side of the trailer two cowboys and at least one horse down. They had been struck by lightening. I grabbed two beach towels I had and covered them up. We stayed until the ambulance came. They guys survived but it was a true awakening for us. Many times we were outside when it was lightening and we didn't take it seriously. Now we do. For a long time the boys at the slightest hint of rain would close the windows and want the shades down. Their daycare provider once commented on how they wanted the window closed even if it was a small shower. I told her this story and she had a better appreciation of what the boys had been through. It had been such a blessing that our guys hadn't been struck. If they had been outside just seconds longer it could have been them. There are guardian angles I have come to believe. The rain always sweetens up the air and I have decided no canned air freshener can compare to the real thing.

I have also been so hot I thought I would burn up in the sun when we got a load of straw bales one summer evening. I think we had two big racks and one small flat bed trailer. We had a crew of about 10 people that were driving, throwing, or stacking straw bales. The air was so thick, so still, and so miserable. Not one breath of fresh air blew during that entire job. I will never forget how lifeless I felt that night.

Winter out here can be a beautiful nightmare. Snow days are not a school kid's dream. Chores have to be done, water has to be checked and all this takes twice as long to get done. The tree branches bend and hang their head like a lost, drunken man. It's nothing to have a couple feet of snow from one storm. The wind does us no favors. We have been without power from minutes to hours. I feel bad for the rural electrical guys and their wives on nights like these. Usually when the weather gets snowy and icy we don't go anywhere. We are usually snowed in at the ranch. Our calving barn has living quarters in it. I think one of the most memorable blizzards I was in, my in-laws, Brian's grandparents, Brian, the kids, and I were all snowed in together. We actually enjoyed a rotten day! We are usually stocked up on groceries and supplies last quite a while. I detest going to town for a gallon of milk. My car is packed with extra gloves, coveralls, pack boots, and blankets. I want to be prepared.

Summer of 1999 we went driving through the back roads by our place to check some fence when we ran into the only thing that makes my husband squeamish, a rattlesnake. We were in "old blue" (good thing she's trusty) bouncing along the hills. It always seems when we are in old blue the boys and Brian find some song they all know most of the words to and sing it at the top of their lungs. (Usually the pick is "Should've Been a Cowboy" or "Stampede.") Anyway we were traveling along and out of no where Brian slammed on the breaks and put the singing to a halt. Out of the pickup he bolted and grabbed a spade. He killed a snake. (We always chuckle when Brian kills a snake. He stands at one end of the spade, barely hanging on to it, and swings. As he swings, he jumps back 5 feet!) This time he swung so hard the spade flew out of his hand and landed on the ground. Brian said, "now what do I?" Logan, our serious son replied, "leave it dad, we'll come back and get it tomorrow." To add to the excitement the boys noted that several tiny baby snakes about the size of a pencil were climbing into holes right out our window. We were screaming and hollering for Brian and he was hollering at me to back the pickup down to where he was because he had spotted a huge adult snake a few feet ahead of where we were parked. I said, "I'm trying to hurry but I can't see to back up very good because this stupid gun is in my way." He said, "You mean I've standing out here whacking away at this stupid snake and you had a gun in the pickup the whole time?" Jeez, what a rush we were on. All the way home we sat as close as we could to Brian. I bet we could've fit three more people into that single cab pickup. Speaking of snake stories, one time the boys were out playing and it had been a pretty uneventful day. It was very pleasant out and Brian had come in for a glass of tea. He and I

160

were talking in our kitchen when we heard Logan give a bone-chilling scream. Brian and I bolted out the door and Brian said he had a feeling the boys had run into a snake. When we got to where the boys were, Logan was sitting on top of the car crying and screaming and little Colter was standing on the ground beside him. Brian asked what happened and Logan pointed to a bull snake lying in the grass a couple of steps beside where we were. I tried to reassure Logan that everything was OK, but he was scared to death. He did not appreciate stepping barefoot on the snake. Brian carried the snake away and Colter looked up and said, "that was a damn big snake, Dad!" and Brian replied, "Yes, Colter, that was a big snake." We have a rule now, no going outside without shoes on.

Our dog 'Snickers' warns us of intruders of all sorts. Last fall we had a 3-foot long rattlesnake coiled up on our cement pad. She fusses at stuff until you go and investigate. She walks with Logan to the school bus in the morning and lays under the trampoline when the kids are jumping on it. If I am on horseback she goes with me; if I travel to the mailbox, she's there; if I hang clothes out she's right beside me. She'll work for Brian, but I can't make a peep or else she's there at my side and we both get in trouble!

We have had about 100 cats in our married life and some of them have had interesting names like Chicken Strip, Attention Cat, Scoop, and John Wayne. I couldn't help but mention their names, as they are the best-fed cats in the county. Colter's job is to feed them every day and believe me he does a good job. He strings feed from the porch door to the end of the sidewalk. He strings it out the way his dad strings out hay for the cows. His nickname is Boss or Bubba. He'll tell me how to open a gate, drive a pickup, back up to a trailer, and he'll tell his great grandpa which bulls to buy and tells his dad how to rope.

One day Logan had a friend out and they wanted to ride sheep. So Brian caught one for them and all three little boys came out of the house in full rodeo gear. Austin was first and he rode his ewe like a pro. Logan got turned out and his ewe dumped him off, got her foot stuck in the fence and pinned him underneath her. Brian went to the rescue and got Logan up. Tears and dirt stained his face and he decided he had had enough. Colter, in the meantime, was telling the other boys what they should've done different and was really playing up the part of his nickname. Brian asked if he was ready to ride and Colter replied, "not today, Dad."

The boys have been accustomed to working with their

dad and I. They have had to take baths in the big sink in the barn and they have had their share of dirt in their ears at a rodeo or two! They both do a great job of pitching in when we do anything at all with the cattle. Logan used to take my tater masher out when we branded and he would brand calves right behind Grandpa Billy. Colter always has a rope in his hands and he has been known to catch what he throws at. Both boys have an interest in rodeo and Logan wants to be a bronc rider and Bubba/Boss wants to ride bulls. Imagine that!

We recently took a calf to the Nebraska Hereford Club Calf Sale in North Platte. This was a first for the ranch, as we usually don't sell club calves. We picked the calf out and preparations started immediately to get him ready for the sale. Brian took the hard job of starting him to get halter broke. It involves putting on a halter and lead rope and letting him (the steer) drag the "stuff" around for a few days. Once they are pretty comfortable with that we lead them around by the lead rope. I have a friend in Omaha who giggles when she thinks about us taking our calves for a walk on a big leash. When Brian brought him home for me to put the finishing touches on, I really didn't have too much trouble. I took a portable radio out and played good old KRVN for him day and night for a few days. Brian has a circular pen in our corrals where he breaks colts and young horses for other people, and I used it for our "show arena." I washed him the day before we headed to North Platte. I had him brushed to perfection and during this whole process I had been trying to get the boys prepared that the steer was not a "pet" and he would be leaving home the next day. I knew I had failed when they named him "Buddy". "Buddy" was loaded up and transported to the sale and the boys and I followed and got him settled in. I, along with Brian's cousins the Estergard's, (another long-time Hereford breeder from Callaway) fed the calves and started preparations to get all the calves ready for the sale. We blew their hair out with blowers (a high-powered hair dryer) and Dick Estergard sprayed the cattle with a solution that made their hair glisten and repel dust. We blew their hair out and combed them just right again. I guess it might sound silly to my friend when she thinks about us putting our cattle on display, but she has no idea how proud we are of our cattle. It is really hard to try and raise an eye-appealing, consumer friendly product.

I was so nervous the day of the sale. Would anyone buy him? Was he good enough? I knew he wasn't as flashy as some but he was thick down his top, and he was not too stocky or short (my old college livestock judging days were haunting me.)

162

We entered the show ring and I remember the auctioneer said a few words about our family but after that I went blank. The steer was doing fine, he held himself like royalty, but I was nervous and prayed it didn't show. He did get sold and I think I asked Brian twice just to make sure. "Buddy" went to a good home by Burwell. We loaded up the trailer and we couldn't find the boys. We found them hugging the steer and soothing him and we overheard them telling him "it will be OK." Man, I'm telling you, mom's heartstrings were tugged. Brian said it was a good lesson for the future because if we have 4H calves, we'd go through the same thing. I think we'll take horses!

I have a feeling Brian and I are just getting started with our adventures on this ranch. It is neat when our boys ask for new chaps instead of Nintendo. Deb Greenough, a professional bronc rider, is our boys' idol. They stayed up just about every night of the National Finals Rodeo to watch him. If they fell asleep good old dad would give them the report of how Deb did that night. We wrote a letter to Deb after the N.F.R. two years ago and in less than two weeks, the boys had a huge manila envelope filled with pictures that were autographed along with a hand written note. We were all surprised. It seems that most people that we meet or are associated with through rodeos, ranch rodeos, or ranching are good people. I am thankful that my boys can grow up surrounded by hard working, fun loving people.

An old college instructor told our speech class that prospective employees like people with farm/ranch backgrounds. He told us that companies like people who are self-starters, hard working, and have a good family background. I didn't pay much attention to him then, but I sure am thinking about it now. We want so much for our children. I feel guilty about not being able to give our kids a lot of material things they see. Brian reminds me though of how much time we spend with our boys and how important that time is with them.

I am also very thankful for how much a part of nature and the outdoors is to my family. While most children learn about animal life in zoos or on TV, my boys experience life first hand. They have watched a live set of quadruplet lambs being born, bottle fed lambs and calves; they've had a pet goat, dogs, chickens and ducks, cats, and hogs. They have seen a c-section performed in our barn and quizzed our vet to death! They ride real horses, and when they are saddled up and riding next to Brian, I can't help but feel and overwhelming sense of pride. I am glad that we live a real life adventure. I like my "little house on the prairie." The boys like their home and these hills and so do I.

Diana Lambson   **Demise and Fall**

This land is full of black holes
in unplowed fields of broken dreams.

Drive-by victims.

Lonely houses with broken windows,
echoing
rooms, all their stuffing pulled
apart, trailed away.

Silence shivers down spectral spines.

Long dead ghost emotions wander,
aimless.

Burdens, like trees downed in high winds,
crushed the edges
and the souls have leaked out, leaving

derelicts,

sleeping in alleys,
standing in empty fields.

Dick Schanou   **Modern Farming**

Meadowlarks squat
In the dry pasture grass
Fluffed against the wind.
A late spring snow
Spits across the frozen ruts.
He heads for the barn
Thinking of the Holstein
That he will hobble
And curse.

He remembers the Guernseys
Who had stood passively
As the milk streamed and foamed

Into gleaming buckets.

He smells the dust in the mow,
The mold in the granary,
The rotting wood.
And there
Among the rust and decay
He lifts his hat,
Scratches his bald head,
Thinks of scabby teats and bag balm,
And vows
To sell the cows,
Scoop no more manure,
Let the barn go to hell,
Give it over to the rats and
mice,
To the pigeons and sparrows,

164

Things were new then,
And fresh.
He remembers
The smell of horses,
Of freshly ground corn,
Of loose hay in the mow.

He unravels the rusted
Baling-wire door latch,
Breaks it, curses,
Crosses the crumbling threshold,
And eyes the cracked leather
Of harnesses he hasn't touched
Since he sold the horses
Over twenty years ago.

There under the fly-specked beams
He listens to the wind
And watches snow sift through cracks
And powder the dried-dung floor.

The mangy cats,
And the barn swallows.
He'll sell the pigs, too,
He thinks.
And the chickens.
No more wallowing in slop.
He'll put up one of those
New-fangled metal-concrete buildings,
Convert to eight-row equipment
And a new lifestyle,

And die
Watching television.

Richard Good   **Depression Days of the 30s and
Armistice Day Freeze—Nov.11, 1940**

Sixty years ago southeast Nebraska's fruit growing
industry experienced a major catastrophe...the Armistice Day
Freeze of November 11, 1940. At that time there were many,
many orchards in southeast Nebraska. In the region from
Plattsmouth to Nebraska City, Peru and Brownville and on into
Richardson county, particularly, apples and some other fruits
were grown commercially. This production had evolved over
many years back to the 1800's. A key ingredient was the Loess
Soil of the region.

Loess Hills are very special and can only be found at two
or three locations in the whole world. Loess (usually
pronounced to rhyme with bus) means "wind-blown silt". These
Loess hills were blown in during the period from 30,000 years
ago to 14,000 years ago. This Loess soil can be up to 200 feet
deep, which makes it very important to the growing of fruit.
Fruit trees can send their roots very deep into the soil for
diverse plant food which made a very special quality of fruit.

I grew up in the 1930's in this beautiful apple orchard
environment. My parents Everett H. and Virginia M. Good and
grandparents M. E. and Ina Good between 1913 and 1924

acquired 160 acres 3 ½ miles southeast of Peru, Nebraska near the bluffs overlooking the Missouri River. All of the land was acquired from John T. Swan who owned the property back to the 1890's. I believe he had the orchards in place when the Good's bought the property. Because of the hilly ground, ravines and timber probably 110 of the 160 acres was in orchard. Most of this was in apple trees with some cherries and a few pears, peaches, grapes and raspberries.

In the depth of the depression my brother Lawrence and I went to "Woodsiding School," which was a one-room country school with one teacher, a very special lady, "Teacher Esther Cole", who taught all grades 1 through 8. There were a total of probably 10-12 students. This school was about one mile from our farm home and my brother and I walked through the Orchard and along a country road to school each day. I remember a few times we walked home during major dust storms of the drought. We couldn't see very far. On cold days we liked to sit closely around the wood-burning stove which was in the middle of the classroom. And of course on those cold days you didn't look forward to going outside to the "outhouse privy."

I still remember that Christmas in 1933. My folks didn't have enough money to buy Christmas presents so my Mom (without telling us kids) went up into the attic and found some old toys we hadn't used for a while and wrapped them up so we would have packages under the Christmas tree and have something to open on Christmas morning.

As a boy I enjoyed working with my Dad in the orchard. I remember driving the horse-drawn spraying wagon up and down between the rows of trees for spraying the apple trees. The tank wagon had a pump with an engine and long hoses with spray guns. In the fall at harvest time, I also drove the team of horses pulling a long wagon to haul the baskets of apples, being picked by a group of hired men, to the apple packing shed. My brother and I also made apple cider. We took it to town and sold it to local grocery stores.

Dad had a variety of ways to market his apples. Many were sold right at his apple packing shed. Regular customers came each year and he had signs on the highway to attract additional customers. Loads of apples were taken to the "Old Market" in downtown Omaha. He had a few truckers who would buy a load and head west in Nebraska to sell them to grocery stores.

This all changed on Nov. 11, 1940, the day that the whole region experienced the famous "Armistice Day Freeze" which killed nearly all the fruit trees throughout the region.

Armistice Day was a national holiday to celebrate the end of World War I on Nov. 11, 1918. In 1954, Congress changed the name to Veterans Day to honor all American veterans.

The week before the "Armistice Day Freeze" temperatures were up in the 50's, 60's and 70's. On Nov. 11th and for the next 4-5 days the temperatures were near zero at night. Temperatures went below zero in several areas. Here are quotes from newspapers of that day:

"Worst November storm in years strikes Sunday

Subzero cold hampers repair crews in state, 11 below at Alliance

Mercury drops to reading of 4 below zero - Lowest November temperature in 22 years."

There are several good orchards in southeast Nebraska today, but not near the number that were there in 1940. My father converted the apple orchard to regular farm crops of field corn and soybeans.

Jill Burkey   Saying Goodbye to Pet after Preg-checking Cows

I found her grazing --
    expertly pushing aside brown dried up grass from summer
with a wiggle of her velvety nose,
    her teeth snipping tender grass underneath,
her strong jaw filling the silence with
    the sound of nourishment

Dust rises and trails behind my hand
    as it slowly slides over her coat,
thickening for a winter she won't see

As I stand with her, I look
    for the pain she must feel,
but quiet and serenity is all
    that surrounds us in the October sky
where light sneaks through slivers of space
    separating the otherwise dark gray clouds

I run my index finger over
    the hard calcium deposits
that restrict her knees and make her lame
    and I realize I have nothing to give her --

167

no corn husks, cake or words
    to say "thank you," "I'm sorry," or "I'll miss you"

I pull up the short green grass
    on my side of the fence
while she nuzzles my hair
    and I feed her fistfuls of it,
trying to fill us both up

I leave her with her
    ears pricked up,
        happy for the visit and
            a little green grass

 from the other side of the fence

Mary Maas   Holy Milch Cow

      I, like everyone else I knew who grew up on a farm, was expected to do my share of the work and never-ending chores. If you don't work, you don't eat. That philosophy was very simple. Well, to some people that idea was very simple.

      It seemed one worked his or her way up through the ranks of household chores, chicken chores, milch cow chores and then to fieldwork.

      I wasn't too happy with the job of washing the smelly, soured milk and cream separator with its hundreds of out-of-shape shields in their little teepee-shaped house. Those same cone-shaped pieces of metal which, after they finally were washed clean of their clotted residue, refused to fit back on their center spindle with any ease. The shields were formed to fit together by the little rectangular grooves on the center neck of each shield. That groove had to line up on the shaft so they would spin the milk out of the cream like they were made to do. Getting them all to line up and stay lined up, so I could put the heavy lid on, was a challenge and quite often ended with them all springing back off to clank and clatter while bouncing all over the kitchen floor. That would be a costly mistake, thus necessitating the re-washing of each piece, while your ears rang from the deafening sound of the steel bouncing on the kitchen floor with one hundred clamorous, non-musical notes and all at the same time.

      So a person might then graduate to washing the unmentionable stuff off the shells of eggs. And that was an even more odious chore. Slightly cracked eggs would decide to split

168

in two and would leak their slimy, stringy innards in the water. Then those innards would manage to coat all the other eggs with unspeakably yucky yolk.

From that promotion you fell next in line to go out to the chicken house to do the chicken chores. Woe was I. I felt lice and mites crawling on me for hours after leaving the coop. I was bruised and beaten by the old cluck hens that refused to give up their fruits of labor in spite of the persuasion I used on them with the end of a stick. I was forced to neutralize their pointed weapons by holding their heads immobile on the side of the nest. Then I could safely retrieve the eggs they had tucked tightly underneath their bellies, which were no longer protected by their talons and beaks. When all else failed, I had to forcefully prod them from their roost with my handy stick, and sometimes it seemed they couldn't lay eggs again, for a day or so. Stress, I would imagine.

Oh, how I remember the ungratefulness of the fowl flock. After I had hand-mixed and carried mash to them for their meals, all they willingly gave me in return were the creepy biting critters from their lousy home.

I really wanted to work my way up to the rank of a gentle cow maiden or herdswoman. I wanted to go out to the pasture in the evening light and follow the lowing cows home to the barn. I wanted to prop myself up near their flanks and use masterful strokes to coax the milk from their full-to-bursting udders. I wanted to have the cats and kittens begging at my elbows for their daily ration of milk freshly squirted direct from the factory.

But the cows were unmindful and blind to my heartfelt ambition. They conspired with the whole herd and none would let down their milk for me. No matter how I stroked, masterfully or not, not one drop would they release into the waiting, empty bucket. I squeezed my hand into a fist slowly. I drew steadily down the length of the teat. I prodded gently with thumb and forefinger. I yanked. I pumped. I pummeled the poor spigots until in exasperation even old Bossy kicked the bucket out from under her, while wrapping a freshly soiled tail around my head, with a flourishing, final swipe across my mouth and nose for good measure.

Sitting upright on the one-legged, T-shaped milking stool was a feat in itself to accomplish. I teetered. I tottered. I fell forward into the cow, then ricocheted backward, holding on to the teats for dear life, knowing what was on the ground behind me. All the while I kept trying to keep the offensively odorous tail pinned captive between my knee and the cow's

hind leg. One was expected to stay upright on the stool, while
one sought to coax milk from the uncooperative appendages,
despite desperate efforts of trying out all the various strokes.
Then, too, one had to be on the alert and ready to dodge a
sneaky jack hammered blow, delivered from out of nowhere and
for no good reason, from a nervous split hoof. All of that was
simply too much to handle.

Holy cow, I said, or words to that effect, when that quick
foot ended up stuck between the handle and the bucket,
resulting in a rodeo cow bucking and bawling out a horrendous
protest at my presence in the milk barn. I was banished from
the parlor.

Back to the chicken roost I went. Abandoned by the
cats and kittens, I was stuck with feathers, and not one bit
tickled. Oh, my brother said I flunked milking on purpose, so I
wouldn't have to get up early in the morning for chores. But, I
knew the real fault laid with the cows for expressing their
unmistakable preference to not have me in the barn again, ever.

Leo Blaha   The Warsaw Precinct

Warsaw Precinct, Canada Hill

In 1871 the first immigrants came to Howard County and
settled west of St. Paul, which became the Warsaw precinct,
and called it Canada Hill.

It was the Scotch Irish who came from Warsaw, Canada, and
they named the Warsaw Post Office in 1873, according to Allan
Kraft from Grand Island. They built the first Ebenezer
Methodist Episcopal Church in 1873 in the Northwest Quarter
of Section 23, Township 14, Range 11. In 1893 the Church was
dismantled and rebuilt in the Southwest Quarter of Section 11,
Township 14, Range 11.

The first Czech settlers came in 1875, and in 1876 Martin
Slobodny donated two acres for a cemetery in Section 10,
Township 14, Range 11 to bury the first baby.

Not having a Church, the Catholics set up a large cross in the
cemetery and gathered around it each Sunday to worship.

In the spring of 1877, the Burlington Railroad gave 40 acres of
land across the road from the cemetery, Section 3 Township 14
Range 11, to the St. Viclas (James) Society of the Catholic

Church to build the St. Wenceslaus Church of Warsaw. Another 40 acres was purchased in 1878 from the railroad for $50.00. In 1901 the Church wanted to borrow $500 and gave a mortgage of the land to the Catholic Workman of St. Paul, Minnesota. No Record of Deeds is to be found for the 40 acres where the church was built. To get a deed they had to pay a mortgage of $220, which the railroad mortgaged to New England Trust Company of Boston, Massachusetts. The railroad mortgaged all the land that wasn't sold to get money to build the railroad. They got a deed in 1901 - Book Z, Page 75.

A small wooden church 16'x28' was built in 1878.

A new brick church was built in 1895 for $2,737.50. The Church blessed on the feast of the patron Saint, St. Wenceslaus on September 28, 1895. The last mass was offered on December 21, 1948. The church was torn down in 1964.

In Warsaw precinct, there were five school districts:
Dist. 13 in Section 25 Township 14 Range 11 Lease 1885   1873 to 1958
Dist. 8 in Section 10 Township 14 Range 11 Deed 1889   1874 to 1971
Dist. 61 in Section 27 Township 14 Range 11 Deed 1888   1887 to 1956
Dist. 27 in Section 34 Township 15 Range 11 Deed 1895   1876 to 1955
Dist. 18 in Section 33 Township 15 Range 11 Deed 1891   1874 to 1965

There were three cemeteries in the precinct:
Section 28 Township 15 Range 11 Bohemian National Grave Yard
Section 10 Township 14 Range 11 St. Wenceslaus of Warsaw
Section 15 Township 14 Range 11 Methodist Episcopal Cemetery or Warsaw

The St. Wenceslaus Cemetery Association of Warsaw was organized in 1989 to take care of the cemetery. St. Peter Paul council are the land managers of the 80 acres and give money to the cemetery for maintenance from the rent of the 80 acres of land.

In 1964 the Warsaw Precinct got irrigation water from the Farwell Irrigation District.

62% of the land is irrigated
2% is canals
36% is pasture roads and hilly farm ground
In 1998, there were 23 farmers, 13 non-farmers, 2 new homes—
non-farmers
In 1900 there were 79 farms

There are 51.3 miles of canals and laterals. There are 10.8
miles of buried PVC pipe within this 51.3 miles.
28.5 sections make up the Warsaw Precinct.

Linn Hamilton   Farmer Stress

He didn't get much sleep all night,
But rose at the first soft light.
Tired from the night before,
His sprits down and his prospects poor.

The market price for his milk and grain
Was not enough to show a gain.
Every bill was much too high
To pay with milk or meat or rye.

He quarreled with his son and wife,
His day was full of stress and strife.
His mood was mean his spirits low,
His temper hot and about to blow.

His work was a never ending tale,
Up when the morning light was pale.
But in the darkest hour of the night,
He would not give up the fight.

Each time a dark tomorrow came
He milked his cows and sowed his grain.
But there is little hope or life,
In today's stress or tomorrow's strife.

He often wondered soft and loud,
Who stole tomorrow from the cloud?
Who took away the hope and light?
And left us in the dark of night.

"Who's this, Grandpa?" Tommy asked, pointing at a snapshot of a diminutive man, face hidden in the shadow cast by the bill of his cap.

Ten year-old Tommy was snuggled close to his grandfather, Mick, on the over-stuffed sofa leafing through the old photo albums. This was his favorite way to spend a rainy Sunday afternoon. He had his grandfather all to himself.

Mick leaned closer to focus the proper tri-focal in the light of the table lamp. "That was my dad, your great-grandfather, Carl. Don't you remember him? He's the one who always hid your candy under his arm and found it in your ear."

"Oh, sure. He was funny," Tommy nodded, smiling. "He's standing in front of the office at our collection center, isn't he? It looks different."

"Well, that was taken in '99. It was still the grain elevator then. Lots of changes since '99."

"Grandpa! There's your Mustang back there. See it?" Tommy jabbed his finger on a bright red convertible parked by the scales of the elevator.

"Sure is, but wasn't mine then. It belonged to your great-grandma, my mom. That car was built in '65. It's almost as old as I am. Think of that."

"Is she in here?" he asked, searching the photo.

"I think she was taking the picture. See her shadow there?"

"Is that you?" he asked excitedly, spying a face barely visible in the office window overlooking the scales.

"Yep, that's me," Mick chuckled. "I think I was trying to hide from your great-grandma that day."

"How come?"

"Well, I'll tell you. Years ago the government used to pay us to store their grain. When they stopped doing that, we had all these big empty buildings. We had to do something with them, so I did some remodeling and rented out space for farmers to store their big equipment. This picture was taken at the end of harvest and the buildings were filled with farm machinery. I was in trouble that day because Mom brought her Mustang down to store it for the winter, and I forgot to save room for it. I sure didn't want to tell her that."

"What did you do?" Tommy asked, studying the woman's shadow.

"I finally found a little space between two combines. By putting the top down and letting some air out of the tires, I could squeeze it under their grain spouts. Had to crawl out over the back to get out."

"Was she mad?"

"Nope. Never did tell her."

"How come you had combines stored?" Tommy asked with a puzzled expression.

"Well, back in '99 most farmers could still afford to own combines. In time though, just got so they cost too much money with all the gadgets on them. Now the National Harvest Co. that cuts all the crops are the only guys that can afford them. That's why you don't ever see a farmer with his own combine any more."

Tommy felt a shiver of excitement down his back, picturing the day The National Harvest Co. always pulled into town. The huge gleaming machines on trucks, the parade of shiny semi-trucks that followed blowing their horns, the noisy clamor of farmers queuing up to register their fields, the clamorous celebrations of farmers and harvesters joined in the coffee shops and bars, the busy preparations at the collection centers getting ready for the onslaught of new grain.

"Did farmers have their own semi- trucks too?" he asked.

"Some did. Most just hauled in old trucks or grain carts. Some even pulled wagons to town with tractors. I remember one fellow who drove a big semi. When I was dumping his grain, I noticed that half his dual tires were flat, so I told him about it. He walked around, looked at them, kicked them and said, 'And here I been cussin' at the county for all that loose gravel on the road'."

"Grandpa, tell me what harvest was like back when this picture was taken."

His grandfather flushed with gratitude at this request. Old people love to tell stories and reminisce, but seldom find such a willing audience.

"Well, things were different back in those days," he recalled as he settled comfortably on the sofa and stretched an arm across the back behind Tommy. "For one thing we had a lot more farmers, but not as many as when your great grandfather, Carl, took over the elevator. Of course, when the first Gordon, that would be your great-great-great grandfather John, started the elevator there was a family on every quarter section. Those were probably the best times for everyone." He could see he was losing Tommy's interest so he quickly moved on. "Anyway, harvest. We'd open up before 7:30, which was way too early for me..."

"But Grandpa, you get up at 5:30 now!" Tommy protested.

"7:30 came a lot sooner back in the old days. I was younger

174

and sleepier...like you," and he gave Tommy a playful nudge. "Yep, sometimes we'd be there till 9 - 10 at night when we had the dryers going. And our harvest started with that first farmer and didn't end until the last combine was wired together good enough so that last farmer could finish. Usually 6 to 8 weeks straight through. Farmers are an independent bunch. They'd quit work to go to a football game on Saturday and then want you there on Sunday so they could combine. Then there were some that wouldn't work on Sundays no matter what. They figured if they couldn't make it in 6 days, they couldn't make it in 7 either. And some were in such a hurry, they wouldn't quit for anything. Those were the ones you had to watch out for. I remember one who pulled on the scale to weigh and darn if his truck wasn't *empty!* He was in such a hurry he forgot to get a load. Drove all the way to town with an empty truck," Mick chuckled, shaking his head. "And didn't even know it. Then I remember one who pulled on with a load of grain, turned around and went right back to the field - he forgot to dump it!"
"Did you try to stop him?"
"Nah, he was going too fast. Couldn't have caught him," laughed Mick. "Besides, we knew he'd be back. Sometimes they'd get in such a hurry they'd take off with their boxes still up in the air and tear off spouting and augers before we could get them stopped. Women were the best drivers. They were very careful. But some would only drive straight ahead. If they had to back up, we'd have to do that for them, but women drivers never caused any problems."

He gently reached down to rub his stiff knee and continued. "Sometimes we'd go to work and find a truck parked on the scales. They'd bring it in the night before and leave it so they'd be first in line the next morning. Then, sure enough, they'd oversleep from working so late and we couldn't weigh any of the others lined up."
"What did you do then?" Tommy asked.
"Oh, we'd just pull them off with the tractor and they'd have to get back in line when they finally showed up." Mick paused, remembering the old days. "They never thought our scales weighed right and they thought our moisture tester was always wrong."
"You had your *own* stuff then?"
"Wasn't like it is now where the weights and moisture goes right to the Ag department through the computer probe. At least now they have to argue with some Ag flunky; *if* they can find the right one. They could always find us to argue with, but not any more. Hell, we knew our equipment was right," Mick stated

with a trace of anger. "We had an inspector for every gadget on the place."

"Inspector?"

"We had the scale inspector, the moisture tester inspector, the insurance inspector, the feed inspector, the grain inspector, the dust inspector, the noise inspector, OSHA inspectors, the State Fire Marshall, the Public Service Commission," Mick recalled as he ticked them off on his fingers. "And then we had the privilege of paying inspection fees! Some of those inspectors were good guys and others were real horse's asses."

"Mom says I shouldn't say 'horse's ass'."

"Right. Don't say that."

"What else was different," Tommy urged.

"Well," Mick paused, thinking. "We didn't have the pneumatic tubes to move grain. We had metal augers. They were like a big screw that turned real fast inside a tube. They were noisy and always plugging up or breaking a belt or a bearing was going out. My dad, your great-grandfather, lost part of two fingers trying to unplug one. He was at the top and had just reached in to pull it when someone threw a switch down below and it started. Nipped the ends of his fingers clean off before they could get it stopped. Good thing he didn't have his hand in there or he would have lost the whole thing; maybe even his arm."

"Wow, augers must have been dangerous!" exclaimed Tommy.

"*Very* dangerous. Seemed every harvest someone would get hurt or killed by an auger. A farmer got killed in '99. He was out in the field alone and his combine plugged up. Guess he tried to kick the trash loose and got his pant's leg caught in the auger. It pulled his leg right in. Somehow he got the thing shut off before it got the rest of him. He managed to unhook an old tractor from a grain cart and drove himself across the field to the neighbors. They loaded him in their pickup and tore off for town, but he lost so much blood that he went into shock and died before they could get to the hospital. Sad thing was his wife didn't know what had happened and when he was late she was driving around looking for him at the same time they were trying to call her from the hospital. Left four little kids, oldest one about your age," he said as he looked down into Tommy's staring eyes. "Never closed the elevator doors during harvest - except that one time - day of his funeral."

Neither said a word, each lost in his own thoughts; Mick remembering the tragedy, Tommy thinking of the loss of a father.

"Know what happened the next day?" Mick abruptly broke the

176

silence. "All the neighbors left their fields and took their combines and trucks over to his farm. They had his crop out in two days. Farmers were like that. They were always trying to get ahead of each other, but if something happened they were the first ones there to help."

"Would the National Harvest Co. do that?" Tommy asked.

"Someone would have to give up his place on the register and move to the end of the line. I don't know if that would happen or not."

"Did anyone besides great-grandpa Carl ever get hurt at the elevator?"

"Yeah, a fella who worked for us hit a nail wrong and it came right back at him and went into his eye. He lost that eye. And another one, Earl, got buried in some milo. We thought he *was* a goner."

"How did that happen?"

"Well, we'd dump the milo in the pit and auger it out the bottom. But sometimes, if it was wet, only the middle part would go down to the auger and the rest would just stick up on the sides and stay there. Earl climbed down in the pit with a rake to pull down the milo that was stuck, but when he raked it, it *all* came down. Buried him up to his chin and kept coming! I grabbed a flat board and stuck it in front of his face to keep the grain away so he could breathe, but every time he took a breath and let it out the milo would pack in tighter around his chest, so he had to take smaller and smaller breaths. He just about suffocated even though we kept his face free. He was stuck in there so tight we couldn't get him loose. Finally, we managed to get a rope worked under his arms and four of us just pulled like hell. We got him out, but he said he was 5'8" when he went in and was 6'4" when he got out," Mick chuckled.

"Did he go to the hospital?"

"Nah. He was tough. He just kept on working."

"Did you ever get hurt?"

"Oh, had a guy drop the endgate of his truck on my head. That hurt like hell."

"Mom says I shouldn't say 'hell' either."

"Right. Shouldn't say that."

"What's 'milo' anyway?"

"A sorghum. Farmers used to raise a lot of milo around here. And wheat, too. Ninety-nine was the last year we took in wheat. Milo finally ended in '07, I think it was."

"Did they raise corn and soybeans then too?"

"Corn, soybeans, wheat, milo and some oats. Corn, beans and

milo all came in during the fall harvest. Sometimes when grain was coming too fast, somebody would forget to close a slide in an auger and we'd dump beans on corn. Then it was scoop shovel time."

"What's a slide?"

"Well," Mick paused, rubbing his chin. "That's like a railroad. The slide is like switching trains from one track to another. If the wrong switch is changed there's a train wreck. Or in our case, beans and corn or milo would end up all mixed together."

"Scoop shovel time?" Tommy asked.

"Scoop shovel time," Mick nodded. "Then we had to collect different taxes on all that grain." Counting on his fingers again, Mick continued, "There was an ethanol tax for corn, an ethanol tax for milo, a check-off tax for corn, check-off tax for milo, check-off tax for soybeans and then sales tax. We were unpaid tax collectors that, by God, had to keep it right for all those inspectors. Then, when we bought it from the farmers, we had to divide it sixty ways from Sunday. For instance, I remember one deal in particular. Two brothers formed a corporation. The delivered grain had to be divided between the corporation, each brother and the landlords who were also two brothers. The grain was split 1/3 to the corporation and 1/6 to each renting brother and 1/6 to each landlord brother. But, the renting brothers also fed cattle and one of the landlord brothers had alfalfa on his property, so the renters used his alfalfa and repaid him with more grain. When the grain was delivered, we had to establish the value of the alfalfa and record that much more grain to the one landlord. To complicate matters even more, some of the grain was delivered to another elevator, so we had to find out how many bushels were there before we could determine the 1/3 and all the 1/6s."

"Grandpa..."

"Don't stop me now, I'm figuring this out. Finally everyone sold their shares except the renting brothers because that would give them too much income for that year so they put it into storage. Then storage expense had to be figured for the brothers' share, but not equally because one brother fed more cattle than the other and he used some of his grain for feed. There was so much record keeping we had to hire a secretary-bookkeeper." Mick took a big breath and shook his head to clear it.

"I don't understand what you told me," Tommy puzzled.

"Neither do I - just trust me; it happened," Mick assured him, patting him knowingly on the head. "Then," he continued, leaning forward, elbows on his knees and gesticulating with his hands, "We had to haggle over the price we could pay to the farmers. That was called 'settling' time. That's when your great-grandpa would get *really* testy."

"How come?"

"They'd always come in and tell us what the other elevator in town was paying and it was always more. Now, sometimes, they *were* paying more all right, but guess what? They weren't taking any grain because they were full. Hell-er-heck, you can offer anything you want when you aren't buying. Or, they'd pay more but charge the farmer to dump his grain there, or they'd charge more for drying or storage. Hell, we were usually paying the same or more, but it sure as hell made us look bad,' Mick declared, chopping the air with his fist. "Actually," he continued, settling back on the sofa, "A lot of the farmers were smart enough to figure that out, not all of course. The worse were the little old lady landowners. Most of them couldn't understand anything but the posted price. I remember in '99 one called back *five* times. Each time your great-grandpa would try to explain it. He finally got so mad he was ready to elevate her corn right out in the middle of the street."

"Is that why Dad doesn't buy grain now?"

"Partly - but not really. You know, that's why I remember the '99 harvest so well. Last one of the century and that's when everything started to change. For years the government experimented with one farm program after another. In '99 it was called the "Freedom to Farm Act'. Farmers went out and planted every speck of land they could find. Then they grew so much grain that there wasn't a market for it. Didn't need all that grain so no one wanted to pay anything for it. Prices got clear down to $1.60 a bushel for corn. Well, at those prices farmers couldn't pay their loans and they stopped buying machinery. Then implement dealers started closing down. There wasn't enough money to feed livestock, so feed companies went broke. That same year two big Ag companies merged and eventually eliminated most of the competition, small family elevators like us. Then they got into the livestock business with the cheap grain and feed and drove out the rest of the livestock producers. That's when the government stepped in and nationalized the farming industry. The government leased all the elevators and that's when we became a collection center. Now farmers are told how many acres of what grain they can plant, how much they'll receive per bushel and which collection center has their account number for delivery."

"Dad says he'd rather do it like you used to do," Tommy confided.

179

"We did a lot of haggling over the prices and weights and everything, but farmers are a good bunch. We'd finally all compromise and end up about where we should be. They were all our friends, not just some account number like now."

Mick settled back on the sofa and glanced out the window. "Rain's ending," he mentioned with a trace of regret.

"That's okay, Grandpa. Mom says I can stay until you send me home," Tommy replied hopefully.

"I think you should stick around for a while."

"Good! So do I. Tell me some more about the harvest when this picture was taken," Tommy urged as he pulled his legs up and tucked them Indian style under himself.

Mick sat back and rubbed his chin, trying to recall that time so long ago. "Well," he started with a chuckle, "This one guy called and wanted to know if I'd stay late so he could dump one more load of corn that night, so I hung around for him. When he was on his way to town, he happened to meet a neighbor, so they stopped in the middle of the road to visit a little. Trouble was, he didn't turn his engine off and talked so long that he ran out of gas, so he called me because he knew I would still be waiting for him and asked if I'd bring him some gas. Well, I closed up the elevator and drove out there with a can of gas, but we couldn't get him started because he had run his battery down, too. Another neighbor came along and tried to jump his battery, but it was too big and burned up the neighbor's battery, so then I went back to town and drove the old Farm-All tractor out to tow him in. I pulled him almost a mile before his engine turned over. I told him not to stop till he got to a filling station and to not stop and talk anymore. Man, that was a lot of trouble for a load of corn!"

Wound up now, Mick continued enthusiastically, "Then I remember a woman who came in and said her husband wanted to sell his grain, so we got the paperwork done and gave her the check. When we balanced the grain that night, we discovered she'd sold her *brother-in-law's* grain; her husband had delivered his grain to a different elevator. That took some straightening out. And then, believe it or not, some people would actually forget they had grain in our elevator. Once a year we'd go through the old accounts and call everyone who had grain stored with us. Some would be surprised, some would argue with us, but they were all pretty tickled to find out they had some unexpected money coming."

"I wouldn't argue. I'd just *take it!*" Tommy exclaimed.

"That was also the year the elevator got broken into 3 times in 6 months."

"You mean you were robbed?!!"

"Nah. About all they took was some dog food samples and a flashlight. An elevator was a damn poor place to break into. They never had any money. But, it cost us a hell of a lot. They wrecked the doors, the computer, the printer, old antique safes, filing cabinets, did a lot of damage. Insurance paid about a third each time. The last time was right after harvest and something scared them off before they destroyed the place again. I remember my dad saying it's a sad state of affairs when you have to be grateful to thieves that they didn't do worse damage."

"Did they ever catch them?"

"No. Our police were like the Keystone cops. We just paid," Mick grumbled.

"Well......hell."

"Don't let your mom hear that," Mick chided.

"Right. Unh...what was the very worse thing about harvest then," Tommy asked, changing the subject.

"Oh, the long hours, no days off. It was damn (I know-don't tell your mother), it was damn hard work. And then trying to keep my dad out of the grain dust. When he was a young man, he cleaned bad milo out of the pit and breathed too much moldy dust. He passed out and ended up with severe dust pneumonia. Soybean dust was the worse. Ended up he couldn't even eat food that had soy products in it. Grain dust started bothering me, too, later on. Just can't breathe that stuff all your life without it finally getting to you."

"Is that why you always puff on that inhaler?"

"Yep, helps me breathe."

"What was the best part about harvest?"

"Well, it was an exciting time. Hard work, but exciting for everyone. And, you would have liked this. When harvest started, your great-grandmother would bake cookies. About every other day she'd show up with a fresh batch and leave them by the coffee pot in the office for us and the customers. You never knew what she was going to bring: gingersnaps, chocolate chip, oatmeal. We really went through the cookies. Then, in '99, we had a bunch of roast pork left over from a feed, so she'd doctor that up in a crock-pot and bring it down with a bunch of buns. Lots of farmers had lunch at the elevator that year. Helped to slow everyone down a little, too, standing around eating and shooting the breeze."

"Yum! Homemade cookies! Did all the elevators do that?"

"Don't think so. We just wanted to do something special for our customers. Everyone was working hard and trying their best.

181

Say! I want to show you something in this album." Mick searched through the pages until he came upon a sheet of yellow paper. "We got this after the '99 harvest. Read it," he said as he handed the dog-eared sheet to Tommy.

Tommy read, "Carl, Thank you for all your help and kindness at harvest. It is nice to do business with people who care and are conscientious about their customers. Please share this with everyone. Delbert."

"Who was he?" Tommy asked.

"He was just an old farmer in a seed corn cap. Sure made us feel good when we got that."

"Dad never gets anything like this."

"That's because they are all just account numbers now."

"Really is different, huh?"

"Yep, really different. Liked it better the old way. That's when it was fun."

Bruce Messersmith   Future Think

Some folks gaze in awe,
Or somethin',
At the engineer in charge
Of that mile and a half
Twistin', turnin'
Sinuous chunk of railroad train.

But shucks,

Bein' raised astride a Super H
Or at the helm of a 656
With PTO, power 3-point,
Live hydraulics, and
F-11 Farmhand with
Stacker head or grapple fork,
Those four levers that
Make this train go,
Fast or slow
Ain't much challenge.

Sometimes I ponder
My cousin's wonder at
My thirty-six hour days
Account I hadn't figured
On runnin' a train after

182

Spending all day workin' cows.

But heck,

I guess cuttin' my teeth
On three a.m. heavy check
And spendin, most the night
Extractin' a ninety pound calf
From an eight hundred pound heifer
Only to stay up all day
Supplyin' hay to four hundred
Hungry mouths and
Scabbin' the sunburnt, frost-bitten crust
From 7257's rear quarter
Musta been good trainin'
For this railroad life.

But now, the cows
Have all gone
To someone else's pastures,
And I'm still here
Shufflin' cars
On a midnight switch

And lookin' ahead.

'Cause we'll keep the land
If we can arrange income enough
To cover the med's
And provide a comfortable retirement
For that gentle old couple who
Dedicated nearly fifty years
To
Hereford cows,
Arabians,
And kids.

And, one day, when I retire
Perhaps I'll still have
A couple mares to foal
And an old bay gelding
To wrap bowed legs around
And ride

Through someone else's cows.

Leastwise
If the animal rightists and
Herbivores haven't yet
Civilized us to the point
Of soybean roasts
And seaweed steaks

By 2017

Amy Rasmussen   A Crazy Ride

I was eight years old and my first hog show was coming
to an end. I had shown my four hogs throughout the day, and
now I was waiting to go in the show-ring for showmanship. I
was standing in my hog pen with my dad and brothers, picking
out the hog I wanted to show for showmanship. I picked out
my red hog because she had been the calmest in the ring earlier
that day. We corralled her into a wash-rack and I hosed her
down. Dad reviewed with me questions the judge might ask:
How old is my pig? What is the breed of my pig? What do I feed
my pig? Where is the ham located? I had all the answers to
these questions from last night's quizzing session with my
brothers. First call for Junior Showmanship echoed throughout
the barn. I started to get ready to go. Double-checking my
whip and brush, I walked my hog up to the show-ring. I almost
lost her in a sea of pigs being viciously whipped by their eight
year old owners. Too many Junior Showmen congesting the
runway made the hogs hot and tired. Thirty kids plus thirty
hogs boisterously crowded through the gate. My hog decided to
be stubborn and ran towards the far end of the ring. I was
chasing after it when I was swept off the ground by a big, ugly,
white pig. It hauled me backward across the ring cutting
through the maze of chaos. I was terrified! I fell off the white
pig and ran over to the railings where my mom was sitting in
the bleachers videotaping. My shouts of dismay could be heard
throughout the building in an attempt to get me out of the ring.
The judge came over and asked if I was all right, but I was
sobbing too hard to even answer him. Somehow, I was able to
find my hog, take my purple ribbon, and head back to the barn.
My experience hasn't discouraged me from showing hogs.
Every year when it's time for Showmanship I can't help but
smile when I think of that embarrassing moment my first year
in 4-H.

Jack Ostergard   Going, Going, Gone

The auctioneer said, "They're for sale, a complete dispersion
now,
And anybody's welcome that wants to buy a cow."
He said, "There's fifty years of breeding here and no one's had
the chance
To buy a set of cows like these; they've not been off the ranch.

They have never been to town before, if you don't buy today,
Tomorrow you will be sorry you let them get away.
The old man had decided he had to sell his herd,
A tough decision age had made, he gave his wife his word.

He knew he couldn't handle the workload anymore,
Each new season took more effort than it had the year before.
He reasoned this was better cause he wouldn't feel the need
To get out in the weather when the cows require their feed.

So he called the local auction barn and consigned them to the
sale,
And loaded up the trucks with every hoof and horn and tail.
He sat silently remembering, not worried about the price,
The decision was his own, he had not sought advice.

He watched as they filed in the ring. He knew each cow by
sight.
As the auctioneer began his chant, he felt his chest grow tight.
Old happenings flashed through his mind, back to days now
passed.
His ranching days were over but the memories would last.

He lived his lifetime over while the cows were being sold,
And was completely lost in reveries, reliving days of old.
He came back to reality as "Sold," somebody cried.
It was then he fully realized a part of him just died.

Suzanne Richards   You Might Be a Rancher's Wife If...

1. Your mud porch doubles as a doghouse.
2. A skunk has ever sprayed your clothes hanging on the
    line.
3. His favorite radio channel is the weather station.
4. He calls to check on the cows, but doesn't ask how you
    are.

5. His idea of quality time is tractor-driving lessons.
6. His idea of dressing up and going out is dinner at the sale barn.
7. You wear out a welcome mat every six months.
8. You can vacuum your whole house from one outlet.
9. Your baby's first word is 'mooo'.
10. Your only television channel is P.B.S.
11. You maybe get one solicitor per year.
12. You have skulls or wagon wheels as lawn ornaments.
13. You mow your lawn with a goat.
14. You call your kids in the house for supper with a cowbell.
15. Your kids' trip to the library is actually the bi- monthly bookmobile visit.
16. You have beef in every meal.
17. He buys you insulated coveralls for your anniversary instead of lingerie and you are thrilled.
18. He buys you fencing pliers for Christmas.
19. Instead of foreplay at night, you check for ticks.
20. Your fridge looks like a veterinarian pharmacy.
21. Your mailbox is full of fertilizer junk mail.
22. Your next-door neighbor is a mile away.
23. It takes a half a tank of gas to get to the supermarket.
24. You have to sweep your kitchen twice a day.
25. You hear tractor and implement commercials on your favorite rock-n-roll channel.
26. You have to put your truck in four-wheel drive to get down your own driveway.
27. You have tractor seat barstools.
28. You wouldn't trade anything in the world for this great lifestyle and hard working, good loving husband.

Raymond Weed   Last Will and Testament of a Farmer

I leave:
To my wife—My overdraft at the bank.
      Maybe she can explain it.
To my son—Equity on my car. Now
      he'll have to go to work to meet
      the payments.
To my banker—My soul. He's got a
      mortgage on it anyway.
To my neighbor—My clown suit. He'll
      need it if he continues to farm as
      he has in the past.

To FHA—My unpaid bills. They took some real chances on me
  and I want to do the same for them.
To ASCS—My grain bin. I was planning
  to let them have it next year anyhow.
To SCS—My farm plan. Maybe they can
  understand it.
To the junk man—My machinery. He's
  had his eyes on it for years.
To my undertaker—A special request:
  Six implement and fertilizer dealers
  for pallbearers, please—they're used
  to carrying me.
To the weatherman—Rain, sleet and snow at the
  funeral, please. No sense in having
  nice weather now.
To the grave digger—Don't bother. The hole I'm
  in should be big enough.
And last: To the monument maker—Set up a jig
  for the epitaph: Here lies a farmer who has
  now properly assumed all his obligations.

Patty Lindgren   The Cowman

He's of a breed that's pretty scarce
From an era long thought passed;
He doesn't care for city life,
He lives for cattle, land and grass.

Cows and horses are in his blood
And he knows them horn to hoof;
His home has grass for carpets
And the blue sky is his roof.

He could no more trade his saddle
For a briefcase and a chair
Than to part with cows and tractor,
And sell his favorite mare.

He's always on the lookout
For a head that's droopin' low,
An eye that isn't bright enough,
An ear that ain't just so.

And when he sees this sick one
With his ever-watchful eye,

187

He won't go in to supper
Till he knows the reason why.

Nothing brings him greater pleasure
At the closing of each day
Than the distant lowing of his cattle
And the smell of new-mown hay.

The men who build our spaceships
He does, beyond all doubt, admire,
But he can put them all to shame
With a pair of pliers and some wire.

To see a game of football
He wouldn't walk across the street
But let it be a calf sale,
And he'll beat you to a seat.

While we'll sit in cold and rain
To urge on our teams with cheers
This guy will brave the hail and snow
To study choice and fancy steers.

Yes, he'll buy and feed and sort his cows
Right to the day his time is nigh,
And his cowmen friends will greet him
In the Big Stockyards in the sky.

Here they never have to worry
About prices and the weather,
And their music isn't that of harps
But the squeak of saddle leather.

The cowman helped to build this land,
A mighty great one, I might add,
And it makes me proud to say it
'Cause one of 'em's my Dad!

Max Malone   Farewell to the Farm

I stopped beside the old farm site,
Where we had lived so many years,
And the scene spread out before me,
Very nearly brought some tears.

The trees around the farmyard,
That once tamed winter's icy breath,
Had been leveled by bulldozers,
Just broken branches marked their death.

The white house had been moved away,
And of the other buildings on the place,
The corncrib and the workshop,
There was not a single trace.

Gone were the tractor shed and granary,
The garden plot and the well,
That they ever had existed,
It was impossible to tell.

There were memories of kids playing,
In their little backyard swimming pool,
Of the bus stopping every morning
To transport them to their school.

And winter nights, in the lambing pens,
Out there among the sheep,
Helping new-born lambs to suckle
Before I had a chance to sleep.

I could still see the cattle resting,
Down by the stream and in the shade,
A respite from the summer's heat,
What a pleasant picture that they made.

Some people call it progress,
But for some, it seems like pain,
For a way of life is passing,
That will be never seen again.

3/25/97

Rose Marie Hulse   Rural Life in Fillmore and York Counties

I was born on a rural farm home in Glengary Township
of Fillmore County. The doctor present for the delivery made the
trip from Tobias. My maternal grandmother Koca was a midwife
at several births recorded in the Delayed Birth Records found at
the Fillmore County Courthouse. This farm, three mile from
Milligan, has been in the Kotas Family since the beginning of

189

Fillmore County.

My ancestors all migrated to the United States from Bohemia, first settling in Illinois before coming to Fillmore County. Some homesteaded and others purchased railroad land. A dugout in the bank of Turkey Creek was the first home of my paternal grandparents who were married in Fillmore County. They built their first wooden frame home and farmyard a half mile from what later became the main highway. This became a hindrance after the car came to the area in 1903 because of the long mud driveway.

I attended a rural one-room country school, a mile from home. The same one my grandfather and father attended. During my eighth years at this school, I had only three teachers. The first one who lived in Crete taught me for five years. She had quite a chore because she had to teach me to speak English. I spoke only Czech, and yet, I had cousins who did not understand Czech. When I was in the first grade, there were four girls in eighth grade, so I got a lot of attention. After that I was the only girl until I was in the eighth grade, when another little girl started in first grade. I hated to play boy games all the time. My second teacher, who now lives in California, taught me for two years and my eighth grade teacher, who lived in Daykin, was one of the girls I went to school with when I was in first grade. Pupils could take four years of Normal Training in high school, which entitled them to be teachers. Teachers in those days could not be married. Before we could graduate from the eighth grade, all rural school eighth graders had to take exams at the County Courthouse in Geneva, the county seat. Later, we all returned to receive our diplomas and had a group picture taken on the courthouse steps. It was at these graduation exercises that I wore my first store bought dress. It served double duty because I had to recite a poem at the Memorial Day program and I had to sing in the chorus that year. The county school never had electricity or water. Two of the older pupils went to the neighbors to get water in a cream can. A large heating stove sat in the middle of the room furnishing heat when it was cold. Coal or wood was used to provide heat in the heater. Outdoor toilets, one for boys and one for girls, were used instead of a bathroom today. Mail order catalogs were used instead of our present day toilet tissue. Of course, it was not unusual to have wasps and mice to scare us even though we were used to outdoor toilets at home.

Farm children were involved in doing chores on the farm at a very young age. I was milking cows at the age of five. Our cows were so gentle we could walk up to milk them any place in the pasture. I never sat down to milk. We had to milk in the morning and at night. The milk had to be separated each time. To separate the cream from the milk, the crank on the separator had to be turned very fast, before you could turn on the milk in the bowl. In the evening, we ran water through the machine to rinse it out, but it had to be taken apart and washed thoroughly in the morning. There were about 60 discs that the milk went through to separate the cream. Our separator was attached to the floor in the pantry. The skim milk was taken outdoors to be fed to the hogs. We would save some of the milk, until it got sour, to feed to our little chickens. The flies were thick in this clabbered milk. Could this be why I can't eat cottage cheese today?

I grew up in the 1930's when we had the terrible drought and the banks went broke. We raised chickens, ducks, geese, rabbits, hogs, cattle and, of course, horses. Our poultry was hatched at home by having setting hens sit on the eggs till they hatched. We were forever exchanging male stock with other people to keep our breeding stock producing. I remember one day when I was a small girl, I loved to gather eggs, but I could not see into the nest. One day, I lifted out a snake, which frightened me terribly. We got dad in from the field who shot the snake that had swallowed many of the eggs whole. Hatcheries became businesses in the farming communities, but those have been extinct for many years now.

We had no electricity or running water. We did have a telephone, the kind you cranked a lever and the local operator asked you the number you were calling. She would relay the call. At that time, there were party lines with as many as five people on the same line. You distinguished your call by the code of a long ring and two short or whatever. The operator had the switchboard in her home and had to be available 24 hours a day.

A windmill would pump water for the livestock. We had a well with a pump by the house. When the house was built in 1909, a big tall metal tank was installed in a room upstairs. We would pump water into it using a gasoline engine. This waster was used for bathing, washing dishes, and our hands. Water for drinking and cooking was pumped by hand daily. We used gasoline lamps and lanterns for light in the house and for chores after dark. We hung the lamps from the ceiling, which lit up the room better, but we had to keep taking the lamp down to pump air into the gas tank for a good bright light. Each lamp had two mantels. Millers would fly into the light mantel and die, but then the light would go out because the lamps did not operate on one mantel. We never used kerosene lamps with the glass chimneys except when we wanted to heat the hand held curling iron to curl our hair.

When I was very small, we used a washing machine that had a hand lever to move to agitate the clothes. The stove for heating the wash water and the wash machine were in the washhouse, which was the first frame house built on this farm. This house still stands on the yard, restored in good condition by my brother who lives on the farm. I remember when I was about eight years old my maternal grandparents came to visit followed by the Maytag salesman with a new washing machine that had a gas engine. A lot of tears of happiness where shed that afternoon.

Cooking was done on a cob and wood burning stove in the kitchen. Cobs were picked up in the hog pen after the hogs chewed off the kernels. This stove had a reservoir that kept water hot for bathing, dish washing, shaving, etc. Can you imagine how hot it got in the house during the summer when the meal had to be cooked! Especially in July, when we cooked for thrashers, baked kolace, crescent rolls and home baked bread. In the 1930's, it was not unusual for the temperature to reach 115 degrees in the afternoon. There was no refrigeration, but we had a nice cool cellar covered with a lean to, on the north side of the washhouse. Before eating a meal, we ran down to the cellar to get food and returned it back again after the meal. This was a job for the kids, except lizards and salamanders liked to rest on the cellar steps, which frightened me to death.

We had a radio that was used sparingly because it worked only when hooked up to a car battery. The battery had to be taken to town to be charged if the radio was used too often.

We tried to be as self sufficient as possible. A large garden was raised every year. We canned all the vegetables, made ketchup, tomato or vegetable soup. We also made cabbage into sauerkraut, canned fruit from the orchard, and made apple butter and jelly covered with paraffin. We would store the potatoes and squash in the cellar. With no refrigeration meat was canned when we butchered, pork was fried down, stored in an open crock with lard poured to cover it. Lard was rendered. The cracklens from the rendered lard were used to make Jelitha, a Czech sausage using blood, barley and garlic. Another Czech sausage made from the pork head was called Jathernice. These were stuffed in the intestines of the animal after they were thoroughly cleaned. Cracklings and old rancid lard were used to make homemade soap, cooked and dried outdoors. Beef

192

was butchered in the late fall and hung to freeze in one room of the washhouse, covered with oilcloth or a clean cloth. Whenever we needed meat, dad would bring in a quarter of beef and cut off what we could use.

Folks enjoyed going to dances or entertainment in town, but many times it rained while we were gone, so the car got stuck on the long muddy driveway. My Dad farmed with horses until after the drought and then he used them for situations like this. While dad harnessed the horses to pull the car out so it didn't freeze in the mud over night, mom made a fire in the heating stove and put us kids to bed than she went back out to the car to guide it while dad pulled it with the horses. We needed the car to go to church the next morning. Other social functions were free outdoor movies in the summer on a vacant lot in town. Us kids would do our chores early and then walk to the highway where we caught a ride to town. Folks would come to town to buy groceries and brought us home. After World War II, movies were shown in the auditorium. You paid admission on Saturday night and received a complimentary ticket to attend the movie on Wednesday night. During intermission time, the business places sponsored bingo, giving away five one-dollar bills and free comp tickets to future movies. You did not hear of babysitters in those days. Children attended all social functions with their parents and when they got tired a room or balcony was available where the children slept. An adult attendant watched over the sleeping children.

Dad purchased a John Deere tractor after the drought but this caused a problem because all of his machinery had hitches for horses. Dad was handy in his blacksmith shop so he converted the machinery to be pulled by the tractor. The binder to cut wheat was not a one-man machine. One person had to drive the tractor and the other had to ride the binder to be able to dump the 8 or 10 bundles on a pile to be made into shocks later. My brother, who was eleven years old, drove the tractor but he would keep falling asleep so dad bought firecrackers and they took breaks to shoot off the firecrackers, quite an undertaking in the very dry wheat stubble. Those bundles of wheat had to be made into shocks before they could be thrashed. Mom and I did this but it was cooler to do it in the moonlight during full moon. Us kids didn't shock at night, but in order to entertain us in the field, folks drove there with the car. We had a small phonograph that had a crank to wind it to work and it had a large horn for volume. We sang with the music or danced in the stubble.

Our cousins liked to come to our house because there

was so much to do. With the creek nearby they loved to walk through the woods searching for stuff nature provides. Fishing was a great pastime. We loved to pour water into the crawdad holes by the creek to force them out. We knew what we would have for supper that evening. Jumping out of the haymow into the hay outside the barn kept us on the move till I got the wind knocked out of me. In the winter, cousins brought their sleds. We had the hills to enjoy sleigh riding. I sprained my wrist once and two cousins got their toes frost bitten, which were painful accidents, but this didn't keep us from doing it again. Skating on the ice kept us moving to keep warm. This sure beat watching television or sitting at a computer like young folks do today.

With the arrival of spring each year dad had the big chore of hauling manure, cleaning out the barns, hog sheds, and chicken houses before spring fieldwork. The manure was hauled out on the garden and fields, the only means of enriching the soil to produce better crops in those days.

After Country school, I attended high school in Milligan, taking a business course. Typing was learned on manual typewriters. I stayed with my maternal grandparents in town the first two years. It was gas and tire rationing because of World War II, so folks couldn't haul me back and forth. The last two years, I rode with the vocational agriculture teacher who farmed west of our place, but I walked that long driveway morning and night. I did not further my education after high school. I did take a correspondence business course through the mail and passed all the classes except shorthand. I lived at home working out to help people pack when they were going to move, helped when a new baby arrived in the family or if there was illness in a family. After I turned 18, I took a Civil Service test and worked for the Quartermaster Department at the Fairmont Army Air Base issuing clothing to the soldiers. No electrical business machines were used. I would have loved to take the manual calculator I used when the base closed.

Shortly after high school graduation, I met a young man from Exeter who poked me with a pool stick in a bar in Milligan while a group of us girls were standing near the jukebox. We dated for four years before we were married. He was called up for military physicals, but didn't pass because of a heart condition. He lived on a farm with his parents but owned a truck, doing trucking as a living. Very few farmers owned a truck. He also made trips to Kansas and Oklahoma buying new farm machinery that local farmers asked him to buy for them. Implement manufacturers would deliver machinery to locations where the machines couldn't be used. He hauled gravel to build the runways for the Fairmont Air Base before I met him. Even though we were not married, he bought us a washing machine with a gas engine down south that was not available in this area.

The war ended so we were married in October 1947. I wanted to live on a farm, so we rented empty buildings north of Exeter in York County. We had laying hens, hogs, and I milked cows. This first farm home had a well and washhouse that was almost a block from the house. We had no electricity. My husband was hauling grain and livestock. Our son was born four days before Christmas, just fourteen months after our wedding. That winter was one blizzard after another with snowdrifts on the roadsides higher than our vehicles. Even though the beautiful sun was out, the wind would redrift the roads and yards. A new baby in the home meant laundry every day. Instead of using the washing machine, I washed clothes on the washboard, which took less water. There were no disposable diapers back then. If the weather was bad for drying clothes outdoors, I hung them inside on clotheslines that were strung from the windows to the doors. We had plenty of moisture inside, so we didn't need a humidifier. Our kitchen stove was divided into two parts. On half of it you could cook with wood and coal and on the other half you cooked with propane gas.

Our landlord notified us that we had to move March first. We rented an empty farm building three-fourths of a mile away. This was a bigger house and the well was closer to the house. I repapered the rooms so the house would be clean. It was a very windy day when I papered the living/dining room. I took a break to eat the noon meal and when I returned to the room, the paper was flying loose from the wall. Does this tell you how cold the house was? If I spilled water in the winter, it froze immediately. We finally invested in an oil-burning heater so we would have heat all day and night. It was a convenience, but filling the tank everyday was a messy job. A skunk was living under the house and every time the baby cried during the night, we were blessed with its aroma. I was raising a crawling baby under these conditions.

Sixteen months after the birth of our son, our daughter was born. This meant laundering more diapers everyday on the washboard. Shortly after her birth, electricity came to the rural area. The landlord would not wire the house so we had it wired ourselves. The mailbox was located one-half mile from our home so I would put the children into the coaster wagon and went after the mail. We bought a new car that had an automatic shift transmission. I figured any dumb cluck should be able to learn to drive this, so I put the kids in the back seat and drove to the mailbox. A year later, I got the courage to get my drivers license. We were asked to move because the buildings were going to be destroyed so the farmstead ground could be farmed.

We were fortunate to rent another farm, but this one had farm ground and a large pasture. I made a deal with my husband that he could continue trucking because by this time he had a semi trailer, livestock trailer, and grain trailer. I farmed the ground with a small Ford tractor, which had mounted two-row machinery. The place had a house that was two houses put together as one. It had electricity, but no running water. We installed running water to the house and my parents bought us a hot water heater so we could enjoy hot and cold running water. We went into the custom farm work business. We baled hay, shelled corn, and combined grain for farmers. As many as five farmers lived in each section, so we had many customers and neighbors. We fed two hundred head of beef cattle and I had a flock of five hundred laying hens, selling eggs to the school lunch program, grocery store, and to a restaurant. Our children helped us accomplish all of this, but after high school graduation they left home to be on their own. Our son served in Vietnam, my brother in Korea, and my father in France during World War I.

Our house was in terrible condition so we moved into a modern house with carpeting, a furnace, bathroom, running water, and electricity. Imagine an indoor bathroom! We added the air conditioning and an automatic washer and dryer. My husband's health had failed him forcing him to live in a nursing home for four years. I continued to farm, telling him on my sixty-fifth birthday that I was quitting. Two weeks later he passed away. I had open-heart surgery in the fall of 1999, and then I returned to the farm to be with nature, my dog, cat and one guinea fowl. This is PARADISE!

Jean Groth   The Best of Me

There were many animals on our family farm throughout the years.
The cattle, the hogs, the chickens, the cats and always a dog.
It is with fondness I recall the benefits of the routine of daily chores.

it was the animals
i think,
that taught me the
reverence for life
in general.

the education
taught
that necessary concern
of another living being
unable to care
for itself.

every working member
of my farm family
will benefit from the carryover
of that kindness
toward another.

as I reflect
on those accountability lessons
that have been instilled
into my character,
i become convinced;

yes,
i do believe
it was the animals.

Marvin Ketelhut   Memories

Have you ever been chased by a bull? Milked a cow and had a
dirty tail swish your face? Taught a calf to drink from a
bucket? Harnessed a horse? Had a runaway with a team?

Have you husked corn? Shocked wheat and oats? Cut grain
with horses and binder? Watched kids kill mice while shelling
corn from the crib? Gone threshing, hauling bundles for six
weeks with temperatures around 100 degrees?

Have you drunk warm water from a sack-wrapped jug? Cut
hemp in the slough with a corn knife - not knowing it was
marijuana? Worked all day for $1 helping neighbors with
haying? Have you eaten at 8th & P Streets in town - all you
could eat for 25 cents; candy bars, 5 cents; a shave, 15 cents;

postcards, 1 cent; stamps, 3 cents?

Have you watched an old cluck hen hatch eggs in 21 days?
Gathered chickens at night from low branches in the Fall to put
in the hen-house? Gathered the eggs from a nest and put your
hands on a bull snake? Made ice cream with your own eggs,
milk, cream and ice from the tank? Hauled water with a tank
wagon from the town's water tower for livestock, because ponds
and wells dried up from the 30's severe drought?

Tubular wells were dug - some with windmills. Dirt silo pits
were also dug and filled with ground corn stalks for silage. In
the 20's, did you watch your uncle cut ice from the pond and
pack it into an icehouse with straw? There was no electricity or
refrigerator, only an icebox.

Have you slept in an upstairs room so cold in winter that it
froze water? Have you slept on a feather tick wearing long
johns and socks and with a heated brick at your feet?

Kerosene lamps and lanterns gave the needed light. Telephones
were on a party line where three or more people could talk and
gossip. Central office in town would ring four longs for
emergency - fires, meetings, etc. Some towns had free outdoor
movies, cartoons, and silent films. Many towns had an annual
picnic.

Have you every butchered a hog or beef? Canned, salt cured,
and smoked rings of meat in your smokehouse? Planted and
harvested three-fourths of a wagonload of potatoes? Cut the
head off a chicken and plucked the feathers?

School buses would leave deep ruts in the road because there
was no rock or gravel.

Have you started a Model T by cranking it from the front? No
glass, just side curtains.

Have you gathered cobs for a kitchen stove? Pumped water
from a well for drinking? Built a dam with horses and scraper
(government project in the 30's).

Milk and egg checks kept some farmers going as there was little
grain to sell. First corn was low yielding, hard husking, non-

hybrid white. Yellow hybrids came later.

Did you see the dust storms during the 30's drought that darkened the sun? Did you put a handkerchief on your face to go outside? Did you see red dust settle on the car from winds from Oklahoma? Did you fight cinch bugs and grasshoppers with creosote and poison bait to keep them from devouring crops?

Have you slopped hogs in a trough and been knocked over? Seen large dry-weather whirlwinds pick up dust and move it across the fields? Ridden a Model A John Deere putt-putt tractor for days - lug wheels, no rubber.

Did you learn to tell time by the shadows from a tree or fence post? Have you stepped on a nail or rake while barefoot? Planted a large garden? Exhibited at fairs?

Have you skinned a skunk? Gone on coyote hunts? Mowed grass with a motor-less push mower? Rescued a pig from a large crack in the ground? He'd been there 10 days. Skinny pig lived.

Neighbor shot my dog; said he was only scaring it!

Have you loaded up a manure spreader and distributed its contents on the fields? There was no sacked fertilizer or weed control solution; weeds were controlled by cultivating and horses - one row at a time.

Have you churned and made your own butter? Have you ever turned the handle on a separator to divide the milk into cream and skim milk? Have you made soap from lye outside in a large black kettle?

There was no running water. Nobody bathed too often. Outdoor toilets really got cold in the winter - no toilet paper rolls.

A baseburner with coal would heat one room. There was no TV. Listened to Amos and Fibber McGee and Molly on the radio. Also baseball games—Babe Ruth and all the rest. Could have saved baseball cards from gum wrappers and been well off today.

Who could have imagined living in the teens and 20's and being here in the 90's or the next century?

There was no beer. Lots of folks made homebrew. Our grandparents drove team and buggy eight miles to visit us. Felt hats were popular with the men and long dresses with women.

House and barn dances were a common get-together. Lots of fights took place. Most small towns had a Marshall, a billy club and a jailhouse.

I put collars on three small red foxes that were found on a railroad right-of-way. I put them in a pen in the hen house. Each night they would grab a chicken. One night they got out. My Dad probably turned them out.

If you see a red fox with a collar, it is probably mine. (No, this happened 70 years ago!)

I see a cloud. I see some lightning and I hear some thunder. The neighbor's trees are turning white. The rains are coming. The rains are coming.

Bruce Messersmith   Priorities

What are they gonna put on the table
When the cowboys have all gone away
When the farmers have all been moved off the land
So the city folks have more room to play?

What are they gonna put on the table
When the cows have been moved off the land
Result of the bovine methane scare
When feedlots and pastures are banned?

What are they gonna put on the table
When farmers have quit growing wheat?
No need for bread or hamburger buns
When soybean extract is the meat.

What are they gonna put on the table
When Ted and Jane, and Debra and Frank
Have pursued their "Buffalo Commons" game
Into a twenty dollar per pound prank?

What are they gonna put on the table
When water rights have all been usurped
By cities, to grow lawns and flush toilets?
Like fine wine greedily slurped.

What are they gonna put on the table
When the result of urban sprawl
Has filled the fields with concrete
And empty shelves at the grocery mall?

Who's gonna tell the folks in the line
At McDonalds and grand Burger King
That there's no fast food left but tofu?
Whose plight are they going to sing?

What are they gonna put on the table
When preservationists and eco-saviors
Have sliced the throats of agri-producers
With a finely honed, multi-word sabre?

What are they gonna put on the table
At the celebration banquet in Washington,
When the last "Scenic River" and "National Monument"
Puts cowmen and plowmen on the run?

What are they gonna put on the table
When generations, raised on the land,
Can no longer steward its water and soil
And it's reverted to wild blowing sand?

What are they gonna put on the table??

Judith Stutzman   **For Richer or Poorer**

It was the spring of 1951 when I asked my mother "are
we going to church on Easter Sunday?"
"That will depend on the weather," she said.
"I get tired of depending on the weather" I said, "I get
tired of living on a dirt road," I complained.
We lived on a farm seven miles southwest of Beaver
Crossing, Nebraska and four miles north of Cordova, Nebraska.
In those days roads were only graveled for the rural mail routes.
We had to walk ¼ mile to the corner to get our mail. To get out
to go to town it was out of the way to go on all graveled roads.
My father and mother were farmers. They tried very hard to
201

provide a good life for my brother and me. They rented 160 acres and work was hard. I remember my dad scooping off loads of corn or wheat by hand because he did not have a grain auger. My mother worked hard also, milking seven or eight head of cows twice a day by hand. I remember how happy she was when they got our first milking machine! She always did all of the milking and dad did all of the other chores. She always used to say, "it's easier for me to do the milking instead of feeding the animals because of my 'little leg'." Her 'little leg' was caused by polio when she was nine years old. She never let it slow her down though, and only walked with a slight limp. "You know," said mom, "if it rains we cannot get to town because the roads will be too muddy."

"I'm never living on a farm when I grow up," I said. "I'm never feeding hogs or milking cows. I'm going to live in the city in a beautiful apartment and have beautiful clothes to wear. If I want to go to church, I won't have to worry about the weather.

"Well I hope you do have an easier life than I do," mom replied, "but we are doing pretty good, considering what your dad and I started out with. The farm is a peaceful life, and good place for you and your brother to grow up."

In the fall of 1964, my husband, Don, and I were driving back to Milford, Nebraska from a visit at his parent's farm. Our six-month-old son, Craig, was sitting on my lap. Don said, "Dad asked me to think about something. He wondered if we would like to move to the farm in the spring and take over the farming."

"What?" I said, very surprised. "What did you tell him?"

"I told him we would think about it," he said.

"Why?" I asked, "We talked about this before we got married and you said you never really wanted to farm."

"I know I did" Don replied, "but I've changed my way of thinking, and I think it would be a good move for us. We could do better than we are now, and it would be a good place to raise a family." Immediately my mind went back to my mom and how hard she had to work.

After some deliberation, we moved to the farm, 3 ½ miles east of Beaver Crossing in March of 1964. We watched the final Class D State Basketball championship game on TV that night. Beaver Crossing took the championship title.

The following nineteen years were full of good times and bad times. Fortunately, the good far outweighs the bad. Over the years we changed the milking cow/calf operation to a hog operation. Our first irrigation well was put down in 1966. At

202

our peak, we farmed 1,100 acres. We added two more sons to our family, Tom, in 1967 and Kirk in 1970. The 70's were very good.

The whole family worked on the farm. When it came time to irrigate, Craig and Tom laid the pipe while Kirk drove the tractor with the pipe trailer. The whole family walked acres and acres of soybeans to rid them of any noxious weeds. At harvest time each of us had a job. Don operated the combine while the rest of us operated the grain truck, gravity wagon, and unloaded at the grain bin. The hog operation went well, too. We had a total confinement-finishing house for 360 feeder pigs. We also raised brood sows. When the oldest was in sports, the next in line was expected to do the chores. The two younger boys made a good team when their brother was absent. The boys loved growing up on the farm. They had go-carts to race in the summer and a three wheeled all terrain vehicle to ride in the winter and a sled to pull behind it. The barn was always a fun place to play as well. The whole family attended 4-H meetings and after the lessons a big lunch was served and all of the children would go out and play games such as "King of the Hill."

Then tough times hit farm operations across the nation. In 1980 the market prices took a turn for the worse, and in 1981 we lost money at harvest time. Things went downhill very fast. To add to our misery, the feeder pigs picked up a disease from new bought pigs added to the bunch. It took them 40% longer to reach market weight. Needless to say, that added to the cost of the whole hog operation. I remember as clearly as though it was yesterday. It was the first week of November 1983 when Don came home from a visit to the bank. "They want us to have a farm sale," he said.

"What? " I was shocked. "I know we've had a little trouble, but they will surely give us some more time to work this out." Tears started to stream down his face, and I knew things had gotten worse than I thought possible.

Craig was a sophomore at the University of Nebraska at Lincoln, majoring in agriculture. His main plan was to graduate from college and return home to farm. Tom was a junior at Centennial High School and also planned to farm. Plans were regularly discussed about the fourth generation of Stutzmans were going to take over.

"We will both get jobs in town," I said. I was not employed out of the home at that time, as I was helping to take up the slack of the boys being busy in school. I had earned extra income for us as a hairdresser for several years. "We can't make enough money, fast enough," Don said, "the high interest rate added to poor grain prices is just eating us alive." I felt like we were spiraling down into a dark hole, fast. All of a sudden the bankers we had trusted and thought our friends became our adversaries. I felt like we were in a melodrama We were the fair maidens who could not pay the rent, and the bankers were the villain.

It was a terribly long winter. Each time Don would explore another possibility to refinance, it would fall through. He would be depressed and dejected. His self worth was deteriorating fast. I would lose patience and become irritable and cranky. I was growing bitterer as time went by. Consequently, we had many arguments, not just with each other, but also with our sons. Kirk, being only in Junior High, witnessed this, and I could see him becoming bitter also.

In March, 1984, we had our farm sale. This was probably the worst day of our lives. To watch people drive off with our farm equipment that we had worked so hard to acquire, was almost more torture than I can explain.

In 1985, one week after Tom graduated from high school, we packed up three generations of belongings and moved out of the house. The farm ground had been sold the previous year, and we were allowed to live in the house until that time. It probably was just as good to move rather than watch others farm the ground and use the grain bins.

Our lives have taken many turns these past fifteen years. We blame the loss for many of the difficulties the boys have been through and failed marriages, financial problems, and personality changes from eagerness to try new things to bitterness and apathy towards others. Don and I had to struggle with our marriage. He battled severe depression. I had little sympathy for him and would become argumentative and tired of struggling.

Don also had a liver transplant in 1994. The doctors told us stress could have escalated the health problems.

We do praise God once again. Our family has survived and is going strong! Things will never be the same again. We know we lover each other are thankful for that. Time spent at the University Medical Center during the liver transplant brought us to a new closeness.

Craig is in the Army; he is married and has two beautiful children. Tom is making and selling hunting equipment; he is back living with us, and we are helping to raise his wonderful daughter. Kirk manages a furniture business and does other ventures. He is married and also has two great children. Don and I are employed at Southeast

Community College at Milford in the Physical Plant.

If it weren't for God, family, and caring friends, we would never have survived. One does wonder why we have to go through some of the things we go through. The Bible tells us that someday when we get to Heaven the reasons will be evident. I guess that until that day comes we have to trust that tomorrow will be taken care of.

Jim Reese   Nightfall after the Banker Stops at the Place

Ronald T.
Select Sire and Proprietor, going on
Thirty-five years.

Ronald T.
Pot bellied
And bald, suspenders holding up what's left
Of his patched up jeans,
Drying the sweat from his face and
Howling at the wind for no apparent reason
We can figure except
Because.

"Stubborn! Just too damn Stubborn!
I know I am.
Won't quit milking and can't.
You expect me to give this all up,
Move to town and start watching the grass grow with Verla?
I ain't ready to be bought and sold—caught in life's grind,
Like some big auction."

Nightfall.
Ronald T.
With a rusted nail stuck in the sole of his work boot
Marking it's own inimitable brand,
Is at the cooler for two more beers.
One for his shirt pocket and the other
Held tight to center of his chest.
He sits back down to watch the moon fill itself,
Like he always does.

"George," he says.
'Cause he's decided on calling me George tonight.

"When it's all said and done

And they come to schmooze
And grease and pave the hardpan over
With some new greed-head's cockamamie scheme,
When they come to repossess the 3020,
It may just be the wind left, to echo
Our call."

Between the Lines

Dale-Marie Bryan   Dad's Dirt

Charlie was right, Ellen thought, as she pulled into the parking space at the nursing home. It probably had been crazy. When she should have been cleaning house or catching up on bookwork, she had dug up a bucket of the rich soil from their best bottom ground. And all for a man that couldn't even remember her name. Why, three weeks before, they had found Dad casually filling the tub in his bathroom at the home with "water for the cows."

"Gotta' make sure the tank's full," he had told Charlie, pushing back the sweat-stained seed cap he still insisted on wearing and wiping his face with a red bandana handkerchief. "Dang drought's gonna' put us outta' business."

"Right, Pop," Charlie had answered, looking outside at the rain that streaked down the window for the fourth day in a row.

As Dad had shuffled across the room that day, Ellen recalled thinking of the first time they'd met Charlie's graying look-alike jumping down from the tractor, striding toward her, removing oil-stained gloves to take her hand in his work-toughened one. From the first, he had made her feel welcome, even when the rest of the family questioned Charlie's wisdom in marrying a city girl. Hard to believe that had been nearly twenty-five years ago.

Sad, what Alzheimer's did to a person, Ellen thought. Charlie's mom had had it better, dying suddenly in her garden of a heart attack. It had been a year after that they noticed Dad was having trouble. He had driven the tractor to the Andrew's place five miles south and forgotten how to get home. Then some neighbors found him wandering down the road in his pajamas. Finally, he'd arrived on their doorstep carrying a suitcase and wearing only his boxers and a necktie. "Came to say goodbye," he said. "Me and Mom are off to Alaska. Feel sorry for those people. Growing season is so short."

As the child who lived closest, it had fallen to Charlie to make the decision that a home was the safest alternative. It was a pretty nice place and, surprisingly, Dad hadn't fussed much about going. The window of his room looked out over a wheat field and the staff provided activities all day long to keep the residents occupied.

"Won't do those arts and crafts, though," Dad had

informed them. "These hands weren't made to cut and paste."
So he'd spent those first few weeks sitting at the table in front of
the window, gazing out.

They had brought a few things to make his room more
homey: family pictures, plants, a cozy lamp made from an old
canning jar filled with wheat kernels, his small-scale tractor
collection. After that, when they visited, he'd be rearranging the
toy tractors and implements on the shelf or spritzing the plants
with the spray bottle Ellen had provided.

Then she'd had the idea about the dirt. "That's nuts,"
Charlie had said. "He'll just make a mess of it."

"Maybe," Ellen replied. "But he might enjoy driving his
tractors around in it. The man needs something more to do.
After all, he worked the ground for sixty years. I don't think he
can give it up just like that."

So, last week, with Charlie looking on dubiously, she
had brought Dad the dirt. As she covered the table with
newspapers, emptying the bucket into a large, flat pan, Dad had
watched from across the room.

"Who's the woman?" he asked.

"Ellen, Pop. You remember her. We've been married
almost twenty-five years."

The old man frowned at her quizzically before turning
back to Charlie. "'Bout time to cut that wheat?"

"We haven't planted it yet, Pop. Should start this week.
Ellen will work ahead of me like she did last year. We'll start on
Martin's Hill."

"Ground's poor up there," Pop said. "Always thought
Old Man Martin should turn it back to pasture. Fertilized that
place but never did yield like it should. Creek bottom. Now
there's good ground. Got ninety bushel wheat off there one
year. Course the rain came just right."

And the next day, she and Charlie had begun drilling the
wheat. It was her job to loosen the soil and kill the weeds with
the tractor ahead of him while he planted the wheat with the
other one behind.

A minor breakdown with her tractor today had given
Ellen a chance to run to town. "Might as well buy groceries and
visit Pop while I'm fixing this," Charlie had said. "Won't get a
chance for awhile after I get this repaired."

As Ellen prepared to open Dad's door, she hoped she
wouldn't frighten him, a strange woman coming to visit. After
all, Charlie wasn't with her to explain who she was.

Dad was sitting at his table when she entered, but he
stood up excitedly when he saw her.

"Look," he said, gesturing toward the table. "Look what's happening."

In the pan of dirt, green, hair-like nubs poked up in tiny rows. The toy tractor and implement used to make them were still parked beside the pan. The lamp made from the jar which had once contained wheat seed lay dismantled under the table on the floor.

When Ellen looked up, Dad's eyes were fixed on her face.

"I know you," he said softly, his smooth hand reaching over to take hers.

"Who am I, Dad?" Ellen whispered, closing her eyes, expecting him to say her name at last.

"You're the one who brought the dirt."

Ellen opened her eyes and looked into his smiling face. Sunlight streaming in from the window highlighted his wrinkles, but something about the innocence of his smile made her think of the little boy he'd once been.

"That's right, Dad," she said, squeezing his hand. "That's exactly who I am."

And then, still smiling, the old man turned from her, picked up the spray bottle, and began to irrigate his crop.

Jack Ostergard   Cattle Feeder Philosophy

This old cattle feeder died and made his way to heaven's gate.
On the way he checked out the markets, and this caused him to be late.
He met St. Peter out in front, checking the admissions.
St. Peter said, "I've some bad news, you might not care to listen."

"Seems our quota's full this month, we've had a rash of cattle feeders
And I don't have an empty pen," said the official greeter.
"But you can wait in purgatory until we add some space.
Small price to pay for feeding cattle, you know you're saved by grace?"

The cattle feeder kicked a chip over by the Pearly Gate
And chastised himself a bit for getting there too late.
Then he noticed a microphone hanging on the post
"Is that hooked up all over heaven?" he asked his would-be host.

"Certainly," St. Peter said, "Would you like to try it out?"
So the cattle feeder grabbed it and gave a shout.
"Attention cattle feeders, got some news I'd like to tell,
The latest rumor quotes fat's at a buck a pound in Hell."

What a rush of cattle feeders, out that gate in one great bound.
They ran over the old feeder, knocked St. Peter to the ground.
They both got up, brushed off the dirt, St. Peter looked about
And said, "You might as well come in, we've room now there's
no doubt."

Now the feeder scratched his head a bit and paused to
contemplate.
He could see he had a second chance and wouldn't have to
wait.
But temptation overcame him and he said, "Though I'm
devout—
If it's all the same to you, Pete, think I'll check that rumor out."

Marjorie Saiser   Otto

who stood at the edge of family pictures
the moving shade of the oak tree
blotching his face
whose hands held his gray felt hat
behind him, rolling the brim
toward the sweat band
whose brown suit grew
season by season too large
each harvest inching farther down
on his wrists toward the large nubs
of his knuckles

whose skin on his high cheekbones
thin as a page of Isaiah
shone in the light from the window
as they figured God's Acre
on the tablecloth
whose voice caught at the start of
his sentences like a plow
settling into a furrow
who did not sing in church
his very clean hands folded over his knees

210

who on summer afternoons
poured cold coffee into his white cup
who said he liked it

who owned a bed in his brother's farmhouse
(no flop-ear brown dog running to the gate
ever known as Otto's
no pipe
no International
no bad jokes
no twenty-two
no girl as far as anybody said
no child of his crying or sleeping
on the second floor in the dark house)

who before reaching up for his hat
on the nail above the separator
would stand
mornings
at the screen door
his hands in his back pockets

Shannon Dyer   Plato's Republic

   A friend of mine from Denver recently made reference to
me and my neighbors here in the Sandhills as being members
of the International Order of Hicks and Bumpkins. Far from
being offended, I am proud to be labeled a hick. For me, it
means I don't have to be up on the latest chic. I'm not required
to pay attention to the trends to keep from embarrassing myself
in the right company. A hick isn't bound by societal
constraints, doesn't have to worry that the dull colors of last fall
are to be replaced with brights this year, that black is out,
brown is in.
   I show my hickness visiting a Starbucks. It seems
everyone in front of me can rattle off their order something like,
"I'll have, a tall skim almond mocha double shot without
whipped cream." But when my turn comes, I ask, "What's the
difference between a cappuccino and a latte?" Audible sighs go
around the shop and the less hickish roll their eyes and nod
knowingly to each other. "Of course, we knew she was a hick
by the black sweater and ridiculously narrow pants legs."
   But some folks equate hickness with ignorance. Now
that's a mistake. A few days ago I was interrupted from reading
an e-mail from my neighbor citing statute and verse of a

legislative bill and how it would impact our small school. A regular customer stopped into the feed store to buy a few bags of grain for his horse. As I wrote up the invoice, we chatted about how busy everyone seems to be these days.

He smiled and tucked the ticket into his shirt pocket. "I was reading Plato's Republic the other day. Socrates was visiting with his mentor -- I can't think of his name just now. But his mentor said, 'Isn't it amazing how many masters we have in our younger days? So many things that call the shots in our lives. We feel we have to serve all these masters: money, success, clean house, serving on committees and doing our time in the concession stand.'"

I stared at him, still stuck on the idea of a regular guy flipping through Plato's works just for fun.

He shook his head. "How many hours do we spend chasing the things that don't matter instead of filling our lives with things that bring us joy?"

Well now, he had a point. A darned good point. A point debated by the world's classic philosophers. Wow. In our little yokel feed store, a Sandhiller was discussing Plato.

He followed me out to the warehouse and helped me load his grain while we chatted about the real meaning of life. Not long after that, a long-time rancher stopped in. Maybe in his younger days he traveled a bit, I don't know. But now, he doesn't like to leave home longer than it takes to get a load of block salt, a bottle of good whiskey, and a loaf of bread. I look forward to his trips to town because no matter what the topic of the day is, he's well versed and ready.

When I worked on a novel set on the Oregon Trail, he knew dates and locations off the top of his head. My next project involved the history of Jerusalem, including Judaism, Islam, and Christianity. Guess what? Without pause, he spouted when Mohammed lived and died and several key events in the vitriolic saga of that city. He's an avid reader and remembers everything.

He has strong, educated opinions on NAFTA, the presidential candidates, IBP's latest insult to ranchers, Hillary's hair, and the conflict in Kosovo.

Hicks? Sure we are. We have manure on our boots, wear Wranglers to even weddings and funerals, eat lots of red meat, and perhaps put "a pinch between our cheek and gum."

But don't come to the Sandhills expecting uncultured ignoramuses. The average rancher knows physiology, entomology, anatomy, biology, geography, the commodities markets, foreign policy, ethics, law, and maybe even a bit about literature, history, and anthropology.

     Go ahead and list me in the International Order of Hicks and Bumpkins. I'll be in good company.

Charles Fort The Poem Found in His Back Pocket at the End of the Plains

They lifted his belongings:
a bundle on a willow stick
and a poem about his father
on a fencepost in swimming trunks,
the ocean rising on the horizon.
His son boarded a freight train
from the Chicago rail yard
to Lincoln with its serpent eye
collapsing into the badlands
winding through the Pine Ridge
as he watched the lightning
leave his father's flared shadow,
a constellation across the plains.
Was this how the poem
skimmed the Platte River,
flattened and ankle deep
driven into the poisoned well,
how it embraced half the world
to the brown and marbled sky?

Jill Burkey   Between the Lines

I'd climb up into Dad's charcoal
pickup and make a place to sit
among ear protectors, sweat shirts,
oil filters and fan belts,
so that my cowboy boots barely
skim the dust covered floor mat.
Together, me and Dad would bounce over
cattle trails or gopher holes
where I learned the basics.
"If farmers fail, grass will grow on city streets"
"Manure has the smell of money"
"When you get a million, keep it"
And in those innocent, dust-filled afternoons,
I learned just what being a Colwell meant.

When he'd pick me up from the gym, sweaty and tired,
my second coach would engrain in my head the two rules
of survival on the court.
"Use your elbows"
"Protect the baseline"
And always he'd drop me off at the game with,
"Give 'em hell"
So for Christmas that year I put a frame around
his moment in time, hoping I'd have one just as good.

Before going out on the town, I'd hear his voice echo in my
mind,
"Everything you've done, I've already thought of," and
"If you're going to get in trouble, just don't get caught"
But I did anyway, and for the same thing he did,
which somehow made us both more human.

Across the dinner table, not many
years left at home now, I'd hear,
"To strive for perfection leads to paralysis"
"There's lots of room at the top"
"Choose your battles carefully"
And when I'd get frustrated with life
in rural Nebraska, he'd teasingly say,
"Why don't you just grow up and move away?"
And I did.

Now he greets me at the door, smiling
"I guess home is where they have to let you back in"
And I want to find my cowboy boots,
or shoot some hoops, but I don't;
I talk about politics and Shakespeare.
And as I leave my visit and my
childhood behind, he says,
"I'm glad you got to see me again"

I am too, Dad.

Gerald Lockhart   The First Look at the Other Side

The train came into our town about 4:00 to 4:30
everyday, and we were usually out of school by the time it
came huffing into town. School in those days ran from
9:00 in the morning until 4:00 in the afternoon. It was a
nice spring day, and we were in school wishing we could

do something else, when at about 2:00, we heard this train whistle. Well, we knew right away something different was going on and thought up all kinds of excuses, from sharpening pencils to going to the outside toilet, so we could look out the window—anything to see what was going on because a thing like a train that time of day had never happened before. What we saw was an engine much larger than what usually came in and it had 36 carloads of Long Horn cattle. The McCarty ranch about 40 miles up the river north of town had gone to Texas and bought the cattle, so the railroad ran a special train with just the cattle cars and the caboose and crew from Texas, as well as McCarty's men, to care for the cattle on the way.

Well, the minute school let out we boys made a beeline for the stockyards--we weren't going to miss out on what was going on. When we got there, the train was on the siding at the stockyards and the men were busy unloading the cattle. We got around on the other side of the yards and by climbing up on the fence, had a good view of the whole thing. Suddenly, as the last cattle came out of the car, we saw something we had never seen before. It was a black man who had come along to help with the cattle. He was a hired hand of the ranch where they had bought the cattle. As far as I know, that was the first black person I had ever seen. We had seen pictures in books, but to see one alive and working was a real surprise. Well, we weren't interested in watching anything else for awhile. He didn't pay any attention to us and went on about his work, as if we didn't exist. By this time, we had sort of tired of the excitement and began to think about suppertime, and they had started putting some cattle in the yard where we were perched on the fence. About that time, the section boss came along and told us we better get down. He was afraid one of us might fall off the fence and those cattle were wild. That sharpened our appetites a little more, so we headed home. We decided that we'd meet in our backyard after supper and play basketball. Dad had the blacksmith shop that sat on the corner and had built a new house a few feet west of it. Being new, it was one of the few houses in town, at that time, that had an outside light on the back. We boys wanted to take advantage of the light, so we rigged us up a basketball hoop on the back of the house.

Our place was about 3 blocks from the stockyards,

215

on the street that went up to the main part of town, which was not quite 2 blocks. We had a game of basketball going full blast and were having a great time. By this time, the men had gotten the cattle unloaded, watered, and hayed for the night and it had gotten dark. As I said, we were having a good game and the ball got away from us and rolled out into the edge of the light. I had gone after it, like a dog after a bone, and when I picked it up, I looked up and there stood the black man. He must have been at least 9 feet tall. To say I was scared would be putting it mildly. I looked at him and glanced toward the house and my good friend, Earl, was already going around the corner of the blacksmith shop. I can see the sand flying up from his feet yet. He had suddenly decided he should go home. If we would have had a stopwatch on him, I think he would have set the record for the 100 yard dash. My 2 brothers and 3 or 4 other kids who were there, were all trying to get in the back door at the same time. It looked like a bunch of calves all trying to get through the door at once.

I looked back up at the black man and he said, "can you all tell me how to get up to the hotel?" My tongue didn't work very good, but I managed to mumble to him to go on up the street to the main street, take a right and he would see it. He thanked me very nicely and went on his way. By that time, my feet came loose from the ground and I started to walk to the house. I got to the back door and looked in and my standby buddies were peeking around the doorway from the dining room, saying "is he gone, is he gone?" They thought I was awful brave to stay there and give the man directions, but what they didn't know was that my feet had froze to the ground like I was standing in cement. Of course, I didn't let them know that. What they don't know won't hurt them. I sure poured it on them about what good standby buddies they had been. Earl didn't bother to come back that night, and anyway, that kind of put a stop to the ballgame for that night. My folks had been to a church meeting while all this was going on, so when we told them about it, they had a good laugh too.

Joan Hoffman   **Smithy**

I would soon forget
how to mark time

if I could not
look forward to
or remember summer.

It is the shape of things for me:
that quick run of days,
the flash of brighter light,
the fixed fire of the
seasonal forge.

My childhood made the case of
defining and refining
the meaning of warm and free.
There was nothing secretive
nor modest about July or August,
no trace of hesitancy,
not a blessed thing withheld
in that wild dance
with the short shadows.

(October 1999)

Lora Lunzmann Black   The Messenger

I was twelve that Memorial Day. I was never one to want
to stay indoors and do housework; I always enjoyed being
outdoors. Give me animal chores, field chores, but don't make
me do the dishes and clean! On this particular day, Mom was
outside taking care of many of her outdoor duties, and today it
was gardening. It was a perfect beginning to summer, sunny
and warm, perfect haying weather, as Dad would say. You
could hear the distant churn of the baler up on the hill. I had
gone into the house for a drink of water, when the phone rang.
"Hello" (I was a great conversationalist) "No, Mom's
outside somewhere". It was my Aunt Bertha: something in her
voice wasn't right. I knew I'd better get Mom. I put the phone
down, and I took off outside. She wasn't in the strawberry
patch. I shouted out "Mom?" But no one answered. She must
be down the hill in the potato garden. By this time, I was
getting a little worried. Something about Aunt Bertha's voice.
The uneasy feeling was beginning to nag at me. And now I can't
find Mom. Where is she? The worry made me hasten my steps.
"Mom......... Mom??"" I couldn't find her. A feeling of dread
came over me. I had to go back in the house and answer that
phone. I ran all the way back up the hill.

"I couldn't find Mom, Aunt Bertha." There was a pause. I waited, breathing hard from my run.

"Would you tell your folks that Uncle Walt passed away?"

I don't remember what I said after that. I replaced the receiver, and for what seemed like an eternity I stood as if glued to that spot. I still didn't see Mom from the kitchen window. Where, oh where was she? But I knew I had to deliver this message, no matter how unbelievably tragic it was. How dare she not be around, and now I have this awful news. I'm just a kid, I don't want to know this, much less believe it. What was I going to do when I found Mom? How can I tell her that her 50 year old brother just died? We just saw him the day before and he was the picture of health. Death just happens to old people and other families. It can't happen to someone we love. I better find Dad. He's way up in the field, but he needs to know. Maybe he knows where Mom is, and he can tell her better than I can.

Off I ran. In the distance, I could tell they were working hard at loading hay. The Allis ÄChalmers WD40 and hayrack moved slowly forward as Dad and his brothers tossed the square bales up on the rack. Just what was I going to say? I've never interrupted the farm work before. Oh please let this be an awful dream. I don't want to do this.

The day had started out to be one of such promise. Sunny, warm, breezy. Perfect for drying the hay, Dad had said. People don't die on perfect days. People I know can't die.

Then suddenly, I was there. I stood waiting as the tractor and rack came to a standstill. I don't think I was crying, but they seemed to know I must need something important to stop work.

"Aunt Bertha just called and said Uncle Walt had passed away, and I can't find Mom," I blurted out. There, I had said it. I remember my Uncle Harold repeating it in disbelief. I wanted to say, I'm not lying, it's true. Dad had jumped off the rack and was on his way to find Mom.

I just wanted to disappear off the face of the earth. I can't handle grown-up things like this. I just want this to be over. I wanted it to be all a bad dream.

I wandered down to my tree house by the chicken coop. My place of solace. Maybe if I stay here long enough this, will all go away. Then I can pretend that the phone call had never happened.

"Lora!?"

I'd never heard my Mom call my name like that before.

218

There was a strained, high-pitched call, almost something haunting about it. I had to answer. I couldn't stay in my tree house the rest of my life.

I jumped out of the box elder tree and ran toward the sound of the strained voice. I saw my Mom as she rounded the chicken house corner with Dad. Oh, do I have to see her? She had never looked old before. But suddenly, she had aged 20 years. She was crying and her face was all contorted.

"Are you sure she said Uncle Walt? You know there are two men with that same name in this county. It can't be my brother Walt."

I felt so helpless. She wants so much to believe that I misunderstood, that maybe I was just playing a cruel joke and was lying. I wanted so much to say all those things. But all I said was "Aunt Bertha said Uncle Walt passed away."

With that final admission, she knew it was true. Her brother was dead. Dad reached and held Mom who sort of crumpled in his arms. He led her away sobbing uncontrollably. As I watched them stumble away, I felt like such a bad person. I had caused my Mom such grief. All I knew was that I didn't want to be around death ever again. I'm just a kid. What do I know? Leave me alone to my imagination and play. My world didn't allow for grief and pain.

I know that Mom and Dad probably went in to town that day to be with the family. I'm not sure what I did after that. My brother and I probably had to go down to my other grandparents for supper. I honestly don't remember the sun shining anymore that day either. Memorial Day would always bear the scars of that day, the pain, the loss. Maybe that was the day I started to grow up. Never again could I go up in my tree house and gain that sense of comfort and peace of perfect childhood. It was gone forever. Gone that Memorial Day, in 1965.

Jim Reese   Cattle Call

for Larry Holland 1937-1999

"The cattle are prowling, the coyotes are howling,
way out where the dogies bawl.
Their spurs are a jingling, the cowboy is singing,
This lonesome cattle call."

I
Haven't seen
A real cowboy

219

For some time now.

Barbed wire barriers
Have been replaced
With electricity.
Instead of horses
They've got
Three wheelers,
And the crack
Of a whip
And a simple
"Yah! Yah!"
Gone to
The firing
Of some kinda'
Taser gun
And a "Run you son of a bitch,
Run!"

David Meyer   My Uncle Paul

Because of a car wreck in the prime of his life some never knew
my Uncle Paul, and that would have been too bad for me and
for you because my Uncle Paul was a very good Man.

When growing up on the farm only ½ mile separated me from
my Uncle Paul. I saw him quite often and knew him quite well,
and that was lucky for me because as you all know my Uncle
Paul was a very good Man.

When I was in 3rd grade and I broke my arm, my parents were
out of town so I felt real down. I was sitting at school
wondering what to do when who should drive up but my Uncle
Paul. Well I was elated but not too surprised because when it
came to caring for me my Uncle Paul was a very good Man

I remember when I was just four years older than eight my
Uncle Paul tried to teach me how to cultivate. Well as you might
guess I was no good but he kept on trying, which just went to
show that My Uncle Paul could be a very patient man.

When I was growing up and my older cousins led me astray, I
remember the day we
All stood against the wall getting a lecture from my Uncle Paul.
Later in life I figured it out He wasn't being nasty or mean or

just spouting off. He was just doing his best to teach us all right from wrong, just doing what all parents should and my Uncle Paul he was a good man

When I went to college off on my own, I remember my phone calls to my Uncle Paul. They would all end the same and they sounded like this.. Keep in touch he would say, because that's what is important. I would reply OK without really knowing why,
because I didn't know then that my Uncle Paul was a very wise Man.

After college I remember my visits with my Uncle Paul, I quickly found out when talking about his grandkids and all that they've done, I had better have more than just a quick minute or two, or even more than three because when it came to his Grandkids My Uncle Paul was a very, very proud man.

Talking about Grandkids, this I could see, but I found it odd he would always talk about relatives that I had hardly ever seen. But, later in life I figured it out, my Uncle Paul knew what most people do not. Politics, football or not even the weather are not things that truly matter. But what is A number 1 top of the list is Family, Family and of course Family. You see my Uncle Paul knew this because he was a very wise man.

Later in life he taught me some more, I learned from him that life is not fair, bad things do happen to good people; although, I still don't know quite why because as you know my Uncle Paul was a very good Man.

But my Uncle Paul taught one last lesson. When bad things happen, you still have two choices, you can sit there and take it and let it consume you or take it head on and keep fighting to do all the things that really do matter to you. As you all know my Uncle Paul he choose the latter, with the help of his wife who was always beside him, he went more places than most healthy men do, Because my Uncle Paul he was a wise and strong man.

I still have his memories, this much is true, but I will still miss him greatly because
My Uncle Paul was a very good man.

But we all must remember, he went to church and he talked to

God because My Uncle Paul he was a very Christian Man.

And now he is in heaven and they are happy to have him because up there they knew all along, from day number one, that my Uncle Paul is a very great man.

Dorothy Boettner   The First Homesteader in Northern Saunders County

On the banks of Danish Langeland Island, just south of Copenhagen and very near the northern shore of Germany, a handsome young Danish lad was staring out to sea. He was pondering a decision he must make very soon—a decision that could and would change his life forever.

On his next birthday he would be of age to be targeted for conscription in the army. He didn't want that or the way it would direct his life. He loved his native Denmark but he wanted to plant and reap and farm like his father and grandfather.

There was only one way to escape serving in the army and that was to flee to America—"the land of the free." But that would mean leaving his parents, his brothers and his beloved land and the North Sea. And he loved his church and warm thoughts came to his mind of the pretty little girl, Christine, who sometimes sat beside him there. Could he leave all this, forever?

Right now there was a ship in the Copenhagen harbor ready any day to sail for America. If he left he promised his mother he would write often and he'd try to come back to visit when he made a lot of money.

When the ship sailed the following week, that young man, Julius Christensen, was on board; so were a couple of other Danish boys from the area.

The passage was a good one and soon they saw the Statue of Liberty on the horizon and they arrived at Ellis Island. They dropped anchor and, as all ships carrying foreign immigrants were required to do, they were quarantined for several weeks for health checks. But the three Danish boys couldn't wait—when the officers weren't looking they jumped overboard and swam to shore. They soon found the "Hiring Agency" they had been told about and started sorting out the best jobs that were offered to them. They finally chose to sign a three-year contract with a logging company in Wisconsin. It offered to pay the best salary; so lumberjacks they were to become! The bosses were tough and crude. The traveling was primitive and uncomfortable and took forever, it seemed. Julius tried hard to push away the question, "Where is this Wisconsin?" Finally, they came to a logging camp in a wilderness of beautiful trees. It was far, far from any settlement but it was next to the eastern shoreline of Lake Michigan and it was cold! Their quarters were bare and simple but the food was good and nourishing. The seasoned lumberjacks were rough and noisy and bossy and not very kind. But the Scandinavian boys got along with them real well.

For three long years they worked from early morning to late at night seven days a week. All this time they never saw any civilization or hardly any other people. They proved their worth, though, for they were excellent workers and they grew strong and rugged. They felled trees and loaded them on to boats for transport to Chicago. Each time a ship left, Julius had a letter to home ready to send with them.

Julius kept accurate count of their days and when the three years were up the company settled with them and they got their money, but the bosses would not let them go on the ship that was ready to sail the next morning because they said that Julius' count was not accurate and they must put in one more week of work and then go on with the next ship.

But after everyone was asleep that night, Julius and the other two jumped in the lake and swam out to the boat; they crept on and hid themselves among the logs. But the next morning as they were sailing halfway down the Lake a terrible storm came up and the logs began to shift and roll. To save themselves from injury or death, they crawled out of their hiding place among the logs and found the crew sick and stretched out limp and quite useless to steer the ship, The three boys, all excellent sailors on much rougher voyages in the North Sea, righted the ship, latched down the loose logs and sailed the boat into Chicago. But again they immediately had to jump overboard and swim to safety on the Chicago shore. They found many places that wanted to hire them. Julius hired on at the U.P. Railroad. He wanted to get down to the Nebraska he'd heard about. He wanted to get hold of some land. He wanted so desperately to farm. But he needed more money and the U.P. paid well.

He worked south and west along the line, he helped build railroad bridges crisscrossing heavy logs as bridge foundations. When he reached Omaha, he heard some startling news that a Chris Christensen was the livery stable manager in Fremont, Nebraska, which was close by Omaha. Could that be his younger brother, Chris? Could he have fled to America to avoid the draft? He kept on with the job awhile longer to earn enough cash to pay down on some land. He wanted a farm, and the soil and plantings and prairie looked so lush in this eastern Nebraska place.

One night while playing cards he beat his opponent so badly that the man owed him $100. However, he didn't have any money so Julius finally settled for a piece of paper that the man told him was worth $80. He said the paper was an application for a homestead—free land, he said. Now Julius had never heard of the Homestead Act of 1862 or of President Lincoln or even much about the Civil War that had just ended a few years earlier. But he took the paper, not that he thought it was worth much, but he couldn't get money out of the guy anyway, and maybe it was better than nothing. He stored it with his meager belongings.

At Fremont he looked up the livery stable and to his everlasting joy and astonishment there was his brother Chris! Chris was dumbfounded to see him—he hardly recognized him because the boy he remembered had matured into a hearty, strong man. Chris and Julius' family had thought Julius was dead, as they had not heard from him for well over three ears. Julius then realized the lumberjacks had never mailed his letters.

Julius wrote immediately to his parents and asked about the girl, Christine. Soon he knew that all was well in Langeland and that Christine had blossomed into a 19-year-old beauty. Now he knew just what he wanted. He wanted to buy some farm land somewhere around Fremont and build a house of sorts and have a family. He showed Chris the slip of paper he had gotten as a gambling debt and Chris shouted for joy! That paper was the first step towards getting a free homestead—80 acres free after living on it for five years! Julius was astounded and wanted to know all about it. He would start homestead proceedings right away. He looked around for a place on which to file a claim. It seemed like most of the land close to Fremont in Dodge County on the north side of the Platte River was gobbled up. So why not go south of the river? No one had risked that yet as everyone said that was Pawnee Indian Territory, and the Indians might become hostile. But that didn't seem to bother Julius. Soon he laid claim to an 80 acre tract of virgin prairie about five miles south of the river on the trail that connected Lincoln and Wahoo to the Lee ferry boat landing on the bluff across from Fremont.

Soon Julius had a small two-room house built along the

trail beside a bubbling brook. He bought a team of horses and a lumber wagon and built a crude makeshift shelter for them on the other side of the trail.

Now he was ready to write to Christine and ask her to come to Nebraska and be his bride. He wanted her to share his dream of making a life on the prairie of Nebraska.

He wrote but to his utter disappointment he received no answer. Several months passed and he still didn't get a reply. His hopes were dashed, but he contacted brother Chris who kept in touch with Christine's uncle who lived in Omaha. And to his overwhelming delight, Christine was already here in America—she was in Omaha at her Uncle and Aunt's place. She had been waiting for word from Julius but not receiving any, she came to America anyway. She had written her answer "yes" to Julius but the letter had never gotten to him.

He immediately hitched his faithful team to the wagon and started off on the little-used trail to Omaha.

When he saw Christine she was even more beautiful than he remembered. They were married right away and soon started back on the trail to his homestead. Darkness and storm overcame them and the trail became invisible so they stopped and Julius took the wagon off the running gears and made them a safe, dry spot to sleep out the night by covering them with the upside down wagon bed. The morning came sunny and bright. Julius got his bearings and they were just over a couple of hills from home. What a homecoming that was! Julius' dreams had come true.

Never was a young couple so in love and so happy. Christine fixed the little two-room house into a lovely, snug home. Together they planted a garden with an asparagus bed and flowers and some trees. The starts for these plantings came from Denmark and friends of brother Chris in Fremont.

Soon Christine found she was carrying a baby and their happiness was even more complete. Baby Andrew William was born a happy, healthy, fine boy. Julius enlarged the house and built a barn on the other side of the trail.   That was usually the practice on the prairie. All was well. The garden grew, the baby grew, and the homestead grew. In a few years their five-year settlement time would be up and they would own their homestead! What pride and joy they felt. It was to be the first homestead in northern Saunders County. The little settlement around Julius' homestead began to grow. Julius' brother Rasmus came and filed a claim for a homestead not far northeast from Julius and Christine's. Other people came, mostly Danish pioneers, many needing help to get started.

Julius and Christine always helped.

The county surveyed the area for roads that would follow section lines. That meant that the section road to the east of Julius' land would eventually be highway #77. The old trail was shut off and abandoned. The first wooden bridge farther down the river to the east replaced the ferryboat.

Rasmus moved his unfinished buildings to be on the east side of the new section road. But Julius and Christine wanted to keep their dwelling by the garden and orchard they had started. The old trail down to their place became their driveway.

As years went on Christine seemed to droop and tire easily. She discovered she was pregnant again and was having a hard time getting things done. Julius helped as much as possible and they both reasoned that the stress was due to her pregnancy. But Julius was uneasy as he could see she was going down hill fast.

1875 dawned and, joy of joy, the homestead became totally theirs. The certificate that states this, and signed by President U.S. Grant, came in the mail. A precious document, indeed. (It is now framed and hangs on granddaughter Evelyn Reid's wall.)

The new baby was born. Brother Andrew was now four years old. Christine was tired and worn out. She began to realize she had consumption (today known as TB)—that dreaded disease that was taking so many lives. The baby must have had it, too. Before 1875 was ended, both mother and baby were dead.

Julius' grief was devastating. Christine had been the very light of his life and she was gone and so, too, the new baby boy! Nothing could help Julius in his darkest hour except little Andrew's great need for him.

Julius buried mother and son side by side in a spot in the garden, which he could see from his chair by the window. For a time he went through the motions of taking care of Andrew and doing the chores and sitting by his window and grieving for his beloved wife. But after a few very hard days he got up with a purpose, bundled up Andrew and drove his team north to Fontanelle, Nebraska, where there was a community of Danish settlers. He advertised for a housekeeper that he could hire to help him raise Andrew and to keep house for him.

Mery Petersen accepted readily. She was a plump little 20-year-old lady with a happy disposition. She was a very capable housekeeper, cook, and seamstress. She did a great job with Andrew and made the little home very comfortable and happy.

Julius worked hard and when he was home he played with Andrew and sat in his chair looking out on the graves of his loved ones. He wanted the best for them and knew they should be moved to a cemetery. So he deeded a piece of land from his homestead to the northeast on the west side of the section road for a cemetery. But he wasn't ready to move his precious ones yet. Let that wait awhile.

Andrew grew and became his father's constant companion. Julius pondered about it and worried that a cemetery should be connected with a church like they were in Denmark. So again near the end of the century he deeded another parcel of land just south of the cemetery for a church. He deeded this to the little community of Danish settlers around his homestead. They had organized a church a few years ago and had been meeting in their various homes because they had no church. They were dreaming of one to build some day so it would be like the "Old Country." This generous gift of land given them by Julius was so wonderful and they were very grateful to him. They went right to work raising money and leveling off the ground. By 1900, they had a little church built just south of the cemetery. They were very proud and happy. Pastors came to offer help and the services were done in the Danish language.

Julius was a wonderful neighbor and helpmate to them all. He was a good farmer and a leader in the community. He enlarged his holdings by purchasing some Union Pacific land across the new road from the church. He was very frugal, almost "tight" some said. He had money saved. He became the "banker" for many of the struggling homesteaders. He never turned down a request for help.

Andrew grew to manhood and was faithful to the church. He became superintendent of the Sunday school and kept that job the rest of his life. He fell in love with Annie Nelson, daughter of a neighbor, and their wedding was the first performed in the new church on December 20, 1900.

Mery Petersen, a very fine lady was a staunch member of the church also and a faithful housekeeper for Julius. She was a wonderful cook and baked the very best Danish pastries around the county.

Julius remained faithful to his beautiful Christine. He kept her grave in the garden. He never could bear to move her. So that was where she was when he died in 1933 at the age of 88.

Claudia Loomis   For Sandy

He uses fencing wire,
strings it trunk to trunk four trees down.
Like a hand to a cross,
he nails it to elm bark
so she can hang
clothes in the same Nebraska wind
that burns and bleeds the
life from her face.

He "can't afford new goddam storm windas."
So she hangs
blue frames, red frames, and waits
for July hail storms
to rip silk from sweet corn,
grind sugar from beets
and doesn't cry when
nothing's left.

He "can't afford a new goddam car."
So she parks a block from the junior high
and waits for children whose
heads hang to the ground.
She drives away slowly,
so that no one sees or hears
who they are or which way
they are going.

He "can't afford a new goddam dryer."
So she hangs
clean clothes between tree trunks
that have grown over wire
strung through elm bark
and the wind dries the clothes like
the cracks in her
farm-wife face.

Ruth Baker   Untitled

I was born in 1930, in a hospital that is no longer there.
Just in time for the Great Depression. My parents, Mr. and
Mrs. Rueben Wallace, has 11 children. I was last.
The first part of my life was spent on the old home place
near Long Pine, 13 miles south on an old dirt road. But that

228

place is all under water now. It looks nothing like it did then. The last few years that I went to country school my Dad got me a Shetland pony to ride, as we lived 3 1/2 miles away. That silly thing was such a joke. He would shy me off so I would still have to walk to school. He knew that I would feed him at school, and he knew that my Dad would give him fits if he came home without me, So he would follow me onto school, far enough away so that I couldn't catch him.

Everyone walked. I can remember my Dad walking out to Buffalo Flats to work for a dollar a day. As it was 18 miles to get there, he stayed all week and came home on weekends. He did this for several years. Not long ago, a local woman gave some blankets to the museums in Ainsworth and Long Pine to honor the fact that Dad was willing to walk so far to work. they were blankets Dad used when he slept.

I had some fond memories of some of my first teachers. There were times when we couldn't get teachers that far out in the country, so I missed a lot of school. We got a teacher when I was 10 and they put me in the fifth grade. Her name was Hazel Schmidt. She kept me in at the noon hour every time she had a chance, for I still had not learned to read. We had all been convinced that I couldn't learn, but she would have none of it. She proved us all wrong. When I took my 8th grade exam I placed third in Brown County, and there were quite a few country kids who took the test. I've often thought if she hadn't gotten that school when she did, I would have been one of those illiterates we hear about on TV.

The school days were very hard, coming from such a large family. There weren't the clothes that other kids had, or anything else.

When I was eight, the folks lost the cattle to T.B. and hogs were burned because of cholera. So with no way to make a living, we spent a year with mother's uncle in Long Pine. Dad was able to get a loan so he could get started again, so we moved back to the home place. My sister, Dolly, Dad, and I were all that got moved in when the lightning struck the house and burned it to the ground. All of our clothes and most of our dishes were destroyed. We managed to save the photos, as Mama had them with her.

One of Mama's uncle gave us a house. Dad got someone from Winner, South Dakota to move it to the farm before winter set in. For the first time, I had a bedroom to myself. I even told someone that "I was glad that old house burned down, cuz this house was better". I got a real scolding for that remark. People from all over gave us clothing and dishes. So once again we were on the mend.

We were still using a horse and wagon when most people had cars. I remember one incident when I was 6-8, when having a car saved a girl's life. We went to visit some folks who had a girl my age. We had never met. She was so excited to see us coming that she cut through the horses pen and got kicked in the head by one of the horses. Her head was laid open and she was bleeding all over. I won't forget that scene as long as I live. Mamma grabbed some clean linens from the clothesline and wrapped her head up tightly while her folks drove them to the hospital. We remained friends over the years and she had a full life. She became a school teacher and lives out in California. Her name is Barbara Jean Dawd. At their anniversary party, her parents introduced my parents as "the ones who saved Barb's life".

In September my sister Dolly gave birth to Eugene. Four months later, Dolly got pneumonia and died, so Eugene became my brother. My older brother froze his ears trying to bring in the doctor. The snow was so deep and heavy-the only way to get through was with a horse. But we lost her before the doctor arrived.

To put the rest of history in order, the older kids were married, in the Army, or otherwise had homes of their own. We got to see them on holidays. My folks lost their oldest son at the age of two. They lost one of their baby girls, Laura, from crib death, when she was just a few months old. To this day, who did it, and why remains a mystery.

Getting back to me and my life...I started high school in Ainsworth as there was no one to board with in Long Pine. Half way through my freshman year my folks retired to Long Pine so I was able to finish high school there. I graduated in 1949 with a class of nine. Shortly thereafter, I married Stewart Warnke. I was 18 and he was about 20 years older than I. Our families had been neighbors. Our oldest child was born on Armistice Day. His dad said that he was going to be in the Army just like his dad and he was. Three years later we had a little girl. Our last child, a boy, came a year later. My great desire was for all three of my children to graduate in Long Pine. But they closed the school, so all had to go to Ainsworth.

Stewart had a stroke shortly after our oldest son was sent to Vietnam, so our other two children helped me care for him. He was in a wheelchair at first. His condition improved over the years, but he never did regain his health. He died a few months after we celebrated our thirty year anniversary.

My father lived clear up into his 90's. He might have

gone longer had he not broke his hip. Dad had enough money he could make loans out. He was still raising a garden to share with others well into his 80's. He was even able to walk from Ainsworth to Long Pine at that age. He sold his car so that we didn't have to tell him to. He knew he wasn't able to drive any more. Both my parents had a clear mind up to the time they passed away. I've been grateful for this, as so many can't do that.

I cared for my father in my home until he died. Then I started caring for other people in their homes. I haven't kept a real accurate count, but a good guess would be about thirty. Right now I have six. I also clean the church and walk every day. Never a dull moment!

Nebraska has been my home for all but five years, when I moved to Denver. This was where I met and married Jay Baker in 1983. He also has three children, so more are added to the Christmas Card list. My three children are still alive. My oldest living sister is 90. I have three more who are 85, 83, and 80. My adopted brother is 58 and living in Oklahoma City.

As I reflect on those 69 years I will always be grateful for the love and the work ethic we were taught. When my parents left this earth, they had enough money to be buried. They also left $2,000 for each remaining child. I am proud to say that my folks never took welfare. They managed on their own. We don't need a lot to survive.

J.V. Brummels   Dead Men's Fences

For all my children's lives I've built a herd,
and no one builds without taking, from an Indian
or some other stranger, at best from some ghost
who can only wander his land as a shade,
his herd and tribe dispersed. It seems
all my life I've mended dead men's fences.

The other day I happened on a grieving girl,
my niece's roommate. Her teacher and a classmate
held her between them, walked her across campus
toward some notion of shelter. Some stranger, hunting
a shelterbelt, found her father not far from where
I live, just the other day, hanging by his neck.

This morning on the street I happened on
my sister-in-law. She told me the story
when I'd only thought to say how lucky

231

my brother and she were, to hit a black cow
on a black night on a back highway and not be hurt.
This morning my brother's hunting used cars.

This December day is clear and warm. Heavy gloves
and chinks are some protection against rusty barbs.
Justice is a fool's theology, like predicting weather.
Last month an unpredicted blizzard blew through and took
a full tithe of the cattle. Today is a bead
in an unexpected chain of lovely December days.

I hammer home another post and move down the line.
What can I do but stretch and splice another strand?
As if a taut fence sorted anything out, or old wire
kept anything safe. As if rusty barbs sheltered not ripped
a heart hammering away in the soft December sun.

Suzanne Richards   Put the Lid on Your Nail Can

I'm going to share a gory story with you in hopes of
spreading my new cause.
It's a simple act that I know we might all slip and miss
sometimes when in a rush.
Some might consider this a ranch hazard; maybe even fines
would be issued by OSHA on some job sites. I would consider
what happened a legitimate workers comp. claim. Of course I
can't sue myself. I wish we had some sort of trauma treatment
coverage though.
The point that I am stressing is even the cause of some
divorces! This is not as drastic in my particular case, but I have
heard it is a strong pet peeve of some folks. The cause that I
am a new true believer in is to...PUT THE LID BACK ON!
If I were to make banners and picket the whole nation,
I'm sure I wouldn't be able to change everyone's habitual
forgetfulness, or slight laziness In most cases we're just too
busy to PUT THE LID BACK ON.
So I'm going to share with you a recent experience of a
lid being off, which has sent me on my mission of finding caps,
lids, covers, or tin foil, whatever I can find to tighten, seal, and
close all.
We, like many folks store our supply of nails and screws
in empty coffee cans. We used to leave the lids off for easier
viewing of what size of nails, or how many screws were left in
the can. The cans are stored on a dark shelf in the back of the
garage.

I know what you might be thinking, that I reached in the cupboard, and grabbed one of the open cans, and sliced off my fingers. No, that didn't happen. What happened was much worse.

Our cans of nails have extra room in the top of them, and quite often there will be miscellaneous items thrown in on top, or smaller cans stacked in them. So digging is essential for finding the correct size for the particular job.

On the snowy day of my mishap I just needed a few nails for a quick project outside. I searched in the dark garage as best as I could with my sunburned eyes, and I found the right size in a can that also included a little ball of string, a baggy with a couple of little screws, and another dark bag with mystery parts in it.

I grabbed a handful of nails and my hammer, and trudged out in the snow to the job site. I wanted to wear my gloves, so before I put them on I stuck a couple nails in my mouth, and put the rest in my pocket. Soon all three nails were used, and I was ready for a refill, but while I was reaching into my pocket, I had to spit out a little hair in my mouth. No big deal when you're constantly working with animals...back to work. After I used the next three nails I had a lot more hair in my mouth, 'Spit! -Spat!' Where was this hair coming from? I just washed this coat. 'Spit! – Spat!' All this spitting made holding the nails in my mouth a little difficult.

Well the job became bigger than I expected, and soon I was out of nails. I re-trudged and spat all the way back to the garage to get more nails from the OPEN CAN. I decided to bring the whole can this time. Again, I was snow-blind, but I found the right can in front, with the two baggies, and the ball of string in it. I took those extras out so they wouldn't be in the way.

I think I finally got all those hairs spat out by the time I got back to my project. I set my OPEN CAN on the ladder, and climbed up. This is where I saw the horror of all horrors. Perched in a begging position laid a dead mouse! I am not ashamed to admit how these lifeless flat forms of fur rather bother me – more so than a live mouse. Just a personal phobia.

Now this little guy had been there for quite awhile. Very dead. This is when I realized what was making me spit hair. Most of his hair had fallen off. He wasn't all flattened out; he was still kind of mushy on the top half. This gets worse; I think my digging around is what caused the oozing hole in what was left on his hide. His tail was starting to 'skelefy' (a personal dead mouse word I invented to describe how they slowly turn into skeletons).

I immediately became nauseous and queasy. Not a good state of being while on top of a ladder. I had to get a grip; I had to finish the job. But I wasn't going to look at my Decon victim each time I needed a nail. I managed with my hammer to dig him out and toss him down. The dogs didn't ease my feeling I had in my mouth when they fought to gobble it up.

Still little hairs lay all over the inside of the can like fashionable little mouse-fur coats for the nails. Obviously I didn't put any more nails in my mouth. I probably never will again. I think the event helped me get my job done faster.

After putting everything away, including finding lids for as many of the cans as I could, you can guess what I did next; brushed my teeth for about ten minutes.

I know asking you all to re-lid everything might be a big request. I just wouldn't want something this horrific, this traumatic, this hazardous, and this disgusting to happen to any of you. Maybe another simple quick tip might be to double-check your can or bag of nails before you pop some in your mouth. Even though all my cans are covered now, I still cautiously double check.

Elaine Phillips   **Things I Am Thankful for this Fall in No Particular Order**

1. Digging potatoes--What's under the dirt? Golf balls or Softballs?
2. Primary Colors--Yellow corn cascading into a red truck under a blue sky.
3. The smell of hot mouse--It means the heater works in the aforementioned red truck.
4. Return of Standard time--its easier to get quieted down and in bed with more hours of dark evening.
5. Turnips--sweet and raw. Why bother cooking them?
6. Contrasts--being chilly and then warm, or both at the same time.
7. Halloween--the return of make believe for everybody and a legitimate excuse to buy lots of candy. Did I really need all this for just for trick or treaters? Yeah, I did.
8. Deep Freeze and microwave--Frozen food becomes hot and tasty supper in minutes for the harvest crew.
9. My mother-in-law--Taking on chauffeuring duty.
10. Always pleasant and helpful people working at the elevators and waiting in line, no matter how long they have been waiting and despite chaff in their eyes and milo dust down their shirts.

"So which end of the cow do you stick that thing on?" I said as I watched my new co-worker, Chester, who was going up and down the stalls of the 4 x 4 Herring bone milking parlor.

Here I was, a transplanted Iowa farm boy on a western Nebraska dairy farm, working on the business end of a milk cow for the very first time in my life. Now I had chased pigs trying to escape castration, sorted cattle that were to be de-horned, put up hay on days when ice tea turned into hot tea the minute you put it in a glass, but this was a Nebraska dairy farm. Strange ground to someone who thought any farm animal that was colored black and white had to be a Hampshire pig or a Black Whiteface cow. It wasn't the end of the world, but you could smell it from there. That was as long as you could get far enough away from the feedlots for the cows!

Chester taught me all there was to know about Nebraska milk cows. How to slap a milker on one without getting kicked or stepped on. How to get a bunch of stubborn heifers to walk through a milking barn for the first time without tearing the building down. The most important fact I learned from Chester, because one week we proved it to be true, was that cows really do give more milk when they are listening to Country and Western music on the radio in the milking barn. All these things I learned, including that cows really can fly.

We had one particularly stubborn first-calf heifer that was very upset that we had taken her calf away from her. She was what you call "flighty" to start with, but after her calf was weaned she got downright wild.

On a dark winter night, after I had helped pull a calf in the birthing shed and had had to pick the calf up and hang it on the fence for a bit to get it to breathe, I learned just how it is true that cows really can fly. This flighty little heifer we named "Airborne" for obvious reasons wanted very much to go investigate the birthing barn, most likely to look for her just weaned calf. As I was bringing the first lot of heifers up to the milking barn, Airborne decided she had better things to do than to walk in and be milked. In the pale light of a moonless night, lit only by the white color of snow on the ground, which made the whole lot look like some kind of surreal black light poster, I saw Airborne glaring at me. I had all the other heifers lined up ready to enter the milking barn. Airborne heard the bawling of that newborn calf and that was all it took to get her off the ground. She sniffed the sub zero air, took one look at the 4.5 foot Powder River gate and without even taking a running start, she cleared that gate with room to spare. Not a single hoof brushed the top rail, she was so high up in the dark Nebraska sky. She ran to the birthing barn desperately seeking her calf, which was nowhere to be found. Then she came trotting back toward me still standing on the other side of the gate. She looked like a child who had been locked out of the house. Now she expected me to open the gate for her to let her back into her lot! But I was just as stubborn as Airborne, so I turned away and began walking back to the milking barn.

     I had taken a few steps when I felt someone push me in the back. I heard the sound of clattering hoofs, and I turned to find it was Airborne nudging me and following me back toward the milking barn. Good thing it was a cloudy night, and that the moon was not out, or Airborne would have likely tried to jump over it too!

Janet Bond   Untitled

The girl of whom I write in my poem is my mother. In 1913, she became the bride of a farmer whose land had been homesteaded by his father.

> Visions of leaves of gold on every tree
> Hers to be had for the picking.
> A land abounding with work opportunities
> Hers to be had for the asking.
> Beckoned and propelled by these sparkling dreams
> With a call loud and clear, "Come over here."
> The fifteen year-old girl bought passage
> To this nation of freedom and promise.
>
> Innocent boldness transcended any fear
> Immersed in joy she packed her meager belongings
> Embarked in February nineteen hundred two
> From Copenhagen, Denmark for this nation.
> Four sisters, three brothers, Mother and Father
> Courageously relinquished their ties
> To delay any appearance of tears
> To deaden the twinge of any parting pain.
>
> Huddled with the poor in the craft's steerage
> Enduring many days of merciless tossing,
> She securely cradled her treasured dreams
> With the resilient fabric of her youth.
> Then spirited on by her fellow traveler's

Dauntless courage and towering spirit,
There came upon the far horizon
The towering torch and then a figure.

Before them loomed the Statue of Liberty
Proclaiming a welcome to this nation.
A solemn silent triumph prevailed
As the polyglot of people tiredly tramped
By the official guards on Ellis Island
Then emerged from the mass the fifteen year-old
Bewildered but beholden unto her dreams
Blinked a tear, brushed her coat, secured her hat.

Again her dreams beseeched and comforted her
Like the warmth of an enveloping sun.
Summoned and caressed her faltering steps
When a train gave notice of its presence
A whistle, a belch of the steam engine
A train making its way to Nebraska.

After many days on a crowded train
She arrived at her destination-
The bustling town of Gresham, Nebraska.

Mae Hiatt   A Kaleidoscope of Years

Hard-surfaced, all weather roads now crisscross the
area near Odell, Nebraska, where I came as a bride on May 10,
1921. This is my story about land that my husband inherited
from an ancestor through a land grant signed by President
Chester Arthur.

Sixty-nine years of my life had been spent on or in close
proximity to this land that I have owned since my husband's
death in 1957. I had served in France and England during
World War I. We settled in what was called a salt-box type
house built by my husband's grandfather as a temporary
shelter for his family when he came to Nebraska in 1878.

This house and others of its vintage, once occupied by
my friends and neighbors, are gone long since. Only one of
these stands lonely and abandoned.

What tales these old houses could tell! Weddings, square
dances, charivaries, quiltings, husking bees, family reunions,
the births and deaths, and funerals!

Gone too, are the narrow, unfenced, dirt roads which
marked the section lines, the wild plum thickets; the huge vines

bearing the pungent little grapes; the clusters of wild roses and goldenrod growing by the roadsides; the indispensable windmills; the big red barns, fairly bursting with prairie hay and housing the horses and the ever constant pigeons; and, the strawstacks spewed from the old-fashioned threshing machines with their coal-burning engines. Where once our fathers walked behind plows, harrows and one-row planters, giant tractors have taken over. The barbed-wire fences and the hand-fashioned posts have given way to steel posts and shiny wire fencing. And I haven't seen a jackrabbit in forty years!

Here, the Hays family lived, a little farther down the road, the Hubkas then more Hays and more Hubkas, the Champs, the Bureshs, and the Novotnys. There too, stood the schoolhouse where my son and daughter later entered school, riding the pony which daily returned to her paddock after delivering the children.

A mile down the road was a church with its homemade pews by our Grandfather on land which he inherited and now part of my farm having reverted to the original quarter section. Across the road is the cemetery also donated to the community by his brother. All of these pioneers and several members of their families lie here in the little cemetery which bears the family name. At the entrance is a huge native boulder with an inscription paying tribute to the pioneers of this long gone settlement.

It is as though on this that I turned a giant kaleidoscope with ever-changing scenes, by seasons and by years.

All is change – change – change! But no, not at all! The land is still here. Inscrutably it lies here! Always the land is basic, yielding its bounty in proportion to the care lavished upon it. Here is land which has given to four generations sustenance and strength to endure and combat drought, depressions, dust storms, hail, grasshoppers, flash floods, blizzards and tornadoes generating each year richness from the ancestral crop residue which lies moldering beneath it.

It is ours and yet it is not ours. We are only its guardians! Now, with the burgeoning spring, as I enter my ninetieth-eighth year, I pause to reflect upon the events of this century, and I pray that the generations which follow us will cherish and respect the intrinsic value of this land which I have loved. Please God, they will protect it from mismanagement, neglect, the vagaries of the elements and the ravages of time.

Ann North   Letter to Santa

This letter was written for Ann's first grade class in Shingle Springs, California, which was lacking family traditions.

December 1991

Dear Santa,

It has been over 40 years since I have written you and it feels so good to say "Hi" and to be writing you again. I remember all the many years that I patiently sat and tried to write as nice as I could with my mother's help, so you would know just what I wanted. I was always worried you would not find my house since I lived on a big ranch and there were no bright lights for you to see. I guess I worried because we did not have any electricity until I was in first grade and our kerosene lamps did not give off much light. Mother always turned them out early to save the fuel. I remember sitting on top of the attic steps waiting for you. All of us kids slept in the attic since our house had only one bedroom. Somehow you always found our house. Guess it was Rudolph's bright nose that gave you the light to find that tiny house hidden on the Nebraska prairie. Or, was it the smoke from the corncobs, after harvest, we burned to cook with, to heat our water and to heat our house?

Santa, I still have the last doll you gave me. She was a Toni doll. She still wears the same dress you put on her--it is a little tattered and faded, but it looks good to me. I lost her socks and shoes somewhere over the years, so I just let her go barefooted. Don't like the new modern shoes they put on dolls. I want her to be the way you gave her to me.

Santa, you must have had a lot of laughs each Christmas Eve after we moved into grandma's BIG house. We had so much room and didn't have to light lamps anymore. We had electricity and INDOOR bathrooms. I bet you also laughed how we always celebrated our wonderful scroungy dog's birthday (Bowser) who was born on Christmas Eve. Remember how we always went to the barn after church and brought him into the house (which he hated) and sang happy birthday to him? He always sat up and ate mints (which were his favorite thing) and would then climb into grandma's favorite chair and try to push her out. She would act disgusted, but loved every minute of it. Remember how this celebration almost ended when he climbed into the wrong chair and scratched mother's dining room chair with his toenails? This went on for 15 years—even though I was grown up then. Miss that crazy old dog. Guess he was a part of my Christmas' for so many years—a fun memory.

Santa, you know that my mother always made special desserts each Christmas--her raspberry Bavarian and pumpkin chiffon desserts. BUT do you remember the fruitcakes she made? They were out of this world. Mom had her own special secret--they HAD to be made the Friday after Thanksgiving or they would be no good. Remember how she chilled them in the old refrigerator in the basement--our first refrigerator that we bought in 1948 when we got electricity--and we were not to open the door to let light in on her cakes? Well, Santa, Dad still has that old refrigerator, and it runs better than the new modern ones. However, there are no fruitcakes to hide anymore since mother has passed away. The refrigerator brings back so many memories. I use and clean it each summer when I go "HOME." Santa, I think I remember you peeking in that old 'fridge and looking at all those desserts and those wonder fruitcakes wishing for a bite. Well, Santa, now that I am grown up, as a family tradition, I make all those desserts each Christmas for MY family, except for the fruitcake. I can't make it like my mom, even though I have tried. That must have bee one secret she didn't have time to teach me. She taught me so many other things. I guess we never got around to it. I wish I had taken the time

I don't want much for Christmas. I guess the memories of our little house on the Nebraska prairie and all the fun times I remember are more important to me. Making the special foods that were important each holiday, sharing the memories of my childhood Christmas'—especially of that crazy dog Bowser--and having a family who appreciates and enjoys my family traditions is the gift I still want each year. I am so lucky that I have these memories and that I still carry them on. In our modern world today, there are so many families who cannot share or enjoy the memories of Christmas' in their childhood. This is my Christmas gift and wish for them--to give their children memories and traditions that they can cherish and carry on to their families someday.

Merry Christmas Santa. Don't peek in my refrigerator or you will find a raspberry Bavarian and a pumpkin chiffon dessert. Sorry there is no fruitcake. This year--take a bite!

In the spirit of Christmas memories,
Ann (Wiggins) North
240

Dick Schanou   Chicken House

It always stunk,
Acrid in wet weather
And winter,
But pungent even
In the dry dust
Of summer.
Outside the freshness
Beckoned with the smells,
Sights and sounds of summer:
Flowers, orchards,
Creeks and fields,
And the drone of bees
Rather than flies--
Roost cleaning was the shits!
Four boys gathered eggs,
Expertly wielded
The chicken hook,
The hatchet
And other accouterments
Of the chicken business.

It was not really
A bad place.
The summer wasps
Usually went on with
Their obscure business,
And if you were over five

You weren't frightened even

Of the hard-beaked,

Ill-tempered setters.

We watched pouncing roosters

Subdue squatting hens--

"Showing them who's boss,"
We said, feeling good
About our maleness,

But roost cleaning--
Hacking away with hoes
At a year's pile-up,
Eyes burning,
Gorge rising,
Gagging, while
Straw in boxes
Where old settin' hens,
Destined for the
Lath crate and then
The stew pot,
Competed for space
With squawking layers.
I often wished
We'd shut the
Damned chicken-house
At night and let them
Roost in the trees!
But the reward--aah!
The filthy lucre for such
Filthy business was
Genuine Royal Crown Cola!
We tossed it down
In small stinging shots
Just as the Cowboys did.

Several summers ago I tore
it down.
The dust smell strong as
ever,
Though the chickens were
long gone.
Standing on the mossy
roof,
Ripping shingles, I paused,
listening
To the intermittent buzzing
of wasps,
And thinking of nicer
times,
When an RC was an RC,
And trees and chickens
Could be anything

But obtuse even when   You wanted them to be.
Surrounded by fecundity.

Kevin Meyer Opportunity Knocks

"Stop! Stop the car!" Grandpa hollered at Dad who was driving Grandpa's '49 Chevy down the graveled road. It was a little after 4:00 on a late winter day. Dad and Grandpa were on their way home from a farm sale.

Dad and Mom had married the year before--1950--and were living at Grandpa's until the house was empty on the farm they had rented near Pilger, Nebraska, and they could move in. Until then, they stayed at Grandpa's and Grandma's, helping with the chores and going to many, many farm sales. They were trying to put together enough equipment for Dad and Mom to farm with, keeping in mind their limited funding.

Today, Grandpa's cousin, Frank, had listed a sale north of town with an International Harvester H and a John Deere B. Dad's first choice was the H, but it brought more than Dad could afford. He settled for the John Deere B and a two-row cultivator.

Frank said they could leave the tractor and cultivator at his place and then on a warmer day drive them to the Pilger farm. Grandpa had bought a few hand tools and things and then suddenly remembered he'd bought some of the same tools at a sale last spring. So Dad and Mom could just as well take them off of his hands, Grandpa said, and use them at their farm.

The day had been successful, but not quite. Last fall after Thanksgiving Grandpa's dog had presented them with six pups. Dad and Mom would take a pup with them, but that still left Grandpa with five pups. He had tried everything to find them homes--newspaper ads, handmade signs, asking the neighbors and all the relatives--but no luck. He still had five pups to give away. Grandpa was too kind-hearted to consider any solution except finding them a home, preferably a home with kids.

Today in a burst of inspiration Grandpa and Dad had decided to take the pups to the farm sale to see if anyone needed a good farm dog. Unfortunately, everyone had a dog. No one needed a pup. What to do? What to do? It was starting to become a problem.

All of a sudden Grandpa saw an opportunity--a golden opportunity. As Dad was driving down the road, Grandpa looked up the hill and saw a country school. It was 4:00.

School was out and walking down the hill were about 15 kids, heading home. Grandpa quickly sized up the situation. Fifteen kids. Five pups. No adults but he and Dad. They were far enough away from home that no one knew them or the car. Thus, the order to stop.

As quick as he could, Grandpa was out of the Chevy and opening the trunk, his eyes gleaming.

"Come kids. Come kids, have a puppy," he said.

It was perfect. The kids were happy. The pups were happy. Grandpa was happy. No, Grandpa was ecstatic as he climbed back in the car, grinned at Dad and gave the order, "Drive like hell."

Then without looking back, he settled in the car seat, readjusted his hat and gave a satisfied grin. Grandpa loved solving a problem with a happy ending.

Molly Noren   Grammy

What a lady she is—
Full of endless energy.
Leader of this, president of that.
Mother, wife, grandmother—superwoman.

She can do anything.
She grows luscious gardens that don't seem to produce weeds,
She feeds every cat within a two mile radius,
She paints china that now sits on the Governor's table,
And enters quilts in national contests.

She takes cruises, travels abroad, goes to flower shows in Iowa.
And in '76 it was "New York or Bust" as she headed for the
        Democratic Convention.

How does she do all of this?
She still finds time to cook, can, make jelly, mend clothes, visit
        relatives, quilt every Wednesday at Church
And she gets her hair done every Friday at noon.

But behind every amazing feat my Grammy accomplishes is my
        equally amazing Grandpa!

Jean S. Gray   Ludvik

Ludvik Alexander Wesely was born in the year 1891 in Saunders County, Nebraska to immigrants from Bohemia,

Czechoslovakia. He came into the world at a time of great changes in the county. The first general store was erected in Cedar Bluffs. Native American teepees dotted the landscape near Wahoo, even though their numbers were dwindling due to disease and starvation. The old saw mill that manufactured ties for the new railroad in Dodge County had long since ceased operating. The cost of shipping timbers into the mostly treeless area was too great. Along with his two brothers, Emil and Ben, and two sisters, Francis and Libby, Ludvik helped carve a new life of his own into the rural plains.

Ludvik grew to be a tall boy and he spent a great deal of his time thinking adventurous boy-thoughts. He would often stop his work and gaze for miles in every direction for the landscape was smooth and undulating like a vast quilt of grasslands and fields billowing in the unrelenting winds. He couldn't help considering the beauty of it as his sapphire eyes scanned the horizon. This was something he did often, far too often as far as his father Frank was concerned, as he tended the fields. Ludvik wiped the sweat from his broad brow leaving dirty smudges. His father was nowhere to be seen. Someday he hoped he would see one of the Pawnee Indians as they wandered from their villages to their holy place, Pahuk Hill, near the Platte River. He had heard stories from neighbors about Indians actually coming to their doors begging food. He thought of how wonderful it would be to see one as he scratched at the dark hair poking from beneath his hat.

"Get busy, boy!" His father's voice boomed across the field at him like thunder. Frank stood next to the barn, big fists on his hips. Even at this distance, Ludvik could feel his anger. "If you're so set on being lazy, we'll leave you to those blasted Indians!"

His parents had warned him and his siblings to run if they saw any savages. Indians were dangerous people and they took children, or so the children were told. Ludvik's older brother Ben was terrified of them, but Ludvik's curiosity tempered his fear and he couldn't help wondering how mysterious and wonderful the experience would be. Clucking to the team, he resumed his drudgery.

Keeping the wildness of the land in check was an endless job of cultivating and weeding, and Ludvik's days were long and sweaty. When not searching for Indians, they were spent looking at the back end of his father's team of horses. It was a job he liked little. The difficulty of the work didn't bother him. He just loathed the horses. They were difficult to understand and they ate too much. More eating meant more

244

mucking for him. They also had to be curried and fussed over.

"Why can't I care for the oxen instead, Father," he complained one evening in the house. One of the brutish horses had stepped on Ludvik's foot and his toes were throbbing like crazy. "Ben likes horses, and he said he would trade."

Ben dropped his eyes quickly to the floor and tried to be invisible.

"Oh, is that right?" Frank spat.

Both boys glanced at each other and began to fidget.

"So you two know what's best, do you?"

Ben bolted for the door and Ludvik was left to face his father's displeasure alone.

"Ludvik, you will tend the horses and that's that. I know what's best. Everyone has chores they don't like and you'll not get special treatment."

Ludvik braced himself for what was coming next. He didn't want to cry. Frank's callused fingers pinched his ear and twisted it ruthlessly to assure the boy got the picture. The tears wanted to spill, but Frank look pained too and that eased Ludvik's indignation. Rubbing his throbbing ear, he limped off to bed. He felt a little sorry for himself, but it would be the last time he complained about horses.

Ludvik also spent a great deal of time secretly wishing he could follow the other children to school. Often he would see them in small bands meandering across the meadows on their way to the one-room schoolhouse not half-a-mile from his home place. He couldn't join them. His time was too valuable. One morning, as the sounds of their laughter reached him like music on the morning breeze, Ludvik could stand it no longer. He approached his mother Marie as she tossed cracked corn to her hens from her outspread apron.

"Mother, when can I go to school, too?"

The conviction in his voice caused her to stop what she was doing and she gazed down on him with soft eyes. She chewed on the stem of her corncob pipe thoughtfully for a moment.

He could hardly breathe.

Finally, she sighed. "I'll speak to your father about it. No promises, but you are such a smart boy. It seems a waste not to let you book-learn a little."

Ludvik's heart almost leaped straight from his throat with his joy. Hugging her he spilled the feed from her apron and looked up apologetically.

"Go on," she cackled and mussed his hair. Her laughter

chased him to the barn.

True to her word, she did discuss it with his father and the following year Ludvik was allowed to attend third grade. For that one short year, he didn't miss a day and consumed the knowledge hungrily. He held it as dearly as his love for his mother and his dislike of horses.

One morning in February of the following year, in the frosty quiet before the roosters stirred, someone woke Ludvik. It was Frank and the expression on his face caused Ludvik's heart to flutter about like a frightened bird in a cage.

"It's your mother, Ludvik. You need to come and say good-bye," he whispered hoarsely.

Ludvik felt disoriented and unreal. Ben and Francis were sobbing softly. He grabbed Emil's little hand and the toddler gazed up at him with huge eyes. They followed Frank into his bedroom. On the featherbed his mother lie very still. She looked as if she was sleeping, but the deepness of the peace on her face and the sensation of her absence in the room gave lead feet to his fear. Marie had simply died in her sleep the victim of a stroke.

After each child had placed a gentle kiss on her cheek, they gathered in the kitchen. Ludvik felt so lost he could barely breathe. He turned swollen eyes to the others as Frank began to sob into his big hands. Ben touched his father's trembling shoulder and encouraged the other children to join him. Engulfing the distraught man, they laid their heads together and prayed until baby Libby's cries brought them back into the moment.

"What will we do, Father?" Ludvik asked, his voice husky from his tears.

"I'll talk to your Aunt Antonia. Maybe she will be able to help with Libby."

Antonia was his mother's spinster sister and Ludvik always considered her his favorite aunt. She joined their family, moving in the day after the funeral, and took on the matriarchal role as naturally as if the children were her own. It wasn't long before Ludvik came to love her almost as deeply as his mother.

An air of normalcy eventually returned to his life. His days of endless work became weeks, and months became years. Ludvik grew older and joined his brother, Emil, in a new farming venture. Emil was eager to marry and Frank had purchased 120 more acres east of the homestead, so Ludvik and Emil, with his new wife Gustie, set about farming it on their own. A small barn and one-room house were already there from the original settlement and the brothers struck a deal. Ludvik would move into the old house and Emil would build a new larger home for himself and Gustie.

The bitter north winds of winter presented them with their first real challenge. Unimpeded on its ruthless quest across the plains, its icy breath oozed through the very walls and made heating the little homes difficult at best. Meeting in the barn, breath freezing before their faces, the two brothers decided without debate that it would be their last winter without a windbreak. Their biggest dilemma was what kind of trees and where to get them. Trees didn't prefer to grow on the plains by choice.

"Cottonwoods grow tall and broad and I've always liked elms," Emil suggested.

"Sounds good to me, but how are we going to get them? We have no crop moneys yet and I'll be damned if I'm asking Father," Ludvik frowned. "We'll have to think of something else."

Emil leaned against the rough wood of the door and looked lost for ideas. Ludvik lit his pipe.

"I know what we'll do," he said. His pipe danced gleefully between his teeth. "I remember seeing a stand of young cottonwoods down by the river where we had that picnic with the Navrkal's last fall. We could dig up the smaller ones."

As soon as the ground thawed that spring, the two brothers hitched a wagon to their team and headed for the river with their shovels. Ludvik had remembered correctly and the trees were in abundance. They spent the entire day digging up as many as they could. They had cottonwoods, elms and a few oaks and box elders for good measure. After the sun had set, they returned home tired and dirty, but ready to plant. The next day they set the trees in the ground to the North, west and south. The new windbreaks were in place.

Then came time to break the black loamy soil for their first corn crop and Ludvik fell behind the horses more eagerly than in the days of his youth. It was his chance to prove himself. It was backbreaking bug-eating work and the cropland proved to be fertile beyond his dreams. The newly planted corn sprouted quickly. There were times, however, when Nature tended to have a plan of her own.

Emil met Ludvik as he surveyed their work. "Gustie heard an owl last night."

"Probably means nothing," Ludvik laughed as he saw his brother's concerned expression. "Those women always have those sayings."

247

"Yeah, but she's usually never wrong."

Ludvik lit his pipe and the brothers raised their eyes to the western sky. Sure enough, dark clouds were peering ominously over the horizon. By late afternoon heavy rains obscured the barn from sight as Ludvik, Emil and Gustie sat huddled at the window watching the wavering world. It was long into the night before the rain ended. Ludvik peered from his window and saw nothing but shimmering water in the moonlight. The Spring Creek, which wound its way through the western 80 acres and usually docile as an old milk cow, had left its banks. Stomach in knots, Ludvik rolled up the legs of his denim overalls, left his little house and waded into the muck. The mud sucked at his feet and the water sloshed about his calves. When he was halfway into the submerged field he stopped, bent down and felt for one of the tender plants. What he had feared most met his fingertips--silt, and a lot of it. He lifted the sorry plant and carried it back to Emil's house. The light was burning.

"It's all gone," Ludvik told his brother and Gustie. They gazed down at the smothered thing. "If the corn had been higher, it may have made it, but these plants are too new."

"We'll plant again," Emil said gazing worriedly at his wife, "as soon as the ground is dry enough."

Gustie put her hand on her husband's sleeve. "It may be too late. I heard the cicadas singing the other day and frost could come early."

The brothers looked at each other over the corpse of the plant and then at Gustie.

"We'll have to try," Ludvik stated so matter-of-factly, no one argued.

Try they did. Ludvik and Emil worked long into the night using the light of the moon as best they could. The new plants sprouted quickly and the weather remained tame enough to allow the corn to flourish, but, just as Gustie predicted, they woke one morning to heavy frost before the ears could fill out. The crop was lost for the second time.

"What will we do now?" Emil asked, his face pale. "What about the cattle and the chickens we were going to buy? How will we eat until spring?"

"We've got my canning," Gustie offered.

"Yes, and the jackrabbits had a good year," Ludvik added. "I've seen plenty of them. They look fat, too."

Emil opened his mouth and Ludvik stopped him before he could speak.

"And we're not asking Father for anything," he said

sharply. "We'll make do."

Make do they did. Gustie's canned vegetables, the rabbits and an occasional pheasant pulled them through. Ludvik ate unusually small amounts and Gustie worried about him, but what she didn't know was that he caught sparrows near the barn and made soup from their tiny carcasses whenever he could. The winter was long, but Ludvik greeted the spring with a new level of confidence. They began again full of hope.

Then the First World War happened. As stories from foreign shores reached home, Ludvik rediscovered his deep yearning to experience the mysterious. Feeling confident Emil could handle things on his own with occasional help from Ben, he drove to Wahoo and enlisted in the army.

"Are you crazy?" Gustie blurted tearfully.

"Don't be such a mother," Emil admonished. "Where will you be going?"

"Camp Funston in Kansas for basic training," Ludvik answered as he hurriedly packed his bags, "and then who knows? I'll send you postcards from wherever I am."

Camp Funston turned out to be a bit of a disappointment as he stepped off the bus. Ludvik wasn't sure what he expected, but this lusterless and dusty spot wasn't it. He listened to the banter of the young men boasting and bragging loudly about their shooting prowess or riding abilities. Having no riding experience and his shooting confined to an occasional rabbit, he began to feel a little inadequate and his eagerness rapidly deflated. Kansas was beginning to seem a dismal place. He found his mind wandering to thoughts of the farm, his youngest sister Libby and his dog, Biddy. Before turning in that evening, feeling sick and alone, he wrote a letter home with hopes of lifting his spirits. The feeling only worsened, though, and his disgruntled drill sergeant sent him to the infirmary.

The doctor shook his head. "Measles. You're the third case this week."

"How did I get measles?" Ludvik couldn't believe his lousy luck.

"Probably from your inoculation. Happens sometimes. See the nurse and she will check you into the ward with the others."

The floor fell out from under his already leaden heart and he sank deeply into illness. The long hours in the infirmary were stark and lonely. It smelled of disinfectant. He was sure he was in hell. Memories of his childhood scolding about leaving his farm work danced through his head. Time slowed to a crawl.

After weeks of lying prone in the drab ward, he was finally checked for release back to duty. He relished the thought of getting back outside and busy again. The doctor's face was grim.

"I'm afraid I have bad news for you," he said. The lack of emotion in his voice made Ludvik's heart skip a beat. "Your fever caused irreparable damage to your retinas."

"What does that mean?" Ludvik asked suddenly feeling very small.

"Your eyesight has been damaged beyond the body's ability to heal it. You will have to wear spectacles the rest of your life and I'm afraid you are unsuitable for further service in the armed forces."

That was that.

Ludvik felt numb as he packed his bags. He had only been there a month and barely began training. Now he was going home. Home. His spirits lifted and by the time he settled onto the bus he was unspeakably happy to be going, and why not? He had gained a new perspective on the mysterious, a new set of eyeglasses and an honorable discharge for his trouble.

After settling back in at home, Ludvik took up the valve trombone to while away the quiet evening hours in his little one-room house. He had always loved Czech music and he found himself quite good at playing it. It wasn't long until word of his abilities spread into the community and he was asked to join The Cedar Hill Brass Band. They were a bouncy bunch playing polkas and waltzes everywhere from haymows to local Legion Halls. Every Sunday after mass at the Sacred Heart Catholic Church on Cedar Hill they would play for the parishioners as the women laid out a banquet of such delectables as fried chicken, liver dumplings, homemade internice sausage and kolaches fit for kings. One of those young ladies, a parishioner named Alice Chromy, caught Ludvik's eye.

One of 12 children born to a thriving Catholic family, Alice was an opinionated, determined, headstrong woman and Ludvik adored teasing her. He loved the way he could get her to grunt, stamp her foot and glare at him from behind her spectacles. She reminded him of a banty rooster the way she could puff up her little frame when provoked. He suspected she grew up the butt of school yard teasings because of the liver-colored birthmark staining the left side of her face, but it didn't

250

bother him in the least. All he had to do was gaze into her chocolate eyes to lose his heart.

One brilliant day in late spring Ludvik gathered his courage and ventured to a neighbor's where he knew Alice tended their garden. He wanted to talk to her alone. He sensed her mother had a problem with him playing in a band and he needed a chance to prove his intentions were gentlemanly before she sent him packing. He approached the fence surrounding the huge garden. Butterflies filled his stomach. She ignored him. He cleared his throat.

Alice looked up through the tomato plants and poked a dirty finger at the gate. Irritation crumpled her mouth into a pout.

"Do you know how to use a gate, or are you a bigger fool than you look?" She snorted, turning quickly to hide the smile threatening to show itself.

"Yes, I know how to use a gate. I'm just afraid you'll bite me if I get too close," he grinned.

"Oh, go on," she huffed. There was a smile now peeking from the corners of her mouth.

Keeping the fence between them, Ludvik lit his pipe and took a deep puff as she wrinkled her nose at him.

"I was wondering if you would like to accompany me to the dance this coming Saturday at Scott's Lake?"

Shock replaced the look of distaste on her face, but her smile bloomed large and honest and full of teeth. It was all the answer Ludvik needed.

"I'll be round for you then," he smiled, turned on his heels and walked home a happier man.

On May 14, 1930, smack in the middle of what the Czechs call "The Days of the Three Frozen Men," Ludvik took Alice to the Scott's Lake social hall. The "Three Days" were typically chilly and damp, but the weather this evening was starry and clear. A warm breeze kept the mosquitoes away. The two must have seen it as an omen for they professed their love for each other as the crickets sang and the band played on. They decided to marry that August.

The morning of the wedding, Alice made the wedding cake and picked her bouquet from her mother's garden as Ludvik cleaned up at home, donned his simple dark suit and pinned a fern to his lapel. He grinned at himself in the mirror. The service was to at the Sacred Heart Church at 10:00 a.m. High Mass would follow. Today would not be the day to raise Alice's ire and he made haste.

A large crowd had already gathered by the time he

arrived. Children chased each other around the legs of the men standing with their pipes and cigarettes. Neither group lent an ear to the scoldings of the women huddled in the shade of a nearby elm tree. Ludvik stopped briefly to exchange pleasantries here and there until his legs became too shaky to stand any longer. He found a small room behind the altar and sat to relax. His groomsmen seized their opportunity to corner him.

"You sure you haven't bitten off more than you can chew?" Joe Vyhildal, Ludvik's friend and best man jeered. "She can be meaner than a wet cat."

"Yeah, I saw her nearly knock the head clean off of a boy once when we were kids," another taunted.

"She's a good woman, just has a funny way of showing it," Ludvik replied harshly.

His jitters were getting the best of him. He all but sighed from relief when the priest poked his head in and informed them it was time to take their places.

When he saw Alice emerge at the head of the aisle, she was a vision in white lace and pearls. At that moment, he forgot all about his nerves and when he swore his life to her it was with a steady conviction deeper than the snows in winter.

After the I-dos, the bridal party clambered into the back of Ludvik's Model A Ford and drove to Alice's parents' home for a celebratory dinner. When they arrived, however, the gate was closed. A stack of hay bales made opening it impossible. They scratched their heads and eyed each other. Joe Chromy, Alice's mischievous brother, leaped from behind the roadblock.

"Nobody passes this point unless they pay a fine," he exclaimed puffing his chest out with an air of authority.

"If that fool grins any harder, the top of his head will fall off," Alice muttered.

"Well, I don't know," Ludvik puzzled.   It was killing him not to laugh at the look of unabashed perplexity on Alice's face. "I may have left my wallet at the church."

He dug in his pockets for effect to the sound of muffled giggles.

"Watch it now, Ludvik. Don't make the misses mad," an unidentified whisper warned from the back seat. "You know she strikes like a snake."

Alice could take no more. "Enough of this already," she spat. "I'm too hungry for all this foolishness. Just pay him, Ludvik and let's get on with it."

Everyone hooted and guffawed.

Ludvik didn't want to upset her further, so he pulled out

his wallet and good-naturedly paid up. They were allowed into the yard with Joe's sweeping bow. Ludvik hurried Alice along, bumping into her when she stopped abruptly on the steps in front of him with a huff. Peering past her, he saw the reason for the delay. A broom lay across the doorway and as Alice bent to pick it up Ludvik could see the group of smiling people inside the house. She lifted the broom and nearly dropped it as cheers erupted all around. She grasped the front of her dress, eyes searching the faces for an explanation. Then she remembered the old Czech custom and laughed too. She had just promised to be a good housekeeper to the end of her days.

That evening, an outdoor dance was held back at the church. Ludvik's band mates provided the entertainment, sans trombone, and everyone whirled and twirled the evening away. When the band took their break, the priest approached Ludvik.

"I just wanted to put a bug in your ear," he smiled. "I don't know if you've heard, but this is the last dance we will be giving on this dance floor. It's getting on in years and we plan to build a bigger one after harvest. I'm looking for someone interested in the timbers," he smiled slyly. "Would you know of anyone?"

Ludvik didn't miss a beat.

"How soon can I start tearing it down?" He smiled.

He made arrangements then and there to pay for it. The timbers felt sturdy and sound beneath his feet and he knew he could put them to good use. He was also secretly tickled to have such a keepsake.

The evening drew on and the moon rose high in the night sky. People began to filter to their cars and head wearily home. Ludvik helped Alice into the Model A and they headed home as well. Emil had since moved his growing family to a farm of his own. The two-bedroom house was now theirs. Instead of pulling into the lane when they arrived, Ludvik turned off the lights and parked behind the trees.

Alice became alarmed.

"What are you doing?"

"You'll see. Just be quiet as you can and come along with me. And stop worrying."

Carefully they made their way, holding hands in the dark, to a small stand of scrub and trees in the south field. They hunkered down to watch the house. Sure enough, after an hour of tense waiting, two cars pulled silently into the yard. Dark figures poured out across the lawn and entered the house. Recognition colored Alice's cheeks in the moonlight and Ludvik began to chuckle behind his hands. She shushed him sharply.

"There'll be no shivaree tonight," he whispered gleefully.

After the luckless assailants left, Alice and Ludvik curled up where they were and slept under the stars, too tired to go any farther.

The next day, though sleepy and a little stiff, Ludvik left Alice to settle in and drove back to Cedar Hill. He spent the day dismembering the timbers of the dance floor and dragging them home, piece by piece, behind the Model A. It took several trips, but it was good wood and it made the trip home perfectly, just as he knew it would. He stacked it next to the house.

"You can't stack that there," Alice barked from the back door as he tossed the second load onto the stack.

"Yes, I can," he grinned at her.

She blinked the shocked look from her face.

"You'll give us mice and snakes in the house. They love places like that to hide in. When the weather turns cold, they'll just move right in and there you'll be." She stamped her foot for emphasis.

"No!" He barked at her gruffly and smiled again.

She stood for a moment with her mouth agape, then with a bang of the door, disappeared into the house. Ludvik decided he would build a garage and cob shed near the house so Alice wouldn't have so far to walk for stove fuel or the car-- but not too close.

In the spring of 1932, as he was setting to plant, Alice walked into the machine shed. The sheepish expression on her face confused him.

"I've been meaning to tell you something all week and I guess now is just as good a time as any." She wouldn't meet his eyes and she was blushing.

"What is it? Are you sick?" He prodded.

"No. I'm pregnant."

That was all she said. Before he could say or do anything, she spun on her heels and hurried back into the house.

Often Ludvik had wondered about their children and his old senses of eagerness filled him once again. He floated about his work. He didn't particularly want to press his embarrassed wife with the subject, but when he came in that evening, smiling from ear to ear, he grabbed Alice, bent her in a dramatic dip and kissed her loudly. She swiped once at him, calling him a fool, and then smiled weakly. He found she didn't feel comfortable discussing it with him, but she seemed happy so he didn't push the subject.

Her silence made the months crawl by. Not able to bear

the anticipation, Ludvik decided to busy himself. Using shovel and pickax he dug out and bricked in a new cellar to store Alice's canned goods. It would also provide them shelter from the fierce spring storms. The old cellar had filled with water and Alice's loathsome snakes.

Then, on October 29, a month after his cellar was completed, Alice woke Ludvik in the early morning hours. She had tossed and turned all night and now she looked pale and frightened.

"Get the doctor," she panted. "I don't know how long I have, please hurry."

Ludvik kissed his wife on the cheek, told her not to worry and sped out the door still pulling on his overalls. Not unfamiliar with the unpredictability of birth among his animals, he didn't spare any fuel. He shoved the groggy doctor into the car and made his way home in record time. The door banged shut behind them as they hurried into the house.

"Move the bed into the kitchen," the doctor instructed Ludvik.

Alice already had water boiling. She leaned against the wall clutching her belly.

"Are you okay?" Ludvik gasped.

"Go outside and stop flustering around," She growled.

The doctor concurred. Ludvik spent the morning pacing the yard. He clenched his pipe between his teeth with such determination it cracked the stem. The dogs grew tired of following him. By the time he wore himself out, the doctor's smiling face emerged from the door.

"Congratulations, Ludvik," he grinned. "You have a daughter."

They named her Dorothy. Ludvik allowed her to toddle after him as he did his chores. He kept a wary eye on the tike for he knew Alice was fretting in the house. She was always fearful something dreadful would happen to Dorothy; one of the cows might step on her, she could get lost in the cornfield, or, God forbid, wander to the creek and drown. Ludvik became annoyed with her constant scoldings and warnings, but he understood it was out of love. Neither had to worry about Dorothy, though, for she had inherited her father's savvy with the land and animals and she managed to survive just fine.

When she turned five, Ludvik gave her a white and black spotted puppy to keep her company.

"I will call him Praz," she announced clapping her hands.

The little dog took to her like a duck to water and the

two became inseparable. One day as Ludvik rounded the garage he stopped flabbergasted at the sight before him. There sat Dorothy on her teeter-totter giggling. Praz perched, tongue lolling, on the other. She pushed him up and down and the dog seemed to enjoy it.

"How do you get him to sit still for you?" Ludvik asked still not quite believing his eyes.

"I just trained him, Daddy," the little girl answered. She simply glowed with pride. "This way he can play with me when you're too busy."

Ludvik couldn't help but smile at her ingenuity.

Just four days after Christmas that same year, Ludvik woke Dorothy as the sun was coming up. He hurriedly drove her to a neighbor's and left the bewildered child to play. By late morning, Dorothy had a new sister. Mildred also had a love for animals and she eventually turned most of them into pets. She had so many favorites that Ludvik found it hard to keep track of them all. A rooster named Benjamin was her most adored friend. Ludvik had to have a talk with her.

"We can't keep all the roosters."

The words fell like bombs on Millie. She puffed up, much in the manner of her mother, to protest, but Ludvik stopped her.

"If we have too many roosters they'll fight and could get mean to us. I'll be thinning them out in the morning so that doesn't happen."

"Where will they go?" She asked. Her large brown eyes glistened with tears.

"To market."

"But please, Daddy," she sputtered as rapidly as she could, "Can't we keep Benjamin? He's such a smart rooster and he won't be any trouble. I'll make sure. I promise. I'll watch him every day to make sure he doesn't fight anybody."

Sighing, Ludvik pushed the memories of his father from his mind and gave in. Benjamin would stay.

The following evening, after he returned home, Mildred greeted him with a tearful sullen look. Ludvik looked to Alice for an explanation.

"That rooster must have gotten mixed in with the others this morning. We can't find him anywhere and she's been like this since she got home from school."

Without hesitating Ludvik grabbed his keys and dashed to the garage. The Model A never made better time as he sped off to Fremont. He spent the better part of the evening searching through hundreds of disgruntled fowl searching for the hapless rooster. Hours later he returned, grinning, with Benjamin tucked safely under his arm.

Shortly after Dorothy turned 13 and Mildred 8 another child was expected, but God had not destined this baby to join them. He was lost before his life could begin. Ludvik was shattered. His sorrow deepened when Alice gave him the rest of the news. He loved his daughters but they would someday marry and move away to farms of their own. A boy could have kept the farm going after he grew too old. He was left only to hope there would be others.

Six long years later Bette was born healthy and happy on December 14. Ludvik loved her instantly. As she grew, though, he found himself fretting after her. On cold mornings he would take time from his chores and drive her to school on the hill so she wouldn't catch cold. She had an adventurous spirit much akin to her father's that couldn't be squelched. She could handle what life threw at her and she brought him endless joy despite his fears. Ludvik couldn't helpchuckling as she raced home from school to grab her bucket and pole and head to the creek to fish, or fly by him racing down the lane on her bicycle, scabby knees pumping wildly.

"Why does mom worry so much?" The quizzical child asked him one day. "She always thinks something bad is going to happen."

"She just loves you," he answered a little taken aback at her directness.

He spoke to Alice about Bette's concern, but Alice was Alice. Ludvik buried his fears for Bette's sake at last.

Ludvik never faltered in his love for his girls. He shared as much of his knowledge with each of them as he could. He tried to never be too busy to stop his work and play with them or to let them help him with his chores. These girls flourished, grew to adulthood, married and went forth into the world using the special gifts he had bestowed on them.

Dorothy married a farming man. She lent him her sharp homemaking, financial and farming skills. Their farm was successful and they in turn helped Ludvik farm his as he grew old.

Mildred put her sewing and drawing skills to use building her own business. She shares her love of the farm and nature with the world through quilts and patterns of her own design.

Bette taught school in Columbus and later became an important part of the Nebraska Groundwater Project. She now helps promote the importance of the health and welfare of

Nebraska's groundwater system to people throughout the state.

Each girl in turn passed her knowledge and love on to her children, who are in turn bringing forth their special talents and children of their own. Ludvik's ability to reach down deep inside to make a difference continues to flow into the world through each of them.

A heart condition eventually prevented him from farming anymore. The livestock was sold and the fields tended full-time by his son-in-law, Richard. Not ready to become useless, he turned his ceaseless grassroots genius to a new hobby of making gates and fences from old windmills. The parts had become readily available after electricity made its way through the county and he wanted to keep his hands dirty. He put some of the fences to use around the farm and others he sold.

Eventually cataracts clouded most of what was left of his eyesight and he had to give this up too. He filled the rest of his days playing solitaire with a magnifying glass and listening to the radio. He never complained. Finally, when he was 87, pneumonia came and took him away. His work was finally done.

Pamela Bowen Anderson   What Makes Them Do It?

What makes them do it?
What drives ranchers to work in the cold and heat and rain and wind?
What inner force cares enough to send them out at 2:00 a.m. to check the heifer that's due to calve tonight?
What strength allows them to work in the hay field for 12 hours straight most every summer day?
What kind of stubbornness makes them keep on after others have failed and quit?

Who knows the answer?
--Probably not their wives.
Each rancher has his own set of reasons.
For most of them, it has to do with love,
Although most are too shy to call it that.

Love for the land itself: the high rolling hills, the creek and river bottoms, the timberland.
Love for the animals they tend, no matter how difficult, how weak, how demanding.
Love for the lifestyle, their independence.

258

Love for the family they support.
Love for the heritage: the history that came before them, the legacy they hope to leave behind.

Lucas Christian Stock
The Stokers
or
"Fort Frederick Deliverance"

In the dark before dawn young Willie got gone,
The men crossed themselves out of respect.
The cowboy was dead and his horse stood unfed,
He had hanged himself right round the neck.

—*"Lonesome Willie's Tech School Blues"*
-Jim Griffith

Billy Settler saw the body before any of the others had arrived. It hung above the great iron stove in the basement of barrack seventeen. This was where they met nightly and divided their work. Sometimes evens and odds, sometimes north fort and south. It all depended on their mood and motivation. Sometimes, against regulation, the four men worked together.

The body moved almost mechanically, like a gear rotating. To Billy, it looked more surreal. It was suspended by a nylon parachute strap, one end tied in many careless knots around the thick wooden rafter beam above the stove and the other in a makeshift, yet effective noose around his neck. The body danced perhaps only by the footsteps of the men above.

Before the pale face and even paler blue eyes of the body met his own, Billy knew in that it was the boy whose grandmother was from Minnesota, and that he would forever feel responsible. He stood at the base of the ladder, as perished looking as the body, as he waited for the others to begin descending into the basement. Hank James came first, as full of tact and candor as ever.

"Jesus Christ, Billyboy, Miss July's knockers look they must have been transposed from your own grandma. When did Playboy start catering to the senior citizen's taste?" Each rung seemed to evoke an equally tasteless rhetorical question. "Am I supposed to be sick or turned on? Frankly, I'm a little bit of both," he said, tossing the weathered gentlemen's magazine over his shoulder and Billy's head before hopping off the ladder onto the hard dirt floor of the barrack basement.

Hank slapped Billy's shoulder as he turned and took a breath in preparation to speak. Instead, he squeezed Billy's shoulder hard and choked on the air as he caught glimpse of the human rag doll in front of him. He turned quickly from the corpse, wincing as though he had been punched right in the stomach.

Billy had become a sullen coyote. He whimpered and his eyes welled, but he never said a word as he watched the body spin around and around. Neither man had spoken when Jim Griffith and Paul Azaria arrived. Jim, a twenty-one year old alcoholic from Cadburry, Iowa, was already one or two sheets into the wind off Bluebeard whiskey when he hopped from the top rung of the ladder and knocked both Billy and Hank to the floor.

The jolt brought the men out of their daze and into a bout of anger that corresponded perfectly with Jim's discovery of the body.

"Jesus H. Christ!" screamed Hank, scowling at Jim.

"Holy shit!" yelled Jim, staring at the body and falling backwards into Billy.

"Fuck!" said Billy.

"Fuck," said Jim.

Paul Azaria, the little Italian from Queens with a propensity for fighting, was not shocked by the scene. He stepped through the other men and picked up the Playboy magazine, tucking it under his arm on his way to examine the body. They watched him as he walked around the body in the counter direction of its slow spin. "Well," he said, "at least this gives a man comfort in the strength of parachute strap nylon."

"When the hell did this happen?" Jim asked Hank.

"I don't know. Settler was here before I was. Ask him," said Hank, pointing at the coyote without looking at him.

"I don't know when," said Billy, staring forward, and halfway into another world now. "But I know who he is."

□

Weeks earlier, before fate bowled the four men into one another, Billy stood outside in the Montana snow at the Ft. Marian Frederick Air Force Base, shivering and sporting an unwanted erection, on night duty for his barrack. It was his job to stay awake through the night, periodically walking through the building and making sure that everything was secure, that all the men were "fit as fuckin' fiddles" as his superior, Staff Sgt. Royer used to say. Billy was outside, rubbing his hands together and smoking a cigarette when the fire alarms went off in a barrack across the fort.

He watched the festivities as one hundred or more galled and confused privates stumbled out into the snow in less than record time, harried the entire time by their two superior officers. As he watched the men dance around in the snow, stuffing their hands in their pants to warm them with the heat of their genital organs, he puffed periodically on his Pall Mall. Unbeknownst to him, a slender blond kid, pale from head to toe, had strayed unnoticed from the blaring barrack and now stood at his side, losing feeling in his bare feet and staring at him through the smoke.

"Minnesota," the boy said.

Billy coughed on his smoke and jumped away from the reticent voice. The boy hadn't moved when the smoke cleared. He stood a gangly six foot three or four and may have weighed in at one hundred and sixty, Billy thought, were he sopping wet and holding a cinderblock. He wore nothing but a pair of white briefs.

"What in the hell did you say?" Billy asked, curtly.

"My grandmother is from Minnesota," the boy repeated. Billy looked back and forth between the two barracks as the void young soldier awaited a response. Billy tromped through the snow and checked around a corner of the barrack to ensure that no one was witness to the queer event.

"Listen, fella," he said upon returning, poking his numb index finger in the kid's bony chest, "I don't know what the hell you want, but you'd better haul back over to your barrack before one of those Staff Sgt.'s has both of our asses on a biscuit." With that, the gangly kid turned away from Billy and shuffled through the snow to his barrack across the fort.

☐

"I haven't seen him since that night," Billy told his confused companions in the basement.

"I don't see what the problem is." Jim Griffith offered opinions in between discernible pulls of Bluebeard. "Let's stoke this fire, cut the bastard down and lug him across the fort. It's as simple as that. Besides, it's on our way to number twenty-four. Their stove will be dying in about forty-five minutes anyway." With that, Griffith tossed his bottle aside, pulled a buck knife from his ankle sheath, and tottered towards the hanging body.

Paul Azaria and Hank ran and each grabbed Jim by a shoulder just as he bumped one of the corpse's legs with his hand, causing it to waver once again. Paul spun Jim around

261

and rose to his tiptoes to become level with the drunk. Face to face, Paul and Jim exchanged odors of whiskey swill and pomade.

"Listen, wino, I don't appreciate your executive decision-making," Paul said. "If you hadn't noticed, I haven't offered my opinion on the issue yet."

With a huff, Jim backed away from the cagey little Italian. He was not drunk enough to fight Paul Azaria. "Alright," he said, stumbling a safe distance across the basement, "whatta *you* think we ought to do with the stiff?" scowling and casting his finger at Azaria. "What do *any* of you think we ought to do?"

Billy could no longer stand the motion of the corpse. It still swayed from Jim Griffith's nudge. He shivered and swooned as he watched in a fit of gagging unlike any he had experienced since the time he tried to swallow a hardboiled egg on a bet in high school. Paul Azaria, noticing Billy's hysterics, stepped forward and grasped the body's legs, jerking it to a stop.

"Personally, I'd like to know his goddamned name before we do anything," Paul said, patting his green wool coat for a wallet, or for anything.

"We know that he has a family," said Hank, sitting on a stump of oak that had become a stool on account of it being too large to fit in the stove.

"That's right," said Paul, "and I'm not so sure that painting him blue by dragging him through the snow is going to do us one lick of good."

Paul felt a lump in the left pocket of the coat and withdrew a worn leather wallet. He unfolded the wallet and quickly began shuffling through a small stack of cards, pitching them one by one to the floor until he came across a Kansas state driver's license.

"William M. Dilling" he read. "2648 Apple St. Rabobek, Kansas." Billy scrambled to pick up the cards at Paul's feet as he recited the information on the license. "Six feet three inches tall. One hundred forty seven pounds."

"Fuckin' beanpole" muttered Griffith, still suckling his bottle of Bluebeard.

Paul tossed some more items from the wallet down to Billy before coming across a stack of pictures. He studied the wallet pictures in the stack. The first three were of elderly individuals, two men and one woman. Each was a portrait shot.

"Looks like I found some family photos here," he said. "I'd guess these to be a couple of grandfathers and a grandmother."

Paul flipped the pictures over and noticed writing on their flipsides. Each picture listed a birth and death date of the individual.

"Looks like they all petered out," he said. "If I had to guess, I'd say his grandma in Minnesota must be the only one he had left, Billy."

Billy took the photos from Paul and studied them carefully. He noticed how one of the men had William's same pale blue eyes while the other shared the same body frame. He touched the grainy surface of the photo of one of his grandfathers and imagined William in a suit and tie. He wanted to think of anything but his dangling body.

Drunk Jim Griffith showed no interest in the photographs. He had finally discarded the whiskey bottle, apparently having gotten a snoot full, and was now occupied with a pen and pad over in his dark corner of the basement. He had a penchant and flair for writing. There were men in their barrack that paid Jim in booze for composing idyllic love letters to their girlfriends at home. "Shakespeare, the souse," they called him.

"Hey, Hank," he said. "Come here and read this." Hank James drew a half-smoked cigarette from his pocket and lit it before abandoning his stump seat to heed Jim's half-stewed call.

Meanwhile, Paul Azaria had stopped tossing pictures onto the dirt floor. Now, he held three more photographs like cards in his hands. He shuffled through the misfit poker hand quickly, checking the back of each one time and again.

"*Jesus Christ*," he said.

Billy came to from the dreamlike state he had been drifting in and out of. He looked up from his helpless position on the ground. The body had ceased moving and now loomed above Azaria as he studied what appeared to be his first significant find in the otherwise insignificant wallet. Billy noticed a look on Paul's face that had never been present during any of the stories about Queens or wisecracks about women. For the first time that Billy could remember, Paul looked intimidated, like he was witness to something more powerful than himself.

"What is it?" asked Billy, almost in a whisper. "What are the pictures of?"

"It's his family, man. His mom and pops, his little sister." Paul gave Billy a look of complete desolation. "They're all fucking dead."

□

One of the first bits of wisdom that Billy Settler had learned in basic training was to never volunteer for anything. This advice had been passed along by a merciful Staff Sergeant named Steinberg. One warm day after marching practice, Sgt. Steinberg pulled Billy aside under a honey locust tree. He was sweating savagely under the high four o'clock sun, which initially alarmed Billy.

"I'm going to tell you one thing, Settler, so listen good" he told him, swabbing his brow with a monogrammed handkerchief. "Don't you ever volunteer for anything here. You're just gonna end up cleaning potatoes or peeling shit."

Billy didn't catch the playful transposition at the time, which made the consequences seem even more horrible. All throughout basic training, he heeded Steinberg's advice. He volunteered for nothing. Anytime volunteers were requested, Billy shoved his hands deep into his pockets. A free hand, in his opinion, could be misinterpreted as a willing one.

After his graduation from basic training, it did not take Billy long in tech school to realize that his abstention from volunteering had not helped his cause. In that new environment, he had been assigned to kitchen duty twenty times, where he peeled and peeled and peeled. As soon as the temperature began to fall, so to did his zeal for not volunteering. Therefore, one wintry December day, Billy, along with three strangers from his barrack, volunteered. From that night forth, it became the duty of Billy Settler, Hank James, Jim Griffith, and Paul Azaria to spend their nights stoking the giant stoves underneath the barracks at the Ft. Marian Frederick Air Force Base in Steeplechase, Montana.

To the benefit of the men, none of the four was ever overly disquieted about their new fraternity. They became acquainted with each other and their new work swiftly. From nineteen hundred hours to sunrise, they trekked from barrack to barrack, descending into the crude basements and stoking the fires that passably heated the shed-like buildings. While they prodded the fire in the stoves, they heaved in logs and exchanged stories about hometowns, glory days, and sex more often than love. Each man's tale seemed to be a catalyst for the next.

On one of the less productive shifts, when the men all hung together, Billy Settler told the others about his grandfather's barbed wire museum in La Crosse, Kansas.

"You know, barbed wire wasn't ever introduced into war until the early twentieth century. Joe Glidden invented the stuff in eighteen seventy-four," he said, hurling a chunk of white oak into the gaping mouth of the black iron furnace. "Before then, it was just used for fencing prairie, mostly."

"Yeah," interjected Jim Griffith, "I remember this one time when I took Lizzie Harris out in the country to watch the stars." Jim chuckled for a moment at his own story. "That's what she thought we were doing, looking at the stars, but I really just needed to get my rocks off, man. Anyway, we got to foolin' around on this bridge and I accidentally kicked her pants off the edge. She told her folks that they got caught up in some barbed wire and she had to leave them tangled up in the fence. You tell your old grandpa he can use that in his museum if he wants."

For a moment after the humorous stories, the men enjoyed a comfortable silence, one subtle sign that they had become friends.

"Cheap as dirt and strong as steel," said Billy.

"What?" asked Paul.

"That's how Glidden described his invention," Billy said.

☐

None of the stokers knew how to react to Paul's announcement. Though none of them knew the real meaning, they were all cognizant to the pain involved in the loss of a family member, let alone all of them.

Jim Griffith rose from his dark corner holding a pocket notebook and a pen. He looked grieved now, not over the death of William Denning, but for his harsh, hasty proposal for handling the incident. "Jesus Pete," he said, head down and crestfallen. "I had no idea."

"None of us did," said Hank.

Paul handed the pictures to Billy and joined Hank and Jim away from the body. They studied it with a new sympathy. They no longer saw a lifeless nuisance of a body dangling above the virile stove. They saw William Dilling now—a fallen, lonely stranger from Kansas.

Hank James saw the quiet, docile man that he had feared becoming. Jim Griffith searched William's eerie, milky gaze and found the tortured soul of his alcoholic father— a man that he loathed and echoed. Paul Azaria saw pain in Dilling's lifelessness. He became nauseous at the thought of how he had celebrated the affliction of pain for so long.

Billy Settler swooned. His head spun and his whole being tingled. He was outside again, erect, freezing, and confused. William Dilling stood before him, pleading with his opalescent eyes for a response. "My grandmother lives in Minnesota," he said. "My grandmother lives..." The wind bit Billy's face, struggling to wake him. He raised his numb index finger again, preparing to drive it into the chest of the young soldier. But now he found the words. "It's cold there," he said. "She must be one tough Betty. You should go back to your barrack now. I'm sure she wouldn't want her grandson in any trouble."

The three men lifted Billy away from the blazing stove and the body. They stood him upright and he returned to them, to the basement.

"Paul," he said, "do you still have a friend in records?"

"Yeah, Billy," Paul answered. "Leland Freeman. We were in basic together."

Billy knew he was in his final moment with the body. He pled forgiveness with his eyes and imagined William finding peace in the warmth of the furnace while he tied his knots and said his goodbyes. Billy looked away from the body and back at his companions.

"What about you, Griffith?" he asked. "Can you still sing praises on paper?"

"Sure, Billy," said Jim. "Sure I can."

Billy eyed the scorching stove. He and the others watched the flames dance inside and saw how the mighty stumps of white oak fell to ashes without contest.

"Then someone needs to help me cut William down," he said. "It's time he be delivered from Fort Frederick."

Alice Heller   Generations

A little boy stands on tiptoe,
Gazing out the farmstead window.
He dreams of helping Dad some day,
But now his farming's only play.

How soon the years go rolling past.
Father and Son now share the task.
Working from sunrise to sunset,
In times of drought and times of wet.

Now at the window another lad,
Dreams of helping Grandpa and Dad.
They wonder if the lad will stay,
Or shall other dreams draw him away.

How soon the years go rolling past.
Father and Son now share the task,
But Grandpa could no longer stay.
God has summoned him away.

Wesley Howe   Memories

Jacob Howe and Pearl Brenneman were married December 25, 1900, at Council Bluffs, Iowa. Pearl said they were both motherless, and at ages 18 and 14, they decided to cast their lot together. They left their homes and traveled to the sandhills near Burwell, Garfield County, Nebraska to homestead. They had Lloyd and Florence and lost stillborn twin boys. Later they had LaTrell and Wesley.

Jake built sod houses for $3.00 per house. They raised cattle. Jake would go in the fall to help farmers near Plainview and Wausa and into Iowa to work in threshing and   corn picking and try to be home by Christmas.

When first homesteading in the sandhills, there were no fences. Pearl Howe and two neighbor girls would herd cattle on the hills. One day the girls wondered where Pearl was. They looked down toward the sod house and saw smoke pouring out so they rode down and called and finally got an answer. Pearl was trying to bake bread and the hay in the hay burner was wet and not burning well. She was laying on her back on the floor and poking at the fire. In those days, they burned hay in a hay burner and if weather was dry, it burned good. A pile of hay was kept outside near the door. People ask, "Why not keep it inside?" but there was no room in a one-room sod house of 16 square feet. Another fuel was cow chips which they gathered from the hills.

A neighbor lady would come to help during childbirth as it was too far from a doctor. Pearl would help other neighbors at such a time.

It seems that so many things would happen when Jake was gone and Pearl was home alone with the children. One time a prairie fire was coming and Pearl put Lloyd and Florence in a half barrel and waded out into nearby Sunfish Lake with them until the fire was past.

Sometimes Gypsies came through the valley. Pearl was afraid of them. Once when she and the children were alone, she saw people coming in a wagon. She and the children hid in a blowout west of the house. It turned out to be an uncle and aunt that had raised her and she almost missed them.

One Sunday about two weeks before Christmas, the Howes went to visit the Walt Graves for dinner. Graves also lived in a sod house. Before Howes left home, they took out ashes from the hay burner. While they were gone, two young people came by to visit. To let Howes know someone had been there, they pushed the container of ashes by the door and put a hay wagon over it. The wagon had a hole in bottom to push hay through and some of the hay slipped through and got on fire. Florence and Lloyd were playing with the two Graves boys in a blowout north of the house where there was a cellar dug for storing food. The boys straightened up and could see the black smoke and ran to the house. Jake and Walt ran to the hill and could see the fire. They took a wagon and team of mules with a cream can of water and gunny sacks but the house was too far gone. Florence remembers that their Christmas things had come from a catalog order and they had begged to get them early to take along to the Graves. They were burned. There was a wagon for Lloyd and a doll for her. The Hardy's lived three miles away and they saw the smoke going straight up on that still day but didn't know for three or four days that it was Jake Howe's house. News traveled slowly.

One year in November an old fellow was burning sandburs and the fire got away. That fall was dry and windy so set much of the country on fire. This fire destroyed all of Howe's hay. The next morning it was raining and then snow moved in, six inches or so, and got deeper and deeper. They had cows to calve, so Jake and two neighbors moved the cattle to some relatives at Atkinson, Nebraska. It took a week to go thirty miles. They had to stop each time a cow calved and then put the calf in the wagon and go on.

Dances were held in the homes. Pearl played for them. She played the organ by ear.

The first Christmas tree Florence remembers was a large tumbleweed which they decorated with popcorn strings. She was age seven before she had a real bed. Before that she slept on a hay tick on the floor.

Things were different in those days.

J.V. Brummels   **Golden**

Mama was a beauty—still is.
And Daddy was a GI Joe,
a dogface so country-fried
they called him Broomcorn,

the only nickname he ever earned.

Mama was a beauty—still is.
This photo, made at graduation,
shows how lovely. And dark,
that's the surprise. But see
this one, made the winter of her birth,
her young parents gathered around her.
How dark they are, how Old-World
they seem, Grandpa Ed's hair piled
high before his cap,
Grandma Anne small beside him.
Though they spoke German,
they look somehow French.
And who's to say they didn't stem
from some Borderline folk.

All those Weyhrich girls
were beauties--still are,
Aunt Jeanette tells me,
and Frances was the sweetest
girl in all the world.
Jeanette and all of Daddy's
people run to redheads and blondes.
Daddy was Mama's old man's hired man
for awhile. Who would have him!
she once thought, but soon
she couldn't if she wanted.
Jeanette tells what Grandma Ida saw.
Mom woke. She'd seen Vernie in her, dreams.
He cried and cried and cried.
That would have been August of '42.
How short the corn stood
on the hills, spare the grass,
and how the hot wind seared Nebraska.
You see, they had him for seven months
and then would not give him leave
to come home before going over there
to England, and on to North Africa
and on to the Anzio beach head
and then up the boot. They had him
for the duration. On the home front—
crops and cattle and winters and wind—
years terrible to endure,

Mama was a beauty, still is,
Did it seem it wasn't meant to be?
How she kept—in the clanging din
of that wartime railroad job,
the coal smoke of locomotives,
the changing geographies
of news from the front,
the drone of fireside chats—
that rosebud beauty, I'll never know
but only suppose it had to do
with the patience not to note much
the seasons, a sort of holding still
till the world turned right again
and set her back down
where she was supposed to be.

                                        *

And how did it end? For Daddy, so far up
the Italian Alps the world's most modern
army packed its ammunition on mules;
below a town, a monastery; and far up a path,
a German officer walking nearer and nearer, holding
a white bedsheet, like some great broken kite.
Some great tear in his world began to mend.
How strange, after so long a going away,
was that first step towards home?
Would they be strangers to each other?
The man who'd traveled four continents
and that river city woman?
It was August of '45,
the corn short on the hills
and the grass spare. Mama a beauty
still, and Daddy come home whole.
An end to a thousand days' enduring,
and what world had hung in the balance?

Why, this one, neither ending nor beginning.
The long flat behind the church in Clearwater
always stretches away to the west.
This is anniversary, this is open house.
This is the slant of sun of this
October Sunday afternoon, always slanting.
Aunt Jeanette tells me Grandma Ida's dream.
They are all here, or nearly all.
The Weyhrich women, beauties still,

smile brilliantly. A handful of old soldiers
march from handshake to handshake, smiling
at their luck. Grandchildren are thick
as grass, and, oddly, blond and red
as the ridges beyond the flat.
Daddy will say again he's the luckiest
man in the world. Mama, a beauty still,
and dark among her plain, fair children,
smiles, not, I think, at luck but that old friend
faith who told her this new world would come to be.

Connie Francis   Summer Vacation with Grandpa and Grandma

      Dennis and I used to go to Grandpa and Grandma's to
spend a week in the summertime. I suppose I was 6 or 7 and
Dennis was 8 or 9. Life was exciting and curious at Grandpa
and Grandma's. They lived on a farm about 10 miles northwest
of Inavale, Nebraska. The dirt road we traveled to get there was
narrow and hilly and rough, unless it had rained. Then it was
slippery and sloppy. Dad always made it through. We never
got stuck!
      At the time, Grandpa and Grandma had no electricity or
running water. Kerosene lamps provided light in the house.
We got water from a hand pump on the back porch or directly
from the windmill out in the yard. Grandma kept two buckets
of water on a little chest in the kitchen. (I think it's called a dry
sink or commode.) There was a dipper that she used to dip
water for cooking or to heat on the cob stove for washing dishes.
We thought it was a big deal to get a drink from the dipper, too.
That water was so cool and refreshing when it came directly
from the windmill, even on the hottest summer day.
      I remember them having a dog named Ponto the first
summers we spent there. He was a black and white border
collie. Grandpa always took him along to get the milk cows.
      The milk cows were in a pasture west of the buildings.
The pasture was a wonderful place! We loved the pond. It was
always a fascinating place to walk around. Sometimes a big
frog would startle us as it jumped into the water. If we were
lucky, we'd see a turtle sunning on the bank. Grandpa would
never let us wade in the pond though. Disappointing.
      The smell of sage still makes me think of Grandpa's
pasture.
      Closer to the barn there was a big anthill. We loved
watching those big red ants scurrying around, carrying stuff

into their hole.

Milking the cows was an event for us. Both Grandma and Grandpa milked by the light of a lantern hung above one of the stalls. Dennis and I would sit in the open barn windows and watch the sky changing colors as evening turned to night. There were always lots of swallows fluttering and swooping to catch the insects of the night. And we'd chatter, chatter, chatter. One night, we got so silly and started laughing so hard that I fell out of the window! That sort of scared the cows and Grandpa, too, so we got sent outside.

Back in the house they would put the milk in the separator to separate the cream from the milk. Because there was no electricity, it was a crank separator. Dennis and I would have fun seeing how fast we could crank until our arm wore out. Grandpa usually ended up finishing the job. Grandma churned some of the cream into butter. They sold the extra cream and butter in town at the creamery.

By the time the separating was done it was usually time for getting cleaned up to go to bed. If it was Saturday night, we'd take a bath in a tin tub in the kitchen. Brushing our teeth was an event! We'd take our toothbrush, a salt shaker, and a glass of water out on the front porch. We used salt instead of toothpaste - and then rinsed our mouth and spit off the edge of the porch! Then we jumped into the feather mattress on the big old black foldout couch in the parlor.

In the beginning, Grandpa had two horses he used to do all the farm work. I'll never forget how proud he was the day we came and he showed us his new "Fordson" tractor! Somewhere there are pictures of all of us standing in front of the tractor.

One of my favorite memories of Grandpa is when he would get out his harmonica, or mouth harp as he called it, and play for us. He could really make music on that thing. The only trouble was, he had to take out his false teeth to play it, and that sort of embarrassed him.

Out in the yard at Grandpa and Grandma's was a big old cedar tree. It was a great place to climb once you got through the prickly needles.

They also had an old push lawn mower. The faster you pushed, the faster the blades turned to cut the grass. Most of their yard was just prickly old weeds, so the mower blades got dull fast, but we expended a lot of energy pushing that thing back and forth.

Oh yes, the outhouse! It was out the back door and down a path about 30 yards north of the house. I never did like that place very well. At night Grandma put a "chamber pot" in the parlor under the bed for us to use so we wouldn't have to go outside.

For a while my great grandma lived with Grandpa and Grandma. She was Grandma's mother. She was a tiny little lady with stooped shoulders and snow-white hair which she always wore in a neat bun on top of her head. I remember the smell of her as sort of soft and flowery. She crocheted a lot and could make the prettiest, daintiest little things. I still have a pot holder she made and some pillowcases she edged.

Deb Carpenter   Grandpa's Tie Tack

I don't remember crying. But I do remember sitting on Grandpa's lap and admiring his tie tack. Grandpa sold parts for cars, pickup trucks, and tractors, and he always wore a suit and tie. This tie tack was a little tractor and was fascinating to a little girl of two years who liked to climb into her Grandpa's lap.

We sat on a chair in the kitchen, and when I got tired of looking at the miniature tractor, I wriggled around and snuggled into the security of Grandpa's arms. And then I must have fussed or whimpered or something because the next picture in my memory is of me being removed from Grandpa's arms and my mommy and my aunts examining my skin. The tie tack had been too tempered and unyielding for the delicate skin of a toddler. I had an impression of a tractor where I had leaned into Grandpa.

That particular imprint faded shortly after it was made that day. But this little girl grew up never forgetting her Grandpa and the imprint he made on her life.

Suzanne Richards   The Bright Blue Stick

After moving from the mountains of Wyoming to the Sandhills of Nebraska, I've come across a few items in my junk-room (some people have junk drawers, we have a junk-room) that remind me of my high altitude memories.

I see my big back pack and realize my everyday life is like a camping trip, so I probably won't use it again. Better keep it just in case. I try not to be too sentimental. But maybe the kids will use it if it doesn't rot away before then.

Then I see the tips of the antlers of 'Charlie' our stuffed elk-head poking up over the boxes. He's too big to fit in our small ranch house. He reminds me of hunting trips near

273

Cokeville and Jackson, Wyoming, and of our last weekend in Wyoming when we saw two colossal bull elk walking on a hill on the Deseret Ranch with a gorgeous sunset glowing on them. So we must keep 'Charlie', we might build a new big house someday where he will fit (yeah, right).

Leaning in the corner, I see my old cross country skis that I recently tried to sell at a local garage sale. I heard one little boy ask his mom what they were and she said, 'I guess they are skis of some sort.' Ughhh! What a difference in territory. Obviously the skis didn't sell at a measly $3.00.

Poking cattle through the alleyways at brandings and etc... (only use one at a time), but it usually makes at least one cowboy ask, 'What the heck is that thing?'

I tell them its my pole/flask/prodder. Then I explain its previous life as a ski pole. Then I pop the handle and expose the hollow where I can pour schnapps (a trick I learned while on the ski team in Wyoming) and the prodder part is usually self-explanatory to most. The last place I worked cows a younger hand asked if he could borrow one of my pole/prodders, and when we were done he asked if he could keep it!

I've also found another useful antidote for my old pole. See the cattle in the Sandhills have never seen anything like these poles before either, and I can scare most any bull of impressive size with ease into the trailer with my bright blue magic wand when we ship or make a vet trip. In fact, that's how I lost my right-handed pole.

I took a young bull with a nasty cut on his leg to the vet in Ainsworth (40+ miles away). I took my trusty pole and brought it out at the vets to help work the bull. Even the vet looked questionable at my choice of equipment. On departure I hooked it on the outside of the trailer and drove off. I was in a hurry to pick up my son from school. I didn't even notice it was gone until we got home. Darn! Someone is going to find one great pole.

About two weeks later I was talking to my good neighbor, Deb. We were comparing calving tricks and methods. She told me her dad starts the cows on ear corn right before they start calving, and when he goes to tag the calves, he throws the mother an ear of corn so she won't hassle him during tagging.

I told her that I figured out a neat trick to keep the cows away from me. I take my ski pole and lay it down between the mother and the calf. Nebraska cows are curious of this pole and they check it out, giving me enough time and space to tag the calf.

Deb heard this and laughed out loud. "What color is your ski pole?" she asked.

"Bright blue, why?"

She just kept laughing. Finally she asked if I lost one.

"Oh yes, did you guys find it?" I was so excited.

"You're not going to believe this", Deb said. Then she explained that her father-in-law, who lives between our ranch and my son's one room schoolhouse, had found it on the road in front of his house. Deb said they just couldn't figure out what it was.

It seems the in-laws had a church group over earlier that day, and most of the visitors were elderly and some have trouble walking. Maybe it was a cane of some sort, they thought. So they called everyone in the group to see if they happened to have lost a blue cane. No one knew what they were talking about, but they kept it anyway. Deb was so ecstatic that she had solved their family mystery.

A couple days after my phone call with Deb some of my friends from Wyoming came to visit. They are fellow down-hillers. They also got a kick out of this ski pole's drama. While they were visiting, Deb's mother-in-law called to say that they would drop my 'ski-stick' off at my mailbox on their way to town. I thanked her and told her that I heard they had pondered over its owner for sometime.

She said "Oh yes, it was very ummm interesting".

My friend Jerry from Wyoming said I should tell her to keep it to show their friends, "Yeah I'll tell them to keep it as a memento from outer space", we chuckled again.

I don't think she wanted to keep it. I was grateful to have my pole/flask/prodder/space maker for tagging/cane/ski stick back.

Joyce Weyenberg   The Terrifying Blizzard

Our Rural Route address was Glenvil; our church and town businesses were mainly Fairfield. Our school was Sandy Creek (I'm sure you've heard of this school because of how well they have done at State Tournaments in Lincoln). Deweese (home of Brian Shaw, Nebraska football hero) and Edgar are also in Sandy Creek.

I was in the kitchen working when the radio began giving startling storm warnings. I told my husband and began praying immediately. Our two precious children were 15 miles from home. Thankfully, they had let school out early. By this time, we had a new tractor with a cab. My husband took the

275

tractor up to Highway 74 to rescue anyone needing it. Sure
enough, the bus was stranded there with our two children and
the neighbors' two children. We couldn't get the neighbor's two
children to their home, but we could take care of them.

Next my husband brought home the bus driver and a
tall, red-haired milk truck driver. My husband went back again
and found a state highway employee in the school bus. That
was all who needed help. The highway man was almost in
shock, but we didn't realize it or we would have treated him for
shock. But sitting him by the stove with a hot cup of coffee
seemed to take care of him. We had them all call and notify
their families that they would be staying with us until the
dreadful storm was over.

Being used to cooking for corn shellers and later for silo
fillers, feeding these people was no problem. We started with a
good canned ham, and I had plenty to go with it. It was the boy
student's birthday, so I wanted to do something special. There
was no time to make a cake, so we just had hot fudge sundaes
and sang to him.

The girl student, Eileen, slept in my daughter's other
twin bed. Her brother slept with my son in his double bed.
While I was trying to figure out the pillows and blankets for
everyone, the milk truck driver kept following me around,
showing me pictures of his grandchildren over and over again. I
looked at the pictures, of course, and they were very lovely
children, but I had some figuring out to do.

The tall one, the milk truck driver, got the longest
couch. Unfortunately, it was in front of two long old farmhouse
windows on the north. I made sure he'd have plenty of covers,
though.

After eating, the bus driver was taken back to his bus on
the highway. He just couldn't leave it there. The bus driver
was glad the highwayman could get shelter in the bus, but he
sure didn't like it that he had been burning pencils and papers
in his bus. My husband saw to it that the bus driver got back
to Glenvil, the start of his route and home.

The highwayman had to sleep on the couch in the family
room, which worked out for he was a very short man. Then we
all settled in for the night with plenty of prayers.

The next morning when I came down to get breakfast I
asked everyone how they had slept. Everyone had slept very
well but the milk truck driver, who said he was too warm. In a
way, it almost tickled me—I didn't understand why he just
hadn't taken off a cover or two. I thought it might hurt his

276

feelings if I asked, so I didn't.

    We had some breakfast and the storm was over by then. Gradually everyone got home. I'm sure the boy student will never forget his 16th birthday and neither will I.

Margaret Nielsen   Remembering Grandpa

He would sink back in his Morris chair in the corner
with Farm Journals, Western Adventures and chaw,
a coal hod for Wastebasket and spittoon,
sleeves of work shirt fastened over his stump,
remains of a tussle with a corn sheller.
A wizened, silent man,
alone in a bustling, cheerful household.

Born to the roar of Niagara Falls
labeled Shelley Bysshe by a romantic
father who died in Andersonville Prison.
Mother brought her family to eastern Iowa,
Shelley and Hal came on to West Blue.
When Grampa built his house on a hill,
he gave a beef each year to Pawnees
wintering in the draw.
Worked from before sunrise to past sunset,
expected his sons to be working
models for the hired man.
Survivor of drouths, depressions, Blizzard of '88.

A neighbor--"everything he touched turned to gold".
A cousin--"shrewdest man in Fillmore County".
His son--"sent a ton of coal to Widow Jones".
His daughter--"quoted poetry when he was young".
Grands was proud if we made him laugh.

Lora Lunzmann Black   Getting High

Riding high on that old, porch swing
lying back,
cool breeze
passing over my childhood face.
Wisps of hair blown in my eyes,
blocking my view of the canopy of tree-topped skies.
"Don't stop, Grandma,
Please push me higher,
Higher."

277

Chains dangled
clink, clink.
Old, worn wood creaked with the girlish weight.
The summer songs,
rhythms at my feet,
cicadas chirping and the mosquitoes buzz.
Summers' eve. Ah.
Cool
After the intense harvest heat.
Can't it last forever?
Life
Perfect peace.
"Grandma, keep pushing-
I love to swing!"
But Grandma had gone on to other earthly tasks,
And my swing had
Stopped.

Marvin Ketelhut   Remembering Christmas

My earliest recollections of Christmas were a long, long time
ago. My three younger brothers and I were born in the teens
and grew up in the 20s and early 30s as teenagers. We lived
with our parents in a large eight-room house in Lancaster
County on a dry land farmstead.

We were poor in those days—no city shopping. Only the small-
town general store, which harbored a pickle barrel, some
merchandise and clothing. Not much in the way of Christmas
tree decorations or presents. Remember this was the day of the
horse and buggy and the Model T automobile.

Our Dad would bring in a small fir tree he found on the farm
and we would somehow decorate it. The coaster wagon that I
wanted so badly would have to wait. I used to make some of my
own presents: bow and arrows, sling shots, tops, and a spool
with a rubber band inside, that if twisted would crawl slowly.

Later as we grew up and had families of our own, we would
meet each Christmas in our large farmhouse where the kids
had the run of the house. The parents would sit or stand and
talk and talk some more. We always measured the height of the
children on the doorframe to see how much they grew each
year. We never had a Santa Claus, as no one wanted to take
over the duties.

The highlight of the family get-together was the meals. Many times Mom would put a large kettle on the stove and my Dad would dump in a gallon of oysters that he paid only four or five dollars for in those days. They were the large, healthy looking, slippery and slick kind that did not disappear while cooking like some we get nowadays. And then if no one liked oysters that meant more for me. My Mom would add the milk, butter, salt and pepper. We always had pickles and celery, plus buns with ham. I am sure there were drinks, salad, cookies, cakes and Jell-O for those who did not like oyster soup.

This Christmas get-together went on for quite awhile until the children grew up and moved away and had their own Christmas parties. As time marches on, we can reminisce about the past glorious times we had at Christmas.

Jason Meyer Grandpa's Story

Growing up on a farm with a Grandpa as special as mine is an experience that everyone should be able to have. One can recall many memories of the times on the farm and recollect the many things that he taught me. I would like to think that a little bit of him is carried on in each of us who knew him. One thing that Grandpa was able to do was make the best out of a sad situation. He had the unique ability to be able to tell stories, most of the time to just about anybody who would listen to him. I would like to think that the part of him that I carry on is the ability to be good spirited and humorous. That is the reason I would like to share a story with you about an experience on the farm that I will never forget.

My memories of Grandpa usually involve the farm. He was a man who truly loved what he did and took much pride in the land he farmed. I don't know much about Grandpa before I was born, but I do know that I got the pleasure of being able to spend the last twenty-one years of my life with him on the farm. One of my favorite memories of Grandpa involved a time when our irrigation system wasn't working properly. We were just discussing last night about how he knew everything about our pivot. He knew every sound that it made and exactly how it was supposed to run. My father once made the comment; "If a sprinkler quit working over the hill he would know it." We don't know how he knew it, maybe it was from years of hard work and experience, or maybe he had extra sensory powers like being able to see through the hill, which he would probably try

279

to tell us he did have. Anyway, on this day the end gun of the
pivot was not spraying water correctly. Grandpa came to the
conclusion that a plug at the end needed to be taken off and
allowed to drain. As usual, he arrived at my house long before
my wake up time of 9:00 A.M. to get started working on the
problem. We proceeded to take our pickup truck to where the
plug was and he asked me to stand on the roof of the pickup
and loosen it with a wrench. So, while he sat in the driver's
seat and gave me directions, I started to pry on the plug. It took
me a while to finally pry it loose. When I eventually did get it
loose, gallons and gallons of water poured out. I was able to
jump out of the way fast enough not to get wet. Grandpa,
though, was not as fortunate. He had every window in the
pickup rolled down and was standing halfway out the door
when the water came gushing at him. He got back inside as
quickly as he could, but it was too late. By the time it was all
over, he was soaked from head to toe and the pickup had
inches of water in the cab. When I got enough courage to go
open up the door to see how he was, the water came spilling out
on the ground and he was dripping wet. With his unique smile
he looked up at me and said, "The next time we come to do this
remind me to bring my swimming trunks."

His special sense of humor was a gift that we all loved.
That, along with the memory of the love he had for his family
and the pride he had for the land he farmed is something that
many will remember him for. It isn't very often that a person as
special as Grandpa can be found. To the grandkids, he wasn't
just a grandfather; he was a friend. He is in a better place now
and hopefully that puts all of our hearts at ease. I know he is
looking over each and every one of us with a careful eye, and I
look forward to the day that I can once again join him in the
fields above.

Fredrick Zydek   Father Dancing

My father liked to dance alone.
Late at night, when he was sure
the rest of the house was sleeping,
he would turn on the old Philco
and dance with the broom.

One summer, when mother sent me
out with his lunch, I caught him
doing the Rhumba in the berry patch.

Music seemed to come from his pores.
One winter, he waltzed for the cows.

I went to the barn to feed the cats.
I found him doing a perfect pirouette.
His arms spun out and up
until he was like a giant top
spinning before the stalls.

The cows were lowing into their cuds.
I could tell they'd seen it all before.
Occasionally he would spin to a stop,
bow, kiss one of them right on the nose,
and two-step back into his turning.

One day I caught him dancing nude
in the small meadow down past our creek.
He and the dance were exquisite as prayer.
I thought of Noah's daughters covering
their father's nakedness, and wondered why.

Leta Olson   Mom's Story

All of my life has been lived in eastern rural Nebraska. I
was born in the Memorial Hospital in Fremont, Nebraska on
March 20, 1956. The once large building is now dwarfed by the
new additions that have been built onto it. My family that
consisted of a brother and my parents farmed 500 acres that
had been farmed by my grandparents and great grandparents
that had come over from Sweden. A quarter mile down the road
from us was my cousin's home. They were a family of 6 and
one of their daughters was the same age as me. Needless to
say, we had a lot of fun! My mom was a school teacher, so
being too young to attend school myself, my aunt would care for
me during the day. It was a warm windy March day in 1960
and the snow that had melted left the ditches filled with water.
I think Leigh and I must have been giving my aunt a rough time
so she sent us outside to play never imagining that we two 4 yr.
Olds would even consider leaving the yard, let alone walk the ¼
mile to my house. But we did, never giving it a thought that
someone would worry about us being gone. We left our boots
on the front porch, took off our wet socks, went upstairs and
got my dolls and came back downstairs to play on my mom and
dad's bed. While we were having a fun time, my aunt and uncle

281

were frantically searching for us. They were looking in the horse tanks, under machinery, in the hog and cattle pens. My uncle just took a whim and drove over to my house. There on the front porch were 2 little pair of boots and 2 pair of wet socks. I can still remember him coming into the house. He must have had a very stressed look on his face because I remember thinking to myself "What's all the fuss about?" Being a parent now myself, I know how scared and heartsick they must have felt before they found us!!!

The years continued to pass by quickly. In the winter we would get out the big bobsled and go around the neighborhood picking up neighbor kids and any adults that wanted to go along and end up at someone's house for hot chocolate and cookies. Then if the snow was good enough we would all go sledding down our country road hills. There wasn't so much traffic then as there is today. I don't ever remember seeing big semis on our road. The hot summers were spent playing softball for the Uehling Rebels and walking beans! My dad always had us get up very early so we could get out walking "while it was still cool". The funny thing was, we never got to quit any earlier in the afternoon! We had a field that had ½ mile rows, so we kept a water jug on one end and drank out of the tile on the other end. Of course, with all the chemical use now, drinking out of the tile is a no-no! But I remember how ice cold that water was, and I'm sure we walked a little faster going that way than back the other to the stale old water jug.

Also in the summer we would play in Han's pasture. Just about ½ mile east of us was a pasture with a creek running through it and lots and lots of trees. The only bad thing about it was the fact that it had a lot of itch weed in it also. We would come out of there with our legs all scratched up and itchy, but it never did keep us from going back to play. My brother and a neighbor boy would take corn knives and cut paths through all the weeds and when they had gone far enough in, they would cut a big clearing out and that would be their fort. Of course, girls weren't allowed and they thought we weren't smart enough to find it ourselves, but we did!

Looking back though, I know what I loved most about being in the country was all the animals we had. My heart's desire was to have a horse, so when I was 8 years old I got my first pony. I was never limited as to where I could ride. You knew all your neighbors and they didn't care if you rode through their fields as long as you didn't trample the crops. My favorite place was the pasture east of our farm. It had a lone tree about in the middle of it and little paths and washouts that were fun to ride through. We also had pigs, cattle, dogs, cats and chickens. Each species holds memories for me. I loved to sing, so I would stand in the feed bunks and sing to the steers. They were a captive audience and polite...they never booed me! (or should I say Mooed me!) We kept around 100 or more laying hens when I was small. Once a year we would move all those hens to the barn so my dad could clean and spray the hen house to get rid of the lice. The moving had to be done after dark so the hens would be easy to catch. I felt so grown up when I could finally carry a hen in each hand. But as soon as we were done Mom would throw us in the tub to de-louse us!!! The pigs were fun but a lot of work. My dad was usually an even-tempered man until it came time to move pigs. We would try to move them up a small chute into the truck and they just wouldn't budge. Finally my dad would pick them up by the snout and tail and literally carry them into the truck. A farm kid could pick up a lot of new words during this ordeal! The cats and dogs were all pets but never allowed in the house...until Mom and Dad were gone for the evening. Then I would sneak them in for a few hours to watch T.V. with me.

I lived in Mead, Wahoo, and Lincoln during my college and running around years but never wanted to live in town for good, and the good Lord must of known this, because I had the good fortune of marrying the "boy next door". My husband Ed lived his life on a farm only 3 ½ miles east of where I grew up. He and his family were dairy farmers and with my love for animals and the country I seemed to fit right in. We have been married for almost 19 years and have seen so many changes in the rural community. Many of our older neighbors that farmed have since passed away and with the farm economy in the tight situation it is made it hard for the next generation to come in and take over. So the houses sit empty and silent and the farm ground is sold to the highest bidder. Many of whom don't even live in the community. It's somewhat ironic, but 2 years ago we were visiting with a couple from Florida and when we told them we farmed around 400 acres, they thought we were rich as kings. They couldn't fathom that we had a small family farm by today's standards and today we both have other jobs to help keep us on the farm. The dairy has always been a good business if you don't mind being home all the time, but even now, with the prices somewhat iffy, we don't know how long we will be able to hold on to the cows. Our quiet country roads have turned into major roads for semis and trucks and anyone from anywhere that feels like driving around at 3:00 in the morning! And where the stars used to shine at night we can now see the Omaha sky line lighting the horizon and we're 50 miles away.

Yes, times have changed and whether it's the fact that I've just grown up from a carefree country kid to a stressed out adult, it still worries me. I don't think that bigger is better. I feel sad that so many kids won't have the opportunities to live life as simply as we did. Their days are so filled with structured activity that they don't need to use their own imaginations.

Can we turn the clock back to a simpler time? I wish we could. Growing up in the country was a great place to be and I'm happy that even now, my girls got to grow up with the freedom of riding horses, playing in a playhouse down in the barn, and just going for walks out in the trees. I feel there is no better way to live and raise a family than on a small family farm. In my mind there is really no "down side" to it. I hope my girls will have great memories to tell their children about growing up on a small dairy farm in Eastern Nebraska, and will hopefully have the chance to help their kids "build a fort in the weeds".

Marjorie Saiser   The Living, The Warm

Aunt Wilma touches the corpse, touches
her Aunt Clara, lays her old hands on top of the hands
in the casket, looks into her dead aunt's face and says
Doesn't she look pretty? So pretty, isn't she?
and it is true, Great-Aunt Clara, 99, looks sharp
and Sunday-best in her turquoise blue suit,
ruffles at her wrist and throat, her eyes closed,
her hair anything but stingy, that shade of blue-white

which she and her sisters, want, a capsule of bluing
in the rinse water to keep a shade of yellow from stealing in.
Yes, she is pretty, and Aunt Wilma lays her hands on,
and keeps them there, and looks into her aunt's face
as if they had the afternoon to talk about plums
or pies or the need for rain. Perhaps it was
the customary thing to lay your hand on the hands
of the dead as my father did when

my grandmother lay in the funeral home.
He invited me, saying *See, she doesn't mind,*

but I shook my head and wiped my wet face
with a kleenex, not wanting to know
if the body is hard, if it is cold, how cold,
the body more or less empty. Perhaps my father
touched his father's hand, that same gesture,
when the body lay in the house
for the night, perhaps in the living room
of that house north of the point where the Niobrara
and the Keya Paha flowed, still flow, together.

I wish I had thought to ask. He would have
told me, if I had sat near his hospital bed,
put my hand on his hand on his arm and said,
Would you tell me of your father's death.

When my father's body lay in the church,
I came early with my mother; the time was there,
I could have laid my hand on the wrist, maybe his
cuff, or his fingers, one cold nail, or his shoulder.
I could have straightened his already straight tie,
but I hung back, as he did in family photographs,
the shy child beside his big sister. My mother
laid her hand on his, my hand on her back,
the ridges of the spine, thc, curve of the shoulders.
I put my arm around her waist, the living, the warm.

After the funeral my aunts sit on brown metal chairs
in the church basement, taking turns talking to blind
Aunt Hattie, the eldest. They laugh about the time
Anna started off to the Black Hills in the Ford.
They laugh about somebody in a bear suit trying to
keep the kids away from the still. My turn next, so
Hattie's hands take mine, clasp them; I'm what's left,
what's here today of my golden-haired father,
Hattie's laugh that same little waterfall he heard,
her hands small quick birds fluttering and resting.
I wonder how it feels to touch the dead but

I don't want to find out. Chicken, as my aunts
would say, though I've been amazed at myself
lately, driving in a hailstorm like it was nothing,
the leaves beaten off the trees, sticking to the
windows, hail smashing on the windshield
and pounding on the roof, smeared images

all around me through the glass. Trees
and grass and the road and the trucks.
Trapped in my car on the road in a hailstorm,
thunder very close, lightning a quick yellow
knife. But I breathe in the smell of the storm
and go right ahead. Not quite scared to pieces,
as my aunts would say. A chain of hands,
coming on down, funeral by funeral. Soon
I'll be laughing at some weak joke, raucous
in a car full of women. I'll move to the back and

let my daughter drive, take my sister's hand or my
niece's. We'll hold hands in the church basement
or town hall. On the table, our lunch waiting.
The cup of coffee, the sandwich, the jello, the cake—
a plate of cake as necessary downstairs as the sermon
was upstairs. That will be after. But first,
at the casket, when my turn comes, maybe I'll
lift my small useful dry old hands and lay them,
unpolished fingers, cool dry palms,
onto the hands of the others.

Marilou Roth A Year in the Life

January 1999: The beginning of a new year and the
start of another cycle for us as a farming family. Soon we will
be expanding our family, as I am expecting for the fourth time
in five years. It has been very busy for us, little hands
constantly tugging, wanting a drink, a book read, or even a
simple hug. God has blessed us richly with three healthy
children already, and He has seen fit to give us another. Right
now I've slowed down a lot so that my pregnancy will last to
term. That means only basic housework, simple dinners, and
relaxing most of the time with our older kids. Something I'm
NOT used to doing, but a healthy child is my most important
goal at this point in time.

Calvin is working in Lincoln again to help supplement
the income from our farming operation. Hogs are at an all-time
low for us, and we cannot stand heavy losses for any length of
time. Right now it costs us $75.00 per head to take a pig from
birth to market weight, but in return, we are only receiving
$40.00 per head from the packing house. That means we lose
$35.00 for each hog that we sell! No one can afford to live very

long like this. Grain prices are not much better, but to dwell on these things only causes unneeded stress for me, so I concentrate on loving my kids, and instilling the values that I hope will allow them to live life to the fullest.

I've been trying to help Calvin by watering the bulls that we keep in a corral by our house this winter. Then he can come in right away when he gets home from work. After being outside all day in the cold, I think he appreciates being able to come into the warm house. He seems so tired. Construction work is also physically demanding. I can understand why he wants to sit all evening when he gets home.

February 1999: We finally get our new arrival. After being in labor most of the day, our little one decides to do a 180 degree turn to breech at the last minute. After an emergency C-section we see for the first time our beautiful baby....girl! She has such big hands and feet, and a deep cry. We thought maybe she was a boy. She looks like her dad: dark hair, dark complexion, and oh, so perfect! We are thankful that she is healthy. So now we have Rebecca Renae, who is excitedly welcomed by Luke Augustus 4 1/2, Morgan Melissa 3, and Toni Rae 20 months. The Lord has provided us with wonderful family, friends, and neighbors who watch the older kids, run necessary errands for me, and bring in meals until I can get on my feet again. What a wonderful blessing to be in a rural area.

March 1999: The month goes by fast and soon it is April. Now it is time to be in the field to prepare for planting. One of Calvin's uncles has passed away. A massive heart attack. He didn't suffer long. He was only 48 and will be greatly missed by us and especially his girls. His youngest is still in high school.

Because of my recent surgery, I am not able to travel, and Calvin doesn't want to go without me, so we stayed home. He did chores for his uncle Roger, over at his dad's and kept up our stuff too. By 'our stuff', I mean his brother and us.

Calvin and Wes are 50/50 partners, so we help each other as best we can when the need arises. He also did as much field work as the weather allowed, which meant long days and short nights. I pray for the Lord's protection over him as he works to maintain our livelihood. Imagine his frustration when his brother wondered why he didn't get more field work done; Wes did not realize the chores and other responsibilities Calvin had taken on. Thank God it rained that week.

May 1999: This month brought a quick and successful planting season, so the men lost minimal time from their other jobs. I think Calvin only missed 2 1/2 weeks from his construction job. In the evenings they have been doing their other farm work which makes for long days and short nights.

I forgot to mention that we calved out 20 cows here in the corral. What a beautiful sight to see a newborn calf suckling from its mama. We did well this year, as we had a set of twins, so our calving percentage was exceptionally high. Now if we can keep them all healthy.

Also, I planted a garden this year. Every spring gives me hope that we will be blessed with a good year and a bountiful harvest from Calvin's fields and my 'field', too. Let's see, we had potatoes (a staple food here), beans, carrots, tomatoes (one of my favorites), onions, raspberries (for jelly), beets, squash, Indian corn (strictly ornamental) and mini pumpkins. I've pledged to try and keep the weeds out better this year. Last year I ended up not feeling so good because of my pregnancy. We still had decent potatoes, tomatoes, onions and garlic. Enough to give me hope for this year anyway!

June 1999: June is windy almost every day, which has made it hard for Calvin to spray for weeds, even in the evenings. Even so, there is always something else to do. No rest for the weary, or for the farmer it seems.

July 1999: Calvin, Wes and their dad were laying pipe to irrigate the landlord's corn when Calvin gets his foot run over by the tractor. His dad didn't even see it happen. Just heard Calvin yelling, and saw him rolling away from the tractor. The men said that dad was backing the tractor around. Calvin had his back to the tractor holding a pipe and putting it on the end of an adjacent pipe with Wes' help. He said he felt the tire against his outside ankle/heel area. He just knew he had to pivot his foot around to keep from having his ankle broken or worse. I say an army of angels were there in that field that day. Only the top of his foot was run over. No breaks. Just a severe sprain. Thank you Lord for sparing us from a greater tragedy.

The rest of this month has been so hot and dry. A person would think that the lawn would slow down in its growth, but there is a lot of subsoil moisture, so it seems to grow at a record pace with all the hot temperatures. With Calvin somewhat laid up, I have decided to try and keep up the lawn, the garden, and of course, my house. It has been a real challenge. By the time I get the lawn done (4 to 6 hours of mowing alone) we've eaten two meals and then I have a day's worth of dishes to do by hand. (I am the dishwasher)

The kids most times need baths from playing outside and from being the farm kids they are. Long days indeed! At least with Calvin in the house, the kids are kept busy and somewhat out of mischief. A change from when he is gone and the ones who won't take naps get into everything while I am out trying to catch up with my garden and lawn. Did I say catch up? I don't think I ever do! I know my husband was getting tired of using paper plates and plastic silverware for meals because the dishwasher was backed up.

I guess there is always next year for a clean garden, and a neatly cut lawn. Calvin only missed three days of work as a result of his foot injury. Work simply does not wait when the extra income is needed to make ends meet.

August 1999: August brought more changes. Our oldest, Luke, started kindergarten. With mixed emotions, I sent him off on the school van knowing that now I have a tighter schedule to keep up with. And now I feel older. In a different phase of life I guess. I am thankful that Luke seems to be adjusting well to the changes school is bringing about for him.

September 1999: This month brings about preparations for harvest. Could it be that time already? I am thinking of our good friends and neighbors who just lost their dad to a massive heart attack two weeks ago. Their eldest son, Layne is expected to take over his dad's responsibilities for this harvest. It is nearly an impossible task when he is struggling to support his own family as well as his mother and younger siblings. I pray that they will be okay and that's about all I can do because I've got my hands full here. We have also said we can listen when they need an ear. I hope it is enough.

October 1999: We finished harvesting in record time

289

with minimal repair costs, and again, not much time lost from Calvin's outside work either. I'm so thankful that we pulled out a decent crop, even though it was hot and dry. It was especially dry at the end of summer right through harvest. I just wish the price of grain could be better. With prices at depression-era levels, literally, there is little, if any, profit left. I know what we grossed which is about half of what most 'small farmers' are expected to gross this year. I also know we only made $4,000.00, after paying off all our expenses. It is not enough to begin supporting our growing family. In fact, it doesn't even pay the grocery bill for this year. Again, I am so thankful that Calvin has been able to bring in extra income from his construction job. At least we can keep going on the farm.

Another bit of sadness. My grandma, dad's mother, passed away around midnight between the 17th and 18th. The first thing I think of when I think about grandma is this: She was a tough old bird. And I mean it with the utmost respect. She lived during a time that I cannot even begin to comprehend. It made her a special kind of person. The time I am referring to is the 'Great Depression'. There is something about the people who made it through that time. It made them tougher than the younger generations living now. I guess it was the penny-pinching nature that the 1930's imprinted in those people's souls that made them who they were.

That was what she tried so hard to pass on to us. Being frugal. Working hard. Pulling oneself up by their bootstraps was her big drive. It almost seemed to consume her thoughts. I think that's common to rural folks. And I think that's why farming people should not be underestimated. I'm thankful that I got to be my grandma's granddaughter, even though I used to resent some of her beliefs. I understand them better now that I have a family of my own. 'Go with God, grandma, and I wish you peaceful rest until He comes again!'

November 1999: Thanksgiving, a time to spend with family. The canning has been done, and it is time to rest from the gardening, lawn mowing and berry picking. The fields lay barren and black waiting for next spring when we start the cycle again.

The cows are on stalks, and we've moved them once already. We also decided earlier in the year that we couldn't keep raising hogs anymore. We sold all our sows and have just a handful of hogs left to sell. I decided that there will always be 'next year' for a neat, clean garden and lawn.

Our children have been growing and changing too fast. Luke enjoys school very much and seems to be adjusting quite well. Morgan is getting eye glasses soon, and has mixed emotions about it. I think that she will be happy to be able to see. Toni is a sweet, quiet little person. At 2 1/2 she does typical toddler things. She has an edge on the first two because she is so quiet. Toni probably can get into more stuff and into more trouble because I don't hear her until it is all done. Rebecca is changing almost daily. Although she has had more ear trouble than the others. We finally believe that we have it tackled. She is such a sweet baby, and she likes her mama. Dad isn't so bad either, but it took her six months to decide that. The bible says that children are a heritage of the Lord (Ps 127:3). What a heritage He has entrusted to us!

December 1999: The year is quickly coming to an end. It is the time to reflect back on the past months, and also to remember our Savior's birth nearly 2000 years ago. We have so much to be thankful for. The family that gathers around us, the home we live in, the faith that has been instilled in us. The faith which sustains us in our daily life here.

There are many things that I have not written about. There just simply is not time to write it all. One last thing I do want to write a little about is our parents. His mom, Jeanene is so helpful. I could not have done all that I did do without her help. Thank you so much, Mom R! My folks live four hours away so they are not able to be here physically as much. We still do appreciate the support that they give us in other ways. Thanks to you.

Everyday we live by grace and hope and faith. We live in a special place and time. I hope our children will be able to live a rural lifestyle; although, with the way the world is now, they probably will never get the chance. I want to be able to preserve their roots enough for them to understand how hard we have tried to give them a good life. A life based on the simple ways of farming, no matter what the technological advances are. Under all this modernity, there is still an uncomplicated answer to rural life. We plant the seed and wait for God and nature to provide. Our faith is what keeps us going day by day, month by month, and year to year. We do a small part, and the Lord does the rest.

Twyla Hansen   The Old Barn

1.

I see my brothers in the hayloft with kitchen matches
and tin, striking and taking turns, yellow flames licking.
Smoke curling up, ashes floating down the hay drop.

The overhead cave where we inhale field dust,
where the rope pulley-hook lilts along its full length,
where the feathertips of a bowl-faced barn owl

sweep past, a ladder rises from composted manure.
We are unable to halt the siding from its own ignition,
the ancient supports, 12 x 12's, a cottonwood tinderbox.

How will we extinguish it without being caught?
What will we explain to father, returning from the field?
We all believe in God and right now He is not happy.

2.

They immigrated to this country for farming and freedom,
grandfather first, returning to fetch his young first cousin.

Grandmother isolated and frightened, this treeless flatland.
No one warned her about raking weather, the relentless wind,
no one knew of drought or typhus or how to save the children.

The new barn, its beckoning rafters, the only height for miles.
He kept the spare rope with him, hidden under the wagon seat.

My brothers and I tasting fear, smelling our own small demise,
one after another calves in the feedlot loping toward pasture.
The air full of shouts, father from a distance detecting trouble.

If our grandparents survived grief and nature, why can't we?
Water holy from the stock tank hitting the blackened wall.

292

At 14,
      pony-tailed and bobby-socked
      she burst her elementary cocoon
      to dance a butterfly social whirl.
18 comes,
      holding court in dorm room castles
      she sees Lancelot in Agrinomics 101,
      plans a farmstead wedding
      and well-browned children.
Of late,
      blank-eyed she stares
      out kitchen windows, waiting
      for the clatter of a clanging bucket jeep,
      elbow deep in last night's
      supper dishes.

Wearing Down to Fit

Robert Richter   **What the Prairie Sky Is For**

There's that one early spring day when I can just smell the mud thawing and the first fresh green emerging. The sun quietly blazes to a certain brilliant hue of golden light, and the sky is the right color of blue. And I know the season is here. I feel the familiar new energy in the flex and reflex of my muscles as I walk across the yard. I start looking for a stick to pick up and swing, or I grab a pebble off the ground and pivot and fire it at the trunk of a tree. Pretty soon, the call will come.

My wife also knows that pretty soon the call will come. She's noticed the change of weather in her own ways and knows what the change means. I can smell the mud, I tell her, and she replies, "Aarrgh. He's going to call, isn't he? I'm going to be the one to answer." And the call always comes a day or so later. I can tell by the groan she foghorns over the phone and the long line of language unbecoming to an English teacher. It's old Spahnie all right, and he's said--or probably shouted--only two words: Play ball! She says, "Not another summer to waste away already, is it?" Spahn just yells, "Play ball!" She says to me, "Here. It's one of your little friends. He wants to know if you can come outside and play." I say hello, and Spahn yells, "Play ball, you bum!"

I am a bum, and that's what we go do.

Come some Sunday afternoon in April, there's a bunch of us bums, stretching and straining old muscles, hearing the aging joints crackle, feeling the soft belly bounce a little more loosely than the year before. We pump protesting legs in a freight train jog across the grass and loosen winter-stiffened arms with easy lobs of the ball. It's something like testing out an old piece of farm machinery after a long winter's storage, wondering what parts are going to need a lube job of Ben-Gay. It's rough going until the old engine warms up and all the worn moving parts get oiled, but then a second sense kicks in, and the game starts getting into the blood with the fresh season's air.

There's the feel of the old, familiar glove on the hand, the smack of the ball into the webbed pocket. There's the comfortable, solid weight of the ball on the fingertips and the power you send through it throwing it back. Then the sharp crack of the bat and the way the bright white ball sails into the season's just right color of blue, and that's what the summer

294

sky is for--fly balls and the long, clean throw to home plate for the tag on a sliding runner.

Baseball has been in my blood since I could stand up and throw, and it's been in the American blood for almost a century and a half. The first pioneers to break prairie sod for houses and new fields on the Great Plains stopped somewhere in the week of endless struggle for survival to kick the buffalo chips out of the way and lay out a diamond on a level patch of short grass plain and to bat a ball into the prairie sky. The earliest local newspapers gave town team scores and accounts of fierce neighborhood rivalries, of how the betting could go and where the opponents' "ringers" really might be from. Baseball grew up with the American farmland culture, and our small towns yielded barefoot pitchers and cover-alled shortstops that played the minor league circuits and made professional teams. My own uncle learned baseball in Lodgepole, Nebraska, and he played in the Cardinals' farm system when they still played in the old Browns Stadium in St. Louis.

Baseball came with the culture, and the prairie land was made for hot ground balls, the wide open sky for long fly balls. The game has helped define this American way of life on the land and also has provided an escape from it. On any given team from any county corner in any American decade you care to pick there's been a cross-section of society's roster--the rich and poor, the righteous and the wretched, craftsmen and wastrels, good old boys and real jerks, winners and losers, and every average man. They are what they are in real life, but for a while, on some summer afternoons, they're all just ballplayers playing their positions, getting in to a great American game.

For a while, for a few innings, it doesn't matter if the roof of your sod house just caved in or if the new $50,000 tractor is broke down again; doesn't matter if the milk and butter business is gone with the last passenger train to stop in the village or if wheat dropped the limit on the Chicago Board of Trade; doesn't matter when the world will end. There's a ball game going on, you're playing well, and the season feels just fine.

There's another long, familiar fly ball, and you think maybe, yes, you can run this one down on the fly this time. It floats up into that just right color of blue, and for a while you know what the prairie sky is for.

Renee Lanik   **Palmyra**

We took the back road into town, driving
slowly past the grain elevator, six stark
churches, Suzi's Saloon, the 5th Quarter Bar, Don's
Grocery and the Mercantile Bank—clustered,
decayed buildings—flashing neon and hope.
Two women were watching as they walked a dog.
I looked to windows for faces—but saw none. We
drove up 7th, then 8th, beyond the barn where
my horse used to be stabled to Taggert Park.
Dusk-lit vines curl through the iron mesh arbor
signifying the existence of this park since 1914.
I smell rain in fields as my son leaps from
the car jumping puddles to climb the rope up the
fort. Once conquered he surveys the park
for his next challenge. I follow along sinking
in the moist, thick, carpeted grass. On the
distant pavement I hear the hum of tires—gone
in a wave of gray to pounding
horse hooves and dust. I tell my son,
"I trained my horse—right here—in this
park—rode him barefoot with a borrowed
saddle. Right there. Under the water tower
around the slide. I'd run him through figure 8's
between the bases of the ball field—everywhere."

I was training my horse and he was training me
from under the brim of his sweat-stained straw
hat. We would talk, passing time, as we rode—
about horses, dogs and life—what it could bring—
how to be careful. He'd tell me "If you're gonna
ride—kindly buy some boots. Someday, your foot
will slip and you'll get drug." It had happened
to him on a drunken night's ride. He was drug
down mainstreet until his hip broke—sliding him
across the graveled, asphalt road. When the
morning paper flew, he was found laying in the
ditch—barefoot-covered with dew.

Minutes earlier, we had stood in his house after
not being there for 20 years—didn't matter—it was
as if I were 19 and full of myself—not 39 and
wearing bifocals, or he at 55 and quick—not 75 and
stiff. He showed remorse as he talked of selling his

horses two years earlier as he watched my son run
his fingers along rows of equine miniatures bright
with gold and glass.

We squeezed every minute into the park, then and
now on the edge of Palmyra.

Chad Koehn   The Shade of a Linden Tree

I bent over to rub the crimson paint off the tip of my
boot when I noticed a crescent of it shining below my
thumbnail. I lifted another shop rag from the stack inside the
porch door, unfolded it, reopened the turpentine, and poured a
few more drops on the clean rag. The eager throbbing of an
engine restrained by low gear caught my attention. As the
throbbing neared, I tightened the lid on the turpentine, refolded
the rag, and laid it on the steps. An old yellow pickup had
halted on the street in front of my house. I turned from the
steps and walked down the sidewalk toward the idling truck.
"Hi, Joey," I said. "I got home a few minutes ago, and
just finished cleaning up."
"Did you get paid?"
"I told her I'd write out a bill and drop it off after the
weekend."
He nodded, raising his dusty John Deere cap, smoothing
the uneven brown and gray hair remaining on the sides of his
head, and dropped the cap into place.
"That didn't take long, Mark. That's the third one since
school's been out, isn't it?"
"The fourth, if you count my lawnmower shed."
I got in and we started down the hill. Both windows
were rolled down, and the air conditioner running. One of the
vents blew a jet of air in my face. I turned the vent to blow at
Joey, looked his way, then draped my elbow out the window like
his was.
"So," he asked, "what's better? Teaching reading, or
painting houses?"
"I don't teach reading. I teach English literature.
There's a difference, Joey."
We coasted through an intersection. Joey wore a smirk
on his face, the same smirk I had seen him wear hundreds of
times during the eight years I had known him. The smirk was
usually followed by a quick check of my expression, and then a
quick look away.
"When I'm teaching, painting seems better," I said, "but

when I'm sweating my ass off painting in June or July, then standing by a blackboard and calling on some half-asleep teenager doesn't seem so bad."

"You know," he said, raising an eyebrow, "Jesus painted a few houses in his day. Don't you think?"

"That's a little before my time. But you probably remember him. Didn't he buy supplies from the Farmer's Union in Galilee?"

"No, he didn't. Joseph did, ordered supplement for the donkeys. I hauled loads of it out there, to the old Christ place. It was pretty close to where Pilate opened that barbecue joint. Lots of weeds there, if I remember correctly."

"At the Christ place, or the barbecue joint?"

A block east of Main Street, on the north side of Fourth Street, grows a row of linden trees. Grandma once said that the Bohemians and Moravians who settled Clarkson planted these trees in remembrance of those growing in the old country. They made honey from the linden blossoms. Joey parked in their sweet-smelling shade, and we walked the rest of the way to Main Street. A handful of other volunteer firemen stood waiting beside the city's wheel loader. An extended cab pickup pulling a gooseneck trailer with wooden planks on it, and a pickup and gooseneck with a mountain of cement blocks, were parked nearby.

Looking north from where I stood, I could gaze down the entire length of Main Street, with the baker's house nestled in trees at the end of the street, an earthen dike behind the house, and green cornfields beyond. If I looked south, I looked uphill at a street that formed a perfect amphitheater. We stood rows of cement blocks, then laid planks across them, to provide seating for the stage show during the Czech Festival. This is what men do in Clarkson on the Wednesday before the last weekend of June.

As a boy, I would sit on the grass beneath Mr. Pavel's catalpa tree and watch Dad and the other firemen stand blocks and cross them with planks. Now, for the ten years that I was out of college, I did it, too.

The volunteer fire department my dad belonged to was composed of men, although the recently-formed rescue squad contained a couple of women. The fire department I belong to has three women members. They man the emergency operations center, fill empty tank trucks, help wash the trucks, and keep the books. I would feel uneasy if any of them donned an oxygen suit and charged into a burning house. I think all

298

the firemen feel the same way. But nobody objects to their presence. If there are objections, it's in the bar after a fire drill and too many beers. I never hear that kind of talk.

Rich, the fire chief, parked his pickup sideways at the top of the hill to block traffic. He was still wearing his brown shop foreman's uniform, and the breeze lifted his gray hair as he descended the hill.

"Here comes the boss," Diane said. She was an attractive woman in her early forties who never hesitated when it came time to volunteer. With her announcement, the idle conversation died, and all eyes were on Rich.

"We'll set blocks halfway up the hill," he said facing us, then he turned and pointed. "Two rows of seats with an aisle down the middle."

"Hey," Joey said, nudging my ribs with his elbow, "that's original. I doubt we could've figured it out." The only change in this job during the last twenty-five years was that seats were no longer needed to the top of the hill.

Diane blocked one intersection with a barricade, and the gooseneck with blocks ascended the hill. Joey and I jumped onto the trailer with two other firemen, and started handing blocks to those on the street. It was hard work, like passing sandbags during a flood. Rich directed from below, straightening the rows with shouts and gestures. The sun surged through every space between house and tree. I constantly wiped my face with my handkerchief.

Those who worked outdoors during the day now moved slowly and deliberately. Those with indoor jobs moved more quickly. They reminded me of the boys I once removed from study hall to practice breaking a full-court press. The boys ran faster, cut quicker, and jumped higher than they ever had during basketball practice after school. When Dad helped the firemen, most of the men worked outdoors at least part of the time. Now, most worked indoors.

Guided by unasked advice, Diane carefully maneuvered the gooseneck loaded with planks around the wheel loader. A round of applause and a lone cheer sounded as she started up the hill. Joey and I mounted the trailer along with two others to unload the planks, which quickly spanned the blocks, with only a couple of fumbled planks crashing and clanking onto the asphalt.

When we reached the midpoint of the hill, the mosquitoes attacked. So many came, and came so quickly, that I couldn't keep up swatting them. They stuck in my hair and on my arms, and lit behind my collar. I envisioned a caribou running along the tundra while it's lifeblood was sucked from it. The gooseneck stopped rolling. Diane jumped into Rich's pickup and drove away. Joey pulled a lighter and a pack of cigarettes from his shirt pocket and lit up while we rested a few moments.

"It's damn hot," he said, wiping his face with his shirt, then coughing. I gave him a sour look.

"I thought you were going to quit. Didn't Frances ask you to?" My hand swiped at a cloud of mosquitoes and smoke.

"They're not biting me, now are they?"

Joey cracked a smile, but it wasn't for me. Diane was coming up Main Street in Rich's pickup. The tailgate was open, and two coolers and a silver tub heaped with ice and cans filled the pickup's box. She parked next to a barricade. As she opened the door, she put her fingers in her mouth and whistled.

"We've got beer down here," she yelled, and several men started downhill. Joey looked over his shoulder, beckoning me to follow.

"I'll just have one," he said. "Have a can of pop. Then we'll head for home. Okay?"

I walked alongside him. The gooseneck trailer was brought around the block and parked near the refreshments, under an enormous elm tree. The remaining half sun infused the clouds above it, forming an orange arch that spanned the gap between the old brick grade school and the Presbyterian church. A band of pink and one of purple floated above the orange arch. Some crows cawed over a pine that guarded the stone pyramid in Memorial Park, a bat flitted over our heads, and a happy row of beer-drinkers aligned on one side of the gooseneck. Another circle of men gathered near the trailer. Joey took the last seat at the end of the trailer, I stood nearby holding a sweating soda can in my right hand, and Rich sat on the rim of a fire hydrant a little ways from us. Diane walked toward us.

"Where's Verbie?" asked Rich, looking at Diane.

"He went to Omaha," she said. "Something with the store."

Verbie owned one of the two grocery stores on Main Street.

"Who knows where he ended up," she said, shrugging her shoulders and taking her hands off her hips. A beer was thrust at her. "No thanks," she said, gently patting the roundness of her belly. "I want to fit in these shorts all summer."

Rich rose from the fire hydrant and walked closer to us. He rested his foot on one of the trailer's wheels, and set his beer on the trailer.

"I heard out at the shop," he said in a low voice, "that Verbie's going to close. He says there isn't enough business for two stores."

"He better not," replied Diane. "I just applied there. Bessie's retiring at the end of July. I'd sooner work there than keep on at the Brass Rail."

Our little group was silent for a moment.

"That would be a shame," I said. "That store's always been there, hasn't it?".

"When we moved here from Tarnov," said Joey, "Verbie was the first to greet us. He delivered a basket of fruit, sort of a welcome-to-town gift."

"They're too expensive," said Rich.

"Too many people shop out of town," replied Joey. "Wal-Mart was full of Clarkson people the last time we were there."

"You can't afford to shop here," said Rich, pointing down Main Street. "You easily pay for your gas to Norfolk with what you save."

"What will you do when you get too old to drive?" said Joey, grasping the edge of the trailer.

"The other store will stay open," I said, hoping to cool the conversation a bit. "It would be hard for some of the older people to drive to the city, let alone navigate Wal-Mart."

I glanced at Rich, and Diane stared down the street at the two stores. Joey glared at Rich. I tried catching Joey's eye by waving my arms, but he ignored me.

Half of the stub clamped between Joey's fingers was composed of ashes; a sliver of sun sliced his eyes.

An alley ran parallel to Main Street, and I as looked across at it, the blood red and chiffon pink blossoms of the rose bushes fixed my eyes. When I was a boy, I helped my grandma and Mrs. Sodomka plant flowers in Mrs. Sodomka's backyard. She was wealthy, Grandma was poor. On first glance, they appeared to hold nothing in common over which a friendship could be built. But there weren't many people to choose your friends from. Grandma often said that the best friendships were formed between people who held little in common. She said their differences could turn into sunshine that would cause them to grow together. Mrs. Sodomka asked Grandma for help with planting her garden. I can remember Grandma on her knees digging a hole for a floribunda, and Mrs. Sodomka slowly treading her back steps with three empty glasses and a pitcher full of iced tea. She knew little about flowers, but had traveled a lot, and often told Grandma about what she had seen. They laid stones in the shape of a heart, and planted roses to fill that heart. All of Clarkson, at one time or another, strolled through her backyard to see the heart of roses and witness the beauty they brought to life. When Mrs. Sodomka got diabetes, her son moved her to Omaha, so he could keep track of her more easily. Shortly after she moved, she had a stroke and passed away. Grandma truly missed her, and their roses still bloomed.

"If you can't compete," Rich said, his eyes locked on Joey, "then you don't belong in business. That's life."

Joey crushed his empty can against the trailer, and lifted his cap to smooth his ruffled hair. His face burned a deep red.

"Maybe nobody will be willing to get your groceries," he said, "when you get old."

Rich stared at Joey, then walked to the coolers to grab another beer. The one he had set on the gooseneck was unopened.

"Put your empties in here," Diane said, pointing to a wire basket in the pickup's box. "The Boy Scouts are collecting again." When she turned from us, the silver that frosted a few strands of her hair matched the sheen of her skin.

"I'm hungry, Joey." I grabbed his shoulder and squeezed tightly. "We better go. Frances won't like me begging a meal so late."

"She won't mind."

Moths clung to the dome light in the pickup. I swatted one with an old newspaper that was lying on the dashboard. I hoped to point out the stripes of crimson paint on the bay window, but it was too dark to see them clearly. We drove the four blocks in silence.

Frances reclined on a lawn chair sitting within the halo of their yard light. Her purple blouse gleamed beneath the silver-blond hair falling over her shoulders, and her flowered shorts bloomed with her full figure. She had a bottle of wine cooler tucked between her flat-spreading thighs.

"I suppose you haven't eaten?" she said with a smile. At the foot of her chair was scattered her sandals, a tube of moisturizing cream, a fat paperback with a coupon for a marker, and an open box of matches. Beside her chair sat a tin bucket with a citronella candle smoldering inside it. A tangle of peonies divided their yard from their neighbor's, and a cloud of fireflies mingled with a burning bush. The full, powder-white moon reigned overhead.

"I don't have anything special," she said, rising from her chair, leaving her sandals behind. "We'll just have to throw something together. Beggars can't be choosers."

"Whatever you throw together will be fine," I said, and held the screen door open for Frances and Joey.

Randall Dunn   Pow Wow Time

The feel of Fall is in the air
Soon they will come from here and there
The Pueblo, Ute, Ponca, Kiowa, Otoe, Lakota
From Hawaii, Alaska, Oklahoma, Arizona, Dakota
And other tribes, from other places
Are mixed amidst the "Umo Ho" faces
They come to renew family ties
Feast on meat, corn, frybread, and pies
The hills come alive, with the beat of the drums
As their songs and dance are begun
When the night air closes around
The drums develop an eerie sound
One can sense the spirits of old
As through their songs, old stories are told
It's as if time has rolled back
Enthusiasm and spirit, they don't lack
I got to visit with neighbors of mine
And share in the food that tastes mighty fine
To learn the tradition and ways of the past
So the ways of my grandfathers will continue to last
Well into winter after camp has broken
My mind retains the beat of the drums and the songs spoken.

Carol Beins   A Few Reflections on the 4-F

Having to drive 50 miles roundtrip to work each day has given me the opportunity to do a little social observing. In particular, the Friendly Farmer Finger Flick, or the 4-F for purposes of brevity.

If you live west of York, Nebraska and tend to use highways and byways other than the mighty 1-80, you know what I mean. The 4-F is the oh-so-subtle method of saying howdy-do to oncoming vehicles used generally by farmers, but occasionally by others.

303

There are many ways of doing this. There is the one finger salute; usually the forefinger on one hand or the other raised gently off the steering wheel. Unfortunately, this can be construed by the uninitiated as the nasty greeting delivered by the neighboring middle digit. While this may indeed be the intent in urban areas, it's a rarity out here unless you've done some colossally stupid bit of driving.

Sometimes you receive the above gesture only doubled. If the deliverer of the 4-F is feeling particularly exuberant you may get all four fingers on each hand raised in greeting. Perhaps because it's rare these days to find a farmer exuberant about much of anything, this one doesn't come around very often. Another sign of the rotten times plaguing those attempting to feed us all.

What if your hands are full of cell phone or coffee or soon to be opened lipstick and a car appears on the horizon? You have two choices: appear rude and stuck-up and do nothing, or else the 4-F option that involves another part of the human anatomy. This one usually is a responsive flick rather than the leadoff. You subtly raise your chin, or tilt your head back, depending on how you look at it. This says, "Yes, I see you and thank you very much for that fine greeting. I hope I remember what your truck looks like so I can get you first the next time."

The 4-F knows no sexual barriers. Since farmers are mostly male, they of course are the majority, but women have been known to flick as well. What is interesting is that they primarily are defensive flickers. It's very rare for me, a woman to receive the gesture from another female. Usually it startles me so that I do not have time to react in kind before she swooshes past. This worries me because oftentimes women are so quick to perceive a social slight.

Like alcohol, drugs, shopping or other vices, the Friendly Farmer Finger Flick can become addictive. My husband has been a user ever since he was a little flicker. He has it so bad that he has been known to flick from the passenger seat. It looks rather inane without the steering wheel as an anchor. One of the most pathetic examples of futility that I have ever seen came when, while flying down the east-bound lane of I-80, my husband attempted to 4-F a car that was passing us. A completely wasted effort, needless to say.

Being a Lincolnite by birth, this social phenomenon is a little foreign to me, but logging all the miles I do in a rural setting have gotten me pretty well acclimated. I wonder how many times the 4-F is given out of habit, without any thought.

But for as thoughtless as the gesture may be in one sense, while out in the middle of barren, quiet nowhere, I find the Friendly Farmer Finger Flick to be ironically full of thoughtfulness.

Lucille Williams Proud to Be from Nebraska

My twin sister and I were born on a farm near Burwell, Nebraska. We moved to a farm near Hartington, Nebraska when I was one year old. I lived on farms near Hartington most of my life except for three years that I lived in Florida in the fifties and half a year that I lived in Washington State in 1990. We moved to the farm where we now live in 1957. I have visited 40 some states and I am still a fan of the Good Old State of Nebraska. Wish we could stay here on our farm forever but know that isn't possible. Someday soon we must move to one of our small Nebraska towns, where a person knows everyone and they still care about their neighbors.

When I rise in the morning, I marvel at the sunrise. Nebraska has to have some of the most beautiful sunrises in these United States. Sometimes you see all the colors of the rainbow and when this happens there is nothing more beautiful. It just takes your breath away. I try always to rise early enough to enjoy this very beautiful time of the day.

This time of morning is when the birds, rabbits, turkey, deer, foxes, pheasants, squirrel and many other wild animals are out to get their exercise and since we have a creek going though the farm, they are satisfying their thirst for the day. We have bird feeders where I can keep an eye on them and they are very interesting to watch as some of the birds bully the other ones and get away with it. So many beautiful birds come to the feeder but I think I like the finches best. They are such colorful little birds. The yellow and black finches are my favorites.

We live in a valley and so I get the benefit of looking out over the fields. In the spring when the corn hasn't yet tasseled and there is a slight breeze outside, the cornfield looks like an ocean of water. It looks like there are waves coming at you. What a sight! At that time of year, I feel like I am living on the coast watching the waves coming in on the ocean. This must be hard for some people to believe but you know corn at that stage is over 90% water.

In fall when the crops ripen, the fields take on a whole new look. When they say, " Amber Waves of Grain", they are so right. The fields are the most gorgeous shade of gold. There is nothing so beautiful to a farmer as a bountiful harvest in the field.

Our sunsets probably are even prettier then our sunrises, if that is possible. The colors are awesome, just wish everyone could see it too. When we are coming home from the city, in the evening and we are heading into the sunset, I haven't words to describe how beautiful it is. In the summer, when everything is beautiful and green and sunset has all those rainbow colors in it, you just wish time would stand still. There is not a camera in the world that will capture the beauty of a Nebraska sunset.

Thank goodness for our four seasons, as they are all so different. When you wake up on a cold and snowy morning and see the trees all dressed up in their new white dresses with diamonds in them it really takes your breath away. The spring with all its beautiful flowers blooming in the field and road ditches with their sprinkling of colors. Then comes summer, warm and sunny, can't beat that. Fall comes in quietly and warms you with all the fall colors, yellows, oranges and browns.

I really never appreciated Nebraska while I was growing up. The longer I live, the more I appreciate where I live. I am so lucky to be a native of this state.

Oh and there is our Cornhusker Nebraska football team, we can't forget them. It is heart stopping when you are sitting in the stadium and the team is coming out on the field with the music being played. What a sight to see all that red. The sounds from the Big Red fans are unbelievable. It really makes you feel proud that you are from this great state of Nebraska. The pride with which we play football is unmatched. The coaches and players handle themselves with honesty and integrity. The players are high in scholastics and just a class act. What can I say? That is our Nebraska!

Marjorie Holland   Nature or Nurture

I'm sitting here at my window
Soft rain is spattering down.
It lands on the driveway and sidewalk.
You see, we are living in town.

Out there on the farm where we once lived
When the clouds opened up with the rain,
It fell on the pastures and cornfields,
It fell on the hay and the grain.

I liked to sit there at my window
On the farm, I saw earth meet the sky.
In town when I sit at my window
I see pavement and cars rushing by.

306

Out there on the farm I'd be lonely
Just sitting and saying—poor me!
But living in town —someone's always around
Folks stop by for coffee or tea.

So it's nature or nurture, I'll have to decide
On the farm—far away from the mall,
Or where street lights are bright, and I can't see the night
But I know I just can't have it all.

Cynthia Boehler   Untitled

Rural Life. How can you explain it to an outsider? A state of
mind? Maybe. A fantasy for some? Most likely. For me, it is
my heritage and daily walk of life. Perhaps it's how the local
sheriff calls to "let you know he'll be out looking for loose dogs
in a few minutes," knowing full well yours has been running
loose most of the day. Or the way your laundry is folded at the
laundromat instead of thrown rumpled in the basket if you
don't get there before someone needs to use that dryer, (only
three of the six dryers work, so they're in high demand). Many
times, it's neighbors, friends, and people you don't even know,
who come to bring in your fields because you've been in the
hospital for a few days. People who would never call in any
favor bestowed upon someone in need. These are the same
people who are experts at organizing and carrying off a benefit
to raise funds to cover expenses for anyone down on their luck.
It's the way my ninety-something neighbor makes his way
across the street with a withered cardboard shell that once held
a "Lifetime Guarantee" light bulb. He had observed me
changing my outside light for the third time that summer.
Clearly scrawled in pencil on the outside of the box were the
words, "June 16, 1974." He supposed I'd been through at least
20 bulbs in the four years since I'd moved to the small town. "I
hain't changed mine since I plopped it in there in '74!" My dear
neighbor passed on this last year, leaving a legacy of tales and
sports accomplishments, and an unbridled love for watching
our local youth in their sporting events. I miss you, Mr. Onnie
Ault, but your Lifetime Bulb still shines brightly across the
street when dusk overtakes the Midlands in this little Nebraska
town.

Vivid memories of my elementary school days intermingle in my mind. In 1952, I entered kindergarten at the tender age of four in the small village of Nenzel, Nebraska, population less than 25. School was three miles from my country home. My mother drove my brother and me to school and picked us up at the end of the day. The school was originally built when three classrooms were needed. During my first few years, students in K-8 were in one room because of the small number of students. The building seemed spacious to a small child. The north classroom was used for storage and wasn't heated. There were offices at each end of the hall, one used for storage, and one for school supplies. We used the middle classroom, and the south room was empty until we were divided up into two rooms. Two sets of stairs led to the basement, which housed a gym, kitchen, stage, boiler room, and restrooms. The basement was a wonderful place with many nooks and crannies in which to play or hide. The boys and girls each had a large coat closet in the hall where we left our coats, overshoes, and lunch boxes. In the 80s the brick school was turned into a house and is still in excellent condition.

I have fewer academic memories of school than memories that included recess and events. Fours girls comprised my class. One girl was exceptionally smart, so I always tried to top her grades. As a beginner, I remember reading the series with the characters Dick, Jane, Sally, and Spot. I also remember doing puzzle pages and phonics. During the early years, I played in the sandbox or with clay when I had completed my work. When I entered the 7th grade, I had a teacher by the name of Miss Palmer. Boy, did she make us work! We had quizzes, tests, and days and days of math facts where every problem had to be right or we started over again trying to have ten consecutive papers with a 100%! Then in the 8th grade, my sister was my teacher, and she made us work hard too.

Recess was a favorite time. I remember running as fast as I could to claim a spot on the softball field. I always figured when we played work-up that I wanted to be a first baseman or pitcher, so I would get a chance to bat before recess was over. We played games such as Kick the Can, Steal Sticks, Pump Pump Pull Away, and Captain May I. Sometimes we played these games in the basement. Probably the most fun was in the spring when we saw little ground squirrels in the field. We ran downstairs, grabbed buckets, old coffee pots, or kettles, took them in the bathrooms and filled them with water, and then ran back up the long set of stairs. Once outside, we poured the water down the ground squirrel hole hoping to drown them out. Sometimes we managed to capture the little creatures when they came up to escape the water. Then we put them in a makeshift cage and kept them in captivity for a while. Those were the days! A few years ago I was thinking about what a mess we must have made when we were hauling the water, but at the time, it didn't seem like we made any mess at all!

I fondly remember the Christmas programs. We recited poems, sang carols, or had a part in a play. If the play was about the nativity, I enjoyed being one of the angels. In later years, it was an honor to be Mary. We practiced for the program for what seemed weeks. It was fun to not have our classes even though when it wasn't our turn to be on the stage, we were expected to sit quietly off stage in tiny chairs.

Once a year we prepared one or two songs for the Cherry County Music Festival. We practiced singing and actions to songs such as "Mexican Joe" and "Don't Go Walking Under the apple Tree With Anyone Else But Me." Our parents took us to the music festival, which was held in the "big" gym in Valentine.

One incident in 1st or 2nd grade made me a little ashamed. I did something bad and for a punishment I was sent to that cold North Room to stand with my nose to the wall for ten minutes. Well, one of my male classmates was also in there. He tried to kiss me. I reacted by scraping my fingernails down his cheek. I kind of liked this boy, and I was really embarrassed to have to go back to the classroom when he had that big scratch on his face.

We celebrated the last day of school by having an outing. I still remember a huge blowout we went to one year. We played in the sand and slid down the sides. I was always pretty "prissy," so I now wonder how I let myself get full of sand. We ate a picnic lunch before heading back to school. Once there, we received our report cards and school was over for another year.

I'm not certain why my grade school memories are so vivid. Perhaps it is because they were good memories, the type I want to remember. School was important in my life. My family held education in high esteem, perhaps because both my mother and father didn't have the opportunity to complete a high school education. I'm grateful that education was important to them, and that I have happy memories of my grade school years.

Rural "extended families" come from the heart and not
legal documents. The term "extended family" was a way of life
in rural communities long before it was coined in recent years
and has quite a different connotation. In rural communities,
past and present, this term has always meant caring about and
helping people in the surrounding area.

Members of rural communities know their neighbors
and still welcome new neighbors with dishes of food, offers of
help, and invitations to their homes, churches, and other local
groups. They are ready to suggest doctors, plumbers, baby-
sitters, and other regular or emergency needs. People quickly
become Marge and Jerry rather than that strange man or
woman next door. However, if you let them know that you want
to be left alone, they will courteously smile and speak when
they see you but they won't invade your space.

The rural family is not limited by miles, church
membership, ethnic background, jobs, economic status, or
other city standards. It is based on familiar faces, school
activities including sports, music, drama, FFA, and fund raising
suppers as well as graduations, weddings, funerals,
anniversaries, and other social events. A little effort and
common sense is all that is necessary to become a member of
the extended family.

The traditions of the rural community have changed
with the times. Many years ago babies were born at home with
the assistance of a country doctor or midwife, but that wasn't
all. Neighbors and friends were there to look after the other
children, cook meals, wash dishes or clothes, and help out as
long as needed. They also brought baby clothes, new or used,
baskets or beds, and other baby needs. Today's babies are
usually born in hospitals, but the same help and things arrive
with the same "oohs" and "aahs" over the little miracle.

Sadly but true, tragedies are often the truest test of the
caring of the extended family. If a farmer is seriously injured or
ill at planting or harvest time, his fields do not go untended.
Magically, a group of men and machinery appear to do the job,
and a bevy of women appear with food to feed them. Less worry
allows more energy for healing. If there has been a death, the
sorrow lessens as the farmer's land provides for the family left
behind.

Some of my fondest memories of childhood were before
the days of the big, complicated machinery of today. Neighbors
shared work, especially for wheat harvesting and putting up

hay. Men had to be fed at noon, afternoon lunch, and probably supper, and they were hungry. Neighbor women came to help with the massive meals often loaning dishes and silverware. My mother got up before dawn to kill and dress chickens and fire up the wood stove oven for pies and cakes. Tables had to be set inside and picnic tables outside to accommodate the men. Of course, the food was all homemade.

When the men came at noon to eat after washing up outside at pans of soap, water, and old towels, the tables were groaning with food. The menu usually included but was not limited to fried chicken, ham, roast beef, mashed potatoes and gravy, green beans, corn, coleslaw, pickled beets, peach pickles, homemade bread and butter and jelly. Dessert included pies: apple, cherry, peach, chocolate and lemon and cakes: chocolate, white, angel food, and sponge. Pots of strong black coffee were ready in addition to pitchers of tea and lemonade as well as water. Ice was purchased for all the cold drinks and to insure food was kept cool in the icebox because there was no electricity yet.

Children carried water to the fields all day in jugs wrapped in wet gunny sacks to stay cool from the water pump. To save time, afternoon lunch was also taken to the field. Yes, they could eat again! Lunch was mountains of sandwiches, cake and cookies, and hot coffee and cold drinks at the very least. If the work continued late, some would have to go home to do chores while others stayed for supper. Leftover chicken, meat sandwiches, potato salad, deviled eggs, coleslaw, assorted pickles, pie, cake, and cookies were served as well as a big watermelon cooled in the horse tank. Modern machinery has changed things much, but neighbors still share work and meals are needed though the full-service supermarkets and delis provide shortcuts as well as the highly technical kitchens of today with their many appliances.

Rural fire departments and rescue squads are volunteer, so it's friends and neighbors who arrive quickly upon the scene. Pagers or other technical devices may have notified them. Because they know you, they also probably know that a family member has asthma, terminal cancer, heart problems, or that a baby is on the way. Accident or illness, they not only treat and transport but will also drive family members to the hospital, make telephone calls, and even baby-sit children or close up the house for you as needed.

Land is often passed down the generations and remains

in the family for a hundred years. Thus, sons or daughters may remain in the neighborhood. Fathers and sons, brothers, and other relatives may farm together or at least nearby. It is not unusual for three or four generations of a family to live within only a few miles of each other or in a nearby small town. The friends of each family become entwined, and they don't have to be well acquainted to help in a time of need. Those that leave the area and travel to far places still have roots in the rural community with the land, relatives, or friends and know when they return, they will be greeted by a friendly face or familiar site.

The appearance of farms and rural communities has also changed. Computers, cell phones, complicated machinery, and the latest scientific and technological advancements are present, but the heart of the rural community remains. The extended family is alive and well and ready to provide a helping hand, a hug of congratulation, or a moment of understanding.

Diana Lambson **Morning Coffee**

Puddles of mid-morning coffee klatchers
gather on the sidewalk outside
the town cafe,
hands pocketed like bridle check-reins;
bending forward like the bobbing
heads of eager Clydesdales,
flared nostrils checking the breeze for last
minute comments;
chuckling to themselves,
minds already busy with the day's projects,
or a nap.
Retired plowhorses
who would still pull a hay rack or wagon
but
whose harness sores and scars won't bear the weight,
so they chew soft oats,
whicker long over coffee mug troughs,
hoary manes
blowing in the conversational
winds of former fields full
of harvested corn, wheat
or trampled
dreams.

I attended a rural school for grades K-8. I started teaching in a rural school in Dodge County the fall of 1947 after graduating from high school.

Each morning I pumped water for the day for the water cooler. The pump was not far from the building. When it was cold, I had to start the fire with cobs and coal in the stove that set in the middle of the room.

Next, I prepared my plans for the day. There were 9 pupils in 5 grades. So my day was busy teaching all the subjects to these students. Some classes lasted 5 minutes while others were 10 to 15 minutes long—depending on learning abilities of the students. Once a week we had art for 30 minutes and penmanship, also, on a different day about that same length of time.

During my first 2 years of teaching, I stayed with a family in the district. They lived 1.5 miles from school, so that was a daily walk to and from school.

Each morning before beginning classes, we said the pledge of allegiance to the flag. Then there was a health inspection, 15 to 20 minutes of music, and then regular classes for each grade. Class for each grade was called, starting with a lower grade first, and the group or individual would come to a recitation bench at the front of the room near the blackboards. Between classes I would help individual students with short questions they might have with a subject.

At Christmas time, it was traditional to have a program. So, in about 3 weeks we would practice recitation, plays and songs for that, omitting classes on various days for practice time. The program was at night and usually lasted an hour. Then Santa made his appearance talking with the students and any other small children present and handing out bags of candy, peanuts, and an orange or apple. The patrons in the district each brought something for lunch which was served after Santa's visit.

This schoolhouse where I first taught was called a "cracker box," because it was so small.

Orange crates were handy items at that time. They held the water cooler and cups for drinking. In the school room they held supplies such as paste, paint brushes, paints, colors, scissors, chalk, paper, etc. They were even made into little chairs for primary pupils. To make their appearance better, there might be a cotton material curtain with a drawstring put

313

across the open side. At Christmas time, by using brick-printed crepe paper, they were changed into a make-believe fireplace for a background in plays.

In may, when school was finishing for the year, there would be a pot luck picnic. Contests were held, such as three-legged races, running races, sack races, and possibly a ballgame between the fathers and the pupils.

After teaching in rural schools for over 20 years, I saw many changes in ways things were done.

Nancy Schroeder   Fontanelle

What tiny village almost became the capital of Nebraska and lost by only one vote? What small burg was original host to Doane College? What Native Americans visited with the first Washington County settlers? Where can you visit one of the oldest ELCA Lutheran churches west of the Missouri River?

All can be found in Fontanelle, NE, eight miles northeast of Fremont in the rolling hills of Washington County. If you cross the scenic Elkhorn River valley and proceed up the hills, you'll discover the Fontanelle Orchards, Salem Lutheran Church, beautiful homes and great history.

Of all the early landmarks of the Fontanelle Store and School, only the red brick fortress church now thrives as an anchor to the community of 100 or so residents.

Fontanelle's allure is its rural peacefulness that can be a soothing balm to our modem and hectic lifestyles. Take a Sunday drive soon and indulge yourself in a bit of memory and nostalgia. Perhaps you'll even locate Grandma's swing on the porch.

Lora Stauffer Family Breakup

Life so brief a scattered plan,
A homestead built by woman and man.
Children raised as best they could,
Then death came, as they knew it
would.

Now money and land to be divided,
Five children quarreling not united.

Then the acres sold, the money spent,
The fortune so hard come by,
easy went.

In later years the children find
discontent, no peace of mind.
Love of money and not each other
breaks the ties between sister and brother.

Angry words and jealous feelings,
In each heart and mind keeps stealing
All the peace they should be knowing.
If only love instead of hate they could
Be showing.

Bob Feurer   The "One-Holer" and the One-Room School

Much ado has been said and written about the one room
school in Nebraska, but precious little has ever been said about
the restroom facilities that accessorized those houses of
learning. District 21, in rural Johnson County, didn't have
running water. The teacher, as part of her job description, was
to bring a pail of water each day to serve the needs of the
students and herself for the noon-time washing of hands and
daily drinking. Needless to say, there was no water for flushing.

The school had large east and west facing windows for
light, an oil burning furnace with an outside tank for fuel oil,
oiled wooden floors and a coat room on the south side the large
classroom of the school in which we often wore five-buckle
overshoes and coveralls for recesses, sledding in the snow and
before departing for home. An adjacent coal shed directly to the
east, used before the oil burner was installed, and two
outhouses, occupied the southwest corner of a section on less
than an acre of land. The lot was surrounded on the east and
north by a dense hedge of, well, hedge! Osage orange was the
tree of choice, and that hedge still separates the school grounds
from the surrounding land.

The most schoolmates I ever had at District 21 was 13 in
grades K-8. So, with myself and the teacher, there should have
been 15 people in attendance on a daily basis in the school's
heyday. An out of tune piano, assorted lift-top desks, teachers
desk, a robin egg blue recitation bench, and a matching colored
wash stand that held the wash basin and the white with blue
stripes stoneware drinking dispenser completed the furnishings

of the school.

But the outhouses, oh, the outhouses. There were two; one for boys and one for girls located a respectful distance from one another, and the school, to the northeast and southwest of the main building itself. Being a poor district, we only managed to have the "one-holer" variety while the school my mom was teaching at closer to town had the extravagance of adding an extra hole! Man, that was living!

The outhouses were great places for hiding behind, we were forbidden to hide inside, during a game of hide-and-seek because if you were fast enough you could beat "it" back to base if you timed everything right. A single south facing window was the only source of light in the "toilet," and access was gained through a large swinging door that made up over half of the south-facing front wall. The small window never had glass, or even a screen, over it at any time during my nine year tenure at the institution to the best of my recollection. The pit was lined with bricks to keep the walls from collapsing and had the strange habit of filling with water as the winter snow melt began.

Imagine the joy young boys had "melting" through that layer of ice or of the horror of having to do "number two" and having the toilet paper and "it" laying on the surface of the ice for the next user to see!

The spring the robin decided to build her nest inside the boy's outhouse was a memorable one. Evidently, mother robin had flown through the open window and made her nest on the two by four at the back of the building just below the roof. Little did we realize the commotion that resulted from the simple act of selecting this as the nest site.

Unfortunately, I was the one involved in starting all the commotion as I had to use the "little boys building" during class time. I quickly walked the 75 or so feet, flung back the door and was about to step into the room when a loud hissing sound greeted me! A huge, at least the way I remember it, bullsnake was about to make an omelet with those eggs the robin had worked so hard to lay! The image of that cold-blooded monster staring me in the face is still vivid in my mind. Of course, I hurried back to the classroom with the appropriate haste and interrupted whatever class was being conducted with "there's a snake in the boy's outhouse!"

My passion in telling the story must not have convinced the teacher as she had to go check my report. I can still remember her leading all of us to the outhouse and her carefully pulling the door open to see the black and yellow reptile still on that two by four by the robin's nest. With my observation now reinforced, I was given permission to use the girl's rest room, the only time in my life that happened! I was careful I didn't go on the seat!

Well, the nearest neighbor got the emergency rescue call as we only had ball bats and broom sticks for fighting this outhouse marauder. This situation called for the heavy artillery-a hoe! Mr. Peterson showed up about 15 minutes later hoe in hand and, though we were not allowed to watch him "execute" the outhouse snake, we were all reassured that the snake wouldn't be bothering anyone anymore.

Outhouse stories could probably be told by countless other students of those rural school days. Placing the toilet tissue roll in a steel coffee can prevented the mice from using it for nest material, and, heaven protect the one who left the lid off when the mouse actually made a nest of the toilet tissue right in the can!

The morning after Halloween was also one of those yearly rituals where all the dads of the district would load the hammers, saws, nails, and some boards into the back of the pickups—ours was a 1949 Willies Jeep—because they knew they would have to set the outhouses back on their foundation. The neighborhood alumni of the last several years always made sure to tilt the outhouses over as a Halloween prank. And, each year our fathers would use their carpentry skills and tools to sit them back in place so that we might sit in place!

My own children have always had an aversion for "outhouses" in the many campgrounds we have visited over our years of camping on vacation. These waterless versions are looked upon as primitive to the "flushing" generation. Back in the late fifties and sixties, having two holes to use instead of one was the real modern convenience!

Marie Raymond   My school years at White Plains School, Lincoln County

I went 8 years to White Plains School, with no kindergarten. The only 2 teachers I remember are Lena Deininger and Marie Dillon.

There were many of my family attending this school. At first we went in a lumber wagon, then when I was in seventh and eighth grade, we rode horses, two to a horse. We had to see that our horses had hay and water after we got to school. I was the oldest of the four of us at that time, so that was my job.

It was great when the teacher started serving hot lunches. They were so much better than those sticky peanut butter sandwiches. It was only cocoa and soup, but good.

We lived three miles from the school. The building was supposed to be in the central part of the district, and there were many arguments about moving the building, but it never happened.

In order to get into high school, country kids were required to take seventh and eighth grade examinations. I don't know if I remember them all. Arithmetic, mental arithmetic, reading, geography, Nebraska geography, art, penmanship, English, history. We "boned" up on that stuff for weeks before the exam.

I loved Fridays—art day. I still remember some of the artists, Rosa Bonhuer, mostly. She painted horses, and of course, we got to do our own creations, too.

I was a tomboy and would rather play football or baseball than "girl" stuff. I broke my collarbone playing football in the sixth grade.

I was not allowed to wear jeans to school, but managed to sneak a pair of my brother's overalls to school to play baseball. But I got caught and had to go back to wearing dresses. How silly!

The Russian Thistles piled up in the fence rows in the early 30's depression and drought years. We somehow could pile them up to make partitions for a playhouse. They were about the only plants that grew. My dad tried salting them to feed the cattle, but hungry as they were, it was a "no-go." Tough years.

My family and I lived in a sod house in Logan County in about 1935. My children think that was pretty great—but it wasn't. We were glad to move on.

I remember helping to milk 30 cows, twice a day and selling cream by the 10 gallon cans every Saturday. That was our grocery money.

I taught myself to drive by watching my dad and brothers carefully. They didn't know I could drive a car, until one day I took the family car, loaded with siblings on a country road. I had trouble shifting, so to go up a hill, I'd start at the bottom in low, then shift gears at the top of the hill. I soon learned how to shift!

Dorm hours at my small Western Nebraska college were 10:00 p.m. Mrs. Lynch, our dorm "mother," hovered under the clock and counted minutes, using the threat of detention in the infirmary of hours to compensate for our minutes lost. But I needed to walk this moonlighted night in the month of April, 1963. My senior year had been full, to say the least, but now I felt it over-flowed with grief, indecision and frustration.

At 8:30, I wasn't certain I could or would be back at the blackout hour, but time and the simple rules I had been so willing to follow now seemed irrelevant to the heavy ticking of my heart. So I pulled on a light coat and ducked into the crystal night to find my place in the world.

My dad had just died a few months before. Such a gentle man. His indirect support had been barely tangible, so I was just now sensing its absence. I recalled that when I had been a freshman in college, I changed my dress style from white, rolled bulges of bobby socks and tennis shoes to hose and tennis shoes; and only then did Dad comment that he liked my hose better. He wouldn't have told me to stop wearing the bulky socks which made my legs look like tree stumps; he only waited until I changed from the current fad and then gave me credit for it.

And how he had protected me in so many other ways. When it came fall and my three pet skunks I'd loved as babies in the spring needed to be released to nature, he just told me he'd taken them one early morning to a plowed field so they could learn to hunt before winter. Yes, he had endured my unusual pets, but he also trained me to release love, to accept the flow of nature.

Even his very death had been a gentle symbol of release. I had been on a USO tour with the college choral group to the Caribbean the month of December. Mom had spoken to me as to what we should do if Dad died while I was gone for he had withered to some 100 pounds with his enlarged heart. The doctors suggested his heart had doubled in size to keep him warm when, as a small boy, he had to herd cattle on the open range to keep them from straying. During the cold winters, he would skate to keep warm. Oh, such a heart was there— enlarged, yes, to encompass both life and death. I knew he'd want me to respond that all was in God's hands, and I could not possess nor change love's direction to fit anyone's destiny, including his.

319

While I was gone, Mom said one morning, early, he saw a light at the end of his vibrator bed. With only north and west windows, they could not imagine reflection from the just pinkening, early eastern light; and though Mom stood with him, she could not see his light. Holding hands, they concluded it was the Holy Spirit.

How proud he was, waiting on his crutches at that small airport for my airplane. Mom said when he saw the sun glint from our wing tips he repeated, "There she is, there she is." Two days later we shared a joyful New Year's Day dinner; and that night, I, being the last to bed, passed my parents' bedroom door. I saw the reflection from the golden glow of his light above his bed. Mom was already asleep in her bed, her feet dangling over its edge to catch heat from the furnace. She was sleeping soundly, for Dad had called himself a "Wild Man from Borneo", and we had all rallied and relaxed in his pep.

I didn't poke into the room to say goodnight for I knew he was reading the Bible. Since he had been down with swollen ankles, he had turned to reading—something a farmer has little time to do—and he had set a goal of reading the Bible all the way through. He made it to the Book of Esther. The Bible lay open, face down on the chest of drawers. I guess I could say that his last words could be taken from those two open pages, which included chapter four through seven. They express the wrath of an earthly king being diverted by Esther so he will not hang Mordecai on the gallows. Oh, how gracious is God who in His love hung his own son so that Dad and I might live eternally.

On that night could not the king sleep, and he commanded to bring the book of records of the chronicles; and they were read before the king." Esther 6:1. There is no doubt in my mind but that Dad is not just sleeping now but is reading the chronicles to His Own King. He must have turned out the incandescent light and met the holy light soon after I had passed by—and there seemed to be no struggle for earthly air as one leg was pulled casually up under the other. Such a blessed passing. So why was I crying? Couldn't I truly release love to its own as his life and training had labored to teach me?

Stars beamed a message, but my head was tucked in my coat and my tears wet the collar as I aimlessly walked. Other moods rang in my ears as I tried to understand how to release my college years too. Such a beautiful trip it had been to the Caribbean—singing three, four times a day—and being paid for what I loved to do! What a joy life was when work complimented one's soul-song.

But now I was student teaching, and my roommates had complained this night that I was pulling away from them, becoming involved with my own interests. I loved those three girls. We had laughed, studied, talked and cried together. They gave me a surprise birthday party, my name sugared in pink frosted roses on the cake. Mom had sent me 21 roses for each year of my life. Was I truly a grown-up adult now? I wanted to keep a heavy-handed hold on that simple, sweet college life, for joy had been there. How could I become so self-centered, so independent of roommates and other secure trapping of youth? Was the labor of teaching my future, or had I just tumbled into that field because I loved to learn myself. Should I try to sing for my living instead?

Yes, indecision, grief and frustration were all clouding my brain though the moon and stars shone clearly. I gradually became aware that I was standing in front of our little Lutheran church, and I said aloud, "I need the Word of God." But how silly! Surely the church was locked; it was dark, and the minister lived on the other side of town.

Pulling on the two big glass doors that faced east, I was very surprised to be granted entry! Then I thought, "Where are the Bibles?" I remembered a few were usually left on a back table in the nave. "But how will I ever see them? I'm not sure where the light switches are, and anyway, I wouldn't turn them on for I may be mistaken as a thief." I felt my way to the table and touched the soft leather of a Holy Bible. I opened it, blindly. Then feeling around the table a little more, my hand fell on a cold object—a flashlight! Beaming it down to the Open Word, I read: "What am I to do; I will pray with the spirit and I will pray with the mind also; I will sing with the spirit, and I will sing with the mind also." Corinthians 14:14-15. I stopped to absorb the words. Reading on in Corinthians 14:19: "Nevertheless, in church I would rather speak five words with my mind, in order to instruct others, than ten thousand words in a tongue."

My God, wasn't that my answer? I was to both teach and sing, and God's tongue would speak for me. Yes, that was to be my mission, my life's work. I was to be a steward to others. Tears tumbled into sobs as I carried that Bible through the darkened church. I returned to the eastern door and leaned on the jamb. Finally looking up to the moon and stars, I stood in complete and utter awe as white, wispy clouds formed a reclining east-to-west cross! The moon shone it pure and white against the cobalt blue night.

Some time later I tried to rationalize a cross in the sky. One just does not see clouds cross in the sky, and certainly not visible at night. Had it been contrails? Cross-currents? How can one rationalize faith? No. It was Dad again. This time using God's hand. The message was clearly written, for me, intimately and personally. We have no more miracles in this modern world, is that our theme? But are we looking for the small personal miracles in our everyday lives.

Through the worries of my daily teaching, I have to search for mini-miracles—with one 16-year-old girl telling me just today that she is pregnant, and another 15-year-old girl describing a suicide list in her old school and of stories of rapes there and of her brother being a drug pusher and of her mother's husband having fondled her and of her own attempt to commit suicide and on and on and...I cry again, this time for a world which needs more gentle father images. I beg for continued strength. The verses I opened and read tonight were Luke 7:36-50 about the woman who sinned yet cried tears, using them and her hair to wash Christ's feet—and she was forgiven the most. Will my girls ever know the peace that passes all understanding in the cool, refreshingly clear, white-air of forgiveness and God's love? I pray with my mind and my spirit. I sing to God's miraculous grace that shines through gentle moon-glow a song of comfort and peace.

And that night? My miracle, my message, my epiphany, God's glory brought to earth again for one precious moment. And yes, time did stand still again, but this time by stopping the moon for I made it back to the dorm by 10:00.

Cassy Holman   **For Which She Stands**

She has been with us
since Betsy Ross,
And if she wasn't here
America would feel the loss.

With thirteen stripes
red and white alternate,
They create a symbol
no man should desecrate.

The upper part
has fifty stars.

322

Through unrest and peace
she will remain ours.

Our flag is a symbol
of honor and peace,
As well as freedom and equality
across all seas.

To our allies she represents
a purpose for determination.
To our enemies she causes
fear and desertion.

Those who show disrespect
for Old Glory,
Obviously do not cherish
the American story.

Many a word has
been written about her,
And every word has helped
a heart slowly cure.

Through good times
and bad,
All Americans have known
what they had.

A land that not a soul
could take away,
And the envy of the world
here to stay.

Jean Hunt   Untitled

I moved from Sioux City, Iowa to Wayne, Nebraska in order to pursue my Master's Degree. I got the degree plus my husband in 1990. We moved to his home in rural Stanton County where we lived for two years. He injured his back at work and had to find a new occupation. As he had always raised livestock on the side, he decided to make it his full-time job. So we bought a ranch in Keya Paha County. My husband had spent his summers out there mowing hay for relatives. He had always wanted to have a ranch out there, so here was our chance. We bought Ray Baker's place in 1993, which had been in his family for over 100 years.

Having grown up is Sioux Falls, SD, I was not accustomed to life on the ranch. Herding cattle simply did not come natural for me. My husband would put me on a horse to help him round up cattle. It was all I could do to cling to the horse, never mind what the cows were doing. I urged him to get a cow dog. They have a natural gift for knowing what to do and even more importantly, they WANT to do it.

I once got chased by a cow who "was just bluffing" as by husband told me. No, she wasn't just bluffing. I thought she'd stop when I reached the safety of a big tree, but she followed me around it several times before running off to rejoin her calf. My days as a field hand were drawing to a close.

Many of the women who I have met work side-by-side with their husbands. Feeding, mending fence, digging post holes, tagging calves, mowing hay...you name it, they do it. It's cold and windy in the winter. Wet and muddy in the spring. The bugs are awful in the summer. Not to mention the heat.

If I thought the work opportunities were limited, entertainment and recreation were even more so. I soon discovered that farm sales and household auctions were a major event. People came from all around, even if it was just to stand around and eat pie with their neighbors. They didn't interest me much until I learned how to bid. My first purchase was a complete set of 1976 World Book Encyclopedias for only $5. I have been hooked ever since.

Our two kids attend country school, which is only two miles away. Eight kids, one teacher, and a part-time assistant. When we go on field trips we only need two cars. Once we went up to Winner, SD to see their museum. They had an old school house close by, to show how education was done "back in the old days". I found this amusing, because it wasn't much different than the one we have now. One of my step-daughters came to visit shortly after we moved here. She lives in Omaha, and was a grade schooler at the time. We showed her our little school and she said "It's so small. Where is the cafeteria?" We told her the kids brought a sack lunch and ate at their desk. She then wondered "where was the gym?" We said that the kids just play outside during recess. Wow. She couldn't believe it.

Last year I bought a telephone with a caller I.D. When I called the phone company to hook up service, they told me that they didn't have this service out here yet. I am happy to say that we just got it last month. My neighbor tells me how suspicious some folks were back in the 1940's when they were bringing electricity to these parts. Someone said "If we ain't careful, they won't even let us own a flashlight!"

Last week I went to the Christmas party at one of the local churches. Around here, you don't just sit around and visit. You play games. At one point we had to scoot the older women (over 80) out of the circle so we could play "Upset the Fruit Basket". If you've never played this game, it is similar to Musical Chairs. One woman hurt her nose in a collision with another gal, and two others fell to the floor after missing their chairs. Each time something happened, I thought that they would stop the game, but they didn't. Tough girls. Just having fun.

We've been here now for more than seven years. Our boys were both in diapers when we arrived. For them, this is home. I am a "transplant". But of all the places to end up, I'm glad that fate brought me to the Sandhills of Nebraska.

Jim Reese   Euchre at Two

■ for Jack Lammers

Picture Main Street.
Pick-ups in a row like a used car lot,
Chevy vs. rusted Ford—late November after harvest.
The bar full of farmers sitting at round tables,
clean overalls and all—the stench of stale beer and
urinals run dry.
Hear fists slamming down on oak,
the louder the better hand.
See Ernest and Linus Cummins, the 57-year-old
identical out-of-towners,
pause between bites of pie
to see for themselves.

Imagine a more serious affair
than prices dropping $3.00 a bushel—Bankers pockets
swelling off of sweet deals
while every decent man's job runs awry.
Hear Edsel Crampit holler,
"More money in selling the kernel to
Earl May for lawn ornnets or dee-cor
than giving her away!"

Like ghost feathers—there's a muffled
"Open, in, and come on."
Loose change impatiently
moving from one pocket to another.
Squinting lids, shiftin' pupils, and
wide eyes showing all their white.
Hands holding five bid, no bid, Busch Light.

Fist against table,
table on top of floor,
floor covering foundation,
foundation over this
land
they pound.

Shannon Dyer   Social Life in the Sandhills

I got up before dawn on Saturday morning. On an
important day like that, I had to start early so I could get my
chores done before the big event. I had been looking forward to
this for a few weeks and didn't want to miss it. At the stroke of
noon, my husband dropped by the house to pick me up and we
were on our way. A few minutes later we pulled into the
parking area, looking over the pickups and cars for old friends,
checking out license plates to see how far some folks had
traveled. Several couples headed toward the door. A mom and
dad with two grade school-aged boys hurried past us, the
mother extracting promises of good behavior from the boys.

We waved to people we hadn't seen for a long time,
stopped to visit with neighbors, then we, too, made our way to
the entrance.

No, it wasn't opening night at the theater or a museum
show. It wasn't a celebrity benefit or awards banquet.
Nevertheless, it was a big social event, about as big as they get
in the Sandhills, not counting weddings and funerals. It was an
annual bull sale.

Bull sale? A social event? Some of you folks think it is
purely business. And it is business, important for buyers as
well as sellers. But I don't own cattle, don't know much about
genetics, wouldn't know a bad scrotum measurement from an
adequate one. I glanced at the cattle once in a while as they
were ushered into the ring, displayed, the most revealing details
of their existence related over the microphone, poked, prodded,
admired, and eventually purchased. I didn't know if ranchers

were getting good buys or not. Still, I enjoyed the bull sale.

It's a funny sort of social life we lead here in the Sandhills. We really don't need an excuse for a party, so any event has the potential to become one. An older friend once told me, "You know, since our kids graduated from high school, we don't have much of a social life anymore. We miss traveling to all the games."

Maybe because so many folks live many miles away from neighbors and town they don't get a chance to casually visit the way city folk do, they make an occasion of the simplest get-togethers. In our town, anything can turn into a social event: bull sales, school board meetings, high school sports, music programs. An unexpected meeting of two or three women friends in front of the grocery store constitutes a party, and if they bring their husbands to town and those men meet up in the hotel, you might as well plan on making a night of it.

City dwellers have cocktail parties (so I read in magazines), office parties, grand openings, special moments involving dressing up, eating fancy foods, gathering at unusual places. Since we don't have access to that level of culture, we rarely get out of jeans and boots and a steak tastes just as good with spurs on as it does in spectator pumps, maybe better because your "dogs" can breathe. We don't have to prepare for a social event. We're always ready.

In my opinion, the bull sale turned out to be a big success. I caught up on news and gossip, told a few jokes, learned some new ones. The food was great and there was plenty of it. Everyone seemed to have a wonderful time. All in all, a perfect social event.

What's that? You want to know the sale average and how many bulls changed hands? Gosh, I don't keep track of trivial details like that.

Margie Bonta   Untitled

I taught in a little rural school six miles from my home. I had 12 students total in all eight grades. I worked hard to get the two eighth graders ready for spring tests they had to pass in order to go to high school.

The winters were very cold with lots of snow. I stayed with a family near school. The kids took turns bringing in fire wood and coal for the pot belly stove. Many times a member of the school board would scoop snow and light the little stove. The kids brought potatoes to put in the coals beneath the stove for dinner; we placed Jell-O and ice cream in the snow.

We decorated the windows and put linoleum on the floor. We played games and had art on Friday. We had great fun preparing for the Christmas program. In the spring, I drove my Model A on the muddy roads (There was no such thing as gravel).

I received a Two Year Teaching Certificate by going to summer school at Wayne State and passing the State Boards. It was a great experience for me. I was only 16.

The parents were all so good to me.

Mick Scarlett   Rural Life Expectancy

What is the life expectancy of our rural communities? Before I try to answer that question, let me explain what I mean by rural communities. I don't mean areas within easy driving distance of large cities or towns where jobs and services are plentiful. These areas, although technically rural, are filling up with people who work in these cities and towns. When I talk rural, I mean areas ten to thirty miles from a town of one to two hundred people and fifty to one hundred miles from a larger town or city. In other words, I am talking about the boondocks.

Although I have lived seven and one half miles west of Bartlett, Nebraska for fifty years, I could happily live thirty miles north of Mullen, Nebraska with no problem. These are what I consider rural areas. I think life expectancy in these areas is perhaps one to two generations from extinction. Even with better county roads and better vehicles, most people would shy away from being quite that isolated. Even television can't entertain people enough that they would enjoy these areas as permanent residents. Can you imagine visiting Wally World only twice a year?

I am lucky as I married a rural pearl named Kathy. She may not be as rural as I am but she is definitely rural. The drive through town (Bartlett, population two hundred) once a day to clean out my trailer for me is as close as she cares to get to socializing. Her yard, dog, and our few cattle are all the company she needs. I thank God for her every night. The physical labor and mental stress she has endured the last twenty one years since I fell from a windmill and broke my back would overwhelm many lesser women. She is a television person and loves any kind of sports, with football at the top of the list and hockey at the bottom.

Although I drive truck and talk to many people every

day, I would be perfectly happy working alone in my shop on an old two-cylinder John Deere or my 1941 Dodge Luxury Liner. My relaxation time is usually spent just reading a good book. Any book. We never had television until I was eighteen years old, so I never became addicted to the boob tube as we called it. When I was growing up, if more than the mailman passed our place during the day, we ran to see who it was. Now vehicles pass all times of the day and night, usually someone working at the feedlot up north.

Being rural to me not only means living in an isolated area but loving to live in an isolated area. As I said before that generation of people is nearly extinct. They may never become extinct but their numbers will be so few that they might as well be. One could hold a reunion for these kind of people once a year but no one would come. They would all be too busy entertaining themselves. They are not unfriendly snobs or social rejects. In most cases, in fact, they usually love to visit and can carry on quite a conversation when the opportunity arises.

One of the main reasons they are usually good conversationalists is because they don't sit in the coffee shop three hours a day and aren't all talked out. Like myself, they usually enjoy conversations with strangers since they may learn something new from them. I recall a fellow bumping into my dad from behind at a farm sale one time, thinking he knew him. When dad turned around the fellow said, "Oh I'm sorry I thought you were someone else. I guess I don't know you." Dad replied, "I know you if you're going for coffee." Off they went and fifteen minutes later they were no longer strangers.

The summer I graduated from high school I rode pastures and cared for cattle on a large ranch of thirty-six sections. I don't even remember what I got paid. It really didn't matter what the pay was because as I look back now I would have done it for nothing. There were no cell phones and no two-way radios. It was just me, my horse, and an imagination that was as free as the wind. Now that was rural. I had my lunch in one saddlebag, a vaccinating gun and vaccine in the other, fence pliers, my lasso, and a .22 rifle in the scabbard. Every day when I left the ranch I rode back into the past a hundred years. Now the pastures are checked with four wheelers and in pickups and airplanes.

Things sure have changed in rural Nebraska. They are as different as night and day. I guess you call that progress. Like I said before, I am a rural person but I would draw the line on one thing. I wouldn't live so far out that the radio wouldn't pick up CORNHUSKER FOOTBALL. One of my favorite memories of my dad is seeing him standing at the end of a cornfield by our old WC Allis Chalmers and two row picker with a six transistor radio up to his ear listening to Nebraska and Colorado play. I got back with an empty wagon and our old B John Deere just in time to hear the final play. The Colorado ball carrier was stopped on the three-yard line to keep them from scoring as the clock ran out. Put another squeaker in the win column for the Cornhuskers, throw the old six transistor in the toolbox, and let's pick some more corn. Some things just don't change.

Steven P. Schneider   Chanukah Lights Tonight

Our annual prairie Chanukah party
latkes, kugel, cherry blintzes.
Friends arrive from nearby towns
and dance the twist to "Chanukah Lights Tonight"
spin like a dreidel to a Klezmer hit.

The candles flicker in the window.
Outside, ponderosa pines are tied in red bows.
If you squint,
the neighbors' Christmas lights
look like the Omaha skyline.

The smell of oil is in the air.
We drift off to childhood
where we spent our gelt
on baseball cards and movies,
cream sodas and potato knishes.

No delis in our neighborhood.
Only the wind howling over the crushed corn stalks.
Inside, we try to sweep the darkness out,
waiting for the Messiah to knock
wanting to know if he can join the party.

Gerald Lockhart   My First Rodeo

Let me say that I was born and raised in Nebraska. We lived 18 miles east of Burwell, in Garfield County, for many years. I am now 82 years old, so my first Rodeo at Burwell was either in 1921 or 1922. I would have been seven or eight years old at the time.

Today we buzz over the hard surface road and eighteen miles don't seem very far. But in the days of Burwell's first Rodeo, it was a different story.

I have to think of the preparation that it took to get ready to go. We made sure the old Model T had a tank full of gas, was full of oil, and had a 5 gallon can of water tied to the running board to replenish the radiator, as needed. My mother would fry a bunch of chicken and prepare a big lunch that we would eat when we got there. No fast food places in those days.

Our neighbors, who lived about a quarter of a mile from us, were making the same preparations, as we planned to go at the same time. That way, we could help each other if needed. I remember the anticipation and excitement of going to the first Rodeo. But we still had 18 miles to go over a so-called road that was nothing more than two tracks across the prairie, up hill and down.

We were finally on our way. It was about 10 a.m., and that gave us two hours to go the 18 miles, eat our lunch and be ready for the Rodeo to start at 1 p.m. After stopping a couple of times and filling the radiator, we were going down the big hill east of the river, across the old bridge and into Burwell and the Rodeo grounds. We had time to eat our lunch and get in to the bleachers before it started. I remember I was so excited about the whole thing I could hardly eat any lunch. I just couldn't wait to see my first Rodeo.

At that time, they had one grandstand that wasn't very large, and on the east end of that, they had a set of bleachers. That was where we sat right out in the open. The sun was quite hot, but we didn't mind. Right east of the bleachers there was a set of corrals that held the stock. The track was laid out, but was only fenced on the side past the corrals and grandstand. The rest was open arena.

The stock was let out of the shoots into the track and everything took place right in front of the bleachers and grandstand. Talk about ring side seats, we had them. Between events, they would have a horse race. There were no jockeys, as we know them now. These were just cowboys that had a horse they thought could outrun someone else's.

331

The race we enjoyed the most was the relay. Each contestant had three horses and a helper. They would ride one horse around the track to the starting point. Then they would jump off and put their saddle on the next horse as fast as possible, jump on, and around they would go again. Some would jump on before they had the cinch fastened good, and start off and a kerplunk! they would fall off, saddle and all. Talk about mass confusion, when there were six or eight horses, and men trying to get changed and away.

There was no P.A. system at that time. The announcer was riding a horse and used a megaphone to call the events and times, etc.

The grand finale was the wild horse race. Two men and one wild horse made up the team. They had to saddle the horse, while their partner tried to hold it, then get on, if they could, and get around the track with just the halter and lead rope for a guide. There were usually six or eight horses and men in this event. What a scramble! Some made it around the track and some didn't. Some even ended up going around the track the wrong way, and of course, that didn't count.

We must remember that the stock for these first rodeos was brought in off the ranches and had never been to town before. They performed because they were wild and afraid.

Yes, the first rodeos were much different than now, but I believe we enjoyed them more, probably because they were not so professional.

Marjorie Finley   Change

"Change" is the word that can describe rural life throughout the century in modern Nebraska. Technology in communications and custom building of new highways (especially through the central part of the Sandhills area) brought together the borders of our state.

Education helped build awareness of economical change. Our educated children went for higher salaries and better jobs with personal family benefits. Agriculture machinery became larger and did more of the "work" letting people do cleaner chores. Cattle feed lots, hog confinement, and chicken farms are now a part of the country scene.

In rural northwestern Nebraska, the agricultural life

style appears to be substantial with cattle but more recreational with hunting (elk, deer, big horn sheep, wild turkey) and tourism (camping, family reunions at Fort Robinson and scenery of the Pine Ridge).

Schools have merged. Children are now taught at home, in private or public schools.

Churches have expanded into new "starts" and/or ethnic congregations.

Apathy has finally diminished spiritually among the people. Folks care about what is happening in their neighborhoods and communities.

Historical events, family reunions, alumni activities, senior citizen centers, assisted living housing, investments, money, retirement, jobs, conservation, recreation, transportation, utilities and communication are all becoming topics of daily and general conversation.

E-mail, the internet, and computers are now changing the rural lifestyle in Nebraska. Libraries are still information centers and there is a better standard of living for more people.

The world is becoming smaller and yet "rural" income is still low. Yields are better than ever but some people are starving. More people are helping the poor and yet material goods are plentiful, but income is low for rural laborers.

Computer shopping, E-mail, and Internet activity will keep people informed but may change the fellowship of activity in modern rural society.

Historical territory is being relived through the Oregon Trail, Mormon Trail, California Trail, Pony Express, and Hiking-Bicycle Trails. More people are aware of the environment and ecosystem of our state. Stories of the past are popular, and western, rural "character" is appreciated as people seek peace in the country.

Perhaps Nebraska will remain a "full" state yet into the future.

Together we could make the Bridge (Gateway to the West) in Kearney and the Long Pine Hidden Paradise in the north canyon (off Highway 20) places of joyful happiness for the dedicated rural citizens of agriculture (and others) who have never seen either one, because they go through Nebraska instead of stopping for recreation and rest.

Rosalyn Jones   Here Lie Plain Folk

I have been a bone hunter on the Great Plains, and bone hunters attempt to draw conclusions about things, including communities, that are only skeletons of their former selves. We examine scattered, osseous fragments, like those of the oreodont I found while browsing in the forbidden sediments of a quiet arroyo. I tried to visualize it wandering in prehistoric grass, lazing through the heat of high noon, looking away with distance-bemused eyes. Time, in turn, had clamped the oreodont in a relentless hold until erosion worried it free. For all that I held its wind-polished bones in my hands, I could not flesh the creature out. I had it and I had it not.

I experience the same haunting frustration when confronted by the remains of Great Plains communities. How should one articulate what is left? If the Great Plains have gotten a bad press, so, too, have the folk who live here. The suspicion is that they are boneheads for coming. We've chosen to describe them as spare, angular stock, picked clean by the ebb and flow of great tidal winds, inclined to jut a stolid haunch into flinty heat or steely cold. Sometimes, they just hunker down and make a virtue of obstinacy.

Still, it is difficult to fault them for setting up their cardboard cutout towns to cast at least a temporary shadow into the openness.

Amherst is one of those myriad small towns. In many ways, it is a centenarian dinosaur lumbering and creaking down the trail to possible extinction. The railroad that supplied it has already settled into oblivion. Someone has come by and pried up the steel femurs. Grass and trees have come hesitantly to claim the right-of-way. The trains are out of track. The town is out of time.

In the town itself, there are so many empty lots. It seems a contradiction in terms. Parts of the town shut down slowly and are become miniature boneyards. Both grocery stores, the lumberyard, and two gas stations—all are closed. The bank folded up and died years ago. The brick carapace slouched in crumpled glory at the corner of Garfield Avenue and Main until, cumbered not so much with the weight of time, but simply weary of shouldering Nebraska weather, it collapsed into itself and was unceremoniously carted away. The old ledgers and their fossilized record of debits and credits are gone. A community center has risen in the lot the bank once occupied.

A rising up, a lying down to near oblivion—that is the inexorable way of things. Perhaps future bone seekers will somehow tap into memory's aquifer and resurrect the shadowy people of this place. They will see them home on dark country roads, graced with speech, laughter, and the memory of light

that misted from town windows. Perhaps they will plumb the
collective memory of the venerable old men who presided over
the town tavern. They will see them gathered in smoky gloom,
weathered trilobites, well-grounded in local sediments, only
seeming to peer out from inward-looking eyes.

In the community center gatherings, there are many
who could trace their origins to immigrants of German-
Lutheran stock. A few miles from what would become our town,
they organized a church in 1883. Having wrested the initial
church from sod, they graduated to a frame building in 1889.
The Immanuel Lutheran Church was a rural landmark until it
was razed in 1970. A stone monument is all that remains to
mark the altar site. During high summer, it is hidden in the
willowy greens of alfalfa, bromegrass, and foxtail. Then, the
quietude is shattered by a swather that comes to sever the
exuberant growth. It makes its rounds and retires from the
field, pausing briefly to survey the grassy carnage fallen in
strangely ordered ranks.

A few steady rows of somber cedars, the unkempt and
the nicely trimmed, rise up together to mark the other
community of fallen in the church cemetery. It lies at the top of
a hill, in the corner formed by our pasture and the road.
Schools and cemeteries are often seen slouched on hilltops. I
suspect that good drainage is a consideration. Every fall, the
road crew sets up a picket fence to keep the snow from blocking
the road. The pickets, for all their mighty clattering in tight
formation, yield to a fine floury assault and the road is closed at
least once each winter.

At least twice each year, someone is hired to mow the
cemetery. They do a perfect, painstaking job, even though most
in this quiet neighborhood are not their people. Those who
lived out their lives in disparate economic spheres are all
returned to the same sod. If some remain unconvinced that
death has reduced them all to equally low estate, the mower is
here to enforce the dictum.

The hired mowers have also taken the terror out of
Memorial Day eve, which was usually the time we remembered
what we had forgotten—to mow our lots. In good years, when
memory served, my parents' house was close enough to the
cemetery that we could push the mower up the road and get the
job done. We were then compelled to comment, along with
everyone else, about the so-and-so who never mowed his lot or
set the mower at a height different from surrounding lots and
"just ruined the looks of the cemetery for everybody." We could

feel superior for having better remembered relatives who had shrugged off a load and lain down to take their ease for good. Those meaningful glances at the lots of the nonmowers were part of our Memorial Day tradition. More than a few times, we were in that select group marked for community opprobrium—until we found redemption the next year in an early mowing.

There is no underground sprinkler system here, no manicured bluegrass conceit. There is just sober, unassuming buffalo grass, liberally interspersed with weeds. It is not flashy, but has staying power in the face of unforgiving summers and winters. The folk who tenant these lots probably thought of themselves in the same terms. There is Henry Herbst who marched off to fight in the Civil War. He survived Andersonville, a cannonball in the shoulder, and came home to find a hill he couldn't take. It took him. His stone is an older one on the east side of the cemetery. It is a fine gray block. There is Wilhelm Trennt. His marker rises east, yet, of Henry. As captain of a sailing vessel, he might have found a greater measure of affection for the wind that chisels these plains.
There is no "lost at sea" inscribed on his stone. He, too, returned to this landlocked boneyard. Therese Schipper has two markers at the south end. She was brought out to the cemetery in a wagon box and buried at night, during a rainstorm. There was a plague upon the land—diphtheria. At 34, she was gone. The thinking was that a prompt burial would slow the spread of diphtheria. Sometimes, thinking didn't seem to make much difference.

If I walk up in the cool of the evening, these and other stones are still warm from the heat of the day. They remind one not so much of death, but hearths that move one to pause in warmth and recollection. Here, among stones and bones, in this formal boneyard, is a good place to brush away the accumulated debris of daily routine. There is occasion to sift through pieces of memory until the last dirt is removed and that one polished piece is lifted intact into bright and sharpened sunlight. I recall one such shard vividly.

One summer, some 16 years ago, my sister and I painted my grandmother's house. She lived in town then, at 81 the world's greatest seamstress, cook, and oracle of common sense. A few years later, we gathered on a fine October morning and brought her out to the country one last time. We started work in July, when scraping paint under wasp-infested eaves made for unbearable heat and discomfort. I'd like to paint again among wasps and heat.

Marjorie Saiser   Wearing Down to Fit

A spoon worn down cattywampus
from stirring against the bottom of pots,
she gets ready for church, paints her nails,
scalloped corn baking,
a ham under foil in the oven,
chickens fed. He's finally ready,

her shoes a Sunday sound
against the boards of the porch,
a Sunday sound up the aisle
of Zion Lutheran Evangelical,
into her pew, purse on her lap.
Lean up to speak to the neighbors,
how much rain or how bad we need it.
The ham warming, staying juicy

under its tent, the corn and the eggs
and the milk firming under their layer
of buttered crumbs. No bread in the freezer,
have to make biscuits, no big deal oven's hot already,
set the table while they brown,
maybe Dan and Esther will come,
made the jello last night and

the cake yesterday. Just a cake,
a little ice cream. Sunday dinner:
an old spoon, heavy, silver, worn
down to fit, years,
cream sauce and pudding
and gravy, don't think about it,
another Sunday, another week,
another ham or pork or beef.

Michael Lynch   Hand-Waving Story

Nobody waves anymore. He supposed he deserved it.
When he was a teenager, all his friends used to flip off
everybody driving highway ninety-two. Then somebody's mom
heard about them giving the bird. That behavior came to a stop
right quick.
   So they started doing their own wave. They must have
seen it on an MTV video. Who frigging knows. But anyways,

337

they would do this thing where they would whip out one hand, close to the windshield, with all fingers spread straight. It looked as if they were casting a spell on approaching vehicles.

This waving lasted until he got out of high school. About that time he started to favor no wave at all. Guess he figured he'd be going to college at Johnson County down in Kansas. The only tooling around he did was through regions alien to him. Plus he was just sick of all that country hick waving.

But he always did admire a good wave. It was something like a solid handshake. Or maybe a square meal that stuck to your ribs, and you leave patting your belly. Dale Grotstsky farmed out near Valley County. Well, you'd see him out there on Hwy 92 in his old green Dodge pickup. Straight jawed and checking fields, he would raise one arm from the elbow straight up. A set of fingers limp and crooked from age and rheumatism were suspended in mid air. His arm was extended as if he just had a brilliant idea come to mind, or he wanted to pull you over so he could tell you something he'd forgot. Or you'd see Tip Stonacek raise a trigger finger from the steering wheel. Just as the other car was about to drive by, ole Tip would shake that finger with the force of a dog tugging on a bone. Then ole Tip would let go and allow the car to pass.

Don't know about Dale or Tip, but he always hated tough guys. Born again cowboys usually. They'd be out tearing around in their king cabs and big tires, like some frigging gods on wheels. If they'd wave at all, it would be a slow peel of their first finger from the wheel. Immediately the finger would drop with the weight of the world. It was as if they were saying you ain't hardly worth the effort.

Later on he went to school in Kansas City, Kansas. Nobody waved there. In fact, it was best if you didn't wave at all. He was told not to make any defining gestures or else a guy could be tailed and get his ass kicked in a parking lot someplace. He also heard not to flick high beams at somebody with only cruise lights on at dusk. Street gangs were supposedly driving these vehicles. These gangs would turn around, track you down and kill you as initiation into their frigging gang.

Of course, once he couldn't wave at anyone, all he wanted to do was wave at everyone. So, that's when he started taking backroads home. Over breaks from school, he worked on perfecting his wave. Starting off with an open palm, it evolved from a "howdy pardner" swing to a calculated two finger turn of the wrist. Resting in perfect symmetry on the wheel, he would simultaneously extend salutations while maintaining course. Steady as she goes and all that. What came to be known as the "two finger pheasant head lift" didn't quite suit him. Finally, he settled on resting the right palm against the wheel. Holding his hand at two o'clock, he would gradually raise all four fingers in a generous sweep.

Driving up Hwy 81 during deer season, he noticed nobody waving. It was early in the morning so he figured the sun was right behind him and oncoming vehicles couldn't see all too well. By midday, there were still no waves to be had. So, that's when he decided this new development was the handiwork of Kansans who don't like out of state plates. He figured things would be different once he got back to Nebraska. This did not prove to be the case, though. Hardly any movement was being flushed out from the driver sides the further north he drove.

He began to wonder if it was his sunglasses or his long hair. Cars went by so fast, depending on weather and road conditions, he could barely make out any drivers passing by him in the next lane. Then he thought it must be the car. His pile was built right here in the U S of A. It wasn't pretty, but at least it worked. People should really be waving purely out of sympathy. About then it was decided if he were in a pickup this dilemma would never have come up.

But an idea would not escape him. He remembered back to when he was young. He began to think that somehow flipping off farmers caused this rash of anti-waving. He couldn't get it out of his head. People were tired of greeting a perfect stranger and not having that greeting returned. Or worse yet, to get the finger.

One of the few good things of plains living was becoming eradicated. His sophomoric behavior had no doubt contributed to its demise. A thought came to mind. He realized that something had to be done. He felt individually responsible to act. So, he took it onto himself to begin a hand waving revival campaign.

Any car he saw, any make or model, any slickness or toughness, he would wave at it. Any time, thin daylight or tired clouds, he would go out of his way to acknowledge the presence of another fellow driver. Even when the sun was setting directly in his eyes, and there were merely tall shadows in the passenger seats, he'd wave. But he did draw the line when it came to divided highways, or a row of cars behind a slow moving vehicle. Or driving the interstate, because he just felt like a freak or a pervert.

But, when driving on the open road, with clear skies and no threat of high winds, rains, snow or deer, he is the one who's waving.   .

Jean Groth   Rural 2000

As I look at the diminishing farm families around us,
I notice that many of the farms are being rented out or sold as
acreages.
The people who actually work the land are accumulating more
and more acres.
And there are people from the city filling those homes that were
once harboring the
"American Farmer."
This poem reflects one of those situations of a stock trader
moving to a rented farm.

farm turned acreage
collecting rent   no taxes paid
escaping urban business
retraction to rural quiet
tired of the exchange of time for money
imac the computer
the internet connection
the ameritrade brokerage account
wake up
hay the horse
feed the dog
check the cats
8:30 am the stock market opens
day trade in – day trade out
e-commerce....e-business....e-webb
simple clothing
slippers on feet   smell of coffee
quiet background
market closes 3:00 pm
sun sets
life on the farm
as good as it gets

Many of us have hobbies, from collecting coins, to baseball cards, to beanie babies. Some people take their hobbies very seriously, spending lots of money to buy the most recent beanie baby. Some spend a good part of their life going through antique store after antique store looking for an eighteenth century tea kettle. But how many of you have a hobby which would cause you to spend your summer days, the hottest, driest, windiest, days, sitting on a horse twirling a rope?

My father team ropes for a hobby, a very expensive hobby if you count the cost of ropes, horses, and roping steers. Most people who have this hobby of team roping are referred to as "ropers," an entirely different breed.

"Ropers" is also the term applied to the longhorn cattle that the human "ropers" use for practice. Many animal experts have placed the sheep as the dumbest farm animal, but trust me when I say that sheep have five times the brain of a roping steer. It is true, roping steers are the dumbest creatures alive, just barely beating my brother. Their horns could only be three inches long and they would still manage to get their head stuck in a hayrack. Or if you have them squeezed as tight as possible in a narrow alley, barely three feet wide, the animals would manage to get turned in the opposite direction thereby becoming almost suffocated by the push of the rest. From my own experience, I would have to insist that the roping steer is the stupidest creature alive.

When it is time to go to a roping jackpot, we round up the roping calves on horseback or with the four wheeler. After you manage to load all the roping steers and horses into the trailer, you race home to change. If you wish to be able to ride a horse you must wear jeans. I once tried to get away with wearing shorts and still riding; it was a very, very painful experience. Your knees will be red and raw for the entire week. So you have a choice of wearing jeans and dying of heat or of wearing shorts and suffering through a week of red blisters. Given the two choices I choose jeans.

A common sight at a roping is all the little kids, ropers in training, riding around on horses, entirely unsupervised. Most are six years old or even younger. These kids are set on top of the gentlest horses and allowed to roam free. Their legs are so short that they stick out horizontally from the saddle. The older kids are busy trying to tie each other up with ropes or harassing the steers by throwing rocks, sticks, or whatever else is handy. There are a few women who accompany their husbands along, or even rope themselves, but the majority of ropers tend to be divorced. In fact one of the leading topics at a roping is who has been recently divorced and how much the wife took him for.

During the roping, the kids' job is either to help push cattle, unrig (take the ropes off the steers' horns), or keep out of the way. A roping will last the whole afternoon and into the night, if the arena has lights. This is the hottest and windiest day of the year, so it is necessary to apply sunscreen periodically during the day. All of that sunscreen will cause nearly half of the dirt in the arena to stick like glue to your skin, the other half is either in your teeth or in your eyes.

Going to the bathroom during a roping is a tricky operation. It's much easier for the men I'm sure, but for the women, it takes a bit more effort. There is not a real bathroom anywhere near the arena so it is necessary to use the only other concealment, the cattle trailers. It works best if you go in pairs, while one is in the trailer doing her business the other stands guard. Inside the trailer, it is a whole different world from the hot and windy outdoors. Inside it is at least fifty degrees hotter and not a breath of wind, not to mention the few inches of manure on the floor.

However the most interesting cultural experience of roping is the ropers themselves. Their attire may range form the diehard cowboys in long sleeved shirts and cowboy hats to the more modern attire of muscle shirts and baseball caps. But they all have one thing in common, horrible grammar. My English teacher would pass out cold if she heard all of the "ain'ts" and "I seen's" that constitute most ropers' vocabulary. For roping itself they have completely different terms that an outsider would find impossible to understand. The CIA could merely use the roping language for completely foolproof codes. For example: the term "puked", which means in standard English, "He missed the Steer". Or going "nine-o", going very fast. And "fishin it on" is when the header tries to "fish" the rope onto the steer's horns.

While ropers may seem like an odd race with very few characteristics similar to normal people, they are the most open hearted and down to earth people I know. Sure, their lifestyle is not the best, and they enjoy spending the night at a bar. But they would do anything for a friend to help him out, from lending him money, which they can't afford, to helping with the guy's chores.

    While the roping itself is a very serious and hot affair, afterwards it is party time. Every roper brings a cooler full of refreshments for afterwards and everyone shares with everyone else. After the exhausted steers and horses are loaded up, the entire party goes to the nearest bar. The ropers who placed at the top spend a good part of their winning buying refreshments for their less lucky fellow ropers. My favorite part is the food. Everyone is starving after spending the entire afternoon either roping or pushing cattle so everyone orders a steak: paradise. It is usually around one to two o'clock in the morning when you finally get to bed after the ride home and after putting the horses and steers up.

    Even though roping may be an expensive and time consuming hobby there are certain points about it which make it fun. Such as meeting a totally different culture from your usual high school buddies. Roping is an enjoyable pastime for those who wish to put the time and effort into it.

Peter Beeson   **So It Goes**

A dusting of snow highlights deep green winter wheat
and a bow of bright yellow leaves frames a fading blue sky.
Tall white sentinels, stuffed of unwanted grain,
stand guard over rusty ribbons of steel that run westward,
leaving town like so many others have over the years.

Bare trees cast afternoon shadows over faded seed and feed signs
while grain dust and road dirt share the air
with the silence of boarded school house windows
and the creaking of abandoned swing sets
that move lazily in the breeze that drifts in across the empty fields.

Streets, vacant, cracked and worn, turn to gravel,
then dirt; running away into a setting sun;
marking off unplowed fields, assets of a bank gone under.
Homes, gray and worn, mostly empty,
recede; shrinking from bright red "For Sale" signs.

A tattered gray cat, a left-behind mouser,
wanders from porch to porch,
crossing the church steeple's long black shadow

that creeps down main street running back to
peeling white paint, dust laden pews, and empty collection
plates.

Like cattle at a feed trough,
a few mud splattered pick-ups line the curb,
staring into dark storefronts,
whose windows reflect less and less comings and more and
more goings
and stare back as empty reminders of better days and lost
friends.

The only sounds are the rustling of leaves on old brick streets
and the faint talk of the weather drifting from the tavern
where gray stubbled faces with farmer tans
and sad, weather worn eyes blankly search the Hamms beer
sign.

Rolled up coveralls hover over old scuffed boots
that shift with discomfort at the mention of foreclosure.
In each other's faces they see the loss of friends and family,
survivors or hangers on, not sure which, or if it matters;
together, they share the passing of a way of life.

11-2-98

Biographies

Pamela Bowen Anderson (p. 258) is a ranch wife, mother of three, and part time church secretary living in northwest Nebraska. She and her husband, Dale, own land that has been in the Anderson family for four generations. Her great respect for the pioneers who settled the land and their descendants who remain on that land prompted this writing.

M.J. Anthony (pp. 66, 150) has always lived on a working farm except for college years. She is the treasurer of a family farm corporation and is still learning about computers. Her greatest joy is her family; one husband of fifty years, three children, and six grandchildren.

Curt Arens (p. 13) and his wife live on his parent's old homeplace near Crofton, NE. He is the fourth generation of his family to live and farm that land. In addition to farming full-time, Curt is a staff writer for two local papers and a news correspondent for the Norfolk Daily News.

Ruth Baker (p. 228) is now living in Ainsworth, Nebraska. She was the 11th child of Mr. and Mrs. Rueben Wallace and was born on September 11, 1930 at Long Pine, Nebraska. She has lived in Brown County all but 5 five years she spent in Denver after her first husband passed away.

As a writer and news editor of The Times, **Elizabeth Barrett** (p. 27) is privileged to practice her craft and learn about day-to-day happenings in the progressive farm community of Gothenburg. The escapades of Barrett's 4-year-old daughter Betsy and hot dog throwing attorney husband Steve Potter are related in many of her columns. Barrett has a bachelor's and master's degree from the University of Nebraska-Lincoln and taught journalism at the University of Nebraska at Kearney for 10 years.

Peter Beeson (pp. 17, 343) came to Nebraska in 1970 to attend the University of Nebraska-Lincoln. While working on his Ph.D. he taught at the university, worked at the Lincoln Regional Center, coordinated research, and directed the evaluation of a community corrections program. He is currently the Administrator of Division of Strategic Management Services Division of the Nebraska Health & Human Services System. Dr. Beeson has also been involved with rural mental health advocacy, policy, and research for many years. He is the current President of the National Association for Rural Mental Health.

In 1992, he received the Victor I. Howery Award for significant contributions to rural mental health. Dr. Beeson has written a number of articles and reports on rural mental health and other topics. He has also served on a number of national and state advisory groups such as the National Rural Health Advisory Committee. Dr. Beeson's photographs and poetry have been used to illustrate national and state reports. He has also contributed poetry and photo essays to Nebraska Life magazine.

Carol Beins (pp. 75, 303) is enjoying 5 kids and a new husband. She holds an undergraduate degree in Journalism and a graduate degree in American History/Museum Studies from the University of Nebraska-Lincoln. If someone would pay her to do it, she would love to be a college student forever. If this person is out there, please call.

Lora Lunzmann Black (pp. 217, 277) grew up on a farm 1&½ miles east of Johnson, NE, in the southeastern part of the state. She graduated from JHS in 1968, attended Dana College in Blair 2 years, and graduated from Peru State College in 1977. She firmly believe that she was very fortunate growing up in the rural lifestyle. Every opportunity She had when she was little, she'd run out of the house to go find her father in the field, just so she could ride along with him on the tractor- the Allis-Chalmers WD45. Her love of nature and the outdoors comes from these experiences. She has her parents to thank for that. Presently, she is the weekday afternoon host of Afternoon Concert, and Friday's Classics By Request for the statewide network, Nebraska Public Radio. Her hobbies include working in her garden; watching and cheering her daughter Rachel's many softball, volleyball and tennis teams: her son, Zach's many Lincoln High music concerts; visiting her older son, Andrew and his wife, Jen and her first grandchild, Katharine Anne. She is married to James Black II, and they just celebrated their 30th wedding anniversary.

Leo Blaha (p. 170) is the fourth generation of the Blaha family to live in the Warsaw Precinct. His great-grandfather, Matthew Blaha, came from Czechoslovakia and settled in the precinct in 1875. Leo still lives on the family farm, is married and has two daughters. He has been active in local organizations, raised certified seed, and is now retired.

Florence Blanchard (p. 313) was born on a farm 10 miles northwest of North Bend. She attended North Bend H.S. She began teaching in rural schools in 1947, and in 1978 she graduated cum laude from Midland Lutheran College. She and her husband have two grown children, are retired and live in North Bend.

Carlene Bodlak (p. 154) lives at Emerson, Nebraska with her husband, Marvin, and their four children. They raise corn, soybeans, and alfalfa. During the school year, Carlene volunteers an afternoon a week helping her children's teachers. She also teaches Sunday school. Her hobbies include reading, writing, and crocheting.

Cynthia Boehler (p. 307) thinks that living in two different small south-central communities with her family has been perhaps one of life's biggest blessings.

Dorothy Boettner (p. 222) lived in Saunders County, Pohocco Precinct all her life until December, 1999 when health problems and loneliness caused her to move to Fremont, NE. She graduated from UNL and took graduate classes at the University of Iowa. Though she is a farmer at heart, Dorothy also loves to teach, and taught American History at high schools in Hickman, Cedar Bluffs, and Fremont for nearly 30 years. She is an avid quilter and china painter, and even headed the committee which painted the 24 place settings of china for the Governor's Mansion in 1987.

Janet Bond (p. 236) lives in her own home in the village of Gresham. She has two sons who live in Arizona and California. The woman of whom she writes is her mother.

Margie Bonta (p. 327) was born in 1930 and graduated from Sholes High School. She taught rural school in Wayne County for two years and was married in Randolph, NE. She and her husband operated the Fillmore County News for nearly 40 years. She has 10 children, all of whom have college degrees. She is now retired and living in Exeter, NE.

Mary J. Borm (pp. 34, 121) grew up on a small farm in the Platte River Valley of central Nebraska. She moved to the Sandhills in 1990 and lives on a ranch eleven miles northwest of Purdum with my husband Dewey Keys. She has been writing for only six years or so, and describes her pieces as "mostly incoherent ramblings." And, for the past five years, she has performed 'cowboy poetry' in public.

Poet, novelist and short-story writer **J. V. Brummels** (pp. 25, 78, 138, 231, 268) grew up in northern Nebraska, first on a rented quarter section in Cedar County and later on a ranch in the Sandhills. After his graduate work at Syracuse University, he joined the faculty of Wayne State College, where he coordinates the Plains Writers Series and edits *Nebraska Territory,* a review of the literature of the Northern Plains. His poems have been widely published in journals and little magazines. His most recent collection is *Cheyenne Line,* due out from The Backwaters Press this year. He has received a number of awards, including a Literature Fellowship from the National Endowment for the Arts and The Mildred Bennett Award from the Nebraska Center for the Book. Brummels is the publisher of Logan House. He lives in western Wayne County, Nebraska, where he and his family run a horseback cattle operation.

Dale-Marie Bryan (p. 207) has been writing forever, it seems, and is inspired most often while behind the wheel of a tractor. She has had both fiction and non-fiction works published. The mother of four and a former teacher, she especially enjoys writing for children. Dale-Marie farms with her husband, Floyd, along the Nebraska border near McCook.

Jill (Colwell) Burkey (pp. 52, 167, 213) grew up on a ranch southwest of Hay Springs, NE. She attended Nebraska Wesleyan University and received a B.A. in English and Business Administration with an endorsement in Secondary Education. She and her husband, Todd, moved back to the family ranch in February 2000 where they are the fourth generation to carry on the ranching tradition in her family. Earl & Jeanette Colwell, Jill's great grandparents, brought Pepper Creek Ranch into existence in approximately 1916.

Rose Burrows (p. 319) was born in the western Nebraska Panhandle and was raised in the same area as her first cousin, Mari Sandoz. Her grandmother Elvina Sandoz Burrows was a sister to Old Jules, father of Mari who is the well-known author of Plains writings. Rose graduated valedictorian from Hay Springs High School in 1959 and cum laude with a BA from Chadron State College in 1963. She majored in Speech, Theatre and English with secondary teaching. After four years teaching in Colorado and one year traveling in Europe and Mid-East, she returned to CSC for her MS in 1970. She retired from 29 years teaching at East High in Cheyenne, WY in 1999. Her talents include singing, painting, landscaping and writing. She has published poetry and a travel journal to the Orient. She has completed a 64ft x 5ft mural of Wyoming history shown at the Old West Museum in Cheyenne, and another 25ft x 5ft mural displayed at the Wyoming Hereford Ranch. She is presently working on illustrating her children's books and projecting iron works of life-size scenarios of a sheepwagon, shepherd and sheep and a cattle drive for public display.

Deb Carpenter (pp. 150, 273) lives in rural northwestern Nebraska with her husband and two daughters, just a few miles from where her great-grandfather homesteaded in the late 1800s. Deb is a writer, poet, songwriter, and performing artist. She currently teaches in the Humanities Department at Oglala Lakota College on the Pine Ridge Reservation in South Dakota.

Mickee Cheek (p. 61) lives in the Nebraska Sandhills. She and her husband raise cattle and have a couple goats, three horses, one wild burro, a bunch of barn cats, and three dogs. In addition to working the ranch, she crochets, embroiders and quilts. She also plays the dulcimer. (And writes the occasional poem.)

Betty Chittenden (p. 139) was born and lived all her life in Johnson County until 9 years ago when she moved to Lincoln. Three times she took her camera to the farm to preserve the history of the barn, only to leave empty-handed rather than record its deterioration. The barn is now gone, but her memories remain.

Faye Tanner Cool (pp. 31, 59, 116) was born in Canada in 1926 and came to Colorado when she was five years old. She grew up in the small town of Sterling, Colorado during the Depression years. She taught in the elementary grades in the 1940's. She married a farmer/rancher and they raised a family of four children on the plains of northeastern Colorado. In the 1970's, they moved to the Sandhills of central Nebraska, and are now retired. She was bitten by the "writing bug" very early, and began being published in the children's magazines and in various poetry publications. Since the 1990's, She has written feature articles for The Nebraska Fence Post and had poetry published in Cappers and Nebraska Life Magazine.

Callie Danehey (p. 341) will be a senior at Silver Lake High School during the 2001/2002 school year. She lives with her parents, Pat and Dianne Danehey, and her two brothers, Sean and Keenan, three miles north of Bladen, Nebraska. Callie helps her parents with fieldwork and raising cattle on their family farm. She participates in competition speech in school, and hopes to go into a law or an agricultural field after completing college. She enjoys watching her pets, two cats, Sophia and Ann, and six kittens, play in the garden. This work was inspired by her father and his friends' obsession with roping.

Katie Deerson (p. 51) is a native Nebraskan who grew up on a family farm located south east of Mead. She graduated from Mead High School and plans to pursue a degree in horticulture at the University of Nebraska Lincoln. Agriculture has played a huge part in Katie's life and she hopes to continue her agricultural influence.

Lyn DeNaeyer (pp. 36, 130) is a third generation Nebraska Sandhills rancher, newspaper columnist and free lance writer. She has also worked in the field of mental health, and claims "it's pretty much like handling stock; just make it easy for them to do the right thing." Lyn has participated at Cowboy Poetry Gatherings in Canada and most of the western states and is affiliated with both the Nebraska Arts Council, and Nebraska Humanities Council. She has one published book of poetry, and has a couple of other projects in progress. Lyn and her partner, Deb Carpenter, recently released a CD and companion book, entitled, "The Heart's Compass, a Journey of Faith," produced by Andy Wilkinson, which is based on the diaries of pioneer women. In addition to personal appearances, Deb and Lyn are available for workshops in schools or other writing groups.

Kathy Disney (p. 85) is originally from Wymore, Nebraska and currently lives and works in Lincoln. She is a member of Chaparral Poets of Lincoln.

Randall Dunn (p. 303) is a farmer in northeast Nebraska raising crops and feeding cattle. He recently began a new farm business, making livestock tiremats for various livestock applications out of recycled tires. Randy has been researching his family history for many years, including the oral history of Indian blood. He enjoys writing poetry, participating in a family circle letter, and going to auctions and farm sales in his spare time.

When **Shannon Dyer** (pp. 211, 326) saw the Nebraska Sandhills for the first time, she decided she'd never live in a place so desolate and lonely. That was the last time she said never. Evidently, love overcame prudence and she married a rancher and moved to the Sandhills in 1982. Since then, the sand has shifted into her veins and she can't imagine living anywhere else, at least not for a very long time. Shannon is a freelance writer, with articles published in Guideposts, Catholic Digest, Lutheran Witness, and many others. She is a contributor to Leaning into the Wind.

Janet Eckmann (p. 140) is a farm wife, mother and grandmother from Bloomfield. They own and operate a grain, hog, and cattle farm near Lindy, located within the boundaries of the Santee Sioux Indian Reservation in northeast Nebraska. Janet started writing freelance as a new bride while learning to be a farmwife, milkmaid and mother. She started a column called "Rural Accents" in the Bloomfield Paper in Nov. of 1994. She is member of the Knox County Extension Board, the Knox County Farm Bureau Board, Nebraska Press Women, the Northeast Nebraska Resource Conservation & Development Council and a member of Northeast Nebraska Travel Council.

Jason A. Elznic (pp. 45, 111) has lived in small, rural Nebraska towns most of his life, the latest being Winside, in Wayne County, where he lives with his wife and two children. Trees seem to be sprouting-up in his writing fairly often lately, as he works part-time for a Certified Arborist while studying for his graduate degree in English at Wayne State College. Most recently he assisted with the Black Elk Young Writers Workshop, sponsored by the John G. Neihart Foundation, and is working on a chapbook, tentatively titled The Unholy Plow.

Becky Faber (p. 76) lives in Lincoln, but comes from a rural background. She was raised on a farm in southwest Iowa. Prior to moving to Lincoln, she lived for 15 years in Dawson County, NE. She holds a Ph.D. in English from UNL where she works as an academic adviser for the College of Arts and Sciences. She is also a manuscript reader for Plainsongs, a poetry journal published through Hastings College.

Bob Feurer (p. 315) was born in Humboldt, NE, and grew up on a farm in rural Johnson County, graduating from Tecumseh H.S. in 1973. After attending Kearney State College, he took a job teaching science at North Bend, a job he still holds after 21 years. He has been involved in coaching, and has been president of the Nebraska Scholastic Wrestling Coaches Association and the Nebraska Association of Teachers of

Science. He was the 1994 Nebraska Presidential Award Winner for Secondary Science Teaching.

Marjorie Finley (p. 332) is the wife of Charles and mother of two, plus grandmother of six children. Four of the six children are young adults. She and her husband are retired and enjoy traveling, golf, genealogy, antiquing, and reading.

Charles Fort (pp. 115, 213 holds the Reynolds Endowed Chair in Poetry and is Professor of English at UNK. A MacDowell Fellow, he has received major awards for his poetry. His books include *The Town Clock Burning, Darvil, We Did Not Fear the Father*, and *As the Lilac Burned, the Laurel Grew*.

Connie Francis (pg. 271) lives in North Platte, Nebraska where she is an Extension Educator with University of Nebraska Cooperative Extension in Lincoln County. Her major areas of responsibility are working with individual and families to build strong families, character development in youth and adults, and small business development. Connie and her husband, Dick, have two married daughters. She enjoys playing the piano, reading, weaving and gardening.

Elaine Frasier (pp. 18, 101) resides with her husband Ken on their Nebraska Pioneer Farm north of Max in Southwest Nebraska where they raise Angus cattle, corn, wheat and alfalfa. They have three grown children and two grandchildren. Farming and ranching has been a life long adventure for Elaine and she enjoys sharing her experiences through the Ag in the Classroom project and through written memories of her childhood and present day life in rural Nebraska.

Suzanne Glendy (p. 156) grew up in Bassett, NE and went to Northeast Community College in Norfolk. She received her veterinary technician degree. While there, she met her husband, Brian. They, along with their two young sons, Wm. Logan, and Colter Hughes Glendy, raise Hereford cattle near Oconto. Suzanne is pursuing a degree in Respiratory Therapy in Omaha, and hopes to be in nursing school in Kearney by this fall.

Richard H. Good (p. 165) is a native of Peru, NE. In 1951, he graduated from Iowa State University with a degree in Animal Husbandry and Agronomy. He served as County Agricultural Agent in Dodge and Douglas Counties in the 50's before going with the Omaha Chamber of Commerce as Agricultural

Manager. In 1959, the Good family moved to Grand Island where he served as C.E.O. of the Chamber for over 32 years. In 1976, he was elected Chairman of the American Chamber of Commerce Executives.

Jean S. Gray (p. 243) was born and raised in Lincoln, Nebraska. She moved away in 1993. Her grandparents and most other family members were farmers living in or near Saunders County. She spent a lot of time visiting their farms, especially during the summers, and had many adventures embracing the life there. Her writing is a hobby and a dream.

Jean Groth's (pp. 30, 196, 340) childhood was spent on a farm and her rural ties continue as she and her husband, Stan, live on an acreage near Pilger, NE. For 22 years, she has been teaching school and coaching volleyball. Her time is filled with photography, reading, writing, other people's children, and the outdoors. Her adage for living is: "I Can Do Everything through Him Who Gives Me Strength."

Agriculture and rural Nebraska form the basis for **Pat Grothe's** (p. 173) life experiences. Her childhood was spent on a 160 acre dry-land farm in Boone County. She met her husband at UNL and has lived since then in Geneva, NE, a town of 3000. Her husband, Charles, is the owner of the family feed and grain business. Their son is presently purchasing the business and represents the fourth generation of ownership.

Anneke Gustafson (p. 83) lives on her family's farm north of Mead. She enjoys nearly ever aspect of farm life. She is attending the University of Nebraska at Lincoln.

Mark Gustafson (pp. 33, 88, 124) was raised on the farm he and his family now work near Mead, Nebraska. He is a fourth generation Nebraska farmer. He earned B.S. and M.S. degrees at the University of Nebraska, Lincoln and a Ph.D. at the University of California, Berkeley in Agriculture and Natural Resource Economics. He worked two years in Brazil and a year for the University of California, Berkeley before returning to the family farm in 1977. Mark and Dianne have two children, Christopher (22) and Anneke (18). He and his family enjoy many activities including traveling, reading, community service and trail running.

Norman Gustafson (p. 69) was born in 1914, on a farm south of Mead, Nebraska, homesteaded by his grandfather, Christoffer

Gustafson. After graduation from high school, he attended UNL where he received a bachelor degree of science. Norman taught vocational agriculture in Loup City and Mead, and then purchased a farm in the Mead area. After retirement, he has enjoyed community service activities and the passage of the farm to son Mark, his wife Dianne, and Norman's two grandchildren: Christopher and Anneke.

Linn Hamilton (pp. 85, 172) is a retired dairy farmer from Washington, PA. He is sixty-four years old and has been married to Louise Hamilton for thirty-five years. They have two children. Linn sold his 230-acre dairy farm in 1997 on which they maintained a herd of seventy milking Holsteins. Linn was the sixth generation of Hamiltons who worked the family farm in Washington County.

Twyla Hansen's (pp. 82, 292) books of poetry are In Our Very Bones and How to Live in the Heartland. Her new collection, Love Songs from the Plains, is currently seeking a publisher. Her writing has been published in national literary periodicals and anthologies. Her BS is from the University of Nebraska; she was employed as a horticulturist for 25 years. She grew up in northeast Nebraska on land her grandparents farmed as immigrants from Denmark in the late 1800's.

Nancy Peters Hastings (pp. 108, 120) grew up on a farm near DeWitt, near the Big Blue River. She lived in Lincoln until she was 33, and then moved to New Mexico. She still loves the people and landscape of Nebraska.

Alice Heller (pp. 116, 266) was born October 2, 1937, on her parent's farm south of Wisner, NE. She and her husband, Warren, raised their five children on the farm where he was born. They still reside there. Some of the things Alice enjoys are writing, reading, music, and attending church and family activities.

Mae Deck Hiatt (pp. 68, 131, 237) lived in Gage County until she moved to Lincoln in 1948 where her husband was in the real estate and building business. She taught school in Iowa as a young woman, and served with the YMCA during World War I in the Overseas Women's League. Mae passed away in 1991, but the farm she writes of is still in the family.

Sarah Hilkemann (p. 120) lives on a dairy farm in Pierce County with her parents and four siblings. She enjoys writing and reading, and has been home-schooled since kindergarten.

Joan Hoffman (pp. 98, 216) is a long time ranch wife from Antelope County, a contemplative, bluebird watcher, and a poet.

After years of rural living, **Marge Holland** (p. 306) and her husband renovated a 1913 family house and moved into Wisner. In addition to writing, she enjoys antiquing, genealogy, and gardening. Marge is a "perennial student" and often enrolls in continuing education classes at an area community college. She considers her computer the best toy she ever owned.

Cassy Holman (p. 322) is 16 years old and a junior at Scottsbluff High School. She lives in rural Scottsbluff and is very active in 4-H, her church, and community service activities.

Wesley Howe (p. 267) was born January 20, 1922 near Chambers, NE. He attended rural schools in Holt and Garfield Counties. He joined the Army in 1943 and served 2 years in the south Pacific, starting in northern Australia and moving to the north. He was in Japan when the armistice was signed on the Missouri. He started Fremont Body & Frame in 1965, and operated it until he retired in 1997. He and his wife will celebrate their 52nd anniversary in late 2000. They have 2 daughters and 1 son.

Rose Marie Hulse (p. 189) was the first-born child of John H. Kotas and Anna R. Koca Kotas, March 15, 1926, near Milligan, Nebraska on the Kotas Family Farm. She graduated from Milligan High School in 1943. She worked at the Fairmont Army Air Base during World War II, until it closed. She was married in October 1947 to Merlin K. Hulse. They lived in empty farm buildings north of Exeter in York County. She was a rural housewife who did not know how to drive. In 1967, They purchased a farm where she lives today. Merlin Hulse passed away in March 1992, following four years of living in a nursing home. Rose Marie divorced him in 1990 to keep from losing the farm, even though she loved him dearly. She quit farming in 1992. She has two grown children.

Jean Hunt (p. 323) was born and raised as a "city kid" in Sioux Falls, SD. She lived in Iowa for 10 years prior to moving to

Nebraska in 1988. Jean has lived in a ranch in north central Nebraska for the past 7 years. She is employed as a therapist and educator.

One of the fifth generation to call Nebraska home, **Maxine Bridgman Isackson** (p. 107) writes of the land and people she knows. She fits her writing in between the demands of being an active farm/ranch wife-mother/grandmother. She has one book published, The Sandhills Beckon and is currently working on a novel based in the Sandhills. She has had short stories published in a variety of magazines and in several anthologies. She also does feature articles for the Nebraska Fence Post. Home is twelve miles north of Brady, Nebraska.

Susan Johnson (p. 308) was born on Dec. 4, 1947, at Valentine, NE, and spent her first seventeen years at her parent's ranch located 3 miles east and 1½ miles south of Nenzel. The ranch was homesteaded in 1888 by her Polish grandfather Stanislaw Krajeski and later operated by her father Paul Krajeski until his death in 1994. Susan's son Mark operates the family ranch today along with her mother, Ruth Krajeski. Susan is married to John Johnson and lives at Cody, NE. She is the Curriculum Coordinator at St. Francis Indian School at St. Francis, SD. Susan especially enjoys the history of the area and the antiques and photographs that belonged to her family.

When **Rosalyn M. Jones** (p. 333) is not teaching Spanish, she may be found on the poor, but peaceful, half section known as the family farm. After a decade of planting trees, she is best known for the high arboreal mortality rate in areas where she has worked. With the exception of 300-odd days a year, she wouldn't think of living in any other state.

Marvin Ketelhut (pp. 197, 278) spent nearly five decades on his family's homestead in rural Walton, Nebraska. After marrying, he moved to an acreage in Lincoln, but continued to raise milk cows, pigs, goats, sheep, horses, chickens—and four children. Marvin discovered the allure of writing at age 80, and continued to write until his death at age 86.

Chad Koehn (p. 297) earned a B.A. from the University of the State of New York. He won the 1998 Kathy Gibson Prize for Short Stories. His articles on disabilities have appeared in *St. Anthony Messenger* and *God's Word Today*. He wrote and narrated the CD *A Crown of Thorns: Faith in the Midst of Great*

Adversity. He lives in Clarkson, a small town in northeast Nebraska.

Mel Krutz, (p. 149) a retired professor of English from rural Seward, where she and her family have lived and farmed since 1963, was born in Curtis, Nebraska, grew up in Ohio, and received her graduate degrees at UN-L. She is pleased to share the pleasure and power of the plains with her husband, children, and grandchildren.

Diana Lambson (pp. 28, 142, 164, 293, 312) has been married to Ivan "Skip" Lambson for almost 32 years has two children, Marlis, who is 30, and Trevor, who is 24. She is a freelance writer and a regional correspondent for the Hastings Tribune. She also writes for three local weeklies, the Harlan County Journal, the Oxford Standard, and the Beaver City Times-Tribune. In addition to being a reporter and poet, she writes short stories, short mysteries, children's stories, magazine articles, book reviews, inspirational pieces, devotionals and sermons. She is very involved in her church and has edited a small press magazine, and co-founded an annual artist's and writer's conference.

Renee Lanik (pp. 38, 119, 296) was born in Lincoln, Nebraska the youngest of three children. Currently Renee is working as an Illustrator for the University of Nebraska Institute of Agriculture and Natural Resources. She and her husband Rod and six-year-old son Wyatt, share an acreage near Hickman with a horse, pony, cat and dog.

Kurt Lewis (p. 151) grew up in Bladen, NE where his parents farmed. He spent many enjoyable hours irrigating on their family farm. Kurt is now a lawyer in Denver, CO.

Vesta Linderman (p. 143) was born in 1921 near Falls City, NE, and was educated in the local schools. She graduated from Peru State College and taught in rural schools for 12 years. In 2000, she received the RSVP Volunteer of the Year Award. She and her husband, Elmer, are active members of the United Methodist Church. They have two children and eight grandchildren.

Patty Lindgren (p. 187) has lived all her life on the McClean family farm in Saunders County. Patty has gained a love of cattle and horses by helping her father with the calves and baby colts from early on in her life. She married Edward Lindgren in

1974, and in 1976, their daughter was born. Patty and Ed continue to farm, but both also work off-farm to supplement their income. Patty works for Fremont Contract Carriers and Ed does part-time trucking. They worry about the future of the small farm.

Gerald Lockhart (pp. 214, 330) was born in southern Nebraska on the family homestead. When he was five years old, he moved to a ranch that his father had bought from the homesteader. It was in Garfield County—eighteen miles east of Burwell. He grew up on that place and never expected to be anything but a cowboy. Later on he had his own place and ranched and farmed some and had a sawmill for a while. There were good years and bad, droughts and bad winters, all of this while raising a family. He is now retired and living in senior housing in Colorado.

Claudia Loomis (pp. 84, 155, 228) grew up on a 7,000 acre farm and ranch in western Nebraska, five miles northeast of Bridgeport. During the farm crisis of the 80's, her family was forced to sell out after 100 years of living on the land. Claudia now resides east of Lincoln and is mother of an eight-month-old son and an English Second Language teacher.

Born in central Nebraska, **Michael L. Lynch** (p. 337) has lived throughout the Midwest. Lynch received a Bachelors of Fine Arts in Painting from Northwest Missouri State University and a Masters of Fine Arts degree in Painting from Washington University in St. Louis. Currently, Michael L. Lynch is Art Department Head at Northeast Community College in Norfolk, NE.

Mary L. Maas (pp. 104, 168) is a lifelong resident of Nebraska, born on a farm in Stanton County and lived there until marriage. She is married to Curtis Maas; they have three children and six grandchildren. She is employed at Norfolk Public Schools as payroll clerk. She is a part-time student at Wayne State College. She works as a free-lance writer for the Stanton Register and Norfolk Daily News. She proofreads copy for the Stanton Register and has proofread the annual literary magazine, Voices From Out of Nowhere for the past five years.

James Magorian (p. 102) was born in Palisade, NE. He attended the University of Nebraska. His family farm was started in Hitchcock County in 1909 with a sodhouse and a windmill.

Max Malone (pp. 88, 188) is a retired farmer. Except for 1935, when he lived in Colorado, and four years in the Army Air Corps during WWII, he has spent his entire life in Nebraska. As a young man, he lived in Cheyenne County, but has spent his entire adult life in the eastern part of the state, living 50 years on the same farm near Waverly. During the war, he spent 13 months overseas, mostly in the China-Burma-India theatre, serving as a gunner on a B-29 combat crew. His writing is a hobby, which he developed in recent years, mostly reflecting experiences of a lifetime on the Great Plains of Nebraska.

Joyce Maser (p. 143) is a farm wife from western Nebraska and the mother of three married sons and grandmother of two. Both she and her husband are third generation family farmers, with their grandfathers and fathers preceding them, and two of their sons are now involved in the family farm.

R. F. McEwen (p. 102) is a professor of English at Chadron State College in Chadron, NE. He has been teaching and writing for almost 30 years. His first book, <u>Heartwood and Other Poems</u>, gained national prominence when it (and its author) were showcased on a segment of "CBS Sunday Morning."

Yasmin McEwen (p. 64) is a runner and a writer.

Bruce Messersmith (pp. 151, 182, 200) has had several poems published in <u>Dragonfly</u> and <u>Nebraska Life,</u> but is either too busy or too lazy to gather this poetry for more permanent publication. Bruce works as a locomotive engineer for the Burlington Northern RR and raises registered Arabian horses with his Dad. The railroad income allows Bruce to travel to four or five poetry gatherings and personal appearances a year where he recites his original poems, as well as, "classic" western poetry. He has been most interested, of late, in the history of western poets and sharing their works with audiences who may not be aware of the historical oral tradition. Bruce's recitations have taken him from Alberta, Canada to Arizona and Elko to Omaha.

David Meyer (p. 220) was raised on a farm 9 miles south of Dodge, NE. He graduated in 1982 from Midland Lutheran College with a BA in Biology and Natural Science. He went on to get his Masters and Ph.D. in Plant Breeding and Genetics from the University of Nebraska-Lincoln. He is currently employed by Mycogen Seeds at York, where he is the Station Manager in charge of corn breeding.

Jason Meyer (p. 279) is a twenty-two year old senior at the University of Nebraska - Lincoln. He read this story at his grandfather's funeral hoping to help people in their grieving and enlighten people to the side of his grandfather that not everyone had the pleasure to know.

Kevin Meyer (pg. 133, 242) was a farmer in the Pilger, NE, area, having grown up here and lived there his entire life. He worked as a field staffer for the Farm Crisis Hotline in the 1980's, through the Center for Rural Affairs based out of Walthill. His family liked to call him the "unofficial historian" for the Pilger area, and he was the family genealogist. He had just found the perfect job--Pilger's librarian--before he died in November of 1999 at the age of 48; he loved to read, and was the only person his wife knows who read the entire World Book Encyclopedia from A to Z--every page. He would be quite happy to learn his work has been accepted for Rural Voices.

Shirley K. Miller (p. 310) was born on a farm near Stella, Nebraska and lived there until her family moved to Wahoo where she graduated from high school. She attended Peru State Teacher's College for 2 years and earned a teaching certificate. She married, had one son, was widowed in her twenties, and returned to teaching while earning a degree from Midland Lutheran College in Fremont. She taught in the small rural town of Mead for many years and married an Agricultural Education teacher adding three stepchildren. Rural Nebraska is in the blood of both she and her husband, though no one in her family farms today. She and her husband farm their yard in Wahoo and their livestock are three indoor cats and birds and squirrels they feed year round. Her memories of farm life are still vivid. She supposes it's true, "You can take the girl off the farm, but you can't take the farm out the girl!"

Gaylen Mosel (p. 110) was born and raised in Neligh, NE. He attended a country school for 8 years. He has lived in Nebraska all his life.

Margaret Stine Nielsen (p. 277) was born in Fairmont, Nebraska and grew up on a farm north of town. She graduated from Doane College, and taught in Upland for one year and Blair for two years. She met her husband, Vance, in Blair.

They have one son who is a pathologist at Methodist Hospital in Omaha, three grandchildren, and one great-grandchild.

Molly Noren (p. 243) was born February 27, 1967 in Saunders County to Larry and Mary Brown. She graduated from Cedar Bluffs H.S. in 1985, and from the University of Nebraska-Lincoln in 1990, later earning a Master's Degree in Speech. While working as a speech pathologist in the Omaha Public School system, she married Bob Noren. She has put her career on hold to stay home with their two children: Jessica and Grant.

Ann Wiggins North (p. 239) was born and raised in Gothenburg, Nebraska. Her home was on Wiggins Ranch just south of Gothenburg where her family raised cattle, hogs and grain. Her elementary school years were spent in a one-room schoolhouse without indoor bathrooms or running water. After graduating from Gothenburg High School, Ann attended the University of Nebraska. There she earned her teaching degree. Writing has always been a joy for her. Ann's writing "Dear Santa" expresses her love of her family's ranch and all the traditions her family gave her. She is married with one son and two grandsons.

Leta Olson (p. 281) lives with her husband Ed and their 2 daughters Penny and Kalee. They own and operate a dairy/farming operation in Craig, Nebraska. Along with this, Ed auctioneers with Marreel and Associates from Hooper, Nebraska where Leta helps with the clerking

Jack Ostergard (pp. 29, 89, 131, 185, 209) is a fourth generation rancher raised in Custer County. He used to be an amateur rodeo competitor, is a Korean War veteran, and served on Nebraska Cattle Association boards.

LoRee Peery (p. 40) lives in the country, on an acreage east of Lincoln. When she yearns for the farm, she goes camping close to a high hill that overlooks distant wetlands. She is an editorial assistant at UNL, a past editor of a large church women's newsletter for 10 years, a freelance writer, and an unpublished novelist. She is also a grandmother, a machine quilter, and an avid reader.

Stephanie Peters (p. 20) grew up on a diversified family farm in Custer County, Nebraska. She holds a degree in Agricultural Economics from UNL and worked for 14 years in corporate agri-marketing. She and her husband served for 2 years as U.S. Peace Corps volunteers in Samoa, after which time she is pursuing a Masters degree in Health Administration at USF-Tampa in Florida.

Elaine Phillips (pp. 60, 117, 234) is a farm girl who returned to the farm with her husband after college, marriage and 5 years "out in the world." In addition to the usual activities of a farm wife, a good bit of her energy is spent in volunteer activities. She has been active in 4-H, County Extension, church and school. She has held the part time job of substitute rural mail carrier since 1980 with the Beaver Crossing Post Office. Elaine is married to Ted Phillips and they have 3 children: Lane, a computer engineer, and the twins, Adele and Eliot, currently students at the University of Nebraska-Lincoln.

Amy Rasmussen (p. 184) has lived on a farm all of her life. She enjoys country life and has learned many life skills from living on the farm. With the help of her three brothers and parents, Amy has participated in many agricultural projects. Amy has been actively involved with 4-H for 10 years where she has shown livestock and entered home economic projects. Amy feels that living on a farm has given her a strong work ethic and has instilled pride in her family's farm.

Andy Raun (pp. 51, 118) grew up on a diversified family farm south of Norman. He graduated from Minden High School in 1989 and went on to the University of Nebraska-Lincoln, where he earned a bachelor's degree in journalism in 1993. He has worked for the Hastings Tribune for the past seven years, first as city reporter and now as region and farm news editor. His wife, Ruth, teaches first grade at Hastings' Longfellow Elementary School. For Raun, creative writing is a longtime interest sporadically pursued. For inspiration, he draws heavily on his farming experiences, family relationships that are rooted firmly in the Nebraska soil, and his ties to the Osco community in southern Kearney County.

Marie Raymond (p. 317) was born in Custer County, the sixth of nine children. She grew up on farms in Custer County, Logan County, and Lincoln County. She attended and graduated from country school in Lincoln County, attended high school for three years in Stapleton, and graduated from Broken Bow. She married Floyd Raymond in 1940, and raised six children. She now resides at Sherman Lake, Sherman County, and is thoroughly enjoying it.

Jim Reese (pp. 123, 205, 219, 325) is a writer and photographer, and the Imagining Editor for Logan House Press. He is currently working on a Ph.D. at the University of Nebraska at Lincoln. His work has appeared in Dig Magazine, The Backstage Pass, Nebraska Territory, NebraskaLife Magazine, Plains Song Review vol. 1 and 2., The Platte Valley Review, Poems of the World, and numerous other publications. He has been a selected reader for the Western Literature Association, Nebraska Literature Festival, Plains Writers Series, and the John H. Ames reading series in Nebraska's Heritage Room. His first book, "As Worthless As Tits On A Boar" was published by Cacthouse Publishing in 1995. He is currently at work on a screenplay, The Great American Road Show, with Nebraska writer, J.V. Brummels. Jim lives in Lincoln with his beautiful wife Linda and snoring dog Doo Rite.

Suzanne Richards (pp. 185, 232, 273) moved to the best-kept secret in the United States, the Sandhills of Nebraska in 1996. Ranching (cattle, pigs, pheasants, quail, etc.) was a new experience for her, and she thinks that helps her see the funny side of this lifestyle that folks who have been born into it just take for granted as everyday life. With her husband, she has one son and two daughters. Suzanne has been writing for Fence Post Magazine since 1997, and plans on publishing some short children's stories about a young cowboy and his cow dog in the near future.

Robert Richter (pp. 33, 294) lives on the remnants of a family homestead in Perkins County where he farmed dryland wheat for twenty years before surrendering to economic impossibilities in 1995. He now conducts escorted small-group tours of Mexico and continues to write. Robert published the mystery, Something In Vallarta, in 1991, and the second mystery in this series, Something Like A Dream, was published in 2000 as well as a novel, Homefield, which is set in Nebraska, and a biography of a presidential candidate in Mexico. In 2000, he received the Distinguished Merit Award from the Nebraska Arts Council for nonfiction.

Marilou Roth (p. 286) is a mother of four and the wife of a farmer near Milford, Nebraska. She grew up on a farm in rural Boyd County. She graduated from Spencer-Naper High School, and then attended UNL, where she majored in Animal Science. This is also where she met her husband, Calvin. When she has free time, she enjoys reading, gardening, cooking, and writing.

Mary Ruff (pp. 52, 103) lives in the rural Kearney/Gibbon area where she helps neighbors with their cattle and is involved in other aspects of rural living. She is in the antiques business and occasionally performs. She has a cassette tape addressing the experiences of pioneer women on the trails.

Marjorie Saiser (pp. 39, 78, 210, 284, 337) received a fellowship in literature from the Nebraska Arts Council in 2000, and the Literary Heritage Award in 1999 from the Nebraska Literary Heritage Association. Her work has been published in *Prairie Schooner*, *Georgia Review*, *Crazyhorse*, other literary journals, and in a full-length collection, *Bones of a Very Fine Hand*. She is a speaker for the Nebraska Humanities Council.

Mick Scarlett (p. 328) was born in Boone County near Petersburg. He graduated from Wayne St. College in 1969, and after a year of teaching, returned to the farm. He has written a series of three paperback fiction books about the Sandhills. Mick now hauls hogs and lives on the home place with his wife, Kathy.

Dick Schanou (pp. 19, 58, 99, 164, 241) was raised on a farm a few miles north of Shelton, Nebraska. He had an idyllic childhood, although he certainly did not realize this at the time. Dick graduated from Hastings College with a BA in 1963, and from the University of Nebraska in 1970 with an MA. He has taught high school English since 1963, at Aurora High School since 1969. In the mid-eighties he took several sessions of the Nebraska Writing Project taught by Les Whipp. These classes inspired him, changed his life and his teaching. Most of his "rural" poetry is autobiographical.

Steven P. Schneider (pp. 26, 81, 330) is an associate professor of English at the University of Nebraska-Kearney, where he teaches contemporary American poetry and American literature. His poems and articles have appeared in Prairie Schooner, The Literary Review, The Iowa Review, The Beloit Poetry Journal, The North Carolina Literary Review, among others. His critical books include A.R. Ammons and the Poetics of Widening Scope and Complexities of Motion: New Essays on A.R. Ammons's Long Poems.

Nancy Schroeder (p. 314) was raised on a farm near Fremont and Fontanelle, NE. She currently lives in Grand Island, with her husband Joel and three sons. Professionally she is an elementary vocal music instructor in Grand Island and a church organist. Creative pursuits include volunteering at St. Paul's Lutheran, 4-H, camping, music, writing, and reading. She is a 1975 graduate of Midland Lutheran College in Fremont.

Izma Buethe Seeba (p. 87) is a retired farm wife, mother of four and grandmother of eight. When she and her husband left the farm, they stayed in the country. She has been active in church, school, politics, NFO, and authored the Heritage Cookbook. She has the Special Occasions cake business, is a history buff, and an avid gardener.

Carolyn Seger (p. 67) is Nebraska born and bred, daughter of a grocer in a town of less than 5,000, married to a professor of education at Peru State College, mother of four fine adults from 21 to 34 years old, and grandmother to two tiny little boys. She currently represents several marketing companies in southeast Nebraska, pursues the arts as a member of the Jefferson County Art Guild, and chases Nebraska sunsets and hidden oasis's while looking for wildlife with her husband of 36 years. She began writing "family stories" only a year ago to save memories for her children and grandchildren, and to remind herself of the special life she has lived.

Lora Stauffer (pp. 115, 314) was born to Henry and Flo McCann. She was the second of three children. At an early age her father died and the family had to work very hard to support themselves. She married Henry Stauffer from Banner County and they lived on family homestead for many years, ranching and farming wheat. As her husband approached 50 they departed the family homestead and bought property in Scottsbluff County out along the Nine-mile creek. There she and her husband raised beef and beets and corn. She has seen her children (Joan, Charles and Connie) all grow to adulthood and marry. She is now the proud Grandmother of nine and Great Grandmother of fifteen.

Hilton Stedman (p. 53), Ret. Farmer; b. Unadilla, NE. Aug. 4, 1920; s. of Sherman S. and Lydia Ann Stedman; att. UNL Coll. of Agr ; m. Mary Jo Sandsted ; children : Ann (Mrs. Roger Overleese), Paula (Mrs. John Ellis), Shari (Mrs. Terry Gray) ; 4-H Leader ; USAF 1942-46 ; VFW ; Past ch. Upper Little Nemaha Watershed ; Past Pres. Otoe Co Farm Bureau ; Past mem. and officer Capitol Pork Producers ; Recip. Pork Awards ; Presbyterian Elder, trustee, deacon, Sun. Sch. Teacher.

Bruce Stock (p. 109) was born September 26th, 1948 in Lincoln, NE. He is a fourth generation farmer outside of Ashland, NE, where he resides with his wife Connie, and two sons, Spencer and Lucas.

Lucas Christian Stock (p. 259) was born on a kitchen table in Murdock, NE in 1981, the son and grandson of southeastern Nebraska farmers. He is currently studying English at the University of Nebraska-Lincoln and plans to become a writer. Lucas was the recipient of the 2002 Vreeland Award.

All of **Algene Stohl's** (pp. 46, 113) grandparents were Swedish immigrant farmers. She attended a one room, country school. She married a farmer and is a mother of four. She made soap, churned butter, canned vegetables, fruits and meat. She baked from scratch: using a wood burning stove, had no indoor plumbing, water or electricity for years. Algene continues to write and witness as a Christian.

Sandy Straus (p. 62) was born in Omaha, March 15, 1938. Her name at the time was Sandra Jean Fiedler. She was raised and educated in Omaha, later attending the School of the Art Institute of Chicago, where she received a BFA in 1976. During that time, she had two children. After graduation, Sandy moved to New York with her children. She is a professional artist, having exhibited around the world. She has works in major collections. She currently lives in New York City and Accord, New York.

Judith Stutzman (p. 201) is a mother of three sons and grandmother of five grandchildren. She and Don, her husband of 36 years, were both born and raised in the Beaver Crossing, Nebraska area. She graduated from Beaver Crossing High School, Reece & Sybil School of Beauty and Southeast Community College, Lincoln from the Dietary Manager Program. She is currently employed at Southeast Community College, Milford, as a custodian. Her interests and hobbies include learning about Nebraska history, writing poems and short stories, feeding wild birds, teaching Sunday School and playing with her grandchildren.

Carole Tharnish (p. 91) lives in Grand Island, Nebraska with her husband, Mark, and sons, Brad and Jeff. She was raised on a farm north of Raeville, Nebraska, attended the St. Bonaventure church, and was married there in May 1983. In

August 1984 she graduated from Kearney State College and worked ten years at Mutual of Omaha. Giving up a fast-paced career, she instead chose to stay home with her children when relocating to Grand Island. In May 1999, she received a Masters of Arts in Teaching degree from Hastings College with an emphasis in English. Currently, Carole teaches at Central Community College and enjoys being a Cub Scout den leader, a "soccer-baseball-basketball" mom, and church volunteer.

Effie Thompson (p. 71) was born in Desoto, NE, one of 12 children of Lewis and Minnie Wise. She grew up on a farm and went to school in North Dakota. She married Pete in 1937 and he died in 1986. She lives alone and is content in an apartment at Cromwell Memorial Home. She still has two sisters and one brother.

Paul Timm (p. 87) is a senior Agricultural Education major at UNL from Lyons, NE. He is active in FFA, FarmHouse Fraternity, and Navigators Campus Ministry. He is grateful for both his hometown and his family, and the love of agriculture they have instilled in him.

Raymond Weed (p. 186) was a farmer in western Nebraska.

Stacy Wegener (pp. 47, 148) grew up on a farm near Humphrey.

Don Welch (p. 100) is a native of Nebraska, a former high school teacher of English and French, as well as a coach, who taught English and Philosophy at the University of Nebraska for almost forty years.

Anita Lorentzen-Wells (p. 69) teaches at the University of Nebraska at Kearney and is working toward the completion of a Ph.D. in English through the University of Alberta in Edmonton. She was raised on her parents' farm in Axtell, NE. She now lives on another farm in the same area with her husband and three children, cats, dog, chickens, and the occasional 4-H livestock.

Joyce Weyenberg (p. 275) is a Nebraskan through and through! She is trying her hand at a little writing. She also does some artwork.

Cathy Wilken (p. 48) is a full time legal assistant, wife, mom, and community volunteer. She only began writing seriously in her 40's for her own satisfaction and to record memories for her children, then friends encouraged her to take it further.

Lucille E. Holcomb Williams (p. 305) was born in Burwell, Nebraska and has a twin sister, Lois. She attended high school in Belden, Nebraska and one year at Wayne State College, Wayne, NE. She was married in 1953 and owned and operated a dairy farm near Hartington, with her husband. They had four sons and two daughters. Her husband, Dean, passed away of a heart attack in 1984. In 1989, she married Alfred Williams, and they enjoy living on the family farm, although the land is now rented out.

Harold Wilson (p. 235) is a transplanted Iowa farm boy, who left the Army for the flat-water country of Nebraska. His inspiration is farm life and a special lady from Oklahoma.

Fredrick Zydek (pp. 38, 63, 76, 106, 153, 280) is the author of four collections of poetry: *Lights Along the Missouri, Storm Warning, Ending the Fast,* and *The Conception Abbey Poems.* His work appears in The Antioch Review, The Hollins Critic, Michigan Quarterly Review, Poetry, Poetry Northwest, and other journals. Formerly a professor of creative writing and theology at the University of Nebraska and later at the College of Saint Mary, he is now a gentleman farmer when he isn't writing. Most recently, he has accepted the post as editor for Lone Willow Press.

Rural Voices

Literature at the Millennium

Available at Dirt Road Press
1020 CR Q • Mead, NE 68041
dirtroadpress@hotmail.com

Order Your Copies

Mail a check written to Dirt Road Press to:
Chris Gustafson 1020 CR Q Mead NE, 68041

$12.66 ($11.95 + .71 sales tax) per book
     X ____ copies= _____
Please add $2 shipping for first book and $1 each additional

          Total Enclosed= _____

Name: _____
Address: _____
City: _____ **State:** _____ **Zip:** _____

Authors retain all rights to their work.